*Labor in the
Twentieth Century*

STUDIES IN LABOR ECONOMICS

Richard B. Freeman, Series Editor

Department of Economics
Harvard University
Cambridge, Massachusetts

Labor in the Twentieth Century

Edited by

JOHN T. DUNLOP
*Department of Economics
and
Graduate School of Business Administration
Harvard University
Cambridge, Massachusetts*

WALTER GALENSON
*Department of Economics
and
New York State School of Industrial and
Labor Relations
Cornell University
Ithaca, New York*

ACADEMIC PRESS   New York   San Francisco   London
A Subsidiary of Harcourt Brace Jovanovich, Publishers

ACADEMIC PRESS, INC.
111 Fifth Avenue, New York, New York 10003

United Kingdom Edition published by
ACADEMIC PRESS, INC. (LONDON) LTD.
24/28 Oval Road, London NW1 7DX

Library of Congress Cataloging in Publication Data

Main entry under title:

Labor in the twentieth century.

  (Studies in labor economics ; v. 1)
  Includes bibliographical references.
  1. Labor and laboring classes——History——Case studies.
2. Trade—unions——History——Case studies. 3. Industrial
relations——History——Case studies. I. Dunlop, John
Thomas (Date)   II. Galenson, Walter (Date)
III. Series.
HD4854.L26   331'.09'04   78–3335
ISBN 0–12–224350–1

CONTENTS

INTRODUCTION

JOHN T. DUNLOP

1. THE UNITED STATES

WALTER GALENSON
ROBERT S. SMITH

2. GREAT BRITAIN

A. W. J. THOMSON
L. C. HUNTER

3. THE FEDERAL REPUBLIC OF GERMANY

HANS GÜNTER

GERHARD LEMINSKY

4. FRANCE

FRANCOIS SELLIER

5. JAPAN

TAISHIRO SHIRAI

HARUO SHIMADA

LIST OF CONTRIBUTORS

Numbers in parentheses indicate the pages on which the authors' contributions begin.

JOHN T. DUNLOP (1), Department of Economics and Graduate School of Business Administration, Harvard University Cambridge, Massachusetts 02163

WALTER GALENSON (11), Department of Economics and New York State School of Industrial Labor Relations, Cornell University, Ithaca, Ithaca, New York 14853

HANS GÜNTER (149), International Institute for Labour Studies, Postale 6, CH-1211 Geneva 22, Switzerland

L. C. HUNTER (85), Department of Social and Economic Research, University of Glasgow, Glasgow G12 8RT, United Kingdom

GERHARD LEMINSKY (149), Economic and Social Research Institute of the German Trade Union Confederation, 4 Dusseldorf 1, The Federal Republic of Germany

FRANCOIS SELLIER (197), Les Erables 63, 55 Boulevard de Charonne, 75011 Paris, France

HARUO SHIMADA (241), Department of Economics, Keio University, 2-15-45 Mita, Minato-ku, Tokyo, Japan

TAISHIRO SHIRAI* (241), The Japan Institute of Labour, Chutaikin Building, 7–6 Shibakoen 1-chome, Minato-ku, Tokyo, Japan 105

*Present Address: Faculty of Business Administration, Hosei University 2-17-1 Fujimi-cho, Chiyoda-ku, Tokyo, Japan 102

ROBERT S. SMITH (11), Department of Labor Economics, New York State School of Industrial and Labor Relations, Cornell University, Ithaca, New York 14853

A. W. J. THOMSON (85), Department of Social and Economic Research, University of Glasgow, Glasgow G12 8RT, United Kingdom

*Labor in the
Twentieth Century*

Labor in the Twentieth Century

INTRODUCTION

JOHN T. DUNLOP

THE WORKER'S CENTURY

A reader of this volume must conclude that the twentieth century is likely to be known as the century of the *worker* or of the *employee* in advanced democratic societies. Unprecedented improvements in the living standards, social status, economic security, political power, and influence of industrial workers have occurred in this century. In taking the measure of this epoch, however, it should not be forgotten that this century generated at least two periods of world wide warfare.

Sumner H. Slichter enunciated something of the same theme in 1948 when he said

> the United States is gradually shifting from a capitalist community to a laboristic one, that is a community in which employees rather than businessmen are the strongest single influence. A community in which employees are the principal influence will have its own way of looking at things, its own scale of values, its own ideas on public policies, and, to some extent, its own jurisprudence.[1]

One of the great merits of the perspective of a century is that underlying tendencies and fundamentals stand out in sharper focus. Cyclical phases and climacteric events in the aftermath of war, depression, or social upheavals, as occurred in the later 1960s in many countries, are more soberly perceived and assessed. Moreover, the first three-quarters of the century provide a desirable frame of reference to consider the course of developments out to the year 2000, recognizing that simple extrapolations are seldom warranted.

[1]Sumner H. Slichter, "Are We Becoming a 'Laboristic' State?" *New York Times*, 16 May 1948. Reprinted in *Potentials of the American Economy, Selected Essays of Sumner H. Slichter*, by John T. Dunlop (Cambridge: Harvard University Press, 1961), p. 255.

1

The comparative method of reviewing labor in five advanced democratic countries has the further reward of helping to highlight both the common elements and the distinctive features of each country during this remarkable period for the worker and the employee.

A common initial outline was adopted for each chapter, although each author was urged to stress those elements and develop those themes that were of particular significance to his country. Every chapter contains statistical series, carried as far back to the start of the century as the data permit for employment, unemployment, wages, hours, and labor disputes. The growth and operation of labor organizations, collective bargaining institutions, the political activities of labor, and labor legislation are common features. Each chapter also seeks to identify the major future problems and prospects.

LIVING STANDARDS

Despite very different starting dates in industrial development, and quite diverse policies of industrializing elites, not to mention differential rates of growth in particular decades, unprecedented changes in the economic and social status of ordinary workers have taken place in these five countries in the twentieth century. The magnitude of these changes is without an historical parallel, and such changes do not seem likely to be repeated on the scale of this century.[2] These changes occurred in the process of industrialization. "The industrial system everywhere has its managers, its managed and a pattern of interaction between them."[3]

1. Workers and employees have become quantitatively the largest component by far in economic activity. Moreover, their absolute numbers have also grown rapidly with natural population increase and, in some of these countries, with immigration or temporary migration in some periods. Workers and employees are numerically dominant.

The production structure, to use Kuznets's[4] term, reflects significant relative declines in employment in agriculture and the primary sector. Correspondingly, there have been marked relative increases of workers

---

[2]For some purposes in some countries a different 100-year span, such as 1860–1960, might produce even larger changes. But this perspective utilizes an even century in the Gregorian calendar for all countries in the comparison.

[3]Clark Kerr, John T. Dunlop, Frederick Harbison, and Charles A. Myers, *Industrialism and Industrial Man* (Cambridge: Harvard University Press, 1960), p. 15. Also see by the same authors, *Industrialism and Industrial Man Reconsidered* (Inter-University Study of Human Resources in Rational Development, Final Report, Princeton, N.J., 1975).

[4]Simon Kuznets, *Economic Growth of Nations, Total Output and Production Structure* (Cambridge: Harvard University Press, 1971), pp. 309–313.

and employees in the service sector and public employment, with small or larger relative increases in the goods-producing industries.

The participation of women, particularly married women, in wage and salary employment has grown significantly in most countries, particularly in the post-World War II period. These changes are said to be related to higher education levels, smaller family size, reduced hours of work, rise in clerical and service occupations, and other factors.

There have also been significant changes in occupations associated with reshaping the production structure, as in the relative decline in agricultural laborers and domestic servants and in the growth of professional, technical, and administrative as well as clerical and service employees.

2. The compensation of workers and employees, after allowing for changes in consumer prices, has increased dramatically thus far in this century. E. H. Phelps Brown has documented this point in his outstanding studies of a closely related hundred years. "In the short span of time since the Fourth Ice Age, men have achieved two bursts of technical progress so concentrated and extensive that they deserve to be called Revolutions. One was the Neolithic Revolution, that came about ten thousand or more years ago. The other was the Industrial Revolution."[5]

In the 75 years after 1900 it would appear that real wages increased on the order of 3 to 5 times among the five countries. (Brown's data for the 100 years from 1860 to 1960 range between 4 and 6.5 times for four of the five countries common to these two volumes.[6])

The rise in real wages was accompanied by marked reductions in the average hours of work. In the 75 years after 1900 it would appear that weekly hours worked were reduced in a range of 25 to 35% among these countries. The scheduled weekly hours now converge around 40 hours or a little less.

There also has been a significant shift in the lifetime distribution of education, work, and leisure. In the United States, for instance, life expectancy for men in 1900 was 48.2 years—10.0% spent in preschool, 16.6% in school, 66.6% at work, and 6.5% in retirement. By 1970 life expectancy for men had risen to 67.1 years—7.4% in preschool, 18.0% in school, 59.7% at work, and 14.8% in retirement. The rise in life expectancy and the greater fraction of time spent in education and in retirement, with a smaller fraction of time at work, is a notable measure of the change in the status of male workers and employees.[7]

---

[5]E. H. Phelps Brown with Margaret H. Browne, *A Century of Pay, The Course of Pay and Production in France, Germany, Sweden, The United Kingdom, and the United States of America, 1860–1960* (London: Macmillan, 1968), p. 25.

[6]*Ibid.*, p. 31.

[7]Fred Best and Barry Stern, "Education, Work and Leisure: Must They Come in that Order?" *Monthly Labor Review,* July 1977, p. 4.

3. The average number of years spent in education has increased sharply in the period after 1900, and the fraction of the age group going on to higher education has increased very sharply, particularly since World War II. The access to higher education has become more generally available in these societies over the period studied. Chapter 5 describes the active role of education and manpower training in Japan as an important policy tool deliberately used to achieve the goal of industrialism in that economy.

4. In the perspective of the period since 1900, there appears to be no discernible trend in the average rate of unemployment. If any tendency emerges in these countries, it is for a decline in the variability of unemployment rates around the mean.

5. All of the five countries examined have become welfare states with a spectrum of public policies designed to protect workers, employees, and citizens generally, from the risks of illness, retirement, accidents, disabilities, involuntary idleness and to facilitate housing, training, and other assistance.

It is difficult, at best, by resorting to these generalizations or by reference to the detailed statistical series for the separate countries to capture fully the quality of the changes in the economic status of workers and employees. Another means is to refer to autobiographical material and reports on the conditions of life and work at the turn of the nineteenth century and to make comparisons with today.[8]

INDUSTRIAL RELATIONS AND POLITICAL ROLE

In the twentieth century, labor unions have established a secure place in the economies and societies of these five countries, despite the wartime repressions that occurred in three of them. As is discussed in Chapter 3, unions in Germany "tend to see themselves as a central part of the democratic infrastructure." The role of labor organizations in the economic, industrial relations, and political lives of these countries today stands in

---

[8]While the representativeness of individual reports are open to question, such social history can be a useful supplement to general data. See, for instance, Eli Ginzberg and Hyman Berman, *The American Worker in the Twentieth Century, A History Through Autobiographies* (Glencoe, Ill.: The Free Press of Glencoe, 1963), pp. 27–144. For a more general type of presentation, see, Stephan Thernstrom, *Poverty and Progress, Social Mobility in a Nineteenth Century City* (Cambridge: Harvard University Press, 1964) and *The Other Bostonians, Poverty and Progress in the American Metropoles, 1880–1970* (Cambridge: Harvard University Press, 1973). For the British condition, see, E. H. Phelps Brown, *The Growth of British Industrial Relations, A Study from the Standpoint of 1906–1914* (London: Macmillan, 1959), pp. 1–113.

marked contrast to the weaknesses and restraints that characterized their positions in 1900.

In the mid-1970s these five countries—all leading powers of the democratic world—had an aggregate population of almost 500 million, with a combined labor force of approximately 220 million, one-fourth of whom were reported to be members of labor unions. The figures ranged among countries from approximately 20 to 45%. At the turn of the century, the range was more likely to have been 5 to 10% of the labor force. Moreover, the meaning of being a member of union has changed significantly over the years since 1900.

In the mid-1970s in England and West Germany labor parties and their political allies constituted the governments; in France and Japan the unions were mainly allied with the parliamentary opposition to the elected governments; in the United States the unions were not as formally related to political parties as in the other four countries, but sought to use their considerable electoral and lobbying influence for particular candidates or legislation. In all these countries, unions had grown to be a power in the economy and polity.

The chapters in this volume underscore the importance of the background of the industrialization process in a particular country, the policies of the industrializing elites, and wartime transformations in shaping the distinguishing features of the industrial relations system and its political role at formative stages in each country.[9]

The speed of industrialization and the need to attract labor in a sparsely populated country, or to recruit and train a labor force from agriculture, or acquire it through immigration are shown to be significant factors in an industrial relations system at various stages in Japan, Germany, France, and the United States.

As is stated in Chapter 2, "the influence of history has been stronger in Britain than elsewhere.... Britain had the most evolutionary system of industrial relations in the twentieth century."

The trauma of war and its aftermath were decisive in shaping the current arrangements in both Japan and West Germany, while in Chapter 4, reference is made to the "rapidity of the social transformation that has taken place in France since World War II."

The attitudes of employers toward workers, unions, and employer associations as well seem to have been influential in shaping industrial relations. In Britain, "employer associations were less antiunion than those in other countries [Chapter 2 of this volume]."

There appear to be differences among countries based on whether labor organizations created political parties (as in England) or political

---

[9]John T. Dunlop, *Industrial Relations Systems, 1958,* (Arcturus Books Edition, Carbondale and Edwardsville: Southern Illinois University Press, 1977).

parties helped to organize labor unions and their federations (as in Germany, historically).

There have been sharp historical differences among those labor organizations that advocate reformist social and political policies and those characterized as revolutionary.

Thus the economic and political environment in which unions, managements, and governments evolve and interact, combined with their policies and objectives, appear to have affected significantly the distinctive industrial relations system that has evolved in each of the countries examined in this volume.

However, the systems in each country have also developed a number of common or similar features, which are discussed here as well.

1. The history of these five countries reflects that there have been both periods of marked growth and breakthroughs in union membership and organization and other periods in which unions have languished. Moreover, any simple relationship of union growth to economic fluctuations, prices, or unemployment does not appear to be helpful in understanding the main ebbs and flows of union organization.[10] Rather, the major emphasis should be placed on those social and political forces that are at times related to prolonged depression, the aftermath of wartime, the widespread social upheaval and change in particular sectors or population groups that generate union surges.

Unions appear to have been generally stronger initally in blue collar occupations and goods-producing industries and, only more gradually, have come to organize white-collar positions and service industries, which, outside the public sector, often still remain relatively underorganized and weaker.

Unions have tended to develop a strong hold among public employees, derived in part from the critical role of political processes in influencing their wages and conditions and from the character of public management and administration.

Unions have generally been able to organize larger and medium-sized firms within an industry or sector to a greater degree than small enterprises.

2. Everywhere, collective bargaining, at different rates, has become an established institution involving the negotiation and administration of agreements, although each national industrial relations system reflects

---

[10]The attempts to explain union growth in terms of formal models do not appear to me to be particularly insightful or helpful. As an early illustration, see, Orley Ashenfelter and John H. Pencavel, "American Trade Union Growth," *Quarterly Journal of Economics,* 1969, pp. 434–448. Membership, which grows with employment in older sectors, is to be distinguished from long-run breakthroughs into new occupations, industries, and regions. Membership, vitality, and power are not to be confused.

quite distinctive arrangements. There is a serious danger in using the term "collective bargaining" to encompass such disparate structures unless the differences are fully recognized.

Among the sharpest differences in industrial relations are those concerned with the plant, or work place, level of industrial relations and the applicability of an agreement negotiated at an industry or sectoral level to the work level. The flexibility and adaptability of the institutions of collective bargaining—labor, management, and government—are nowhere better portrayed than in a comparison among these five countries as to the handling of work place questions. One of the significant benefits of these historical studies is to reflect that the work place levels, outside of the United States, have been the subject of considerable discussion and substantial continuing evolution. One should expect further changes in the next several decades by evolution as well as by legislation.[11]

Outside the United States, the work place institutions of workers' councils, shop stewards' councils, and enterprise unions operate in ways that present a challenge and counterpoint to the national labor unions and the labor and management centers. These institutions have significant influences in accommodating the many diffuse currents and groups at the work place.

Agreements differ among these national industrial relations systems as to their usual duration and the circumstances under which new negotiations may be undertaken. The distinction between the negotiation of agreements and their administration and between issues of rights and interests (including final and binding arbitration) is not generally observed outside the United States.[12]

These industrial relations systems also differ in their administrative procedures, including the extent to which they use professionals—union officers and staff, personnel managers, and private or public mediators—partly because of the factors just mentioned. This in turn influences the level of dues and fees and the financing of unions and management organizations.

The role and the frequency of the strike or lockout, or other means of economic pressure, differ among these industrial relations systems. The strike may be used as an organizing device, a means of general protest, as a political demonstration, or it may be regarded as an integral part of the collective bargaining process used to induce agreement.[13]

---

[11]See, Hugh Clegg, *Trade Unionism Under Collective Bargaining, A Theory Based on Comparisons of Six Countries* (Oxford: Basil Blackwell, 1976), pp. 55–67.

[12]See, Benjamin Aaron, Ed., *Labor Courts and Grievance Settlement in Western Europe* (Berkeley and Los Angeles: University of California Press, 1971).

[13]The application of elaborate models to international comparisons of strike statistics do not seem to me to have produced significant results, nor are they likely to do so, because of these differences. Moreover, periods of several decades reflect industrial relations systems at

3. The experience of these five countries since 1900 reflects an increasing role of governmental agencies everywhere in prescribing the terms and conditions of employment. The method of legal enactment is an increasing alternative to the method of collective bargaining.[14] The government's activities are illustrated in the chapters in this volume by manpower and training policies, in conflict with traditional apprenticeship; by measures to affect disadvantaged groups according to race, sex, area, and migration, in conflict in some countries with the interests of those already employed; and by incomes policies to restrain wages, salaries, and benefits, in conflict with free collective bargaining. The ideology of equalitarianism combined with the push for protective legislation have been vital forces in some countries. The governmental penetrations into the scope of collective bargaining, particularly through incomes policies, have generally proven to be suspect to unions and to managements alike, except in wartime. The accommodation of these differences is a source of continuing tension in industrial relations systems and in political parties.

It should be recognized that these five countries have differed significantly from the onset of labor organizations, and continue to differ widely, in the extent to which the terms and conditions of employment are specified by governments. The French experience probably reflects the greatest detailed specification by governmental processes. As is stated in Chapter 4, "The collective agreement, an institution that is now more or less general for workers in the private sector, is, in fact, a relatively recent phenomenon in France . . . law had great importance." The authority of a ministry of labor to extend the terms of a collective agreement to others in the same industry or sector (apart from the determination of terms and conditions for government purchases and contracts) is a distinctive arrangement that is a general feature of these governments.

4. The chapters in this volume develop the relationships that exist between unions and political parties and their ideologies. The contrasts between reformist and revolutionary unions, and the evolution of their political policies since the outset of the century, are decisive to the operation of these industrial relations systems. They also reflect the great increase in human rights and industrial democracy for the individual worker through industrial jurisprudence and political processes.

---

quite different stages, and are influenced substantially by the dates selected. See, Douglas A. Hibbs, "Industrial Conflict in Advanced Industrial Societies," *The American Political Science Review*, December 1976.

[14]Sidney and Beatrice Webb, *Industrial Democracy* (New York: Longmans, Green, 1914), pp. 173–221 and 247–278.

ISSUES FOR THE FUTURE

The course of the future of workers and employees in these countries will be shaped both by some factors peculiar to each country and by others common to all advanced democratic societies. Among the more significant of these common elements, the contributors to this volume suggest the following:

The composition of the labor force will continue to change, yielding in the next several decades an older population in which the age of retirement and social security-related issues are likely to receive increased attention. The educational systems are turning out college trained people in increasing proportions, and the productive structure seems to require relatively more professional, technical, and white collar occupations—although the supply of some categories of education may exceed the demand for some periods. These developments affect the substance and processes of collective bargaining and government enactment.

The issues of unemployment, inflation, and incomes policies are likely to continue to be central questions in the interactions of unions, management, and governments. These questions involve important relations among unions and the political parties with which they are either aligned or opposed. The intensity of concern with these problems will be affected by the rates of economic growth in the period ahead.

The competition between collective bargaining and government prescription of the terms and conditions of employment is likely to become more acute and complex in the five countries. The combination of these instruments of regulation is likely to vary significantly by issue and by country.

The thrust of the labor unions in these five countries toward industrial democracy, worker participation, worker members of board of directors, socialization of pension funds, and related movements is difficult to gauge but is likely to be cautious. German codetermination appears to be a distinctive and pragmatic response to these issues that does not adversely affect "economic efficiency," which is referred to in Chapter 3 as "a prime stabilizing factor for the social and political order that was adopted after the World War II." Institutional developments in other countries are likely to take quite different forms.

The tension between ideology and pragmatism, revolution and reform, political activity and collective bargaining is likely to continue everywhere, tending toward workable compromises except where an industrial relations system and political stability are displaced in the aftermath of war, prolonged depression, or social upheaval. The quality and response of managements to these developments will play a role in shaping industrial relations and political responses.

The issue arises as to whether the future is likely to reflect more convergence among these countries.[15] The reader of this volume will surely come away with the impression—apart from precision in concept or measurement—that the condition of the worker and industrial relations are relatively more similar today within and among these countries than they were in 1900.

The institutions that workers have created, and the industrial relations systems of which they are a part, have proven remarkably flexible and adaptable to changing conditions and aspirations. It would be surprising if they did not continue to be in the main pragmatic and tractable.[16]

Labor organizations and their political partners in most of these countries enunciated at the end of the nineteenth century programs and aspirations for workers and society that seemed far beyond their possible reach.[17] In retrospect their dreams have been widely achieved. The formulation of new objectives for themselves and for a democratic society are everywhere in lively debate, in the large and in specific programs and sectors.

[15]Clark Kerr, John T. Dunlop, Frederick Harbison, and Charles A. Myers, *Industrialism and Industrial Man* (Cambridge: Harvard University Press, 1960), pp. 266–296. A large literature has developed around the question of convergence in industrial societies with the main issues concerning different social systems.

[16]For a discussion of the outlook in the United States, see, John T. Dunlop, "Past and Future Tendencies in American Labor Organizations," *Daedalus*, Winter 1978, pp. 79–96.

[17]See, for instance the programs of the Second International, Lewis L. Lorwin, *The International Labor Movement* (New York: Harper, 1953), pp. 19–41. For the United States, see, John R. Commons and Associates, *History of Labor in the United States*, Vol. II (New York: Macmillan, 1936), pp. 509–510.

Labor in the Twentieth Century

1. THE UNITED STATES

WALTER GALENSON
ROBERT S. SMITH

THE WORKING POPULATION

Significant changes in the characteristics of the working population and of the work performed have occurred since the beginning of the twentieth century. Some of these changes are the consequences of individual or collective decisions by workers and firms as they faced the economic and social environment; others represent the outcomes of social choices as reflected in legislation. The purpose of this section is to document the major changes in the characteristics of both workers and their jobs that have occurred since 1900.

Labor Force Characteristics: Sex and Age

One dimension of the extent to which a given population works for pay, or seeks such work, is the proportion of the labor force. Previous definitions of the labor force have varied from the current one, but the differences are not so large as to render comparisons over time meaningless. From 1900–1930, the labor force was defined as those "gainfully occupied." People were considered gainful workers if they reported themselves as having an occupation at which they usually worked, regardless of whether they were at work or seeking work at the time. In 1940, the concept of "labor force" replaced that of "gainful worker," with the result that inexperienced people looking for their first job were now included, whereas experienced "usual" workers not looking for work owing to seasonal factors were excluded. Because the changes in definition in 1940 affected only a small portion of the unemployed (who are themselves a small proportion of the entire labor force), and because the two changes tended to have offsetting effects on labor force counts, it is the judgment of those intimately familiar with the data that intercensal comparisons of labor force and labor force participation rates are meaningful.[1]

[1] See Clarence D. Long, *The Labor Force Under Changing Income and Employment* (Princeton: Princeton University Press, 1958), p. 45.

11

TABLE 1.1

Labor Force Participation Rates of Those over 14, by Sex,
1900–1970

Year	Total (%)		Men (%)		Women (%)	
1900	54.8	$(100)^a$	87.3	$(100)^a$	20.4	$(100)^a$
1910	55.7	(102)	86.3	(99)	22.8	(112)
1920	55.6	(102)	86.5	(99)	23.3	(114)
1930	54.6	(100)	84.1	(96)	24.3	(119)
1940	52.2	(95)	79.0	(91)	25.4	(125)
1950	53.4	(98)	79.0	(91)	28.6	(140)
1960	55.3	(101)	77.4	(89)	34.5	(169)
1970	55.8	(102)	73.0	(84)	39.9	(196)

Sources:
1900–1950: Clarence D. Long, *The Labor Force Under Changing Income and Employment* (Princeton: Princeton University Press, 1958), Table A-2.
1960: U.S. Department of Commerce, Bureau of the Census, *Census of Population, 1960: Employment Status*, Subject Reports, PC(2)-6A, Table 1.
1970: U.S. Department of Commerce, Bureau of the Census, *U.S. Census of Population, 1970: Employment Status and Work Experience*, Subject Reports, PC(2)-6A, Table 1.
[a] Index numbers, with 1900 = 100, are shown in parentheses.

Table 1.1 shows the pattern of labor force participation over the century. It can readily be seen that whereas the overall participation rate has been virtually constant, the aggregate stability is the result of large and offsetting shifts between males and females. While the participation rate of males over 14 years of age has fallen by 16% since 1900, the rate for females has almost doubled.

Disaggregating the within-sex participation rates is equally revealing, as can be seen from Tables 1.2 and 1.3. For men, the largest decreases in participation were among the very young (a 41% decrease) and the very old (a 63% decrease). In contrast, males in the "prime age" groups exhibited only tiny declines in labor force participation (2–6%). The patterns of change in labor force participation for males imply that although they are indeed working less now than they did in 1900, the decrease is almost entirely the result of a shortened work life. On the average, men begin their work life later and retire earlier than they did in 1900, but they have almost the same propensity to work during their prime years.

The disaggregated changes in participation rates for females (Table 1.3) show that the largest increases have occurred in the "prime age" groups, with a huge 242% increase registered for ages 45–64, when children are presumably grown. Consistent with the data for males, the female data also show the effects of the tendency to begin work later and to retire

TABLE 1.2
Labor Force Participation Rates for Males, by Age, 1900–1970

Year	14–19 (%)		20–24 (%)		25–44 (%)		45–64 (%)		Over 65 (%)	
1900	61.1	(100)[a]	91.7	(100)[a]	96.3	(100)[a]	93.3	(100)[a]	68.3	(100)[a]
1910	56.2	(92)	91.1	(99)	96.6	(100)	93.6	(100)	58.1	(85)
1920	52.6	(86)	90.9	(99)	97.1	(101)	93.8	(101)	60.1	(88)
1930	41.1	(67)	89.9	(98)	97.5	(101)	94.1	(101)	58.3	(85)
1940	34.4	(56)	88.0	(96)	95.0	(99)	88.7	(95)	41.5	(61)
1950	39.9	(65)	82.8	(90)	92.8	(96)	87.9	(94)	41.6	(61)
1960	38.1	(62)	86.1	(94)	95.2	(99)	89.0	(95)	30.6	(45)
1970	35.8	(59)	80.9	(88)	94.4	(98)	87.3	(94)	25.0	(37)

Age groups

Sources: See sources cited in Table 1.1.
[a] Index number, with 1900 = 100, are shown in parentheses.

earlier. The only age group for which female participation rates declined was the teenage group (14–19), and the smallest increase was in the "over 65" group. Although clearly offset in the latter case by the overall trend toward a higher fraction of women working, the tendency for earlier retirement did serve to minimize the increase in participation rates among women over 65.

The decline in labor force participation rates among teenage males and females alike is associated with sharp increases in the years of formal schooling attained and the length of the school year. A portion of this increased schooling represents added leisure that a wealthier society can

TABLE 1.3
Labor Force Participation Rates for Females, by Age, 1900–1970

Year	14–19 (%)		20–24 (%)		25–44 (%)		45–64 (%)		Over 65 (%)	
1900	26.8	(100)[a]	32.1	(100)[a]	18.0	(100)[a]	14.1	(100)[a]	9.1	(100)[a]
1910	28.1	(105)	35.5	(111)	21.0	(117)	17.1	(121)	8.6	(95)
1920	28.4	(106)	38.1	(119)	22.5	(125)	17.1	(121)	8.0	(88)
1930	22.8	(85)	42.5	(132)	25.4	(141)	18.7	(133)	8.0	(88)
1940	18.8	(70)	45.1	(141)	30.2	(168)	19.8	(140)	5.9	(65)
1950	22.5	(84)	42.5	(132)	33.0	(183)	28.6	(203)	7.6	(84)
1960	23.9	(89)	44.9	(140)	38.9	(217)	41.6	(295)	10.1	(111)
1970	25.5	(95)	56.3	(175)	47.8	(266)	48.2	(342)	10.4	(114)

Age groups

Source: See sources cited in Table 1.1.
[a] Index numbers, with 1900 = 100, are shown in parentheses.

afford. In part, however, education is an investment required for entry into an increasing number of jobs. As such, one would expect school enrollments to rise if the pecuniary or psychic returns to schooling rise. That the pecuniary rates of return to schooling remained relatively high between 1939 and 1958, in the face of sharp increases in years of schooling, is testimony to the existence of strong forces at work to make education a good investment on financial grounds alone.[2]

The declining participation rates of males over 65 is probably the result of (a) the voluntary preference for leisure induced by higher incomes and increasing pensions, and (b) compulsory retirement rules often associated with pensions. In 1951, a Social Security Administration survey found that 11% of all retired males had been forced to quit by an employer decision under compulsory retirement rules, whereas an identical survey in 1963 showed 21% of retired males in this category.[3]

Declining participation rates will be achieved in an environment of increasing compulsory retirements only if those who retire do not remain in the labor force. This has come about partly as a result of earnings limitations on the eligibility for social security benefits. But perhaps the greatest influence is simply the increasing availability and size, since 1940, of public and private pensions. Older workers do not have to work in order to live.

Explaining earlier retirements as a function of pensions and compulsory retirement rules, however, cannot satisfactorily account for two important facts: (a) the substantial decline in the labor force participation rates of older males prior to 1940, and (b) the fall in labor force participation of older males in rural areas. With respect to the latter, Table 1.4 shows quite clearly that the decline in rural areas, which include farms and small plants less likely to have pensions and compulsory retirement rules, has been even more pronounced than in urban areas. It would seem reasonable to suggest that earlier retirement among men is also influenced by the general rise in income and wealth over time, independent of the effects of pensions.

The Rise in Female Participation Rates

The large increase in female labor force participation rates, especially when compared to the decline for men, is closely related to the "household" role assigned to wives by custom. Whereas wives have experienced a 600% increase in labor force participation since 1900 and a 30% increase from 1960 to 1970, single women have shown an overall decrease in participa-

[2]Gary Becker, *Human Capital* (New York: National Bureau of Economic Research, 1964), pp. 128–130.

[3]Fred Slavick, *Compulsory and Flexible Retirement in the American Economy* (Ithaca, N.Y.: New York State School of Industrial and Labor Relations, 1966), p. 7.

TABLE 1.4

*Rural and Urban Labor Force Participation
Rates of Males over 65, 1900–1970*

Year	Rural (%)		Urban (%)	
1900	70.4	$(100)^a$	63.1	$(100)^a$
1910	60.9	(87)	54.0	(86)
1920	61.6	(88)	58.1	(92)
1930	62.2	(88)	54.2	(86)
1940	46.4	(66)	37.0	(59)
1950	44.1	(63)	40.0	(63)
1960	30.8	(44)	30.4	(48)
1970	24.1	(34)	25.1	(40)

Sources:

1900–1950: Clarence Long, *The Labor Force Under Changing Income and Employment* (Princeton, N.J.: Princeton University Press, 1959), Table A-3.

1960: U.S. Department of Commerce, Bureau of the Census, *Census of Population, 1960: U.S. Summary*, Table 84.

1970: U.S. Department of Commerce, Bureau of the Census, *Census of Population, 1970: U.S. General Summary*, Table 215.

^{a} Index numbers, with 1900 = 100, are shown in parentheses.

tion since 1910, and widowed or divorced women only a relatively modest 22% increase since the turn of the century (see Table 1.5). Hence, the brief analysis that followed will be heavily weighted toward understanding the labor force status of wives.

Two important factors in the increasing tendency of wives to work are: (a) the general increase in wages, and (b) the introduction of labor-saving devices for the home. The former influence has increased the opportunity cost of being a full-time housewife, whereas the second has reduced the time required for house care. Although the invention and spread of labor-saving devices in the home may have been partially induced by the rising propensity of women to work, there is some independent evidence that the labor force behavior of women is responsive to the alternative costs of performing household chores. One study found that where the cost of domestic help is lower, other things equal, the labor force participation rates of wives are significantly higher.[4]

The steepest increases in the labor force participation rates of married

[4] William G. Bowen and T. Aldrich Finegan, *The Economics of Labor Force Participation* (Princeton: Princeton University Press, 1969), p. 161.

TABLE 1.5
Labor Force Participation Rates of Females over 16 Years of Age, by Marital Status, 1900–1970

Year	All females (%)		Single (%)		Widowed and divorced (%)		Married (%)	
1900	20.6	$(100)^a$	45.9	$(100)^a$	32.5	$(100)^a$	5.6	$(100)^a$
1910	25.5	(124)	54.0	(118)	34.1	(105)	10.7	(191)
1920	24.0	(117)					9.0	(161)
1930	25.3	(123)	55.2	(120)	34.4	(106)	11.7	(209)
1940	26.7	(130)	53.1	(116)	33.7	(104)	13.8	(246)
1950	29.7	(144)	53.6	(117)	35.5	(109)	21.6	(386)
1960	35.7	(173)	42.9	(94)	38.7	(119)	30.6	(546)
1970	41.6	(202)	50.9	(111)	39.5	(122)	39.5	(705)

Sources: 1900–1950: Clarence D. Long, *The Labor Force Under Changing Income and Employment* (Princeton: Princeton University Press, 1958), Table A-6.

1960: U.S. Department of Commerce, Bureau of the Census, *Census of Population, 1960: Employment Status,* Subject Reports PC(2)-6A, Table 4.

1970: U.S. Department of Commerce, Bureau of the Census, *Census of Population, 1970: Employment Status and Work Experience,* Subject Reports PC(2)-6A, Table 3.

a Index numbers, with 1900 = 100, shown in parentheses.

women have occurred since World War II. In the first 40 years of this century, their labor force participation rate rose by an average of 2.1% every decade. Since 1940 the average increase has been 8.6% per decade. This suggests that the experience of women working during the war may have altered the attitudes of both women and employers. It is noteworthy, however, that the largest increases in the postwar period have come *after* 1950, suggesting that if the war were causal in changing attitudes, its full effect was delayed somewhat.

Other factors commonly thought to have given rise to increased female labor force participation are the growth of clerical jobs,[5] reduced work hours that permitted women to work both in the labor market and at home, and increased income aspirations of families, leading to a desire to employ a secondary worker.[6] The above factors are all plausible; however, none can be clearly identified as causal. All of them could be *induced*, to some extent, by the fact of greater female labor force participation itself.

Labor Force Characteristics: Race

For the population as a whole, economic growth has been associated with shorter working lives for men and increased opportunities for women

[5]Long, *The Labor Force,* pp. 135–140.

[6]Bowen and Finegan, *Economics of Labor Force,* pp. 227–241.

to pursue careers outside the home. It would appear that rising real incomes have widened the scope of effective choice, enabling people to pursue leisure or work alternatives previously not feasible. This interpretation of labor force behavior receives additional support from an analysis of participation rates by race.

It is clear from Table 1.6 that the overall experience of nonwhite participation rates has been contrary to that for native whites.[7] Nonwhite labor force participation has been falling while native white participation has been rising. However, one must examine the data by sex to understand why the experience of each group has differed.

The data for males show that both native white and nonwhite males have withdrawn from the labor force over time, but that the withdrawal for nonwhites has been greater. Nonwhite males began the century with participation rates above those for native whites, but by 1960 such rates were substantially below the native white rates. Nonwhite females were reducing their participation for 40 years while white females were increasing theirs. After 1940 females in both groups were increasing participation, although the rate of increase for nonwhite women was such that by 1960 their participation was not even up to its 1900 level. However, the nonwhite level of female labor force participation is still higher than the level for native white females.

That male participation rates have fallen faster for nonwhites is not surprising. From 1939 to 1962, the median wage and salary income of nonwhite males rose from 41 to 57% of that for white males,[8] suggesting that nonwhite incomes have risen faster over time. It is an interesting and puzzling development, though, that poverty seems now to be accompanied by lower rates of male participation in contrast to the higher rates in 1900. Much of the current differential is among teenagers, who have faced increased difficulties in securing jobs in the black slum areas. However, rates of participation among nonwhite males are lower for all age groups, although they are higher for all female age groups except teenagers. These

---

[7]Native whites were chosen as the reference group to avoid the problems introduced by the rather distorted age distribution of foreign-born whites (who are much older than others). Separate analysis of foreign-born whites is omitted for the sake of space, but the general patterns of change are rather similar across age groups to the patterns for native whites (the single exception being teenagers, where foreign-born participation rates have declined substantially relative to those for native whites). The comparisons of native whites and nonwhites were truncated at 1960 because data in the 1970 census were not reported in a form comparable to earlier years.

[8]See U.S. Bureau of the Census, *Historical Statistics of the United States, Colonial Times to 1957* and the *Continuation to 1960, 1962, and 1965*, Tables G169–190.

TABLE 1.6
Labor Force Participation Rates, by Race, 1900–1960

	Both sexes (%)				Males (%)				Females (%)			
Year	Native white		Nonwhite		Native white		Nonwhite		Native white		Nonwhite	
1900	51.9	(100)[a]	66.2	(100)[a]	85.7	(100)[a]	89.9	(100)[a]	17.1	(100)[a]	42.2	(100)[a]
1910[b]												
1920	53.5	(103)	65.8	(99)	84.8	(99)	89.5	(100)	21.8	(128)	41.7	(99)
1930	52.8	(102)	64.9	(98)	82.5	(96)	88.2	(98)	23.0	(135)	41.8	(99)
1940	51.7	(100)	57.8	(87)	78.7	(92)	79.9	(89)	25.0	(146)	36.8	(87)
1950	53.8	(104)	56.3	(85)	79.9	(93)	76.8	(85)	28.7	(168)	37.0	(88)
1960	56.0	(108)	56.3	(85)	79.0	(92)	72.2	(80)	34.1	(199)	41.7	(99)

Sources: 1900–1950: Clarence D. Long, *The Labor Force Under Changing Income and Employment* (Princeton: Princeton University Press, 1959), Table A–4.

1960: U.S. Bureau of the Census, *1960 Census of Population,* Subject Reports, PC(2)-6A, Tables 1 and 3.

[a] Index numbers, with 1900 = 100, are shown in parentheses.

[b] Data are not available for 1910.

facts may reflect the greater incidence of black men as "second earners" in a female-dominated family.[9]

The relative poverty of nonwhites and the higher incidence of female-headed families among blacks are obviously important reasons for the historically higher participation rates of nonwhite women. Market work has been a virtual necessity for women whose families needed second or even prime earners. As nonwhite incomes have risen both absolutely and relatively over time, and as the welfare programs aimed at female-headed families have expanded, some of those previously working out of necessity have quite likely withdrawn from the labor market to pursue more attractive alternatives. This tendency has not quite offset the postwar forces operating to increase female participation rates, but its existence probably explains why the increases for nonwhite females have been so small.

Education

One significant change in the characteristics of the labor force, associated with the declining propensity of teenagers to seek work, is the rise in the level of formal education. In 1900, the average member of the labor

[9]Daniel P. Moynihan, *The Negro Family* (Washington, D.C.: U.S. Department of Labor, March 1965), pp. 30–31.

TABLE 1.7

Years of School per Member of the Labor Force, 14 Years and Older, 1900–1957

Year	Mean years of school completed	Indices of school attainment (1900 = 100)	
		Unadjusted	Adjusted for length of school year
1900	7.70	100	100
1910	7.91	103	112
1920	8.12	105	127
1930	8.41	109	145
1940	9.02	117	175
1950	10.10	131	209
1957	10.96	142	252

Source: Theodore W. Schultz, "Education and Economic Growth," *Readings in the Economics of Education,* ed. Mary Jean Bowman (Paris: United Nations, 1968), p. 286.

force had completed 7.7 years of school, but by 1957 the typical worker had almost 11 years of schooling (see Table 1.7). This apparent 42% increase is, in fact, even larger if one considers the gradual lengthening of the school year from 99 days in 1900 to 159 days in 1957.[10] Adjusting for the longer school year (Column 4 of Table 1.7) implies a 152% rise in the level of educational attainment from 1900 to 1957.

Increases in educational attainment have continued since 1957 to the point where the median years of formal schooling completed by members of the labor force is 12.3 for both men and women.[11] In 1970, fully 7.5% of the Gross National Product (GNP) represented expenditures by primary, secondary, and university-level schools. The proportion of GNP allocated to formal schooling has more than doubled since the late 1940s, a period in which private pecuniary returns to education were high and education was seen as a vehicle for economic and social advancement.

Job Characteristics: Hours of Work

There are two well-known caveats that must be acknowledged when interpreting data on average weekly hours of work. First, average hours

[10]Theodore W. Schultz, "Education and Economic Growth," *Readings in the Economics of Education,* ed. Mary Jean Bowman (Paris: United Nations, 1968), p. 281.
[11]U.S. Bureau of the Census, *Census of Population: 1970,* Subject Reports PC(2)–5B, Tables 5, 6.

"paid for" will exceed average hours actually worked, because of paid holidays, sick days, and vacations. For our purposes of indicating work effort, hours worked is clearly more meaningful than hours paid for. Because the official statistics on work hours published by the Bureau of Labor Statistics relate to hours paid for, we must look elsewhere for the necessary data. Second, hours of work per week vary inversely with the unemployment rate as companies eliminate overtime and adopt shorter schedules. This fact means that we must control for cyclical influences in reaching conclusions about long-run trends in work hours. However, it also reminds us that not all reductions in work hours are necessarily accompanied by increases in human welfare.

Table 1.8 contains a series on weekly hours worked for manufacturing production workers. Whereas many of the yearly averages between 1920 and 1947 are interpolations from a benchmark, and although the data from 1900 to 1919 are based on *scheduled* hours, this series is carefully constructed and the best available. Comparing the peak employment years (1901 and 1969) of the earliest and latest cycles covered by our data, in a crude first attempt to filter our cyclical variations in hours, it can readily be seen that the decline in weekly hours of work has been enormous over this century. The 1901–1969 decline of 16 hours of work per week suggests that a typical full-time production worker has an extra waking day per week of leisure time now, as compared to the turn of the century.

Economic theory suggests that because both commodities and leisure time combine to produce human welfare, a simultaneous increase in both real income (the "command" over commodities) and leisure signals a clearcut increase in social well-being. It is therefore useful to note that the 30% decrease in average hours worked cited above has been accompanied by increases in the wage rate so that real weekly earnings have increased. Thus if more goods (including leisure) do produce greater happiness, the welfare of the typical worker has improved substantially over the first seven decades of this century.

In analyzing the large decrease in hours worked, economists have usually emphasized the theory of labor supply, the obverse of which is the preference for leisure time. Briefly put, these analyses suggest that the increments in income made possible by the increased wage rate have induced a greater desire for leisure time, despite the fact that the price of leisure time (approximated by the wage rate) has risen. Analyses stressing labor supply theory, however, appear unable to account for the entire pattern of the decline in hours worked. Table 1.9 shows average hours worked for the peak employment years in each business cycle (excluding World War II). The data indicate that the decline in hours worked has taken place in three stages. From 1901 to 1929, average weekly hours

TABLE 1.8

Average Weekly Hours of Work, Manufacturing Production Workers, 1900–1975

Year	Hours	Year	Hours	Year	Hours
1900	55.0	1925	47.9	1950	38.7
1901	54.3	1926	47.8	1951	38.9
1902	55.4	1927	47.4	1952	38.8
1903	54.3	1928	47.6	1953	38.6
1904	53.6	1929	48.0	1954	37.8
1905	54.5	1930	43.6	1955	38.5
1906	55.0	1931	40.2	1956	38.2
1907	54.3	1932	38.0	1957	37.8
1908	50.3	1933	37.6	1958	37.3
1909	53.1	1934	34.4	1959	38.3
1910	52.2	1935	36.4	1960	38.1
1911	51.7	1936	38.7	1961	38.0
1912	52.4	1937	37.9	1962	38.5
1913	50.9	1938	35.0	1963	38.5
1914	50.1	1939	37.3	1964	39.1
1915	50.4	1940	37.6	1965	39.1
1916	51.4	1941	40.0	1966	39.1
1917	51.0	1942	42.3	1967	38.4
1918	49.6	1943	44.1	1968	38.6
1919	46.1	1944	44.2	1969	38.3
1920	48.1	1945	42.4	1970	37.9
1921	45.3	1946	39.2	1971	37.7
1922	47.9	1947	39.2	1972	38.0
1923	48.9	1948	38.8	1973	38.0
1924	46.6	1949	38.0	1974	37.6
				1975	36.8

Sources: The data for 1900–1957 were taken from Ethel Jones, "New Estimates of Hours of Work Per Week and Hourly Earnings, 1900–1957," *Review of Economics and Statistics,* November, 1963, pp. 374–385. The data for 1900–1919 were obtained from *scheduled* hours of work per day and the days of plant operation. The data from 1920–1932 are based on data from the National Industrial Conference Board bench-marked to 1929, when several independent surveys (yielding approximately the same results) were averaged. Data from 1933–1946 were obtained by interpolating between surveys in 1933, 1935, 1937 and 1939. Data for 1947 on (including data after 1957) were calculated from all issues available since 1947 of the *Census of Manufactures* and *Annual Survey of Manufactures,* which contain man-hours worked (exclusive of vacations, sick leave, and holidays).

worked declined by 2 hours per decade, whereas from 1929 to 1948 the decline was close to 5 hours per decade. However, from 1948 to 1969 hours worked fell by only .2 hours every 10 years.

TABLE 1.9

Average Weekly Hours Worked by Manufacturing Production Workers, Peak Employment Years in Each Business Cycle, 1900–1976 (excluding 1940–1945)

	Average hours worked	Average decline in hours worked per decade
1901	54.3	
1906	55.0	
1913	50.9	
1919	46.1	2.2
1923	48.9	
1926	47.8	
1929	48.0	4.6
1948	38.8	
1953	38.6	
1956	38.2	.2
1969	38.3	

Sources: See sources cited in Table 1.8.

The more rapid reduction in average hours worked in manufacturing during the 1929–1948 period may have been the result of the Fair Labor Standards Act of 1938, which required time and one-half payments for weekly hours worked in excess of 40. The act, though not establishing maximum hours of work—as the states had for women and children in the late 1800s and early 1900s[12]—did increase the cost of employing workers for more than 40 hours per week. Thus, when recovery from the depression, with its short workweek, came, average hours worked in manufacturing rose above 40 only during the war years.

It is remarkable that there has been very little decline in working hours in the postwar period. Indeed, the data in Table 1.8 may overstate the decline. An estimate of hours worked by men in nonagricultural industries, adjusted for growth in vacations and holidays, indicates that the decline was only from 41.6 per week in 1948 to 40.9 per week in 1975.[13] The more inclusive data in Table 1.8 are biased because of a change in the sex composition of the labor force.

A number of econometric studies have attempted to explain this long period of stable working hours, but thus far, none has yielded plausible results.[14] The fact that the number of paid leisure hours per week has

[12]The state laws on maximum hours had little impact on actual work hours, since the average workweek was 4 hours less than the average state maximum throughout this period.

[13]John D. Owen, "Workweek and Leisure," *Monthly Labor Review* 99, (August 1976), p. 3.

[14]See John D. Owen, *The Price of Leisure* (Rotterdam: Rotterdam University Press, 1969); idem, "The Demand for Leisure," *Journal of Political Economy* 79, January–February 1971, p. 56; and Thomas J. Kniesner, "The Full-Time Workweek in the United States, 1900–1970," *Industrial and Labor Relations Review* 30, October 1976, p. 5.

increased by at least one since 1948[15] makes it even more difficult to understand why working hours have not fallen more. It may be that a 40-hour working week has become a powerful conventional norm; thus, the scheduled working hours of 80% of all plant workers was precisely 40 hours in 1973–1974.[16] However, the 1976 collective agreement in the automobile industry, which provided for 12 additional single days off per annum, may be interpreted as the beginning of a drive toward the 4-day week.

Industrial Distribution of the Labor Force

Shifts in the industrial distribution of jobs have been very large since 1900. Agricultural employment declined from 38.1% of the experienced civilian labor force to just 3.8% by 1970, and almost the entire loss of jobs in this primary sector has been picked up in the service, or tertiary sector (see Table 1.10). The latter sector has more than doubled its share of employment since 1900, and now is larger than both the agricultural and goods-producing sectors combined—commanding over 56% of all civilian jobs. The employment share of goods-producing industries, after rising somewhat, began to decline after 1960.

A detailed examination of the reasons for the large sectoral shifts in employment is beyond the scope of this chapter.[17] Suffice it to note that the real income gains made possible by productivity increases in agriculture and manufacturing are disproportionately spent on services. The largest increases in the service sector have been in retail and wholesale trade (9.2% in 1910 to 20% in 1970), and government administration and education (3.2 to 13.2%). These two categories alone account for two-thirds of the percentage-point increases in the service sector share since 1910. By contrast, domestic services have fallen by 4.5% (to 1.5% of employment in 1970), and other personal services have remained fairly constant.[18]

Occupational Distribution

Changes in the mix of jobs performed throughout this century reflect changes in industrial composition. There was a huge reduction in the number of farmworkers. Manual workers, who are heavily represented in the goods-producing industries, maintained an essentially constant share of employment. Clerical, professional-technical, and "other" service workers recorded large increases in their share of employment, a fact consistent

[15]U.S. Department of Labor, *Handbook of Labor Statistics 1972*, p. 156.

[16]U.S. Department of Labor, *Handbook of Labor Statistics 1975*, p. 186.

[17]For the most searching analysis of this question, see Simon Kuznets, *Economic Growth of Nations*, (Cambridge, Mass.: Harvard University Press, 1971).

[18]See the sources listed in Table 1.10.

TABLE 1.10
Employment Distribution^a, by Major Industrial Sector, 1900–1970

Year	Agriculture (%)[b]	Goods-producing industries (%)[c]	Services (%)[d]
1900	38.1	37.8	24.1
1910	32.1	40.9	27.0
1920	27.6	44.8	27.6
1930	22.7	42.1	35.2
1940	18.5	41.6	39.9
1950	12.1	41.3	46.6
1960	6.6	41.4	52.0
1970	3.8	39.8	56.4

Sources: 1900–1940: U.S. Bureau of the Census, *Historical Statistics of the United States, Colonial Times to 1957,* 1960, Table D57-71.

1950: *U.S. Census of Population 1950,* Subject Reports, Vol. IV, Chapter 1D, 1955, Table 15.

1960: *U.S. Census of Population 1960,* Subject Reports, PC(2)-7F, 1967, Table 1.

1970: U.S. Census of Population 1970, Subject Reports, PC(2)-7B, 1972, Table 1.

^aFrom 1900 to 1930, employment refers to "gainful workers." From 1940, employment refers to experienced civilian labor force. Where applicable, persons not assigned to an industry were assumed to have the same employment distribution as those who were.

^bAgriculture includes forestry and fishing.

^cIncluded are manufacturing, mining, construction, and transportation, communications, and public utilities.

^dIncluded are trade; personal, professional, and business services; entertainment; finance, real estate and government.

with the growth of services in general, and the government (including education) and trade sectors in particular. Table 1.11 records these changes in occupational structure.

Within each of the major occupational groupings some interesting patterns emerge. The most spectacular growth has been in the clerical occupations, which have gone from 3 to almost 18% of the labor force. This growth has been associated with the large increases in female labor force participation. In 1900, only 4% of women in the labor force had clerical occupations, and only 24% of clerical workers were females. By 1970, 34% of women were in clerical jobs, where they comprised 74% of the total.[19] To what extent the growth of female labor force participation caused or resulted from the growth in clerical jobs is not known. It should be noted, however, that clerical jobs require general skills and are therefore

[19]See the sources cited in Table 1.11.

TABLE 1.11

Occupational Distribution of Experienced Civilian Labor Force[a], 1900–1970

	1900 (%)	1910 (%)	1920 (%)	1930 (%)	1940 (%)	1950 (%)	1960 (%)	1970 (%)
White collar	17.6	21.0	25.0	29.4	31.1	36.6	42.2	47.5
Professional and technical	4.3	4.6	5.4	6.8	7.5	8.6	11.3	14.6
Managers	5.9	6.5	6.6	7.4	7.3	8.7	8.5	8.1
Clerical	3.0	5.2	8.0	8.9	9.6	12.3	14.9	17.8
Sales	4.5	4.6	4.9	6.3	6.7	7.0	7.5	7.0
Manual	35.8	37.5	40.2	39.6	39.8	41.1	39.7	36.6
Craftsmen	10.6	11.4	13.0	12.8	12.0	14.2	14.3	13.9
Operatives	12.8	14.4	15.6	15.8	18.4	20.4	19.9	17.9
Laborers (nonfarm)	12.5	11.8	11.6	11.0	9.4	6.6	5.5	4.7
Service	9.1	9.4	7.9	9.8	11.8	10.5	11.7	12.9
Domestics	5.4	4.9	3.3	4.1	4.7	2.6	2.8	1.5
Other[b]	3.6	4.5	4.5	5.7	7.1	7.9	8.9	11.3
Farm workers	37.5	30.4	27.0	21.2	17.4	11.8	6.3	3.1
Farmers and farm managers	19.9	16.3	15.3	12.4	10.4	7.4	3.9	1.8
Farm laborers	17.7	14.2	11.7	8.8	7.0	4.4	2.4	1.3

Sources: 1900–1950: U.S. Bureau of the Census, Historical Statistics of the United States, Colonial Times to 1957, (1960), Table D72-122.
1960: U.S. Bureau of the Census, Census of Population 1960, Subject Reports, PC(2)-7A, 1967, Table 1.
1970: U.S. Bureau of the Census, Census of Population 1970, Subject Reports, PC(2)-7A, 1972, Table 1.

[a] From 1900–1930, employment data relate to "gainful workers." From 1940 on, data relate to experienced civilian labor force.
[b] Included are attendants, barbers, cooks, guards, janitors, police, practical nurses, ushers, waiters, and similar jobs.

well suited to the needs of women returning to the labor force after periods of not working for pay.

Another interesting development has been the decline of low-skilled jobs. In 1900, the fraction of jobs in the operative, laborer (farm and nonfarm), and service worker categories was 52.1%. In 1970, these jobs comprised only 36.8% of the total. This is due largely to the decline in farm labor jobs, since the share of low-skill, nonagricultural jobs has remained almost constant. Technological change has not substantially reduced the need for low-skill workers in the goods producing and service sectors, but it has in farming.

Unemployment

In the United States, the unemployment rate is defined as the ratio of those who want and are seeking work, but are without any sort of job, to all those in the labor force. As a measure of employment stability, the unemployment rate is crude because it ignores hours of work. As a measure of hardship, it is even less useful, since it does not take account of wage changes and the existence of unemployment compensation. Nevertheless, a brief review of the evidence on unemployment rates, particularly with respect to their stability over time, may prove useful in outlining some important changes in job characteristics over the century.

Table 1.12 contains the best continuous, historical series of unemployment rates for the United States. However, the number of people unemployed in years prior to 1940 cannot be measured directly except in the census years 1900, 1910, and 1930. In the intercensal years, unemployment was estimated by the difference between estimated employment and labor force. Errors in estimates of either employment or the labor force in the pre-1940 years can therefore have large effects on the estimated unemployment rates. The rates since 1940, however, are based on direct estimates from monthly household surveys, and are therefore much less subject to error.

Although the pre-1940 estimating procedure imparts no clear-cut bias to the unemployment rates, it does lead to greater *variability* in unemployment rates (when compared to the post-1940 rates) for two reasons:

1. The procedure is subject to greater error.
2. The calculation of the labor force cannot account for the "discouraged worker" effect of reduced employment opportunities on the labor force, which tends to damp fluctuations in the unemployment rate over the cycle.

TABLE 1.12

Unemployment Rates, Civilian Labor Force over 14 Years of Age[a], 1900–1976

Year	Rate	Year	Rate	Year	Rate (old series)	Rate (new series)[b]	Year	Rate (new series)[b]
1900	5.0	1924	5.5	1947	3.6	3.9	1971	5.9
1901	2.4	1925	4.0	1948	3.4	3.8	1972	5.6
1902	2.7	1926	1.9	1949	5.5	5.9	1973	4.9
1903	2.6	1927	4.1	1950	5.0	5.3	1974	5.6
1904	4.8	1928	4.4	1951	3.0	3.3	1975	8.5
1905	3.1	1929	3.2	1952	2.7	3.1	1976	7.7
1906	.8	1930	8.9	1953	2.5	2.9		
1907	1.8	1931	15.9	1954	5.0	5.6		
1908	8.5	1932	23.6	1955	4.0	4.4		
1909	5.2	1933	24.9	1956	3.8	4.2		
1910	5.9	1934	21.7	1957	4.0	4.3		
1911	6.2	1935	20.1	1958		6.8		
1912	5.2	1936	17.0	1959		5.5		
1913	4.4	1937	14.3	1960		5.6		
1914	8.0	1938	19.0	1961		6.7		
1915	9.7	1939	17.2	1962		5.6		
1916	4.8	1940	14.6	1963		5.7		
1917	4.8	1941	9.9	1964		5.2		
1918	1.4	1942	4.7	1965		4.6		
1919	2.3	1943	1.9	1966		3.8		
1920	4.0	1944	1.2	1967		3.8		
1921	11.9	1945	1.9	1968		3.6		
1922	7.6	1946	3.9	1969		3.5		
1923	3.2			1970		4.9		

Sources: 1900–1954 (old series): Stanley Lebergott, "Annual Estimates of Unemployment in the United States, 1900–1950," *The Measurement and Behavior of Unemployment,* NBER Special Committee Conference Series no. 8 (Princeton, 1957), pp. 213–239.

1955–1957 (old series): U.S. Bureau of the Census, *Annual Report on the Labor Force,* Current Population Reports, Series P-50 (1955, 1956, 1957).

1947–1966 (new series): U.S. Bureau of Labor Statistics, *Employment and Earnings,* vol. 13, no. 7 (January, 1967), Table A-1.

1967–1976: U.S. Bureau of Labor Statistics, *Employment and Earnings,* vol. 24, no. 7 (July, 1977), Table A-1.

[a]After 1966, unemployment rates only for those 16 and over are published. The differences between the rates for these over 14 and over 16 in the years where both were computed are very small. Therefore, a parallel series in this table was not considered necessary. The rates shown from 1967 on relate to those over 16, and the prior data related to those over 14.

[b]In 1957 the definition of the term unemployed was changed to include those who

1. Were waiting to be called back to a job from which they had been laid off; or
2. Were waiting to report to a new wage or salary job scheduled to start within the next 30 days (and were not in school during the survey week); or
3. Would have been looking for work except that they were temporarily ill or believed no work was available in their line of work or in the community.

Prior to 1957, part of group 1 above—those whose layoffs were for definite periods of less than 30 days—were classified as employed, as were all of the persons in group 2 above.

This new definition was also applied to unemployment data for the years 1947–1957.

The Level of Unemployment Rates

Perhaps the best place to start is with the least controversial estimates in the nonwar, nondepression years prior to 1940, namely, the census years 1900 and 1910. The unemployment rates in these years—5% and 5.9%, respectively—are strikingly similar to the unemployment rates (using a somewhat different definition of unemployment) in the latest three census years: 5.3% (1950), 5.6% (1960), and 4.9% (1970). Although definitional changes alone appear to raise the postwar rates by .4 percentage points over the old series, it is interesting that the rates should be so similar.

Although it forces us to use less reliable, interpolated estimates, broadening the scope of comparison to the first 15 (nonwar) years of the century and the 12 years between the Korean and Vietnamese wars is also instructive. The 1900–1914 mean unemployment rate was 4.4%, and the median rate was 4.8%. By way of comparison, the mean rate from 1954 to 1965 was 5.3%, and the median was 5.5%. Even including all the years since 1954 only lowers the mean to 5.0% and the median to 5.2%. Given the impact of postwar definitional changes, the evidence suggests that there has been no long-run trend in unemployment rates.

This ignores more than 30 years of upheaval associated with three major wars and the Great Depression. But the apparent failure of the average unemployment rate to fall during "normal" periods over this century, despite the emergence of Keynesian tools for economic management, is most interesting. One can only speculate on the reasons. It may be, for example, that the absence of unemployment compensation in the early part of the century kept unemployment low by forcing workers to accept any jobs that came along. More recently, the constraints imposed by fear of inflation may have prevented the government from attempting to drive unemployment down.

The most notable change in unemployment rates during periods of "normalcy" is that their variability has fallen. From 1900 to 1914, the unemployment rate varied from .8 to 8.5%, with a standard deviation equal to one-half of the mean unemployment rate (2.2/4.4%). The range from 1954 to 1974 was from 3.5 to 6.8%, with a standard deviation equal to one-fifth of the mean (1/5%).

Cyclical stability in the demand for labor can be enhanced if product demand becomes less variable, or if the demand for workers becomes less responsive to change in output. The relatively recent emergence of fiscal stabilizers, improved methods of inventory control, and a growing service sector all suggest a greater stability of output now compared to the early years of this century. In addition, however, employment is probably less sensitive to changes in output than it used to be. Employers may be reluctant to lay off workers for whom they have made large training outlays, and it is likely that these outlays have been increased in size and extended to more workers as technology has become more complex.

TRADE UNIONISM AND
COLLECTIVE BARGAINING

Trade-Union Membership

The modern history of American trade unionism begins in 1886, when the American Federation of Labor (AFL) was formed. The mainstream of the labor movement has continued to be this organization, despite several challenges from the Left.

Membership statistics since 1900 are presented in Tables 1.13 and 1.14.[20] The year 1935, which witnessed the formation of the Congress of Industrial Organizations (CIO), was a cataclysmic one, accounting for the break in the series. For several years thereafter, membership was difficult to estimate because of the great organizing drives that were in process. From 1938 to 1950, AFL and CIO memberships are shown separately. Thereafter, there is a combined total for the merged AFL–CIO.

American trade-union membership has not shown a monotonically increasing trend. From a high point of 5 million in 1920, there was almost a continual year-to-year decline until the bottom was reached in 1933. The big breakthrough came in the Roosevelt era, and by 1945, total union membership was 4.5 times as great as it had been in 1933. Although the rate of growth moderated sharply thereafter, the trend was generally, if not always, in an upward direction.

The degree of organization represented by the membership data is not easy to specify, in part because of the variety of labor force bases against which membership can be measured: total labor force, nonagricultural labor force, employment in manufacturing, "organizable" labor force. To take an illustrative example, the percentage of organization in 1900 was 3, measured against the civilian labor force, and 6 against nonagricultural employment. The comparable figures for 1920 were 12.3 and 19.5.[21] One might conclude that progress in organizing farm workers had been made

---

[20]Preliminary data for 1976 indicated that union membership had declined by 767,000 during the period 1974–1976. This was the first overall drop in membership since 1960–1962. Of the total decline, 400,000 represented women workers, probably as a result of heavy unemployment in industries employing large numbers of women. AFL–CIO membership decline from 1974 was 300,000. "Unions' Rolls in Nation Down 769,000 in 2 Years," *New York Times*, 3 September 1977, p. 8.

[21]Leo Troy, *Trade Union Membership, 1897–1962* (New York: National Bureau of Economic Research, 1965), p. 2.

TABLE 1.13

Trade Union Membership in the United States,[a] *1900–1934, in Thousands*

Year	Total membership	Membership of AFL	AFL membership (percentage of total)
1900	791	548	69.3
1905	1918	1494	77.9
1910	2116	1562	73.8
1915	2560	1946	76.0
1920	5034	4079	81.0
1925	3566	2877	80.7
1930	3632	2961	81.5
1934	3249	2608	80.3
1935	3728	3218	86.3

Source: U.S. Bureau of the Census, *Historical Statistics of the United States,* p. 97.

[a] Includes Canadian members of labor unions with headquarters in the U.S.

between these two years. In fact, there was a sharp decline in the relative share of farm employment between the 2 years, which accounted in part for the more rapid increase in the first measure of degree of organization.

If one simply takes the ratio of total trade-union membership to the number of employees on nonagricultural payrolls, a statistical series that is available only since 1919, the results are as shown in Table 1.15. It would

TABLE 1.14

Trade Union Membership in the United States,[a] *1938–1974, in Thousands*

Year	Total	AFL	AFL percentage of total	CIO	CIO percentage of total
1938	8,265	3,623	43.8	4,038	48.9
1940	8,944	4,247	47.5	3,625	40.5
1945	14,796	6,931	46.8	6,000	40.6
1950	14–16,000	7,143	47.6	n.a.	
1955	17,749	16,062[b]	90.5	—	—
1960	18,117	15,072[b]	83.2	—	—
1965	18,519	15,604[b]	84.3	—	—
1970	20,752	15,978[b]	77.0	—	—
1972	20,894	16,507[b]	79.0	—	—
1974	21,585	16,879[b]	78.2	—	—

Sources: U.S. Department of Labor, *Handbook of Labor Statistics,* (Washington, D.C.: U.S. Goverment Printing Office, 1976), p. 297; *Statistical Abstract of the United States* (1976), p. 384.

[a] Includes Canadian members of U.S.-based unions.

[b] AFL–CIO.

TABLE 1.15
Trade Union Membership as a Proportion of
Employees on Nonagricultural Payrolls,
1920–1974

Year	Percentage
1920[a]	18.4
1925[a]	12.4
1930	12.3
1935	13.8
1940	27.6
1945	36.6
1950	33.2
1955	35.0
1960	33.4
1965	30.5
1970	29.3
1974	27.6

Sources: U.S. Department of Labor, *Handbook of Labor Statistics,* (1975), p. 105;
Tables 13 and 14.
[a] The data for these years may be overstated by
a fraction of a percentage point due to use of
different sources.

appear from this table that the trade unions achieved their maximum penetration of the labor market around 1945, and again in 1955, but lost ground thereafter. This is true in a sense, but an intervening factor, structural changes in the labor force, complicates the conclusions that can be drawn from the data.

In 1945, service-producing employment constituted 57% of total nonagricultural employment. This rose slowly to 60% in 1955, and thereafter began to rise very rapidly, reaching 68% by 1970. In the United States, as well as in most other countries, the service industries have been less susceptible to trade unionism than those producing goods. There are some exceptions, notably transportation, but the relative growth of service employment has been a major factor behind the trend shown in Table 1.15. For similar reasons, the relative strength of U.S. and European unions cannot be assessed by a simple comparison of union membership and employment, since the United States is more service oriented than any other major industrial nation.

Available estimates of the sectoral distribution of trade-union membership bear out these points. Of the 21.6 million trade-union members in 1974, some 12.5 million were in goods-producing industries, whereas 9.1 million were employed in service industries. This amounted to 51% trade-union penetration for goods and only 17% for services.[22] When it is recalled that employment in the goods-producing sector includes white- as well as blue-collar jobs, and that a substantial proportion of those white-collar employees are not organized, a more accurate picture of the extent of the strength of American unions among blue-collar employees emerges.

There is a substantial body of literature devoted to a discussion of the factors that have determined changes in union membership. On the economic side, the level of unemployment, the rate of change of money wages and prices, and profits, are among the variables that have been cited. Among the political factors are the attitudes of both the government and the public toward unions, as well as labor legislation. Sociologists tend to emphasize management attitudes, the quality of union leadership, and various aspects of the working environment. Historians have pointed to the impact of such events as the two world wars and the Great Depression.[23]

There have been recent efforts to determine the causative factors more precisely through econometric analysis. One such model uses as explanatory variables of changing union membership the following: the rate of change of prices, the rate of change of employment in the union sector, the level of unemployment in the preceding trough of the business cycle, the degree of unionization, and, as a proxy for political pressures, the percentage of Democratic members of the House of Representatives.[24] The model has been subject to considerable criticism,[25] and it cannot be said that satisfactory results have been achieved.

If one examines the membership data, it appears that the advances have occurred in bursts during periods marked by major political or economic events. After a period of gradual growth from 1900 to 1915, membership almost doubled from 1915 to 1920, years of war and postwar economic boom, a period in which, for the first time, the labor movement was treated as a representative group by the federal government. There followed a decline from 1920 to 1929, despite a relatively favorable economic climate, for reasons that are not yet entirely understood. The Great

[22]These figures are calculated from data in U.S. Bureau of Labor Statistics, *Handbook of Labor Statistics, 1975*, p. 105. The percentages are subject to some overstatement, since Canadian members are included in the membership totals. Moreover, most of these are probably in the goods-producing sector, which might result in a relative upward bias of this sector by a few percentage points. Union membership in goods-producing industries was secured by adding the data for manufacturing, mining, construction, and public utilities in the source.

[23]For a summary of the literature, see Albert A. Blum, "Why Unions Grow," *Labor History* 9, (1968): pp. 39–72.

[24]Orley Ashenfelter and John H. Pencavel, "American Trade Union Growth: 1900–1960," *The Quarterly Journal of Economics* 38, August 1969, pp. 434–448.

[25]See in particular R. B. Mancke, "American Trade Union Growth," *The Quarterly Journal of Economics* 85, February, 1971, pp. 187–193; and George Sayers Bain and Farouk Elsheikh, *Union Growth and the Business Cycle* (Oxford: Blackwell, 1976), pp. 33–45.

Depression, which began in 1929, exacerbated this decline, and between 1929 and 1933, union membership fell by more than 20% from an already low level. One has to go back to 1916 to find a membership total as low as that for 1933.

The New Deal, bringing in its wake both legislation and government administration favorable to the labor movement, ushered in a second period of rapid growth. From 1934 to 1939, union membership almost tripled. The third and final burst came during World War II, total membership rising by 65%. During the 27 years between 1945 and 1972, membership rose by 40%, whereas the nonagricultural labor force grew by 80%. Since 1960, the most notable growth of unionism has been in government service, and there has also been an increase in the number of associations that bargain for their members in a quasi-union fashion.

It hardly seems possible to capture in a simple model, quantitative or otherwise, the complexity of the forces that have molded the fortunes of organized labor under greatly varying circumstances. This does not mean that satisfactory explanations are not available from the historical context in which trade union development occurred. There is no mystery about the great surge of unionism in the 1930s, or the further advances during the war years. More general models, theoretical or empirical, do have the advantage over ad hoc explanation by facilitating prediction. However, new social phenomena keep intruding, and render extrapolation of the past hazardous.

Trade-Union Structure

American trade-union structure has been relatively simple from its beginnings to the present day. Apart from the CIO, which was formed in 1935 and went out of existence as a separate body 20 years later, the American Federation of Labor has been the dominant organization. As Tables 1.13 and 1.14 show, three-quarters of all union members have belonged to organizations affiliated with the AFL throughout the twentieth century, except for the years of the CIO split. Indeed, the CIO was the only federation that ever offered any real challenge to the central position of the AFL, and this was a relatively short-lived one. The decline in the AFL–CIO percentage after 1955 was due primarily to the expulsion of the large Teamsters Union in 1957 and the withdrawal of the United Automobile Workers in 1968.

The AFL–CIO is a coordinating body for the labor movement, representing it in national and international affairs. The basic operational units are the national unions,[26] organized on the basis of craft, industry, or a

---

[26]Some of the national unions have the word "international" in their titles because they have members in Canada and Latin America.

TABLE 1.16
Number of National Unions Affiliated with the AFL–CIO

Year	AFL	CIO	AFL–CIO
1900	82		
1905	118		
1910	120		
1915	110		
1920	110		
1925	107		
1930	104		
1934	109		
1938	102	42	
1940	105	42	
1945	102	40	
1950	107	30	
1955			139
1960			134
1965			128
1970			120
1972			113
1974			111

Sources: U.S. Bureau of the Census, *Historical Statistics of the United States,* p. 97; U.S. Department of Labor, *Handbook of Labor Statistics* (1976), p. 297.

combination of the two. Each national union is financially independent, and the AFL–CIO does not have a central strike fund. The number of national unions has been remarkably stable over the century (see Table 1.16). There was a sharp increase when the CIO was formed, due in part to the establishment by the CIO of new unions rival to existing AFL unions, but with the merger and subsequent consolidation, the total number in 1972 was very close to what it had been near the beginning of the century. This is in.marked contrast to countries that have had a proliferation of national unions due to the prevalence of rival federations.

The 10 largest national unions and their average 1972–1973 dues paying membership are shown in Table 1.17. Two of the 3 largest, the Teamsters and the Automobile Workers, were not affiliated with the AFL–CIO in those years, but all the rest were. It is interesting to note that concentration of membership has fallen somewhat over the years. In 1900, some 52% of all union members belonged to the 10 largest unions.[27] The

[27]Martin S. Estey, "Trends in Concentration of Union Membership," *Quarterly Journal of Economics* 80 (August 1966), p. 349.

TABLE 1.17
Average Membership of the Ten Largest Trade Unions in the United States, 1974

Union	Members (in thousands) (1974)	Number of local unions (1973)	Average members per local[a]
Teamsters	1973	783	2519
Automobile workers	1545	1575	981
Steelworkers	1300	5675	229
Electrical workers	991	1647	602
Machinists	943	1929	489
Carpenters	820	2435	337
Retail clerks	651	215	3028
Building laborers	650	890	730
State, county, and municipal workers	648	2289	283
Service employees	550	364	1510

Sources: U.S. Department of Labor, *Directory of National Unions and Employee Associations, 1973; Statistical Abstract of the United States, 1976,* p. 386.

[a] Membership in 1974 divided by the number of locals in 1973. 1974 data on number of locals are not available.

comparable figure for 1972 was 45%. As one student of the problem put it, "The power represented by control of union membership is now more widely diffused among international unions than it was 30 or 60 years ago. The shift in membership concentration, therefore, reflects, and is an index of, underlying shifts in the direction of greater structural democracy."[28]

There is no general rule for the scope of local union organization, but several key factors tend to determine structure: the size of productive units, and the scope of labor and product markets. In the case of the Teamsters, for example, local jurisdiction based upon large urban areas, because of the mobility of the work, tends to produce large locals. Construction craft locals are generally coterminous with product markets, and there are many independent locals in small communities, so that average local size is not large, for example, in the case of the Carpenters and Building Laborers. Jurisdiction of the locals of the Retail Clerks and the Meat Cutters tends to coincide with labor markets, and it is the size of the retail chain stores, where organization is concentrated, that creates relatively large locals. In the case of the Automobile Workers, large production units raise the average local size.

Local unions play a more important role in the United States than in most other countries. There are no works councils or internal commissions, free of identification with specific unions, that bargain on local issues. Shop stewards, grievancemen, or business agents, as they are variously called, are officers of the local union. They must follow union policy, and may be removed by local union officials if they fail to do so. Their role is generally

[28]*Ibid.,* p. 352.

limited to the first-step handling of grievances involving the interpretation of collective agreements. They almost never bargain over changes in wages or working conditions.

This is a structural fact of far-reaching significance, and is a consequence of an organizational principle that has characterized the American labor movement from its origins: *exclusive jurisdiction*. This principle became a basic element of national labor legislation when it was embodied in the National Labor Relations (Wagner) Act in 1935. What it means is that there can be no more than one union representing the workers in a single bargaining unit—the union that is chosen by the majority. This does not necessarily imply that there can be only one union in a manufacturing plant. For example, separate units can be established for blue- and white-collar workers, or for craftsmen. But within each specifically designated unit, the majority union represents all the employees, whether or not they are union members. The authority of the local union cannot be diluted by interunion committees of shop stewards, a phenomenon that is the cause of considerable structural weakness in many countries.

Although the main organizational line of the American labor movement is the federation, the national union, and the local union, there are various coordinating bodies. Directly under the AFL–CIO are the state federations of labor, which perform at the state level the same functions as the AFL–CIO does nationally, mainly working with state legislatures. There may be links between a national union and its locals in the form of district or company councils to coordinate collective bargaining, where appropriate. In large cities, local unions of different national unions often form central labor councils to represent their political and economic interests at that level. The coordinating structure is not neat, having developed in response to need. Taken as a whole, however, the structure is an impressive one, providing working people with representation at every level required by their economic interests.

American labor unions have been relatively well financed, particularly in recent years. As Table 1.18 shows, total union assets were over $2.3 billion in 1970,[29] up by $767 million from 1960.[30] About 40% of these assets were held by national unions and 52% by local unions, the rest being in the hands of intermediate bodies. These figures, however, do not reflect accurately the relative financial strength of national and local unions. The latter held a good part (46% in 1970) of their assets in cash, presumably for paying current expenses, and only 15% in investment assets other than short-term government notes. The national unions held 18% of their assets

[29]Total assets in 1974 were $3.16 billion, but this figure is not comparable with those for earlier years because for the first time it included the postal employee unions.

[30]By comparison, the estimated assets of British trade unions in 1969 amounted to $320 million. Leo Troy, "American Unions and Their Wealth," *Industrial Relations* 14 (May 1975), pp. 134–144.

TABLE 1.18

Assets of Labor Unions, 1960 and 1970
(millions of dollars)

	1960	1970
National unions	730.8	935.6
Intermediate bodies	101.7	175.7
Local unions	719.9	1208.1
Total	1552.4	2319.4

Source: U.S. Department of Labor, *Union Financial Statistics 1960–1970,* Table 1.

TABLE 1.19

Total Revenue and Net Assets of Large National Unions in the United States, 1966

Union	Total assets (thousands of dollars)	Assets per member (dollars)	Total revenue (thousands of dollars)	Revenue per member (dollars)
Teamsters	45,002	30	22,974	15
Steelworkers	23,021	26	62,435	71
Automobile workers	59,526	52	47,010	41
Electrical workers	18,184	30	57,071	93
Carpenters	27,641	39	16,328	23
Machinists	32,282	49	20,449	31
Retail clerks	7,206	18	9,323	23
State, county, and municipal workers	518	2	3,514	15

Source: U.S. Chamber of Commerce, *A Financial Survey of the Major National and International Unions of the United States,* Miscellaneous Pamphlet No. 272 (Washington, D.C.: Chamber of Commerce, 1966).

in cash and 38% as investment assets. The bulk of the reserves of the labor movement are thus concentrated in the national unions.[31]

There is great variation among national unions in income and wealth. Table 1.19 presents data on union assets and revenue in 1966 for those unions listed in Table 1.7 for which data are available. Although the Auto Workers are shown as having the largest per-member volume of assets, they were subsequently forced to borrow money from the Teamsters to help finance major strikes that involved large numbers of members. The revenue figures primarily reflect the dues structure, which in turn depends largely on the wage level. None of the unions on the list is a craft union; some of the older, small crafts unions are much wealthier. The Bricklayers

[31]Data are from U.S. Department of Labor, *Union Financial Statistics 1960–1970.* Leo Troy has pointed out that American unions have been very conservative in their investment policy, despite their reputation as business-like organizations. In 1969, only 8.1 percent of their total assets was invested in corporate stock. Holding so much cash meant a substantial loss both in income and potential capital appreciation. Troy, "American Unions."

TABLE 1.20
Membership and Financial Data for Seven Large Local Unions, 1966

Union	Membership	Total revenue (thousands of dollars)	Revenue per member
Local 743, Chicago, Teamsters	22,000	1886	86
Local 600, Dearborn, Auto Workers	31,200	2547	82
Local 3, New York, Electrical Workers	30,100	3127	101
Local 837, Hazlewood, Missouri, Machinists	17,600	1161	66
Local 876, Detroit, Retail Clerks	25,900	1697	66
Local 300, Los Angeles, Building Laborers	14,800	1111	75
Local 342, New York, Meat Cutters	11,800	1053	89

Source: U.S. Department of Labor, Financial and Administrative Characteristics of Large Local Unions (1969).

Union, for example, had assets of $235 per member in 1966; the Lithographers, $248. But the older unions that were transformed from craft to industrial unions after 1935—the Electrical Workers, the Carpenters, and the Machinists—tend to be relatively well off both in income and wealth. In any event, all of the unions listed in Table 1.19, and most of the rest of American national unions, are quite affluent compared with unions in other nations.

A special 1966 survey of 100 large local unions showed that many of them are also well financed. Table 1.20 contains data for the largest single locals of the national unions listed in Tables 1.17 and 1.19, for these national unions for which data are available from the survey. A substantial portion of local union revenue is paid to the national union as an affiliation fee, but the locals themselves keep a good deal of the money, as comparison of the data in Tables 1.19 and 1.20 reveals. This ratio is quite different from union to union, and depends, among other things, on the existence of strike funds and other beneficial funds at the national and local levels. Some large local unions—Local 3 of the Electrical Workers Union is an example—run a wide variety of welfare programs for their members, and are both larger and wealthier than many of the national unions affiliated with the AFL–CIO.

The use to which funds are put at the local level seems to depend to a considerable extent upon the size of the local. The larger locals spend about half of their disbursements on basic administration and operation: 21% for affiliation payments, 21% for salaries and expenses, 5% for office and administration. The rest goes for various types of benefit payments and investments. The smaller locals, however, spend almost all their receipts on affiliation payments and costs of administration, with little left over for member benefits.[32]

[32]U.S. Department of Labor, Financial and Administrative Characteristics of Large Local Unions (1969), p. 48.

American unions have always paid their officers well. With a few exceptions, they have not followed the common European custom of restricting officers' salaries to the level of top earnings in the trade, largely because of the lack of a socialist tradition. The accepted rationale has been that trade union officers must be skilled negotiators and administrators, dealing on a day-to-day basis with highly paid business managers. In the absence of ideological motivation, people of ability could be attracted only by paying sufficiently large salaries.

Salaries of national union officers have been the subject of considerable interest for some time,[33] but only since the enactment of the Labor–Management Reporting and Disclosure Act of 1959 has comprehensive information regarding local union salaries become available. The heads of the 100 largest locals in the United States in 1966 received between $5000 and $80,000 a year. But salaries of less than $10,000 were paid in only 8 locals, 5 of which were in the Automobile Workers, a union known for its tradition of low salaries. Some 13 locals paid $30,000 or more to their presidents. There was an even chance that the highest-paid officer in each of the 100 large locals would receive a salary at least half of the highest paid officer in his national union.[34]

Tenure in union office has been of long duration at the federation level. Since its establishment in 1886, the AFL (later AFL–CIO) has had only three presidents (except for a single year)—Samuel Gompers, William Green, and George Meany. There has been a somewhat higher turnover at the national level. The Labor Department found that over the decade 1960–1970, "three-quarters of the national unions (133 of 174) have replaced the individual occupying the office of president. Turnover was higher in unions that were not affiliated with the AFL–CIO; some 85% of these organizations replaced the incumbent between 1961 and 1970, compared to 72% of the unions affiliated with the Federation."[35]

Turnover tends to be more frequent in smaller unions. From 1971 to 1973, only six unions with over 100,000 members had leadership turnover. In one case, the president retired after 26 years in office; another died; and another was removed after a rank-and-file revolt against corruption (the United Mine Workers).[36] Few union constitutions specify an automatic retirement age for officers, and despite the fact that officers must stand for reelection every 2 or 3 years, the rule for the larger unions is long tenure.

[33]See, for example, Philip Taft, *The Structure and Government of Labor Unions,* (Cambridge, Mass.: Harvard University Press, 1954), pp. 105–110.

[34]U.S. Department of Labor, *Financial and Administrative Characteristics of Large Local Unions* (1969), pp. 59–63.

[35]U.S. Department of Labor, *Directory of National Unions and Employee Associations* (1971), p. 59.

[36]U.S. Department of Labor, *Directory of National Unions and Employee Associations* (1973), p. 62.

TABLE 1.21
Turnover of Local Union Officers, 1962–1967

Compensation (in dollars)	Continued in office	Not continued in office	Percentage turnover
5,000 or less	15,665	8,311	35
5,001–10,000	623	204	25
10,001 or more	977	311	24

Source: L. Applebaum and H. R. Blaine, "Compensation and Turnover of Union Officers," *Industrial Relations* 14, (May 1975), pp. 156–157.

Turnover is higher at the local level, but again, it is much more frequent in smaller local unions paying lower salaries, as Table 1.21 indicates. American workers, it is clear, have opted for a well-paid, professional leadership, with relatively long terms of office, for their trade unions.

How much the financial and organizational status of unions has changed during the twentieth century can be appreciated by comparing the present trade union situation with that which Samuel Gompers, the founder of the AFL, described in a letter in 1887:

> Money is coming in very slow, in fact so slow that it is discouraging. . . . If I only had the means I wouldn't care a straw but as it is I will have shortly to decide upon giving up the position, take a post at my trade or starve.
> If the unions of the country don't want a federation, then they don't and that settles it. If they do they ought to pay a little for the protection its very existence affords and should not insist upon doing what we protest against employers doing, i.e., exacting work without pay. There can be no question that I did a great deal of that in my long connection with the labor movement and am willing to do so again if I get a chance to get back at my trade. But with a large family depending upon me for support I cannot give my entire time without recompense.[37]

Collective Bargaining

American trade unions, from their start, favored what the Webbs termed the "method of collective bargaining," as opposed to compulsory arbitration or the "method of legal enactment."[38] This implied a readiness to enter into written agreements with employers governing all terms and conditions of employment. Although legislation has been enacted to bolster the bargaining process, union loyalty to free collective bargaining has never wavered.

Employers, however, were much more reluctant than unions to engage in collective bargaining, and because of union weakness, the growth

[37]Quoted in Philip Taft, *The AFL in the Time of Gompers* (New York: Harper, 1957), p. 44.
[38]See Sidney and Beatrice Webb, *Industrial Democracy* (London: Longmans, Green, 1902).

of bargaining was a slow process. Lack of data makes it impossible to estimate accurately the extent of bargaining at the beginning of the twentieth century, but it was not widespread in the context of the entire economy. The earliest studies of written agreements, covering the Commonwealth of Massachusetts, indicated that 43% of local unions in 1911 and 56% in 1916 had written agreements with employers. In the latter year, however, only 170,000 workers in all were covered by agreements; moreover, Massachusetts was a relatively well organized state.[39] In 1926 the Bureau of Labor Statistics reported that it was collecting about 2000 agreements annually, but that its compilation was not complete.[40]

The breakthrough came in the 1930s with the enactment of the National Labor Relations Act (1935) and the subsequent expansion of union organization. The act, which is the most important landmark in American labor legislation, made collective bargaining compulsory if a majority of the employees in a bargaining unit desired it. A Federal National Labor Relations Board was created to prevent employers from interfering with the right of employees to choose their bargaining representatives, and to specify the rules under which bargaining was to be carried on. Reaching an agreement was not made mandatory; in the event of failure to agree on a contract, a work stoppage could take place. But, by Board ruling, once an agreement had been reached, it had to be reduced to writing if either side demanded it.[41]

By 1945, out of the 29 million employees in occupations in which unions were organizing and attempting to obtain written agreements, about 13.8 million were covered by written agreements. Some 67% of production wage earners in manufacturing were similarly covered, and in nonmanufacturing industries, about 34%. A number of major industries were in the 80–100% coverage category, including automobiles, clothing, newspapers, basic steel, rubber, nonferrous metals, coal mining, construction, railroads, and trucking.[42] Of these industries, the only ones that had been as well organized in 1938 were clothing, coal mining, newspapers, and railroads, whereas the rest had lesser degrees of coverage.[43]

---

[39]National Labor Relations Board, *Written Trade Agreements in Collective Bargaining* (Washington, D.C., 1940), pp. 214–215. By interpolating between the 1910 and 1920 population census data for Massachusetts, and applying the 1920 labor force participation rate, it can be estimated that the Commonwealth's labor force for 1916 was on the order of 1.95 million. This would mean that only about 9% of the state's labor force was working under collective agreement.

[40]Bureau of Labor Statistics, *Handbook of Labor Statistics* (1924–1926), p. 372.

[41]For a good account of the impact of the 1935 legislation, see Harry A. Millis and Emily Clark Brown, *From the Wagner Act to Taft–Hartley*, (Chicago: University of Chicago Press, 1950).

[42]Bureau of Labor Statistics, *Extent of Collective Bargaining*, Bulletin no. 865 (1945), pp. 1–2.

[43]National Labor Relations Board, *Written Trade Agreements*, p. 218.

TABLE 1.22

Collective Agreement Coverage, Metropolitan Areas, 1960–1974[a]

Years	All industries (%)	Manufacturing (%)	Nonmanufacturing (%)	Transport and communication (%)	Wholesale trade (%)	Retail trade (%)	Finance, insurance, real estate (%)	Selected services (%)
				Plant				
1960–1961	73	79	61	95	56	39	—	56
1963–1964	70	77	58	—	—	—	—	—
1964–1965	69	77	57	94	57	36	—	54
1965–1966	69	76	57	94	56	37	—	53
1967–1968	68	76	56	93	55	37	—	53
1969–1970	67	76	53	92	55	35	—	50
1971–1972	65	76	51	91	57	33	—	48
1972–1974	63	75	49	90	55	31	—	46
				Office				
1960–1961	17	12	20	65	9	17	3	11
1963–1964	15	12	17	—	—	—	—	—
1964–1965	15	12	17	62	7	14	2	12
1965–1966	16	13	17	63	8	15	1	11
1967–1968	15	13	17	61	8	14	2	8
1969–1970	15	13	16	61	7	13	2	7
1971–1972	15	13	16	63	8	12	2	8
1972–1974	14	12	15	61	7	12	2	8

Source: U.S. Department of Labor, *Handbook of Labor Statistics 1975*, pp. 420–421.

[a] Data relate to percentage of workers employed in establishments in which contracts covered a majority of workers in the respective categories.

The systematic collection and publication of collective agreement coverage began only in 1960. The relevant data are shown in Table 1.22. The first thing to note is the consistent decline in coverage, during the 14-year period of 1960–1974, for almost all categories. The precise reasons for the decline are not apparent from the data, but in all probability the main factor has been the changing composition of the labor force. There has been a relative increase in the number of white-collar as compared with blue-collar workers, and the former are less susceptible to union organiza-tion.[44] This is less true in manufacturing than in nonmanufacturing indus-try, but even in manufacturing, there has been a similar trend. The very sharp decline in manufacturing contract coverage in the Western part of the United States, from 83% in 1960 to 68% in 1974, supports this thesis, since much of the new high-technology industry that requires a great many technicians was located there. In the North Central states, where the bulk of traditional heavy manufacturing has been located, the percentage of contract coverage stood at 86 both in 1960 and in 1974.

Apart from transportation and communications, contract coverage in nonmanufacturing has been substantially below that in manufacturing, as Table 1.22 shows. Only wholesale trade showed an upward trend in cover-age. Office, as distinct from plant, employees were largely unorganized; this remains the frontier for union expansion.

Two major groups are omitted from the tabulation—employees in construction and employees in government service. Workers in heavy and commercial construction are almost entirely under contract, whereas those engaged in building private homes are largely uncovered by union agree-ments.

The situation for public employees is more complicated. Union or-ganization has grown very rapidly in the past decade as public bodies have conceded to their employees the right to bargain collectively. Half of all federal government employees were union members in 1968, but their right to bargain is limited, and the strike is denied them both in law and in practice. Some 38% of state and local government employees, excluding teachers and transportation workers, were unionized in 1970; most of them worked under collective contracts. Teachers and transit workers are cov-ered by collective agreement to a greater extent than any other group of public employees.[45]

The only other major piece of federal legislation dealing with collective bargaining was the Labor–Management Relations Act of 1947 (the Taft–

[44]Plant workers would include technicians and other nonmanual employees who were working directly in the plant and were covered by the same agreements at the manual work-ers.

[45]The data are from Jack Stieber, *Public Employee Unionism,* The Brookings Institution, 1973, pp. 11–13.

Hartley Act). Adopted over the strenuous opposition of the trade unions, this law added to the Wagner Act, which had specified only employer unfair labor practices, an additional set of union practices that were banned. The basic framework of the collective bargaining system remained unchanged. Employers had been arguing that the Wagner Act gave the unions too great an advantage in the bargaining process, and they were able to convince Congress that some redress in the balance was needed. Although there has been subsequent legislation regulating the internal affairs of labor unions (the Labor-Management Reporting and Disclosure Act of 1959), the legal framework of collective bargaining has remained essentially unchanged since 1947.

One of the outstanding characteristics of the collective agreement in the United States has been its broad scope. Matters that in many countries are handled by legislation are regularly dealt with in the United States through collective bargaining. The collective agreement is usually a long and complex document, drafted with great care.

All agreements contain wage provisions, and on this score, American agreements tend to be more precise than those of other nations. The wage rates specified in the contract are usually those actually paid, not minimum or average rates. The wide range of subject matter included in addition to wages is illustrated by Table 1.23. So-called union security provisions involve some variant of the union shop, whereby employees are required to join the union as a condition of employment.

A unique characteristic of American industrial relations is the manner in which shop grievances are handled. Virtually all agreements provide for compulsory arbitration, if grievances cannot be resolved by discussion between union representatives and management. There are no labor courts; the arbitrators are selected and paid jointly by the parties. Their awards are final and binding. It is virtually unknown for the losing side to refuse to abide by an arbitration award. Any portion of the agreement is subject to interpretation through the grievance procedure, and as a result of the thousands of awards that have been made since 1945, when the system became fully operative, there is a system of informal industrial jurisprudence that is in many ways more important than legislation or formal judicial action. The major arbitration awards are printed and distributed by private publishing services, and help guide both those who are revising agreements and the arbitrators who interpret them. Many believe that this common law of labor relations is the outstanding achievement of the American system.

There are some major national agreements, but the decentralized character of American collective bargaining is indicated by data on the number of workers covered per agreement, shown in Table 1.24. There are national agreements in apparel, steel, automobiles, and telephone, but bargaining by employer associations, which is common in Europe, is quite

TABLE 1.23

Substantive Content of Collective Agreements Covering 1000 Workers or More, July 1, 1973 (percentage of total agreements including specified subject matter)

Subject	Percentage
Union security	83
Dues checkoff	80
Management rights	60
Antidiscrimination	92
Labor–management safety committees	28
Restrictions on posting or distribution of union literature	47
Job evaluation	17
Production standards	28
Time study	21
Incentive wage payments	31
Wage progression plans	38
Travel time	25
Meal allowance	32
Lodging allowance	17
Transportation allowance	36
Work clothes	45
Cost of living indexing	41
Pay for time spent on union business	57
Retention of seniority in layoffs	74
Limitation on subcontracting	53
Interplant transfers	36
Restrictions on work by supervisory personnel	66
Advance notice of layoffs	45
Supplemental unemployment benefit plans	16
Severance pay	33
Grievance arbitration	99
Ban on strikes and lockouts	94

Source: Bureau of Labor Statistics, *Characteristics of Agreements, July, 1973,* Bulletin no. 1822 (1974).

rare in the United States. From the start, American employers have preferred to do their own bargaining rather than entrust it to professional negotiators. Nor is there any provision in the United States for the legal extension of agreements to nonbargaining employers as is the case, for example, in Germany.

Strikes

Violation of contract through strike action is rare in the United States. American unions take the position that once an agreement has been reached, all disputes should be settled by resort to the grievance procedure stipulated in the contract. However, they have been unwilling to submit

TABLE 1.24

Coverage of Major Collective Agreements, by Number of Workers Covered, 1973

Number of workers covered	Total	Manufacturing	Nonmanufacturing
All agreements	1,339	723	616
1,000–1,999	623	391	232
2,000–2,999	216	115	101
3,000–3,999	135	67	68
4,000–4,999	82	34	48
5,000–9,999	155	72	83
10,000–24,999	93	27	66
25,000–49,999	23	8	15
50,000–99,999	6	4	2
100,000 or more	6	5	1

Source: Bureau of Labor Statistics, *Characteristics of Agreements, 1973* Bulletin no. 1822 (1974).

disputes over new contracts to arbitration, either by the government or by private arbitrators. Because of the complexity of agreements and the high income level of the American worker, which permits him to remain on strike for long periods, the incidence of strikes in the United States has been high.

There are a number of alternative measures of strike incidence: the number of strikes, the number of workers involved in strikes, duration, man–days lost, the ratio of workers involved to the labor force, the ratio of man–days lost to total man–days worked. The most useful for our purposes is the ratio of workers involved in strikes to trade-union membership. There are not many strikes among unorganized workers, so that this measure yields a good approximation of the extent to which union members resort to strikes as the result of collective bargaining failures.[46] However, since nonunion workers sometimes join in strikes called by unions, the results are overstated if they are taken to measure the proportion of union members involved in strikes.

The relevant data are shown in Table 1.25. For the first quarter of the century, the strike ratios are very high. During these years, the labor movement was small and struggling to organize, and most employers were unwilling to engage in collective bargaining. Thus, in 1905, 37% of all strikes were called in an attempt to achieve union recognition. But in 1916 these strikes formed only 19% of the total; in 1920, 18%; and in 1924, 20%.[47] Many strikes were spontaneous outbreaks against what were per-

[46]The proportion of strikes called by labor organizations increased from 47% in 1881 to 75% in 1905. Florence Peterson, *Strikes in the United States 1880–1936*, Bureau of Labor Statistics, Bulletin no. 651 (1938), p. 32.

[47]*Ibid.*, pp. 33 and 39.

TABLE 1.25

Workers Involved in Labor Disputes as a Percentage of Union Membership, 1900–1974[a]

Year	Percentage	Year	Percentage	Year	Percentage
1900	65.4	1932	10.9	1954	9.2
1901	50.1	1933	41.6	1955	14.9
1902	50.3	1934	42.5	1956	10.3
1903	41.2	1935	31.8	1957	7.5
1904	27.7	1936	20.2	1958	11.4
1905	15.0	1937	30.4	1959	10.3
1916	60.5	1938	9.7	1960	7.3
1917	42.4	1939	15.6	1961	8.4
1918	38.0	1940	7.3	1962	7.0
1919	108.8	1941	28.4	1963	5.3
1920	30.6	1942	9.2	1964	9.1
1921	24.1	1943	18.3	1965	8.4
1922	42.2	1944	17.6	1966	10.2
1923	22.1	1945	28.4	1967	14.6
1924	19.6	1946	37.2	1968	13.1
1925	12.9	1947	16.1	1969	12.2
1926	10.0	1948	14.6	1970	16.0
1927	9.9	1949	22.4	1971	15.9
1928	9.6	1950	17.9	1972	8.2
1929	9.0	1951	15.1	1973	10.6
1930	5.8	1952	23.4	1974	12.9
1931	10.9	1953	14.8		

Sources: 1900–1954: Arthur M. Ross and Paul T. Hartman, *Changing Patterns of Industrial Conflict* (New York: 1960), pp. 204–205.

1955–1974: Bureau of Labor Statistics, *Handbook of Labor Statistics 1976*, pp. 297–298; *Statistical Abstract of the United States* (1976), p. 386.

[a] There are no strike data for the years 1906–1915.

ceived to be substandard labor conditions, so that union membership may not be an appropriate base.

After some major strikes in the years 1921–1923, including an unsuccessful attempt to organize the steel industry and a futile effort by the coal miners to protect wage standards in the face of falling coal prices, trade unions were unable to exercise any direct pressure on employers for almost a decade. The first years of the Great Depression, 1930–1932, were marked by a very low strike incidence. The outburst of organizational efforts that began in 1933 and continued until 1938 are clearly reflected in the data. Thus, in 1935, the major issue was union organization in 47% of the strikes, and in 1936, 50%.[48]

For 5 years after the end of World War II, strike activity continued to be high, primarily reflecting the failure of collective bargaining to resolve

[48]*Ibid.*, p. 61.

wage issues in a period of rapid price inflation. Labor–management relations improved during the 1950s, leading to a declining strike trend that was continued into the first half of the following decade. The years 1960–1965 showed the lowest strike incidence of any similar period since 1900. The strike curve rose thereafter, but there was no American counterpart to the great wave that affected most major European countries from 1968 to 1971.

These are the broad outlines of strike activity in the United States over three-quarters of a century. There have been a number of attempts to relate strike trends more precisely to various economic, social, and political variables. The following observation was made with respect to the period 1881–1936:

> The trend of strikes since 1881 indicates a general tendency to follow the business cycle. In the main, strikes tend to diminish when business activity declines and job opportunities disappear. Business recovery is generally accompanied by revival of trade-union activity and industrial disputes. However, this relationship does not occur with year-to-year regularity. There has been less strike activity in some years of business prosperity than in depression years. . . . It would appear that other conditions such as the political situation, the state of mind of the workers, and the type of labor leadership have as much to do with the amount of strike activity as the purely economic factors of prices and business conditions.[49]

Another analysis of strike statistics, from 1952 to 1967, yielded the conclusion that "the aggregate level of strike activity is behaviorally related to the degree of tightness of the labor market and previous rates of change in real wages."[50]

Trade-union leaders have always known that a recession is not the best time to call a strike. In 1888, Samuel Gompers wrote as follows to the president of a local union that was contemplating a strike:

> Unless present appearances are very misleading strikes of any kind will not be successful for some time to come, if the strikes are for an advance of wages. As a matter of fact, the tendencies of the present situation are in an opposite direction owing to a powerful combination of the employers. . . . My advice is bide your time until you can take practical action; then plan your organization by all means at your command in the full belief that your time will come if you have the courage to wait. Lost strikes break up your organization faster than any cause.[51]

At early stages of organization, as Gompers pointed out, unions risked not only defeat but dissolution if strikes were lost. As the labor movement

[49]*Ibid.*, p. 21.

[50]Orley Ashenfelter and George E. Johnson, "Bargaining Theory, Trade Unions, and Industrial Strike Activity," *American Economic Review* 59, (March 1969), p. 47.

[51]Quoted in Philip Taft, *The A.F. of L.*, p. 49.

grew in strength and power, this threat diminished. When continued existence was assured, and strike funds were built up, the risk element became lower. Depressed economic conditions were still an important deterrent to strikes, but other considerations may have assumed greater importance than they had in the past.

This proposition can be illustrated by comparing strike experience during several periods that were marked by relatively high unemployment. The year 1894 was the second year of a depression. A total of 1404 strikes were recorded that year, of which 31% were for the purpose of securing wage increases and 28% to protest wage cuts; that is, there were almost as many defensive as offensive strikes.

The outcome was favorable to workers in 43% of the cases, unfavorable in 45%, and the rest ended in compromise.[52] Among these strikes was the famous Pullman Car Company strike, which was called by a new union against the opposition of the AFL railway brotherhoods. The strike record of 1894 has been characterized as follows:

> The year 1894 was exceptional for labor disturbances. The number of employees involved reached nearly 750,000, surpassing even the mark set in 1886. However, in contradistinction to 1886, the movement was defensive. It also resulted in greater failure.[53]

There were depressions in 1907–1908 and in 1914–1915, but strike statistics are not available for these years. The next downturn came in 1921, when unemployment reached 11.9% of the labor force, and when the threat to union existence was still a real one. Only 5% of the strikes called in that year were for wage increases, whereas 41% were to protest wage cuts. Of the reported outcomes, 56% were won by employers, 21% by workers, and the rest ended in compromise.[54] This was a bad year for unionism on every count, and ushered in a decade of labor weakness.

Compare this with what happened in 1933, a year in which unemployment reached the highest level in American history—24.9% of the labor force. Despite the highly unfavorable economic climate, the number of strikes called in this year was more than double that of the preceding year. Nor were the strikes primarily defensive: 32% were for higher wages compared with 13% called to resist wage cuts, and a large additional number involving the demand for union recognition. The outcome of the strikes was far better than might have been expected. Some 37% resulted in substantial gain to workers, and 26% ended in partial gains or compromise.

[52]Peterson, *Strikes*, pp. 33–34.

[53]John R. Commons, David J. Saposs, Helen L. Summer, E. B. Mittelman, H. E. Hoagland, John B. Andrews, and Selig Perlman, *History of Labour in the United States*, vol. II (New York: Macmillan, 1918), p. 501.

[54]Peterson, *Strikes*, pp. 39–40.

Only 31% ended with little or no gain.[55] The major explanatory variable, of course, was the political climate ushered in by the New Deal, with its emphasis on the desirability of trade unionism and collective bargaining, affording the unions much greater protection than they had enjoyed in the past.

There was a recession in 1949, though not a major one, with unemployment reaching 5.5%. Strikes were nonetheless at a high level; the number of man–days idle was the second highest on record. Wage increases were the major issue in 29.5% of the total, whereas wage decreases accounted for only 1.7%. There are no data on the outcome of the strikes, but the results were generally favorable to workers.[56]

Finally, a relatively high degree of unemployment prevailed in the years after 1971. Nonetheless, the strike level remained high. Essentially, the strike had become simply a normal part of the collective bargaining process, with none of the overtones of a fight to the finish that had characterized an earlier era.

In sum, despite occasional predictions of its demise, the strike remains very much alive as an integral part of industrial relations in the United States. It is a controlled weapon, however, and not a species of guerrilla industrial action or political warfare, as it has become in other countries. Most wildcat strikes involve few workers and are of brief duration. Political strikes are almost unknown; contract-negotiation strikes normally account for between 80 and 90% of working days lost due to stoppages.[57] Despite occasional calls in the press and the legislatures for the substitution of compulsory arbitration for the strike, there is little likelihood that the American labor movement would be prepared to agree to any limitations on the right to strike, or that it might be possible to force it to do so through legislation.

The Political Role of Organized Labor

The American trade-union movement is perhaps the only one in the world that does not advocate some form of socialist society. The United States is one of the few democratic countries that does not have a political party that primarily represents the interests of the industrial worker. This is often taken to mean that American unions are nonpolitical. In fact, they have been very much involved in politics on both a local and a national basis.

The American Federation of Labor, from its inception, was opposed to the adoption of socialist doctrines despite the efforts of a sizable bloc of

[55]*Ibid.*, pp. 64, 69.

[56]Bureau of Labor Statistics, *Analysis of Work Stoppages During 1949*, Bulletin no. 1003 (1950).

[57]Bureau of Labor Statistics, *Analysis of Work Stoppages 1972*, Bulletin no. 1813 (1974).

unionists to push it in that direction. During its 1902 convention, a resolution that would have committed the AFL "to advise the working people to organize their economic and political power to secure for labor the full equivalent of its toil and the overthrowal of the wage system and the establishment of an industrial co-operative democracy" was defeated by the narrow margin of 4897 to 4171 votes. The Socialist party ran a candidate against Samuel Gompers at the 1912 convention, and gained about one-third of the total vote, being supported, among others, by the Mine Workers and the Machinists.

A famous statement made by Gompers at the 1903 AFL convention epitomizes the attitude toward socialism held not only by Gompers, but by the great majority of the AFL leadership as well:

> I want to tell you, Socialists, that I have studied your philosophy; read your works upon economics, and not the meanest of them; studied your standard works, both in English and German—have not only read, but studied them. I have heard your orators and watched the work of your movement the world over. I have kept close watch upon your doctrines for thirty years; have been closely associated with many of you, and know how you think and what you propose. I know, too, what you have up your sleeve. And I want to say that I am entirely at variance with your philosophy. I declare it to you, I am not only at variance with your doctrines, but with your philosophy. Economically, you are unsound; socially, you are wrong; industrially, you are an impossibility.[58]

The formation of a labor party was opposed on purely pragmatic grounds. There was a firm conviction on the part of the AFL leadership that such a party would not be successful. As Gompers himself wrote: "The effect of a political labor party will be to defeat our friends and elect our enemies." The federation's operating principle in the political arena was, rather, "Reward your friends and punish your enemies," or, to put it more formally,

> We will stand by our friends and administer a stinging rebuke to men or parties who are either indifferent, negligent, or hostile, and, whenever opportunity affords, to secure the election of intelligent, honest, earnest trade unionists, with clear, unblemished, paid-up union cards in their possession.[59]

Beginning with the 1908 elections, the AFL and its constituent unions supported individual candidates whose legislative voting records were regarded as prolabor. Because of the weakness of the labor movement and its lack of funds, this policy was not conspicuously successful prior to the

---

[58]Report of the Proceedings of the Twenty-Third Annual Convention of the American Federation of Labor (Washington, D.C.: American Federation of Labor, 1903), pp. 188–189.

[59]*The American Federationist* 13 (1906), pp. 293–294.

1930s. Moreover, the political affiliations of the top AFL leadership precluded firm stands in presidential elections. The two most powerful men on the AFL executive council for many of these formative years, William L. Hutcheson, president of the Carpenters Union, and John L. Lewis of the Mine Workers, were strong supporters of the Republican party, although many other members of the council were Democrats. The federation cautiously supported the third party candidacy of Senator Robert La Follette in 1924, when the Democrats nominated an extremely conservative candidate to run against Calvin Coolidge, the Republican candidate. However, the failure of this effort discouraged such actions in the future.

Franklin D. Roosevelt was elected president in 1932 without any endorsement by the AFL. Lewis and Hutcheson supported Hoover, while the garment unions supported a Socialist candidate. It was clear from the voting pattern, however, that there was a massive Roosevelt vote among urban blue-collar workers.

The alliance between labor and the Democratic party began with the 1936 election. The CIO, which had been formed in 1936, led the movement for the reelection of Roosevelt, and though the AFL itself remained neutral, some AFL unions joined in. For the first time, labor contributed a substantial amount of money for the Democratic campaign. The same pattern continued in 1940, though John L. Lewis, the organizer of the CIO, split with his colleagues and returned to the Republican fold by backing Wendell Willkie.

In 1944, when Roosevelt ran for a third term, labor's involvement in the campaign was greater than ever before. The Political Action Committee of the CIO, led by Sidney Hillman, president of the men's garment union, raised $700,000 in support of Roosevelt. Hillman and Philip Murray, president of the CIO, were very much in evidence at the Democratic party convention at which Roosevelt was renominated, and the Republicans made the alleged labor control over Roosevelt a major campaign issue. The AFL again remained neutral, though many AFL leaders served as delegates to the Democratic party convention. However, the AFL claimed some credit for replacing Henry Wallace by Harry Truman as the vice-presidential candidate, an event of great future significance. As in the past, individual congressmen and senators were supported on the basis of their voting records, and William Green, the AFL president, repeated that the "nonpartisan political policy of the American Federation of Labor is based on the principle that the workers should elect the friends of labor and defeat its enemies regardless of their political affiliation."[60]

The enactment of the Taft-Hartley Act in 1947, over the veto of President Truman and against a massive campaign waged by the entire labor movement, moved the AFL to embark upon a new political course. It

[60]*The American Federation of Labor Weekly News Service,* 29 October 1946.

was conceded that the old policy of informing state and city central unions about the voting record of legislators was no longer effective. It established Labor's League for Political Education as a separate body for political purposes. The league was not in any sense a labor party; its function was to pursue traditional AFL policies more efficiently, both at the national and at the local levels.

The 1948 national elections hastened the demise of the CIO by bringing about a split between pro- and anticommunist factions. The former mounted a third party campaign on behalf of Henry Wallace, a former vice president of the United States, whereas the latter were strong supporters of Harry Truman. Before the election, Truman's chances were not regarded as good, and despite his prolabor role in the Taft-Hartley controversy, the AFL remained officially neutral. The Political Action Committee of the CIO spent over $500,000 on behalf of Truman, and was credited with a major share of the responsibility for Truman's success at the polls.

During the next 4 years, labor made a strenuous but unavailing effort to bring about a revision of the Taft-Hartley Act. The Democratic candidate in 1952, Adlai Stevenson, was pledged to the repeal of the act, whereas Eisenhower favored it. For the first time in its history, the AFL decided unequivocally to endorse a candidate, Stevenson, although a few influential leaders refused to go along. The CIO's Political Action Committee spent over $2 million on behalf of Stevenson, and Labor's League for Political Education spent $250,000; but labor's efforts proved futile. For the first time in 20 years, a candidate regarded as antilabor was elected to the presidency.

This election illustrated the weakness of the AFL approach to political action. In 1948, a Gallup poll taken a month after the election showed the following results:[61]

	Percentage of vote		
	Total	AFL members	CIO members
Truman (Democrat)	41	54	58
Dewey (Republican)	53	40	32
Wallace (Progressive)	6	6	10

Although the polls were in error on the outcome, it is clear that although the majority of union members were for the Democrats, a substantial minority voted Republican. The same pattern emerged in 1952, when

[61]This and subsequent references to Gallup polls are taken from various compilations of Gallup poll results.

potential voters were asked (in May) which party they regarded as best serving their interests:

	Percentage	
	Total	Manual workers
Democrat	42	54
Republican	37	37
No difference or no opinion	21	9

Behind the Eisenhower victory in 1952 were such factors as the Korean War and his personal popularity as a war hero, but for our purposes it is interesting to note that the Republican party still had about the same blue-collar adherence as in the previous election. The unions, despite their substantial financial expenditures, were unable to change by very much the political attitudes of blue-collar voters. The traditional neutrality of the AFL hindered the formation of a voting bloc based upon the concept of class that is of such great significance in European politics.

After the AFL–CIO merger in 1955, the political arms of the two movements were merged into a new Committee on Political Education (COPE). Despite its effort, the 1956 election was a rerun of that in 1952. Eisenhower actually gained blue-collar strength, as the following data show (polls of October 10, 1958):

	Percentage of vote		
	Total	Manual workers	Union members
Eisenhower (Republican)	52	45	39
Stevenson (Democrat)	40	47	52
Undecided	8	8	9

It is interesting to note that 39% of union members voted for Eisenhower, even though the AFL–CIO endorsed Stevenson and spent a substantial amount of money on his behalf.

In 1960, the union vote was tipped toward the Democratic candidate to a greater extent than in 1956, although the Republicans still retained a substantial minority. The following data from a postelection poll also show the sharp regional differences that prevail:

	Percentage of vote of union members	
	Kennedy (Democrat)	Nixon (Republican)
East	68	32
Midwest	65	35
South	59	41
West	62	38

The South voted much more heavily Republican than the rest of the country, and union members tended to follow the local trend. Nixon lost by a narrow margin, although Eisenhower had won a sweeping victory in 1956 with only a marginally greater share of the union vote than Nixon received. COPE spent $800,000 in 1960, and total union expenditures were about $2 million. COPE took credit for the high rate of voter participation, and it is an axiom in American politics that high participation favors the Democrats.

The 1964 elections were hardly a contest. The Republican candidate was regarded as strongly antilabor, whereas President Johnson had maintained excellent relations with the unions, and enjoyed a wide popularity among all groups. The Republican share of manual-labor votes reached its nadir, as the following poll data, taken in August and September, demonstrate:

	Percentage of vote	
	Total	Manual workers
Johnson (Democrat)	65	72
Goldwater (Republican)	29	22
Undecided	6	6

The 1968 elections were complicated by the fact that there was a third party candidate, George Wallace, who was running on a populist, anti-civil-rights program that had considerable appeal to white blue-collar workers, many of whom felt that their jobs and property were being threatened by militant black groups. The AFL–CIO came out strongly for the Democratic candidate, Hubert Humphrey, and its efforts are generally credited with bringing him within a hair's breadth of victory, despite the handicap of having been vice-president in an administration that had become increasingly unpopular because of its conduct of the war in Vietnam. The Gallup poll data were not reliable, since there was a massive shift of votes toward Humphrey in the closing weeks of the campaign. Nevertheless, about a month before the election, only 33% of a sample of manual workers indicated that they planned to vote for Humphrey, against 34% for Nixon and 25% for Wallace (the rest were undecided). Almost a third of the manual workers' votes remained with the Republican party.

The 1972 election is an interesting one from the point of view of labor's political participation. The Democratic party lost the 1968 election, even though it had the backing of a well-organized and financed political action arm of a unified labor movement. That election was very close, and it was complicated by the Wallace candidacy and the racial issue. But without the support of the labor movement, the Democratic party's prospects of winning the presidency seem remote; at least, that seems to be the lesson of 1972. Because the Democratic candidate, George McGovern, was viewed by the AFL-CIO leadership as being too far to the left on both domestic and foreign policy, the labor movement returned to its traditional policy of neutrality for the first time in 30 years, shattering what had appeared to be a firm alliance between the Democratic party and the trade unions. Taken 3 weeks before the elections, the following sample poll data show the effect of labor's turnabout:

	Percentage of vote	
	Total	Manual workers
Nixon (Republican)	59	49
McGovern (Democrat)	36	44
Undecided	5	7

For the first time since polls were taken, a Republican candidate apparently received a plurality of the votes of manual workers. Many of these were undoubtedly voters who had favored Wallace 4 years earlier, but AFL-CIO inaction cut heavily into the Democratic vote. The trade unions cannot by themselves elect a Democratic candidate, but they can bring about his defeat.

The election of 1976 saw the trade unions firmly back in the Democratic fold. Angered by President Ford's veto of a piece of legislation that would have liberalized the rules of picketing at construction sites, the AFL-CIO was solidly behind Jimmy Carter, and undoubtedly made a major contribution to his election, particularly in such large industrial states as New York and Pennsylvania.[62] There is little doubt that had the

---

[62] About 65% of all union members voted in the election, compared with an overall participation rate of 53%. Seventy percent of the union vote went to Carter. The political arm of the labor movement used 120,000 volunteers, made over 10 million phone calls, and distributed 80 million pieces of campaign literature. "Meany Says AFL-CIO Willing to Discuss Voluntary Wage-Price Guides with Carter," *Wall Street Journal,* 11 November 1976, p. 4.

labor movement remained neutral, as in 1972, Ford would have been successful in his bid for reelection.

This account of labor's political activities, concentrated as it is on presidential elections, fails to do justice to the full range of labor's political role. At every level of government, there are officials who owe their election or appointment to the support of the labor movement. The AFL–CIO claimed, for example, that 70% of the candidates for Congress whom they backed in 1976 were elected. As a result of such activity at national, state, and local levels, the unions have powerful lobbies that enable them to press for favorable legislation. They are credited with having the most effective lobby in Washington, and although they do not always succeed in having the bills they favor enacted by Congress, it is very difficult for legislation that they strongly oppose to be enacted. Some of the results of the exercise of this power are summarized in the following quotation:

> Without union efforts, workers and low-income groups would have little organized political support, and their interests would be more vulnerable to the pressure of other powerful groups. Through constant lobbying and political campaigning, unions have doubtless helped to give birth to Medicare and to enlarge social security and unemployment and workmen's compensation benefits. In addition, labor's success in registering voters and persuading them to go to the polls must have contributed something to the success of the Democratic Party in maintaining control over Congress in all but two sessions since 1933, and holding the Presidency in all but three terms.[63]

WAGES AND SALARIES

Long-Term Trends

The trend of money and real wages for the past 75 years, for production workers in manufacturing, is shown in Table 1.26. Weekly rather than hourly earnings are used in order to allow for changes in the working week. Although it would have been preferable to have had broader coverage of the labor force, this is the only consistent long term earnings series available from official sources.

There are many conceptual problems involved in comparing real wages over so long a period. This is particularly true when it comes to the consumer price deflator, because of the great changes that have taken place over the years in the composition of consumption expenditures. Neverthe-

[63]Derek C. Bok and John T. Dunlop, *Labor and the American Community* (New York: Simon and Schuster, 1970), p. 424. This book contians an excellent summary of trade union political methods. See also Charles M. Rehmus and Doris B. McLaughlin eds, *Labor and American Politics* (Ann Arbor: University of Michigan Press, 1967).

TABLE 1.26
Average Weekly Earnings of Production Workers in Manufacturing, 1900–1976

Year	Earnings (in current dollars)	Consumer price index (1900 = 100)	Index of real earnings (1900 = 100)
1900	8.66[a]	100	100
1905	9.38[a]	108	100
1909	9.74	108	104
1914	10.92	120	105
1920	26.02	240	125
1925	24.11	210	133
1930	23.00	200	133
1935	19.91	164	140
1940	24.96	168	172
1945	44.20	216	236
1950	58.32	288	234
1955	75.70	321	272
1960	89.72	355	292
1965	107.53	378	328
1970	133.73	465	332
1975	189.51	644	338
1976	207.60	681	352

Sources: 1909–1974: U.S. Department of Labor, *Handbook of Labor Statistics* (1975), p. 254.
1900–1905: *Historical Statistics of the United States* (1957), p. 92.
1975–1976: *Monthly Labor Review* 100, (June 1977), p. 89.
U.S. Department of Labor, *Handbook of Labor Statistics* (1974), p. 301; *Monthly Labor Review*, (June 1977).

[a] Estimated on the assumption that trends in earnings of all workers and of production workers in manufacturing were identical from 1900 to 1909.

less, the data do present a rough first approximation to changes in real weekly earnings over the period, and suggest that they have risen three and one-half times since 1900.

There has been no quinquennium in which real earnings have fallen except by a very slight amount. The growth of real wages has been consistent, but far from steady. There were large increases during the two world wars, and during the latter half of the 1930s, when the nation was recovering from the Great Depression. The post-World War II period, after the inflationary years 1945–1950, was a favorable one, apart from the past decade, when real-wage growth has been very modest.

These figures do not take into account a number of factors that are necessary to translate earnings into consumption and saving, among them, the steadiness of work, fringe benefits, and the impact of taxation. There are no data that permit us to estimate the effects of unemployment; such annual earnings data as do exist are for full-time employees, and they parallel the weekly earnings figures. One might secure an estimate by using the unemployment rate as a deflator, but this would be very crude and the results obvious. Real per-capita earnings would fall during the years of the Great Depression, as well as during such lesser downswings as 1914–1915, 1921, and 1974–1975.

Neither fringe benefits nor taxation were of great significance for the wage earner in manufacturing prior to World War II, but they have been of increasing significance since then. Average annual supplements to wages and salaries per employee in manufacturing rose from $129 in 1945 to $504 in 1959, by one account.[64] This figure is not very meaningful in absolute terms, since it is an average for all employees, whereas the greatest advance has been in the union sector. However, it does suggest progress from a fairly low level in 1945.

More accurate data are available only since 1959, when the Bureau of Labor Statistics began to analyze manufacturing payroll data. The relevant data for the years 1959, 1966, and 1972 are shown in Table 1.27. Fringe benefits have grown rapidly since 1959, as the data in the table clearly indicate. Moreover, the trend is continuing, and future payrolls will probably reveal a declining portion of compensation going out as direct pay.

To summarize, rough estimates for the years from 1945 to 1959 suggest that fringe benefits added about 5% to compensation during the period, with an additional 5.5% being added between 1959 and 1972 (fringes here include everything but pay for working time and leave time).

The impact of income taxes on the compensation of production workers was minimal prior to World War II. It became important only after the war, the timing depending on the dependency status of the recipient (see Table 1.28). It is interesting to note that the tax bite did not increase from 1970 to 1976, despite inflation.

To find out what an individual had available for private consumption out of total earnings, the data in Table 1.26 would have to be adjusted downward by about 18% for single individuals, and by 13% for family breadwinners, between 1945 and 1976. This compares with a 10.5% upward adjustment to allow for fringes.

The upshot is that before the earnings data of Table 1.26 can be accepted as a first approximation to the economic situation of an employed production worker, they must be adjusted downward during the post-World War II period.[65] The magnitude of the adjustment is not great, however, and in view of the fact that social security taxes in particular, and a portion of income taxes as well, return to the individual worker in the

---

[64]*Historical Statistics of the United States* (1957), p. 96 and *Supplement* (1962), p. 16. These were, respectively, 5% and 10% of average annual earnings in manufacturing in the 2 years.

[65]The same conclusion can be drawn from a study covering the periods 1950–1965 and 1965–1970, done by the Bureau of Labor Statistics. Because of differing methodology, however, the magnitudes of the change cannot be compared with those shown above. See Jack Alterman, "Compensation per Man–Hour and Take-Home Pay," *Monthly Labor Review* 94, June 1971, p. 25.

TABLE 1.27

Structure of Compensation of Production and Related Workers in Manufacturing, 1959–1972

	1959 (%)	1966 (%)	1972 (%)
Total compensation	100	100	100
Pay for working time	85.4	82.4	78.9
Pay for leave time	5.2	5.6	6.2
Employer expenditures for retirement programs—total	4.2	5.8	7.2
Social security	2.0	3.3	3.9
Private pension plans	2.2	2.5	3.3
Employer expenditures for health programs	3.0	4.0	5.8
Employer expenditures for unemployment programs	1.5	1.5	1.3
Nonproduction bonuses	.5	.6	.5
Savings and thrift plans	—	.1	.1

Source: Bureau of Labor Statistics, *Handbook of Labor Statistics* (1974), Table 117.

TABLE 1.28

Ratio of Spendable to Gross Average Weekly Earnings of Production Workers in Manufacturing, 1940–1976, in Percentages

Year	Worker with no dependents	Worker with three dependents
1940	98	99
1945	83	96
1950	86	97
1955	83	92
1960	81	89
1965	83	90
1970	80	87
1975	80	87
1976	80	87

Sources: Bureau of Labor Statistics, *Handbook of Labor Statistics* (1974), Table 102; *Monthly Labor Review* 100, (June 1977), p. 90.

form of transfer payments from the government, the real-earnings series is useful in gauging long-run improvement in welfare—remembering that we are abstracting from unemployment.

Skill Differentials

There are few consistent long-run time series for differentials in wages and earnings. Perhaps the best available from official sources are those contained in Table 1.29, which portrays skill differences in the building trades and local trucking, derived from union contracts. The building data

TABLE 1.29
Skill Differentials, Building Trades,
and Local Trucking, 1907–1974
(percentage of unskilled to skilled
average hourly union wage rates)

Year	Building trades[a]	Local trucking[b]
1907	50	—
1910	49	—
1915	47	—
1920	57	—
1925	52	—
1930	53	—
1935	52	—
1937	—	82
1940	55	80
1945	61	83
1950	67	85
1955	70	87
1960	74	88
1965	75	89
1970	75	90
1974	76	91

Sources: Bureau of Labor Statistics, *Handbook of Labor Statistics* (1975), Table
94; *Handbook of Labor Statistics*
(1976), Table 91.
[a] Laborers and journeymen.
[b] Helpers and drivers.

go back to 1907; between that year and 1940, the differential varied within
a narrow range, and it was not until 1945 that it began to narrow. The
process of compression continued for 15 years, but after 1960 the premium
for skill remained almost unchanged. The series for local trucking operated within a narrower range, but there was some compression of differentials between 1940 and 1960, and then stability.

These observations can be supplemented by the results of a few studies
covering shorter periods. One such study compared skilled and unskilled
earnings in representative industrial jobs for the period 1907–1947. The
procedure used involved preparation of a skilled–unskilled index for a
number of industries; the final data show the median and the range for the
aggregates of individual-industry indexes (see Table 1.30). These figures,
like those for the building trades, indicate a marked reduction in the skill
differential from 1907 to 1918–1919, but the subsequent increase in the
premium for skill was not as great as in construction. A substantial compression occurred from 1937–1940 to 1945–1947, paralleling the construction experience.

TABLE 1.30

Relationship Between Earnings of Skilled and Unskilled Occupations in Manufacturing (average earnings for unskilled occupations = 100)

		Indexes	
Year	Median	Range (middle half of all indexes)	
1907	205	180–280	
1918–1919	175	150–225	
1931–1932	180	160–220	
1937–1940	165	150–190	
1945–1947	155	145–170	

Source: Harry Ober, "Occupational Wage Differentials," *Monthly Labor Review* 67, (August 1948), p. 130.

A calculation of the coefficients of wage variation for 141 occupations in 17 industries for the years 1903 and 1956 revealed a decline in the coefficients of from 33.8 to 54.6%, depending upon whether the employment weights for 1903 or 1956 were used.[66]

The conclusion drawn from the building and trucking data, that the decade of the 1960s did not see any significant change in skill differentials, is supported by the figures in Table 1.31, where earnings of skilled and unskilled workers in manufacturing are compared. For the 3 years after 1970, however, unskilled wages rose more rapidly than skilled.

This brief review of the available evidence leads to the following conclusions about skill differentials in American industry:

1. Apart from a temporary compression during and after World War I, differentials remained remarkably stable for the first 40 years of the twentieth century. One of the major contributing causes, up to World War I, was the continuing flow of immigrant labor, most of it unskilled.[67] When immigration was stopped in the early 1920s, declining differentials might have been anticipated but this did not occur. Whatever the explanation, the onset of the Great Depression served to maintain the differential, since skill differentials have tended to widen in periods of low business activity and narrow during recovery.

[66]Paul G. Keat, "Long Run Changes in Occupational Wage Structure," *Journal of Political Economy* 68, December 1960, p. 587.
[67]*Ibid.*, p. 591.

TABLE 1.31

Indexes[a] of Earnings for Selected Occupational Groups in Manufacturing, Metropolitan Areas, 1960–1973[b]

Year	Skilled maintenance	Unskilled plant
1960	100	100
1962	107	107
1964	112	113
1966	119	120
1968	130	131
1970	147	148
1972	169	172
1973	179	183

Source: Bureau of Labor Statistics, *Handbook of Labor Statistics,* 1974, Table 106.

[a] 1960 = 100.

[b] Results refer only to male workers.

2. The labor shortage produced by World War II produced a very substantial narrowing of skill differentials, and this tendency continued into the postwar period, until about 1960. After 1960, however, the narrowing process stopped; in both construction and manufacturing, differentials remained constant for a decade.[68] There is some evidence of further narrowing after 1970, but it is too soon to tell whether this will persist.

These are the facts, to the limited extent that they are available, but the causal factors are still to be explored. The precise relationships between skill differentials, on the one hand, and such variables as the general demand for labor, the supply of labor (demographic changes, participation rates, mobility), education, technological change, and trade-union policy have not yet been subjected to sufficient analysis to enable firm conclusions to be drawn.

Blue-Collar–White-Collar Differentials

Earnings of blue-collar workers rose more rapidly than those of white-collar workers (except for sales personnel) during the 30-year period

[68] A recent econometric analysis suggests that the rise of illegal immigration during the past decade may be responsible in part for the stability of the construction differential. Eliot S. Orton, "Changes in the Skill Differential: Union Wages in Construction, 1907–1972," *Industrial and Labor Relations Review* 30, October 1976, p. 16. However, few of the illegal immigrants work in construction, so that any effect would have to come as a result of a generalized impact on the entire labor market of the availability of low-wage labor. See also Robert N. Schoeplein, "Secular Changes in the Skill Differential in Manufacturing, 1952–1973." *Industrial and Labor Relations Review* 30, April 1977, p. 314.

TABLE 1.32

Annual Rates of Change in Earnings of Full-Time Male Workers, 1939–1969 (percentage increase)

	1939–1969	1939–1959	1959–1969
Blue collar			
Operatives	6.0	6.7	4.7
Craftsmen, foremen	5.9	6.6	4.5
Laborers, except farm and mine	6.3	7.1	4.6
White collar			
Clerical	5.6	6.1	4.5
Sales	6.3	6.9	5.1
Managers, officials, and proprietors	5.6	5.8	5.2
Professional, technical	5.8	6.1	5.1

Source: Arthur Sackley and Thomas W. Gavett, "Analysis of Occupational Wage Differences," *Monthly Labor Review* 94, June, 1971, pp. 5–12.

ended in 1969. For the first 20 years, the blue-collar advantage was quite marked (see Table 1.32). There was a reversal during the decade 1959–1969, however, and the white-collar trades (except for clericals) enjoyed relative wage gains. It is tempting to conclude that the same forces that led to a compression of skill differentials from 1940 to 1960, and stability thereafter, were also responsible for the blue-collar–white-collar performance. However, the two groupings are so amorphous that no valid conclusion can be drawn about their relative skill levels. The one thing that can be pointed out is that laborers, the least skilled group in the blue-collar group, were at the top of the growth list from 1939 to 1959 and near the bottom thereafter, which is in line with previous conclusions. Clerical employees fared relatively poorly in both periods.

What causal factors were at work? One study reached the following conclusions:

> In the 20 years spanning the decades of the forties and fifties, . . . the end of the Great Depression, the tight labor markets during the Second World War, the success of trade unions in organization and bargaining, and the relatively prosperous years of the postwar era had all worked toward a compression of wage differentials between blue-collar workers and the more highly trained and paid white-collar employees. . . . Among those factors which may have influenced changes in occupational pay differentials in the 1960s were the strong demand for certain skilled workers and a change in the demographic composition of the available work force. Skilled workers, especially professional, and clerical workers were needed most.[69]

[69]Arthur Sackley and Thomas W. Gavett, "Analysis of Occupational Wage Differences," *Monthly Labor Review* 94, June 1971, pp. 6 and 10.

This statement raises more questions than it answers. Why did tight labor markets favor blue-collar workers? Why did the relative demand for skills increase during the 1960s? We are up against the same problem as in the case of skill differentials: The facts are reasonably clear, the causes are not yet understood.

Male–Female Differentials

The interest of possible wage discrimination on the basis of sex is of fairly recent origin. The commonly held view before World War II, and for some years thereafter, was that women should normally receive lower wages than men for various reasons: a lower burden of dependency, a lesser attachment to the labor market, lower skill levels due to less education, higher absentee rates, and differences in physical endurance, among others. Indeed, in many countries (though not the United States) the differentials were institutionalized in union collective agreements that specified different wage scales for men and women. It is only recently, as a consequence of the increase in female labor-force participation and a growing awareness of inequitable treatment for women, that analytical tools have been brought to bear on the subject.

Absolute comparisons of differentials are difficult to interpret because aggregate data conceal real differences in the types of jobs held by men and women. Even trends in the differential have to be handled with caution, since there have been changes over time in the structure of female employment. Moreover, until the 1960s, relevant data were virtually unavailable. This made it possible for a book devoted to wage structure, published in 1956, simply to record the fact that "there are no regular statistics of hourly wage rates or earnings classified by age, sex, race, and other personal characteristics of the wager earner."[70]

There is one series, however, covering men and women in bookbinding, that goes back to 1915 (Table 1.33). What is revealed is a trend similar to that for skill differentials: sharp discontinuities in the postwar years of 1920 and 1945; a narrowing of differentials from 1945 to 1960; little change during the 1960s; and some improvement during the 1971–1973 inflation. This picture may reflect changes in skill as well as in sex differentials, so that no clearcut conclusions can be drawn with respect to the latter.

Census data for the period 1939–1966 indicate that there was no general improvement in the position of women. Indeed, it may have worsened, as data in Table 1.34 seem to suggest. The large increase in female labor-

[70]Lloyd G. Reynolds and Cynthia H. Taft, *The Evolution of Wage Structure* (New Haven: Yale University Press, 1956), p. 348.

TABLE 1.33

Indexes^a of Trend in the Ratio of Female to Male
Wages in Bookbinderies, Hourly Trade
Union Rates

Year	Index	Year	Index
1915	100	1950	120
1920	109	1955	125
1925	111	1960	128
1930	108	1965	130
1935	110	1970	129
1940	110	1973	134
1945	116		

Source: Bureau of Labor Statistics, *Handbook*
of Labor Statistics, 1975, Table 95.
^a 1915 = 100.

force participation during this period, with many women entering the labor force for the first time or reentering after long absence, may have depressed the female averages and masked an improvement for those women who were working steadily.

The data for the years since 1961 are more reliable. They are based upon wage surveys, and changes in occupational mix can be eliminated to a considerable extent (Table 1.35). The data are available only for clerical employees, but they do show a remarkable constancy over the 12-year

TABLE 1.34

Median Wage or Salary Income of Males and Females, 1939 and 1966

	Income of female as a percentage of male		Percentage change
Industry or occupation	1939	1966	1939–1966
Manufacturing	61.4	55.96	−5.44
Transportation, communication	70.2	64.30	−5.90
Wholesale trade	67.4	58.17	−9.23
Retail trade	63.6	53.90	−9.70
Personal services	41.5	42.72	+1.22
Professional services	74.0	67.24	−6.76
Public administration	72.7	73.11	+ .41

Source: Vernon T. Glover, *Changes in Differences in Earnings and Occupational Status of*
Men and Women, Lubbock: Department of Economics, Texas Tech Univer-
sity, 1970, p. 18.

TABLE 1.35
Earnings of Male and Female Clerical Employees, 1961–1972[a]

	Accounting clerks, Class B	Female keypunch operators versus male tabulating machine operators
1961	80	—
1962	81	76
1963	80	76
1964	82	76
1965	82	75
1966	81	75
1967	81	76
1968	81	76
1969	80	76
1970	81	78
1971	80	78
1972	81	77
1973	81	76
1974	81	75

Source: Bureau of Labor Statistics, *Handbook of Labor Statistics, 1975,* Table 109.
[a] Ratio of female to male earnings.

period, despite the growth of the movement for affirmative rights for women.

The absolute differentials that are revealed cannot be interpreted to represent "pure" discrimination. A recent effort to eliminate other effects comes up with the following statement, which indicates the difficulty of reaching firm conclusions on this score:

> If we correct for differences in hours worked, educational attainment, job seniority, and absenteeism, we can account for approximately one-third of the difference between male and female earnings. The remaining two-thirds, which are unexplained, may be the result of a variety of factors, such as extra costs of employing women, some of which are justified in economic terms and some of which are unjustified by any real differences in productivity or cost.[71]

Industrial Differentials

Long-term trends in wage differentials among industries must be interpreted with caution because of their sensitivity to technological change. There is also the problem of structural change due to the introduction of new products; electrical manufacturing has undergone a great transforma-

---

[71]Robert Tsuchigane and Norton Dodge, *Economic Discrimination Against Women in the United States* (Lexington, Mass.: Lexington Books, 1974), p. 49.

TABLE 1.36

Average Hourly Earnings of Production Workers in Manufacturing, by Industry, 1947–1973

Industry	Rank, by earnings level		Annual percentage increase in wages		
	1947	1973	1947–1960	1960–1973	1947–1973
Petroleum and coal	1	1	5.19	4.63	4.91
Printing and publishing	2	4	4.67	4.40	4.52
Transportation equipment	3	2	5.06	4.85	4.96
Primary metals	4	3	5.56	4.58	5.07
Machinery (except electrical)	5	5	5.06	4.58	4.82
Ordnance	6	7	5.56	3.78	4.66
Rubber and plastic	7	14	4.54	3.88	4.21
Fabricated metal	8	8	5.10	4.40	4.75
Electrical equipment	9	12	4.71	4.17	4.44
Chemicals	10	6	5.68	4.58	5.12
Instruments	11	11	5.19	4.02	4.62
Stone, clay, glass	12	10	5.15	4.76	4.95
Apparel	13	21	2.45	4.40	3.42
Paper	14	9	5.35	4.85	5.12
Miscellaneous	15	17	4.17	4.40	4.28
Furniture	16	18	4.21	4.31	4.26
Lumber and wood	17	16	4.31	5.06	4.67
Food	18	13	5.44	4.67	5.06
Leather	19	20	3.58	4.21	3.89
Textiles	20	19	3.48	4.71	4.10
Tobacco	21	15	4.98	6.33	5.65

Source: U.S. Bureau of Labor Statistics, *Handbook of Labor Statistics,* 1974, Table 98.

tion during the postwar years with the introduction of advanced electronic technology. It is nonetheless useful to examine the data to see whether they portray any broad uniformities.

An analysis of the data for the period 1899–1950 yielded the following conclusion:

> The interindustry wage structure in manufacturing has been surprisingly stable over the long run.... The ranking of manufacturing industries within the wage structure changed so slowly in the past that many of the high-wage and low-wage industries of 1899 were still to be found among the high-wage and low-wage industries in 1950; that there was little if any long-run tendency towards compression of the interindustry wage structure over the past half-century, although differentials were often narrowed temporarily during both extremes of the business cycle.[72]

[72]D. E. Cullen, "The Interindustry Wage Structure, 1899–1950," *American Economic Review* 46, June, 1956, p. 354. For a similar finding, see Sumner H. Slichter, "Notes on the Structure of Wages," *Review of Economics and Statistics* 32, February 1950, p. 80.

TABLE 1.37

Average Annual Hourly Earnings and Increase in Employment of Production Workers in Manufacturing, 1947–1973

Industry	Percentage increase in annual earnings	Rank increase in annual earnings	Percentage increase in annual employment	Rank increase in annual employment
Tobacco	5.65	1	−1.80	21
Chemicals	5.12	2	1.80	6
Paper	5.12	3	1.67	8
Primary metals	5.07	4	.11	16
Food	5.06	5	−.15	17
Transportation equipment	4.96	6	1.47	11
Stone, clay, glass	4.95	7	.98	13
Petroleum and coal	4.91	8	−.64	18
Machinery (except electrical)	4.82	9	1.55	10
Fabricated metal	4.75	10	1.44	12
Lumber and wood	4.67	11	8.06	1
Ordnance	4.66	12	7.85	2
Instruments	4.62	13	2.39	5
Printing and publishing	4.52	14	1.62	9
Electrical equipment	4.44	15	2.56	4
Miscellaneous	4.28	16	.15	15
Furniture	4.26	17	1.70	7
Rubber and plastic	4.21	18	2.91	3
Textiles	4.10	19	−.92	19
Leather	3.89	20	−1.27	20
Apparel	3.42	21	.57	14

Source: U.S. Bureau of Labor Statistics, *Handbook of Labor Statistics,* 1974, Tables 40, 98.

There was a sharp compression of the differential during the Great Depression, but by the end of the 1930s, the earlier level had been reestablished.

Data for the period 1947–1973 reveal a similar stability in interindustrial wage differentials (Table 1.36). The rank correlation coefficient for the standing of the industries in 1947 and 1973 is high: .84. Nor was there any consistent tendency for wages in low-ranking industries in 1947 to increase more rapidly than those in the higher ranks. On the contrary, over the entire period 1947–1973, of the 10 industries in which the range of wage increase was above the median for all industries, 6 were in the top half of the 1947 ranking, and only 4 in the bottom half.

Although stability is the major finding, there were a few striking displacements among industries. The rubber and plastics and the apparel industries fell substantially in the wage ratings, whereas the paper, chemicals, food, and tobacco industries rose. One possible cause is labor demand: If employment is rising in an industry, the argument runs, relatively high

TABLE 1.38

Average Hourly Earnings of Production or Nonsupervisory Workers on Private Nonagricultural Payrolls, 1947–1973

	Hourly earnings in 1947	Annual percentage increase in earnings		
		1947–1964	1964–1973	1947–1973
Construction	$1.541	5.02	6.88	5.67
Mining	1.469	3.88	5.86	4.58
Manufacturing	1.217	4.40	5.43	4.75
Finance, insurance, real estate	1.140	4.22	5.14	4.54
Wholesale and retail trade	.490	4.43	5.58	4.82
Transport and utilities	a	—	6.42	—
Services	a	—	6.28	—

Source: U.S. Bureau of Labor Statistics, *Handbook of Labor Statistics,* 1974, Table 96.
"Series for these sectors began in 1964. In that year, transport and utilities ranked as the second highest wage sector, whereas services ranked last.

wages must be offered to attract the additional labor. A glance at Table 1.37, where the rates of growth of earnings and employment are compared, shows that there is no simple correlation between the two. The two industries in which employment rose most, lumber and ordnance, had only average wage growth.

Another factor may have been at work: productivity growth. This is suggested by the data for such industries as tobacco and food, where rapid wage growth was accompanied by a reduction in the labor force. A third possibility is suggested by the textile and leather industries, where low wage growth and a falling labor force may have been the results of industrial decline. Changes in the composition of output or of the relative price structure may have also played a role.

Turning to wage relationships among broad economic sectors (Table 1.38) there is again no consistent trend in the postwar years. The ranking of sectors in 1973 is precisely what it was in 1947. The highest wage sector in 1947, construction, had the highest rate of wage growth during the postwar period. Wages rose by roughly similar percentages in all the other sectors.

Regional Differentials

A great deal has been written about regional wage differentials in the United States. Although most of the literature has dealt with the so-called North-South differential, in fact there have been long-standing and persistent differences among the other regions as well.

TABLE 1.39

*Indexes of Average Hourly Earnings of Production
Workers on Manufacturing Payrolls, Selected
States, 1951–1975*[a]

	1951	1975
North Carolina	100	100
Alabama	108	118
Texas	125	130
Massachusetts	127	127
Missouri	127	135
Colorado	131	140[b]
New York	138	140
Illinois	142	154
California	150	148

Source: U.S. Bureau of Labor Statistics,
Handbook of Labor Statistics (1976),
Table 100.
[a] North Carolina = 100.
[b] 1974.

For the prewar years, the following quotation summarizes the situation:

> Have geographical wage differentials remained relatively constant, or have they tended to diminish over the course of time? . . . For manufacturing operations the North–South differential in 1945–46 was considerably narrower than in 1931–32, but about the same as in 1919 or 1907. The premium enjoyed by the Pacific Coast over the remainder of the country declined markedly since that time.[73]

Some relevant data for the postwar years appear in Table 1.39. The states selected are the largest ones in their respective regions, measured in terms of the size of the nonagricultural labor force in 1951. The range between the highest and lowest size did not change by much between 1951 and 1975. Relative gains were achieved by the East South Central (Alabama), the West North Central (Missouri), the East North Central (Illinois), and the Mountain (Colorado) regions. The North-South differential remains very much in evidence, but the Pacific Coast region has lost its traditional premium.

There have been some attempts to explain the origin and persistence of regional wage differentials in the United States, which take on added interest because of the relatively high mobility propensity of the American labor force. Industry mix is an important factor; the South has had a

[73]Reynolds and Taft, *Evolution of Wage Structure*, pp. 343–346.

disproportionate amount of low-wage industry, cotton textiles in particular. Labor supply is another obvious candidate as an explanatory variable; the Pacific Coast premium has been ascribed to this factor. Other possible explanations are the level of urbanization, since wages tend to vary with city size; the level of education and training of the labor force; the differences in the racial composition of the labor force; and the degree of unionization. An effort[74] to disentangle the various strands of causation through multiple regression techniques, standardizing for various qualities of the labor force, does provide some interesting hypotheses, but the study covers only a single year, and tells us nothing about trends.

LABOR LEGISLATION

Social Security

By far the largest public retirement program in the United States is "social security," a pension system now covering 90% of American workers. This program was created by the Social Security Act of 1935, in response to the deteriorating position of the aged as society became more industrial, families became smaller, and the Great Depression depleted savings. Organized labor supported the act, but was only mildly interested in it. As shown in Table 1.40, coverage has been extended to more employees over time, with a particularly large increase coming after 1950.

The original act created a pension system supplemented by an old-age assistance program of relief for the elderly poor. The number of beneficiaries of old-age assistance peaked in 1950 and has since fallen steadily as the proportion of those over 65 qualifying for retirement benefits under social security has risen from less than 20% in the 1940s to its 1974 level of 89% (see Table 1.40).

There have been several changes in the original law, but the most fundamental came in 1939, when (a) benefits were extended to dependents and survivors, and (b) the basis for benefits was changed from total lifetime social security contributions to earnings over a certain period. Both these changes made the social security program more of an income-maintenance program and less of a strictly pension system. The concept of financing was also changed from that of a partially funded trust fund to a "pay-as-you-go" basis, backed only by a fund for contingency purposes. Other changes include disability benefits added in 1956, lowering of the earliest possible retirement age to 62 in 1956 (women) and in 1961 (men), and the addition of medical coverage for the elderly in 1965.

---

[74]Victor R. Fuchs, "Differentials in Hourly Earnings by Region and City Size, 1959," *Occasional Paper 101* (New York: National Bureau of Economic Research, 1967).

TABLE 1.40

Social Security Coverage, Benefits, and Taxes, United States, Selected Years

	Coverage		Benefits			Taxes
			Retirement benefits as a percentage of average monthly earnings, nonagriculture sector			
Year	Percentage of paid employment covered	Percentage of aged (over 65) population receiving social security benefits	Individuals	Married couples	Old age and survivors benefits as a percentage of national income	Old age and survivors tax collections from employers and employees as a percentage of total earnings in covered employment
1940	58.2	1.6	n.a.	n.a.	.02	.9
1945	68.4	7.3	n.a.	n.a.	.10	1.8
1950	66.9	20.5	18.3	31.1	.30	2.4
1955	85.5	42.2	20.2	35.4	1.30	2.9
1960	87.9	63.8	20.0	35.4	2.50	4.1
1965	89.1	76.5	19.5	34.4	2.70	4.6
1970	89.3	84.8	22.1	38.4	3.30	5.7
1972	89.7	86.5	26.7	46.3	3.80	6.1
1974	90.7	88.8	n.a.	n.a.	4.20	n.a.

Sources: U.S. Department of Health, Education, and Welfare, Social Security Bulletin, March 1976, Table Q-2; Table Q-4; Table M-5; Table Q-3.
U.S. Department of Health, Education, and Welfare, Social Security Bulletin Annual Statistical Supplement, 1972, Tables 27 and 29.
U.S. Department of Labor, Bureau of Labor Statistics, Handbook of Labor Statistics, 1975 Reference Edition, Bulletin no. 1865, Tables 180 and 102.

Retirees become eligible for the basic social security retirement benefits at age 65, but can obtain actuarially reduced benefits at age 62. To
receive retirement benefits, one must have at least 10 years of work in
covered employment. Benefits are based on average monthly salary between ages 21 and 62, although salary exempt from the social security tax is
not counted for such purposes. The average benefit paid to a retired
worker in 1972 was $157 per month, or about 27% of the average monthly
earnings of all private, nonagricultural workers. Benefits have been rising
faster than wages since 1950, when benefits were only 18% of average
earnings (see Table 1.40). Payments to retired workers with dependent
spouses averaged $273 per month in 1972, or 46% of the average earnings
in the nonfarm private sector, up from 31% in 1950. These upward trends,
however, have not been steady; in fact, most of the increase came between
1970 and 1972. Recent changes have guaranteed that future benefits will
rise at least by the same percentage as consumer prices, although the failure to do so has not been a problem in the past.

The modestly rising real benefits and the dramatically expanded eligibility for benefits have caused significant increases in the proportion of
national income allocated to the social security program. In 1974, over 4%
of national income was devoted to retirement and survivor's benefits under
social security—as compared to 1% or less prior to 1955 (see Table 1.40).

Benefits are financed by a payroll tax of 9.90%, half paid by the employee and half by the employer, on earnings of up to $17,700 (1978). The
taxable base has risen faster than average earnings over time, especially
since 1971, and tax rates have been almost tripled from their original level.
The increases in the tax base and rates have caused old-age and survivors
insurance taxes to rise from .9% of earnings in covered employment in
1940 to 6.1% in 1972.

One problem with the social security program is that it encourages
early retirement. With longer life spans and more jobs requiring mental
rather than physical skills, early retirement is both costly to society and
unnecessary, yet 62% of the men and 75% of the women awarded social
security retirement benefits in 1972 retired before the age of 65.[75] How
much of this early retirement is due solely to the features of the social
security program is unknown, but benefits prior to age 65 probably encourage both employer and employee to take steps resulting in a reduced
retirement age. By reducing benefits $1 for every $2 in earnings by recipients over $2400 per year (until age 71, when an individual can earn un-
limited income and the benefits remain stable), social security also discour-
ages recipients from working and encourages almost total withdrawal from
the labor force.

[75]U.S. Department of Health, Education, and Welfare, *Social Security Bulletin, Annual
Statistical Supplement, 1972,* Table 54.

Another cluster of problems is created by the method of financing. The payroll tax is regressive. For example, in 1972 the old-age and survivors insurance tax rate on earnings below $9000 per year was 8.1% (combining employer and employee contributions), whereas the average tax paid on all covered earnings was only 6.1%. The employer tax may be shifted to the employee,[76] and to the extent it is not shifted, it may discourage the employment of lower-wage labor.

Unemployment Compensation

The Social Security Act of 1935 also established a public unemployment insurance system. The act provided financial sanctions that obliged the individual states to create separate unemployment compensation systems. Prior to 1935, only a few workers were covered by some form of private unemployment insurance. As shown in Table 1.41, by 1940, 50.5% of all employees were covered by a state unemployment insurance program, and by 1973 this figure had risen to 80.7% (for nonagricultural employees the percentages were 75.0 and 88.2, respectively).

Despite the seemingly broad coverage, the percentage of unemployed who are eligible for unemployment insurance benefits is typically in the 40–60% range and has been falling (Table 1.41). The apparent paradox is the result of (a) covered employees who are disqualified from benefits because they quit voluntarily or are deemed not to be available for reemployment; (b) covered employees who are in the waiting period before benefits can begin (usually 1 week); (c) covered employees exhausting their benefits (usually after 26–39 weeks); and (d) people unemployed because of entry or reentry into the labor force and who have not yet established eligibility for benefits. The latter group, in particular, has been growing in recent years. As a result of the eligibility criteria, those unemployed receiving unemployment compensation tend to be older and more predominantly white males than the unemployed as a whole.[77]

One of the major objectives of unemployment insurance is the replacement of lost income. It is commonly perceived that unemployment benefits replace 30–40% of previous income. This belief is based on data like those in Table 1.41, comparing average benefits per week ($59 in 1973) to the average weekly earnings in the private nonfarm sector ($145 in 1973). Several adjustments must be made to obtain a more precise measurement of replacement rates, however. First, covered workers who be-

[76]See John Brittain, "The Incidence of Social Security Payroll Taxes," *American Economic Review* 61, March 1971, pp. 110–125; and Wayne Vroman, "Employer Payroll Tax Incidence: Empirical Tests with Cross-Country Data," *Public Finance* 29, 1974, pp. 184–199.
[77]See Daniel S. Hamermesh, *Jobless Pay and the Economy*, Policy Studies in Employment and Welfare, no. 29 (Baltimore: Johns Hopkins University Press, 1977), p. 22.

TABLE 1.41

Unemployment Insurance Coverage, Benefits, and Financing, Selected Years

	Coverage			Benefits		Financing of benefits	
Year	Percentage of all workers	Percentage of non-agricultural workers	Percentage of the unemployed	Average benefits as a percentage of average earnings in non-agriculture sector	Total benefits as a percentage of national income	State tax collections as a percentage of covered wages	State tax collections as a percentage of national income
1940	50.5	75.0	16.4	n.a.	.6	2.6	1.1
1945	61.5	74.4	69.2	n.a.	.3	1.9	.7
1950	59.4	75.8	49.1	39.0	.6	1.1	.5
1955	66.0	78.9	49.7	37.0	.4	.7	.3
1960	67.8	80.7	53.7	40.7	.7	1.0	.5
1965	69.5	79.8	42.2	39.1	.4	1.1	.5
1970	72.3	78.8	50.6	42.1	.5	.6	.3
1973	80.7	88.2	31.8	40.6	.4	.8	.4

Sources: U.S. Department of Labor, Bureau of Labor Statistics, Employment and Wages, Second Quarter 1973, 1975, Table A-1.

U.S. Department of Health, Education, and Welfare, Social Security Bulletin, March 1976, Tables M-4, M-36, Q-1.

U.S. Department of Labor, Bureau of Labor Statistics, Handbook of Labor Statistics, 1975, Reference Edition, Bulletin no. 1865, Table 180; Table 102.

come unemployed earn 10–15% less than the average covered worker.[78] Second, unemployment insurance benefits are not taxable, which implies that replacement rates of *net* preunemployment earnings (ignoring employment-related expenses) are probably greater by a third than replacement ratios based on gross earnings, marginal tax rates being 16–18% for the typical covered worker. These two adjustments tend to increase the replacement ratio suggested in Table 1.41 to between 50% and 65%, depending on the state of residence.[79] However, these adjustments fail to take into account lost fringe benefits, amounting to about 10% of pretax money wages, which are not replaced by unemployment insurance. They also fail to account for the waiting period of 1 week in most states before benefits can begin. Making all four adjustments (but using average rather than marginal tax rates), it has been estimated that unemployment insurance replaces from one-half to two-thirds of previous net earnings, again depending on the state.

The duration of benefits is another factor influencing the extent to which lost earnings are replaced. Most states limit benefits to a maximum of 26 weeks, but not all beneficiaries can receive a full 26 weeks of benefits due to restrictions on the ratio of compensation to prior yearly earnings. The best way to gauge the effective maximum duration period is to look at the weeks of compensation received by those exhausting their benefit rights. In 1941, exhaustees received 12.1 weeks of benefits, and since then this figure has more or less steadily climbed to 22.4 weeks (1974). However, if insured unemployment rates are above certain thresholds (generally from 4 to 4.5%), exhaustees can continue to receive benefits for up to 13 more weeks under a special extension program permanently adopted in 1970. (In 1975, a temporary, federally funded benefits program was put into effect, extending benefits for up to 26 weeks beyond the previous 39-week maximum.) Ever since 1942, the percentage of all beneficiaries exhausting their regular benefits has typically been in the upper twenties or lower thirties.

Given the number of unemployed not covered by unemployment insurance, the incomplete replacement of income for those who are covered, and exhaustions, it is not surprising that estimates of aggregate lost-income replacement rates are low. In fact, if one counts aggregate income lost through shorter working hours (not covered by unemployment insurance) as well as unemployment, it has been estimated that unemployment insurance benefits only replace between 7 and 15% of these aggregate losses.[80]

Benefits are financed by a tax, generally falling on the first $4200 of yearly earnings, paid by employers. The tax base has not risen to the same

[78]*Ibid.*, p. 16.
[79]*Ibid.*, p. 18.
[80]*Ibid.*, p. 15.

extent as average earnings levels, nor have tax rates. Hence the tax burden of the unemployment insurance system has declined over time (see Table 1.41). In 1973, state tax collections were less than 1% of total wages. The low tax base and the concentration of benefits in the middle of the income distribution imply that the unemployment insurance program probably has a neutral effect on the distribution of income.

The other major goal of the unemployment insurance system is to reduce unemployment. First, tax rates are based (at least partly) on experience, so that employers with stable employment pay lower rates than others. There is not much evidence on the effectiveness of this program characteristic, however. The key problem is that unemployment insurance taxes are not experience-rated for employers at the minimum or maximum rates. For those employers at the extremes (comprising about one-third of total payrolls), the response to cyclical decreases in product demand may be (in part) to cut workers in order to save unemployment insurance costs, whereas the response to product demand increases may be to increase *hours* of work (for the same reason). Furthermore, if the unemployment insurance tax is shifted backward to employees, even the experience rating on two-thirds of total payrolls may not discourage employers from layoffs.

Second, unemployment compensation is one of the fiscal "automatic stabilizers," tending to produce a budgetary deficit in recessions and surpluses in periods of prosperity. The limited tax base, however, means that the major stabilizing effects come from changing levels of unemployment benefits rather than changing tax revenues.

Minimum Wages

A federal minimum-wage law was passed in 1938 as part of the Fair Labor Standards Act. It covered roughly half the workers in the private sector, the principal exclusions being employees in government, agriculture, retail trade, services, and construction. In 1961, coverage was expanded to 60% of workers with the inclusion of some employees in retail trade and construction, and in 1966 coverage was brought up to 75%, principally through coverage of workers on large farms. Currently the law covers 90% of all workers, owing to the inclusion of domestic servants and government employees.

The minimum wage is established in nominal terms by legislative action. New minima have typically been set at about 50% of the level of average manufacturing earnings (see Table 1.42), but in the years when no legislative action occurred, they were eroded by inflation. For example, in 1967 the newly established minimum was 49.4% of average hourly earnings in manufacturing, and a legislated increase effective in 1968 brought it up to 53.1%. By 1974, however, lack of legislation had reduced the effec-

TABLE 1.42
Changes in Minimum Wage Standards,
1938–1975

| | | Minimum wage | |
| | | Relative to manufacturing wage | |
Year	Amount (in dollars)	Before legislated increase	After legislated increase
1938	.25	—	.403
1939[a]	.30	.398	.478
1945[a]	.40	.295	.394
1950[b]	.75	.278	.521
1956[b]	1.00	.385	.512
1961[b]	1.15	.431	.495
1963[a]	1.25	.467	.508
1967[b]	1.40	.441	.494
1968[a]	1.60	.465	.531
1974[b]	2.00	.364	.455
1975[a]	2.10	.416	.437

Sources: Finis Welch, "Minimum Wage Legislation in the United States," Office of Policy, Evaluation and Research, U.S. Department of Labor, 24 July 1973, p. 2.
U.S. Department of Labor, *Manpower Report of the President,* June 1976, Table C-3.
U.S. Department of Labor, *Minimum Wage and Maximum Hours Standards under the Fair Labor Standards Act,* 19 January 1977, p. 3.
[a]Programmed increment contained in prior legislation.
[b]Legislated amendment to 1938 law.

tive minimum to 36.4% of average hourly earnings. New legislation in 1974 then raised the level to 45.5%.

Because minimum-wage levels are relatively low, only a fraction of those covered by the act are directly affected. For example, the legislated increase from the $1.60 to the $2 per hour minimum in 1974 is estimated to have affected only 7.5% of those covered. This percentage is higher in the South and in nonunion sectors, where wages are lower. Some have argued that the law favors the northern unionized states in their efforts to prevent business from relocating in the South.

There are no separate minimum-wage provisions for teenagers, although a limited number of full-time students may be employed at 85% of the minimum in schools or retail and service establishments, if their employers can satisfy the Department of Labor that such employment will not reduce employment opportunities for others. Handicapped workers, if certified, can receive wages in accordance with their productivity. Roughly .3% of covered workers were qualified for subminimum wages, two-thirds of whom were handicapped, in 1974.

The minimum wage is neither fully nor uniformly complied with throughout the United States. Punitive damages for first-time violations are almost never assessed, although some proportion (typically half) of back wages owed to employees under the law must be paid. With these weak incentives for compliance, only about 60% of those who would otherwise have been paid less than the minimum were receiving the legal minimum in 1975, according to one estimate.[81] However, compliance tends to be highest in regions and sectors where Department of Labor inspections are most frequent: in the South and among nonwhites and females.

It has been argued that the minimum-wage law is at least partly responsible for the high and growing unemployment rates among teenagers. Although there is no consensus on this issue, some studies have found that, other things equal, there is a negative correlation between the real minimum wage and the ratio of teenage to adult employment.[82]

Occupational Safety and Health Legislation

The first comprehensive occupational safety and health legislation at the federal level was passed in 1970. The law covers all private establishments except mines, which are covered by a separate law. Superseding state legislation and preexisting federal regulations pertaining to government contractors, the Occupational Safety and Health Act of 1970 was thought necessary to reverse the upward trend of job injury rates in the 1960s when, as shown in Table 1.43, the percentage of manufacturing workers injured badly enough to miss at least a day of work rose from 2.4 to 3.0. Existing state and federal regulations were considered out of date, poorly enforced, and not stringent enough. In addition, states were viewed as reluctant to promulgate adequate standards for fear of losing jobs to states with less strict safety and health rules.

[81]Orley Ashenfelter and Robert S. Smith, "Compliance with the Minimum Wage Law," Industrial Relations Section, Princeton University, Working Paper no. 98, June 1977.

[82]See, for example, Finis Welch, "Minimum Wage Legislation in the United States," Office of Policy, Evaluation and Research, U.S. Department of Labor (Unpublished mimeograph), 24 July 1973. However, the AFL-CIO strongly denies the validity of findings of this nature, and has persuaded Congress that young people are protected, rather than disadvantaged, by the law.

TABLE 1.43
Disabling Work Injuries per 100 Workers, U.S.
Manufacturing, 1939–1970[a]

Year	Number of injuries	Year	Number of injuries
1939	3.0	1956	2.4
1940	3.1	1957	2.2
1941	3.6	1958	2.3
1942	4.0	1959	2.5
1943	4.0	1960	2.4
1944	3.7	1961	2.4
1945	3.7	1962	2.4
1946	4.0	1963	2.4
1947	3.8	1964	2.5
1948	3.4	1965	2.6
1949	2.9	1966	2.7
1950	2.9	1967	2.8
1951	3.1	1968	2.8
1952	2.9	1969	3.0
1953	2.7	1970	3.0
1954	2.4		
1955	2.4		

Sources: Robert S. Smith, "An Analysis of Work Injuries in Manufacturing Industry," *Supplemental Studies for the National Commission on State Workmen's Compensation Laws,* volume 3, 1973, p. 26.
U.S. Department of Labor, Bureau of Labor Statistics, *Handbook of Labor Statistics 1972,* Bulletin 1735, Table 163.
[a] A work injury is considered disabling if the injured worker had to miss at least 1 day of work.

The act places two duties on employers (though none on employees). First, employers must provide each employee a job free from recognized hazards likely to cause death or serious physical harm. However, this "general duty" only extends to hazards that are detectable by the ordinary human senses and are generally known in the industry. Furthermore, an employer can be penalized for a violation of his "general duty" only if an inspector has ordered abatement and he has refused to comply. Second, employers must comply with some 4400 standards promulgated by the Department of Labor. Virtually all the standards adopted under the act were either (a) those already applying to federal contractors, or (b) "consensus" standards recommended by a private safety organization supported by industry. Over half these standards were considered outdated prior to their promulgation under the act, and only 100 or so are being revised each year.

Enforcement of the act is also a problem. There are so few inspectors that only 10% of employees receive the benefit of an inspection each year, and to cover all employers will take 70 years at the present rate. Inspectors cite so few of the 4400 standards that the suspicion is raised that they either cannot detect, or are unfamiliar with, all possible violations. Fines for detected violations are so small ($26 on the average) that incentives for compliance in advance of inspection are almost nil.

Given the problems of standard-setting and enforcement, and the complete lack of correlation between industry compliance and injury rates, the effectiveness of the act is in doubt. Indeed, the first evaluation of the act has estimated a zero impact on occupational injuries. Furthermore, there is some evidence that only between 2 and 20% of work injuries are caused by the kinds of hazards with which standards can effectively deal.[83] Thus, the maximum potential impact of the act may be limited, at least in the area of safety. Its potential for reducing occupational disease is not known, but there is widespread belief that the major efforts under the act should be focused on occupational health.

FUTURE PROBLEMS AND PROSPECTS

The immediate problems facing American labor are identical with those in almost every industrialized nation: unemployment and inflation. The first will presumably be solved in part by an upturn in the business cycle. However, some structural problems are likely to persist: relatively high rates of unemployment among young people and minority groups. New initiatives will have to be taken if these disadvantaged groups are to be fully integrated into the labor market.

Inflation may prove to be a more intractable problem. It may well be that an inflationary bias is inevitable in a market system in which government is committed to the maintenance of a high level of employment. If that proves to be the case, collective-bargaining mechanisms will have to be adapted to constant wage–price pressure, and governmental intervention, ranging from monitoring to direct control, depending upon the degree of inflation, may become a permanent feature of the system.

Apart from these universal problems, some general tendencies more specific to the American scene can be discerned:

1. The expansion of public sector employment and unionism that characterized the post-World War II period is likely to continue. The demand for governmental services appears to be positively

[83]See Robert Stewart Smith, *The Occupational Safety and Health Act: Its Goals and Its Achievements* (Washington, D.C.: American Enterprise Institute for Public Policy Research, 1975), Chapter IV.

income elastic, and despite the financial difficulties in which some local governments now find themselves, the supply of these services is likely to increase. This raises a number of problems. The present unsatisfactory state of collective bargaining in the public sector will have to be resolved, and the most likely direction will be toward granting public employees the same rights as employees in the private sector. Public unions constitute the major growth element in the labor movement, and will probably play a more important role in policy determination. From an economic standpoint, it will be more difficult to maintain a satisfactory rate of growth, since public sector productivity tends to increase less rapidly than that in the private sector. Since most public activity is in the service sector category, the remarkable evolution toward a service-oriented society is likely to continue.

2. Related to the first point is the increased tendency toward the use of the method of legal enactment as opposed to the method of collective bargaining. Federal regulation in the area of equal pay, discrimination in employment, and pensions is illustrative of this tendency. The increased bureaucratization in the field of safety and health standards, which has created conflict between the regulatory process and collective bargaining, is another recent example. This process has created full employment for lawyers—there is hardly a country in which the legal profession plays as important a role in industrial relations as in the United States—but it also represents a retreat from the traditional attitude of employers and trade unions that they were the ones best suited to determine conditions of labor in their industries.

3. One of the most widely discussed labor problems of the early post-World War II years, the emergency dispute, has all but vanished. One reason is the decline of some industries, notably the railroads, in which strikes created economic emergencies. The steel industry, another in which there were many alarms in the past, has displayed an amazing ability to regulate itself in the interest of smooth production and steady employment. This is not to say that the strike has fallen into disuse. Indeed, once begun, strikes in the United States tend to last longer than in other countries because of the ability of unions and workers to finance them. But these strikes normally do not result in any substantial economic harm, and they can be handled within the regular collective bargaining framework. A major problem in dealing with strikes cannot be said to exist in the United States, except perhaps for stoppages by such local government employees as policemen, firemen, and garbage collectors, which reflect the lack of a well-established bargaining system in the public service.

4. American employers, in distinction to those of Europe, have preferred to deal with unions individually rather than collectively. There are a few industries in which they have federated for bargaining purposes, but these are exceptional. The growing complexity of collective bargaining, in part a function of government regulation, and in some measure due to the impact of inflation, may bring about some centralization on the part of employers, in the form of new or strengthened federations along European lines. Contributing to this is an increasing awareness that the appropriate level at which broad economic, as well as labor, problems may best be settled is the industry, not the individual enterprise or the national economy.

5. There has never been a time since the foundation of the American labor movement when the influence of the Left was at a lower ebb than the present. There are no voices of any influence within the AFL–CIO in favor of socialism in any of its diverse forms. Codetermination on the German model, or other methods of worker participation in management decision making, have few adherents in the United States. Even the Swedish-type experiments with new forms of work organization have aroused little interest among American workers.

This commitment of American labor to liberal capitalism, and its rejection of socialism, has always been puzzling to those unfamiliar with the American scene. The brief account of American labor history in an earlier section of this chapter is scarcely sufficient to provide an adequate explanation. It will have to suffice merely to repeat that this has been the traditional ideology of American workers and their unions, and that there are no signs on the horizon of any change despite the conflicts that are occurring elsewhere in the world. This is not at all to say that labor institutions and beliefs will be immutable; there have been great shifts since the New Deal of the 1930s. But the changes are likely to reflect pragmatic reactions to specific problems rather than to follow along dogmatic lines. Many non-Americans have long regarded this phenomenon as evidence of labor immaturity and weakness. In the United States, it is generally perceived as not only an element of basic strength, but as one of the fundamental pillars of political and economic democracy.

2. GREAT BRITAIN

A. W. J. THOMSON
L. C. HUNTER

INTRODUCTION

· Among all the developed countries, Britain has had the most evolutionary system of industrial relations in the twentieth century, with few major breaks or new directions, at least until the events of the last decade or so. In part, this has been due to the fact that Britain already had a relatively modern economy by 1900 in terms of the structure of its labor force and even its industrial relations institutions, and in part it has been due to Britain's escape from the worst traumatic effects of two world wars. Because of these factors, the influence of history has been stronger in Britain than elsewhere; this has been both advantageous and disadvantageous, with the latter effect being seen as predominant in the recent past as attempts have been made to modernize the system. But despite the relative continuity of the system, there are many difficulties in presenting a continuous analysis of the century. The most notable of these is the absence of statistical series on many important topics, at least on any basis that makes comparative analysis between different periods of time feasible within the confines of this chapter.

THE LABOR FORCE

This section looks at various characteristics of the labor force in Great Britain such as population, total labor force, activity rates, length of work year, industrial and occupational structures, unemployment, and labor market policies. Unfortunately there are no comprehensive statistical series for trends in any of these characteristics throughout the century, although considerable use has been made of a number of working papers produced

Labor in the Twentieth Century

by the Department of Employment in 1974, together with the path-breaking work by Routh on occupational analysis before 1960.[1]

Population, Total Labor Force, and Activity Rates

The population of Great Britain has risen from 38 million at the 1901 census to 54 million at the 1971 census, and there has been a growth in the labor force from 16.3 million in 1901 to 25.9 million in 1976, with an estimated further increase to 26.7 million in 1981 and to 27.8 million in 1986, although some doubt must attach to future labor force growth, since the most recent population estimates indicate a stable or even a declining total population.[2] These figures, however, conceal very considerable changes in the structure of both activity rates and the population itself. Activity rates by age and sex from 1901 to 1977 are shown in Table 2.1, though unfortunately there are no activity rates for young workers before 1921. Analysis of the changes in the labor force between 1921 and 1971 reveals that for men, substantial increases in the working-age population were partly offset by declines in the participation rate, especially for the under 24 and over 65 age groups; whereas for women substantial increases in the activity rate were recorded, particularly in the 35–54-year-old age groups.

This reflects the changing role and structure of females in the labor force. Between 1921 and 1977 the proportion of females in the labor force increased by over 9% to 38.8% and the absolute numbers by some 3.5 million, but this latter figure was composed of an increase of just over 5 million in the participation of married women and a decrease in that of single, divorced, and widowed women of 1.5 million. The increase in married women from 12.9% in 1921 to 67.8% in 1977 of all female participants is the single most important component of change and the main source of additional workers in the labor force. In part, this reflects an increase in the numbers of women who are married, 64% of those over 15 in 1971 compared with 51% in 1921, when the figure was probably reduced by World War I and its aftermath. Nevertheless, there has been a rapid increase in the activity rates of married females of all ages and single women between 35–60 owing to a number of partially interacting causes on both the supply and demand sides. With fuller employment for men, employers have had to look to women for increased labor requirements, especially during the

---

[1]Department of Employment, *The Changing Structure of the Labour Force, 1921–1971* (Working Paper, 1974); *Changes in the Industrial Distribution of Employment 1931–1971* (Working Paper, 1974); and *Changes in the Occupational Distribution of the Labour Force in Great Britain* (Working Paper, 1974). Shorter reports on many aspects of these papers can be found in the Department of Employment Gazette during 1974–1975. G. Routh, *Occupation and Pay in Britain 1906–60* (Cambridge: Cambridge University Press, 1965).

[2]*Department of Employment Gazette,* June 1977, p. 591.

TABLE 2.1

Activity Rates (in Percentages) by Sex and Age, Excluding Students[a]

	Under 20	20–24	25–44	45–64	65+	All ages
			Male			
1901	—	97.4	98.1	93.5	61.4	—
1911	—	97.3	98.5	94.1	56.8	—
1921	63.2	97.0	97.9	94.9	58.9	87.1
1931	84.7	97.2	98.3	94.3	47.9	90.5
1951	83.8	94.9	98.3	95.2	31.1	87.6
1961	74.6	91.9	98.2	97.6	24.4	86.0
1971a	60.9	89.9	97.9	94.5	19.4	81.4
1971b	69.7	89.9	97.9	94.6	24.1	82.6
1977	64.0	88.2	97.9	94.5	19.8	80.2
			Female			
1901	—	56.7	27.2	21.1	13.4	—
1911	—	61.9	29.3	21.6	11.5	—
1921	48.4	62.4	28.4	20.1	10.0	32.3
1931	70.5	65.1	30.9	19.6	8.2	34.2
1951	78.9	65.4	36.1	28.7	5.3	34.7
1961	71.1	62.0	40.8	37.1	5.4	37.4
1971a	55.9	60.1	50.6	50.2	6.4	42.7
1971b	63.0	60.1	51.6	53.8	6.4	43.0
1977	57.2	64.7	61.5	60.8	4.9	46.9

Source: Department of Employment Gazette.

[a] In each part of the table the figures down to 1971a are from the *Department of Employment Gazette.* The raising of the minimum school-leaving age from 15 to 16 in 1973 makes further continuation of this series impossible, but the Department of Employment has provided estimates of activity for the population aged 16 and over from 1971 (*Gazette, June 1977*). These are the figures from 1971b in each part of the table.

world wars, and have been prepared to provide more flexible working arrangements and times, especially through the provision of part-time employment. Furthermore, changes in occupational structure and job tasks have made it easier to employ women, especially with the growth of service industries and occupations. Again, labor-saving devices in the home have reduced domestic responsibilities, families are smaller, and the period required to look after under school-age children correspondingly less. Two further factors, other than the domestic and marital responsibilities that differentiate females from males in the labor force, are that a lower proportion of females go into higher and further education, and that the pensionable retirement age for women is generally 60, rather than 65 as for men. These factors indicate a higher participation rate for single women in the youngest age groups but a lower one in the highest.

The situation of males in the labor force has also altered, but less radically. The main changes have been demographic rather than participatory, but some reductions in activity rates have resulted in an overall increase of somewhat less than 2.5 million, rather than the 4 million that would have occurred had there been no change in activity rates. Indeed, since the mid-1960s the number of males in the labor force has declined absolutely, although it will rise again in the next two decades. For those in the middle-age groups between 25 and 54, there has been little change in participation rates. At the younger end of the scale, the raising of the school-leaving age and the greater numbers going into higher and further education provide the reasons for lower participation. In the case of workers under 20 there has been an absolute decrease, and (excluding students) this group accounted for less than 7% of the male labor force in 1977 as opposed to 15% in 1921. For those between 20 and 24 demographic factors have meant an increase of 290,000 in the labor force despite a drop in the participation rate of over 7%. At the upper end of the age spectrum there have been substantial changes. The activity rate of men aged 65–69 dropped from almost 80% in 1921 to just over 30% in 1971 and to 26% in 1977, whereas that for men over 70 fell from 41 to 8% over the same period. The main reason has been earlier voluntary and compulsory retirement, and the provision of better pensions. Indeed, activity rates in the 55–59 and 60–65 age groups have also dropped as a result of earlier retirement, although only by small amounts.

These factors at both ends of the age spectrum, together with increased life expectancy, mean that men can now expect to spend a much smaller proportion of their lives in the labor force than was true earlier in the century. Not only this, but changes in hours worked per week and length of holidays mean considerably less hours of work during a working year, as we see in the next section. But before we continue, mention should be made of one aspect of labor force composition that is not covered by the tables but which is of increasing importance for policy. This is the number of black immigrants in the labor force, who now comprise approximately 3% of the total.

The Length of the Working Year

At the beginning of the century male manual workers in industry worked an average of 53–54 hours a week, but trade unions were pressing strongly for an 8-hour day. Soon after the end of World War I, standard weekly hours were reduced to 48, and by 1971 a 5-day, 40-hour week was the norm. However, since World War II, overtime has been a significant feature for male manual workers, causing actual weekly hours to diverge from the standard workweek, and contributing to a slower reduction in weekly hours than in most other countries. Thus, full-time manual workers in the 1970s were still averaging 44–45 hours, and in manufacturing industry roughly one-third of *all* operatives worked some overtime each week, averaging 8 hours a week.[3] As a result, over the 20-year period 1956–1976, average weekly hours for manufacturing operatives fell by only 10%.

The high overtime phenomenon in Britain deserves some explanation. At one level of analysis, it suggests a preference for extra money rather than extra leisure, but this in turn requires to be explained. In part, the explanation may lie in the prevalence of industry-wide collective agreements on basic pay, which reduce the scope for employers to compete for labor through wage-rate differentials. In periods of high labor demand such as existed from 1940 to 1970, employers have thus become accustomed to offering high overtime both as a means of easing the effect of labor shortages on output and as a device to raise weekly earnings. A high overtime component in weekly earnings has thus become established, and with it, as Flanders[4] has argued, inefficient practices in the utilization of labor that have helped to perpetuate the labor shortage difficulty. Although in the 1970s the pressure of labor demand has weakened, reliance on overtime remains strong. Rising nonwage labor costs may have encouraged employers to make more intensive use of their employees rather than take on new labor, whereas unions in a period of high inflation have been unable or unwilling to seek a consolidation of the overtime element in pay into a high basic wage. Nevertheless, the high unemployment experience of the mid-1970s has produced more union pressure for a 35-hour week in order to increase job opportunities. Employers have resisted this on account of their uncertainty whether overtime can actually be reduced to the extent necessary, in view of the entrenched attitudes to overtime working and the related work practices.

For full-time manual women workers, standard hours are nominally 40 per week, but in the 1970s actual hours have averaged about 37, since employers frequently permit women to work shorter hours without reducing them to part-time status. Nonmanual workers tend to have a shorter standard workweek and work less paid overtime. Thus in 1975 nonmanual men on average worked 38.7 hours with 1.4 hours paid overtime and nonmanual women worked 36.6 hours with .4 hours paid overtime.

Another major factor affecting the working year has been an increase in the length of paid holidays. Little is known about holidays before World War II, although it has been estimated that about 40% of the labor force were subject to holiday agreements, with manual workers usually having 1 week's paid holiday and nonmanual workers 2 to 3 weeks. Holiday entitlements have increased considerably since World War II; by 1955, 96% of

[3]"Earnings and Hours of Manual Workers in October 1975," *Department of Employment Gazette,* March 1977, pp. 239–249 and 312–313.
[4]Allan Flanders, *The Fawley Productivity Agreements,* (London: Faber, 1964).

manual workers covered by national collective agreements were entitled to 2 weeks paid holiday, whereas by 1971 63% were entitled to 3 weeks, and by 1975 34% of manual workers were due 4 weeks or more, 47% between 3 and 4 weeks, and 18% 3 weeks. A fairly common practice gives extra days of holiday dependent on length of service.

The length of the working year has also been influenced by the amount of part-time working, which is generally defined as working less than 30 hours per week. Men are usually full-time workers, and most of those working part-time (nearly 60% according to the 1966 census) were 65 or older. The percentage of part-time workers among all working males is 4–5 percent. Single women are also generally full-time workers, although they constitute a declining proportion of the working population. Married women, on the other hand, are very different; indications from the 1971 census were that about half the employed married women worked for not more than 30 hours a week, and although definitional and census coverage differences make comparisons difficult, there are also indications that the proportion has been increasing. Indeed, it is estimated that between 1961 and 1971 the increase in the number of married women working part time was greater than the increase in the number of all active women, owing to a decrease in the number of active nonmarried women as a higher proportion becomes married. As might be expected, the number of dependent children is the key factor in deciding how many hours a married woman works.

These various changes in hourly inputs per member of the labor force indicate a drop in the total of hours worked. The Department of Employment estimates that this amounted to some 5.3% between 1961 and 1971, or the equivalent of just over 1 million manual men working 1961 average annual hours.[5] These figures do not take into account changes in unemployment or the amount of absence through sickness or other causes.

Industrial Structure of the Labor Force

Table 2.2 shows the changes in the industrial structure of the labor force between 1901 and 1971, with a projection forward to 1981. The two parts of the table, separately covering 1901 and 1971–1981, are based on different definitions since there is no way of marrying the different census categories, but changes in orders of magnitude can be perceived. Most importantly, the table shows that, by comparison with most other countries, Britain in 1901 was already a relatively mature industrial economy, with only limited scope for productivity gains by transferring labor from one sector to another. Thus agriculture by the turn of the century already

[5]The Changing Structure of the Labour Force, *Department of Employment Gazette*, 1974, p. 12.

TABLE 2.2

Labor Force (in Thousands) by Industrial Structure

Sector (1901)	Total	Percentage of occupied population	Sector (1971)	Total	Percentage of those in employment	Projected 1981
Agriculture, forestry, fishing	1,457	8.95	Agriculture, etc.	643	2.70	540
Mining, quarrying	937	5.75	Mining	393	1.65	270
Total primary sector	2,394	14.70	Total primary sector	1,036	4.35	810
Metal manufacturing, engineering	1,569	9.64	Metal manufacturing, engineering, shipbuilding, vehicles	4,244	17.82	
Wood, furniture	297	1.82	Timber and furniture	303	1.27	280
Bricks, cement, pottery, glass	189	1.16	Building materials, pottery, glass	309	1.30	290
Chemicals oil, soap	147	0.93	Chemicals, coal ovens, mineral oils	531	2.23	540
Paper, printing	323	1.98	Paper, printing, and publishing	623	2.62	690
Textiles	1,352	8.30	Textiles	588	2.47	490
Clothing, leather	1,329	8.16	Leather, clothing and footwear	517	2.17	420
Food, drink, tobacco	917	5.63	Food, drink and tobacco	739	3.10	600
			Other manufacturing	323	1.36	310
Total manufacturing	6,123	37.61	Total manufacturing	8,179	34.35	7,650
Construction	1,219	7.49	Construction	1,707	7.17	1,840
Gas, water, electricity	62	0.38	Public utilities	364	1.53	370
Total production sector	7,404	45.48	Total production sector	10,250	43.05	9,860
Transport and communications	1,436	8.82	Transport	1,583	6.65	1,560
Professional occupations and services	674	4.14	Distribution	3,080	12.94	3,140
Commercial occupations and services	673	4.13	Insurance, banking, etc.	960	4.03	1,240
Domestic and personal services	2,344	14.40	Other private services	2,930	12.30	3,130
Armed forces	176	1.08	Education and health services	2,350	9.87	3,250
Public administration	220	1.35	Public administration	1,720	7.22	2,010
Total services	5,523	33.92	Total services	12,626	53.03	14,330
All others occupied	962	5.91				
Total occupied	16,280		Total in employment	23,912		25,000

Sources: *British Labour Statistics, Historical Abstract, 1886–1968* (London: Her Majesty's Stationery Office, 1971). *Department of Employment Gazette.*

comprised less than 10% of the labor force, and the primary sector as a whole, less than 15%. Nevertheless the internationally observed increasing demand for services associated with a rising per capita income, allied with the higher capital–labor ratio in production industries, has resulted in a shift towards service employment that has been particularly marked in the post-World War II period. The apparent constancy of the production sector masks considerable internal changes, with new industries developing (in engineering, vehicles, and chemicals) as others (notably textiles and clothing) declined. However, manufacturing as a whole has moved into absolute decline in the last 10 years, and this is expected to continue in the near future, resulting in a loss of some 700,000 jobs between 1961 and 1981, a trend that is causing considerable concern.

The service sector has grown consistently over the century from a third to over a half, and the rate of growth has accelerated in the recent past. Again, however, distinctions must be made within the sector, for the beginning of the century saw over 2 million employed in domestic service, compared with a current figure less than one-tenth of this. The main growth in the private sector has been in distribution, and professional and commercial services, but the largest overall growth has been in the public sector, now comprising some 7 million workers. Public administration has grown rapidly, more in local than central government, but the growth in public services has been more rapid still, with education and health increasing by 666,000 in the decade 1961–1971. Indeed, the recent growth of the public sector services has been seen by some as one of the reasons for the decline in manufacturing, and has caused considerable debate about the relative balance of the two. On the other hand, to put the matter in perspective, whereas Britain had the most "mature" employment structure in 1901, other countries had a higher proportion of the workforce in services by 1971.

In keeping with the higher proportion of women in the labor force, there has been a considerable substitution of female for male labor based on earlier sex ratios, but this has varied between industries. The move towards female employment has been greatest in the service industries, especially distribution, insurance and banking, professional and scientific services, and public administration, but it has also been positive in most production industries. Only in textiles and miscellaneous services (which includes domestic service) has there been a significant move away from female employment.

Occupational Structure of the Labor Force

Table 2.3 covers changes in the occupational structure, and even though the two statistical services derived from Routh and the Department

TABLE 2.3

Labor Force by Occupational Structure (in Thousands)

Routh	1911	Percentage	1921	Percentage	1931	Percentage	1951	Percentage
Higher professional	184	1.00	195	1.01	240	1.14	434	1.93
Lower professional	560	3.05	680	3.50	728	3.46	1,059	4.70
Employers and proprietors	1,232	6.71	1,318	6.82	1,409	6.70	1,118	4.97
Managers and administration	629	3.43	704	3.64	770	3.66	1,246	5.53
Clerical workers	887	4.84	1,300	6.72	1,465	6.97	2,404	10.68
Foreman, inspectors	236	1.29	279	1.44	323	1.54	590	2.62
Skilled manual	5,608	30.56	5,573	28.83	5,619	26.72	5,616	24.95
Semiskilled manual	7,244	39.48	6,544	33.85	7,360	35.00	7,338	32.60
Unskilled manual	1,767	9.63	2,740	14.17	3,115	14.81	2,709	12.03
Total	18,347		19,333		21,029		22,514	

Department of Employment	1961	Percentage	1971	Percentage	1981 (projected)	Percentage
Employers and managers	1,973	8.49	2,355	9.85	2,762	11.05
Professional workers	656	2.82	875	3.66	1,423	5.69
Intermediate nonmanuals	1,324	5.70	1,860	7.78	2,484	9.94
Junior nonmanuals	4,803	20.66	5,255	21.98	5,370	21.48
Personal service workers	1,030	4.43	1,271	5.32	1,562	6.25
Foremen and supervisors, manual	566	2.43	600	2.51	649	2.60
Skilled manual	5,700	24.52	5,133	21.47	4,526	18.10
Semiskilled manual	3,500	15.06	3,077	12.87	2,714	10.86
Unskilled manual	1,787	7.69	1,769	7.40	1,802	7.21
Agricultural workers	444	1.91	306	1.28	207	.83
Own account workers	867	3.73	971	4.06	1,307	5.23
Total (includes armed forces and inadequately described occupations)	23,245		23,910		25,000	

Sources: G. Routh, Occupation and Pay in Britain, 1906-60 (Cambridge: Cambridge University Press, 1965), pp. 4-5. "The Changing Structure of the Labour Force," Department of Employment Gazette, October 1975, p. 985.

of Employment are even less comparable than those for industrial structure, the general trends are reasonably clear. There are two basic components of change: (a) movements in the demand for the products and services of different industries, largely reflecting increased affluence; and (b)
movements in the occupation mix within industries, largely reflecting
changes in technology and organization. The major movement has been
the rapid growth of nonmanual occupations, together with some decline in
manual occupations, so that in 1971, manual workers represented little
more than half the labor force, as compared with more than four-fifths at
the beginning of the century. Within the manual groups, the major decline
has been in the skilled and semiskilled workers, with unskilled workers
retaining their relative position. Even within these groups there have been
considerable changes, largely dependent on the fortunes of particular industries; in the skilled category, for instance, there has been a move in
favor of the metal-using industries and against clothing and textiles. Since
the mid-1960s there has been an acceleration in these trends, especially
following the downturn in the economy after 1966, which affected employment in the production industries and consequently a decline in the
manual occupations. The move to the nonmanual occupations has been
continuous with the higher and lower professions, foremen and supervisors, administrators and managers, all doubling in numbers as male occupations between 1911 and 1951. Since then the higher-order occupations
such as professional and managerial have also shown a faster rate of growth
than the lower ones such as foremen and supervisors. In the clerical occupations, growth has been concentrated on the female side, with the dis-
placement of males by females largely completed in the early decades of
this century. In 1911 clerical workers accounted for only 3% of the female
labor force, but by 1951 this had risen to 20%, partly at the expense of
skilled and semiskilled work, including domestic service, and partly because
of the growth in the female labor force. Women have also moved into many
occupations traditionally regarded as male preserves, although there are
still many in which few females are found, and it should also be noted that
in some cases there has been a reverse movement of males into such traditional female occupations as teaching and nursing.

The impact of industrial and occupational effects has affected the
various groups in different ways, although generally the two effects have
pulled in the same direction. Until 1951 the industry effect was the more
important influence for the professions, both lower and higher, and the
semiskilled, whereas for clerical workers, supervisors, and skilled workers
the occupational effect was greater. In the more recent period the occupational effect has been greater, although the industry effect has predominated for intermediate nonmanuals, reflecting the rapid growth of the
health and education industries.

TABLE 2.4
Annual Average Unemployment, 1913–1976

	Percentage of insured workers unemployed		Percentage of registered unemployed			
	Original scheme of 1912	As expanded in 1930s				
1913	3.6	1939	9.3	1948	1.5	1971	3.4
1914	4.2	1940	6.0	1949	1.5	1972	3.8
1915	1.2	1941	2.2	1950	1.5	1973	2.6
1916	.6	1942	.8	1951	1.2	1974	2.6
1917	.7	1943	.6	1952	2.0	1975	4.1
1918	.8	1944	.5	1953	1.6	1976	5.6
1919	—	1945	1.3	1954	1.3		
1920	3.9	1946	2.5	1954	1.3		
1921	16.9	1947	3.1	1955	1.1		
1922	14.3	1948ᵃ	2.0	1956	1.2		
1923	11.7			1957	1.4		
1924	10.3			1958	2.1		
1925	11.3			1959	2.2		
1926	12.5			1960	1.6		
1927	9.7			1961	1.5		
1928	10.8			1962	2.0		
1929	10.4			1963	2.5		
1930	16.1			1964	1.6		
1931	21.3			1965	1.4		
1932	22.1			1966	1.5		
1933	19.9			1967	2.4		
1934	16.7			1968	2.4		
1935	15.5			1969	2.4		
1936	13.1			1970	2.5		
1937	10.8						
1938	12.9						
1939	10.5						

Sources: *British Labour Statistics, Historical Abstracts 1886–1968* (London: Her Majesty's Stationery Office, 1971). *Department of Employment Gazette.*
ᵃ First 6 months.

Unemployment

Unemployment statistics are not reliable before the National Insurance Act of 1911, being dependent upon union unemployment benefit records. Even after 1911, not by any means was the whole labor force covered, although successive extensions were made in the interwar period. Table 2.4 reflects the different series obtained under the original and expanded categories of insured workers. Not until 1948 was there an all-inclusive system that was able to show the number of unemployed registered at employment exchanges. (This method of measurement understates unemployment rates compared with survey methods used in North America and elsewhere: The U.S. Bureau of Labor Statistics has reestimated the British rate on the United States' definition, and this raises the published rate for 1974 from 2.6 to 2.9%, and for. 1975 from 4.1 to 4.9%.[6])

Although there are no accurate statistics for the pre-World War I period, there were major problems of cyclical unemployment, going far beyond the impact on trade-union members displayed by the available data, which bore especially hard on the unskilled in the downturn of the trade cycle, as in 1908–1909. It was in this period, therefore, that unemployment became a major political issue, given widespread dissatisfaction with the existing system of local responsibility based on the Poor Law, leading to passage of the National Insurance Act, which for the first time set up a system of compulsory unemployment insurance in a limited number of industries.

World War I brought full employment and indeed a massive demand for labor, which considerably expanded the labor force. But after a short-lived boom up to 1920, the age of mass unemployment set in. Between 1921 and 1939 the number of unemployed did not fall below 1 million; indeed this was the hard core, on top of which seasonal fluctuations added up to another 3 million in the peak period of September 1932. At this time, some 6–7 million people were living "on the dole" and many others close to it or excluded only by the Means Test. If the intensity of the unemployment at its worst was not as bad as in some other countries, the continuous nature of the problem over the best part of a generation ensured that it was seared on the political consciousness of the country, making it the single most important emotional issue in British politics right up to the present. To make matters worse, the unemployment was concentrated throughout the period in certain industries and localities: the staple prewar export trades such as coal, cotton, wool, iron and steel, and pottery; and areas such as South Wales and the North of England. Although in the more prosperous areas of the South and Midlands there was frictional and cyclical unemployment, in the worst areas it was long term and hard core. As usual, it was the unskilled who suffered most.

World War II finally brought the depression to an end, and since then, there has been a commitment to full employment and Keynesian economics shared by all political parties. In the 1950s employment continued at a high level—indeed labor shortages in some skilled occupations caused bottlenecks in production, and there were also side effects in wage drift and

[6]"International Unemployment Statistics," *Department of Employment Gazette*, July 1976, pp. 710–715.

the fragmentation of collective bargaining. There were, however, still significant areas of unemployment; Scotland, for example, had double the national unemployment average for most of this period, and there were smaller pockets where it was considerably higher still. Then in the late 1960s the national average itself began to creep up as a result of deflationary economic policies designed to improve Britain's international economic situation, and in the 1970s, in common with other countries, the situation has grown worse. In August 1977, 1.6 million were registered as unemployed in Great Britain.

Manpower Policies

A feature of recent British economic policy, in keeping with trends in other countries, has been the development of a much more active set of manpower policies designed to supplement the operation of the labor market in a number of different ways. Most of these have come into operation since the mid-1960s, but intervention in the labor market is by no means a new conception. Labor exchanges, which were set up on a national basis from 1909; numerous measures to deal with unemployment, many based on developing the National Insurance Act of 1911; wartime arrangements for the recruitment, dilution, exemption from military service, and ultimately direction and resettlement of labor; and the beginnings of regional policy in the 1930s were all examples of such intervention, but there was never any real conception of a permanent and comprehensive manpower policy. By the mid-1960s, a general concern about the country's economic performance identified various labor market problems, described in the British report to the O.E.C.D. in 1970 as "persistent shortages of skills, uneven distribution of job opportunities between regions, and frequently an attitude of reluctance to come to terms with industrial and technological change, leading to wasteful use of manpower and retarding productivity."[7] There have been many wide-ranging measures since that time, of which only the most important can be outlined here.

Perhaps the most far-reaching break with tradition has been in the area of training, which had almost entirely been left to employers, and which depended to a very large extent on an apprenticeship system whose origins went back well before the beginning of the century. The Industrial Training Act of 1964 moved in the direction of greater centralization by setting up Industrial Training Boards (ITB's) to supervise the amount and quality of training and to finance it by means of a payroll-based levy on employers. Each ITB, currently numbering 24 and covering two-thirds of all employees, was to exercise its functions in accordance with proposals submitted to the relevant minister and for further advice and coordination

---

[7]*Manpower Policy in the United Kingdom,* (Paris: O.E.C.D., 1970), p. 37.

a Central Training Council was set up. Provision for individuals not in employment or wishing to change occupations was made in the form of Government Training Centers (since renamed Skillcenters) to provide accelerated training for adults equivalent to an apprenticeship. The general effect was to stimulate the quantity and quality of training, but by the early 1970s changes in the new system were felt to be necessary, especially since it did not lead to a sustained growth in the number of people trained beyond the requirements of individual firms, and more fundamentally, because any system based on individual industries had inherent limitations. Under the Employment and Training Act of 1973 the responsibility for training was further centralized under the Training Services Agency to coordinate the ITB's, to promote training in areas not covered by the boards, and to take over the considerably expanded individual training programs (TOPS). Modifications were also made in the financing of training, with the government, then and since, increasing its financial commitment.

A second major development in manpower policy has been in the employment services, which have been held to be the single most important aid in the efficient functioning of the labor market. However, in the depression of the 1930s, the "labor exchanges" became associated with the payment of welfare benefits rather than the finding of work. This image was detrimental to the latter function, so that workers used them only as a last resort and employers did not notify them of vacancies. In the early 1970s, planning proceeded towards the reformulation of the service, most notably through separating payment of benefit from finding work, and building new exchanges for the latter function and renaming them "Job centers." The service as a whole was retitled the Employment Services Agency in the 1973 act, and both it and the Training Services Agency were brought under an umbrella organization, the Manpower Services Commission, which was to be independent of government and responsible for developing a comprehensive manpower policy.

A third component of manpower policy has been the encouragement of labor mobility, which has been carried out in several rather heterogeneous ways. Geographical mobility has been encouraged by the provision of housing in New and Expanded Towns whereas financial assistance has been available through an Employment Transfer Scheme. To sponsor industrial change more directly by encouraging the growth of manufacturing combined with economy in the use of service industries, a Selective Employment Tax was introduced in 1966, based on the taxation of employment in service industries. However, this was withdrawn in 1973, largely because of the administrative problems of differentiating between service and manufacturing establishments and the relatively low net yield. A more general encouragement of industrial change was the passage of the Redundancy Payments Act in 1965, whereby payments are made to compensate for, and reduce the fear of, redundancy. Finally, the transferability of pension rights between occupational schemes was introduced in 1976. It needs to be said, however, that there have been problems with all these encouragements of mobility and that some issues, such as housing difficulties, remain major obstacles to its promotion.

The fourth area, regional and industrial location policy, reverses the previous category by concentrating on capital rather than labor mobility, taking the job to the worker rather than vice versa. Some objectives of regional policy, like some of the other measures mentioned, go well beyond manpower policy as such, but one key objective is to obtain a better balance of labor supply and demand throughout the country, obviating unemployment in some areas and "overheating" in others. Regionally differentiated investment grants, advance factory building, and a regional employment premium paid on employees in manufacturing industry have been positive mechanisms of assistance created for the "development areas" in the last decade. There have also been negative constraints to direct industry away from the more prosperous areas in the form of Industrial Development Certificates and Office Development Permits.

It is difficult to evaluate, or indeed to decide, the criteria for the success of manpower policy in Britain, since its main provisions have coincided with an adverse macroeconomic situation. On the whole the results have not been what was hoped for especially in view of the increasingly large expenditure involved, and the various measures have still not been adequately coordinated into a comprehensive program; but the future is nevertheless likely to be in the direction of more rather than less intervention.

TRADE UNIONISM

Membership

Table 2.5 illustrates the overall pattern of union membership and density throughout the century, in which several phases can be identified. Membership passed the 2 million mark for the first time at the turn of the century, grew steadily up to World War I, and increased sharply immediately after it, reaching a peak density of 45% in 1920. From this point it declined, reaching a low watermark in 1933 at the depths of the depression. It then increased again, accelerating during and just after the World War II. From 1948 to 1965 density remained on a plateau, with a tendency to decrease in the 1950s; membership increased slowly, in keeping with the growth of the labor force. Since 1968 there has been a further acceleration, due in part to a more positive attitude by the state in fostering growth, in part also, to growing recognition by workers of the insecurities created by inflation and rising unemployment. These pressures have been enhanced more recently, and further growth can thus be expected in the future.

TABLE 2.5

Total Trade-Union Membership (in Thousands), and Density (in Percentages) in the United Kingdom: Selected Years, 1892–1974

Year	Labor force[a]	Total union membership	Density of union membership
1892	14,126	1,576	11.2
1901	16,101	2,025	12.6
1911	17,762	3,139	17.7
1913	17,920	4,135	23.1
1917	18,234	5,499	30.2
1920	18,469	8,348	45.2
1923	17,965	5,429	30.2
1933	19,422	4,392	22.6
1938	19,829	6,053	30.5
1945	20,400	7,875	38.6
1948	20,732	9,362	45.2
1950	21,055	9,289	44.1
1955	21,913	9,741	44.5
1960	22,817	9,835	43.1
1965	23,920	10,325	43.2
1968	23,667	10,193	43.1
1970	23,446	11,179	47.7
1972	22,959	11,349	49.4
1974	23,339	11,755	50.4

Source: R. J. Price and G. S. Bain, "Union Growth Revisited: 1948–1974 in Perspective," *British Journal of Industrial Relations,* November 1976, p. 340.

[a]There have been changes in definition, especially in the method of computing the labor force in 1972, for which the reader is referred to the original article. The labor force series includes the unemployed, but excludes employers, the self-employed and members of the armed forces.

The overall statistics inevitably hide major changes in the composition of membership. At the beginning of the century there were large sectors where there was little or no organization: manufacturing outside engineering and textiles, domestic service, agriculture (although there had been several short-lived agricultural unions in the nineteenth century), and those service industries that were predominantly based on nonmanual clerical occupations. Geographically most union members were concentrated in the North of England, in Central Scotland, and South Wales, whereas the Midlands and South of England were relatively sparse in organization, with the exception of some occupations in London. Table 2.6 gives the approximate pattern of density by industrial sector as it existed in 1901.

Unfortunately there are no statistics disaggregating union membership throughout the century, but a valuable recent article by Price and Bain has gone a long way toward providing the comprehensive picture in the

TABLE 2.6
Density (in Percentage) of Union Organization, 1901

	Trade-union members	Labor force	Density
Metals engineering and shipbuilding	339	1644	21
Shipbuilding	78	128	60
Mining and quarrying	531	944	56
Textiles	246	1462	17
Cotton	189	546	35
Construction	250	1336	19
Transport	180	1498	12
Railways	76	322	24
Clothing	66	1396	5
Printing	47	139	34
National government	45	146	31

Source: H. A. Clegg, A. Fox, and A. F. Thompson, *A History of British Trade Unions Since 1889*, vol. 1 (Oxford: Clarendon Press, 1964), p. 468.

post-World War II period shown in Table 2.7, which gives union membership and density by industry in 1948 and 1974. Three main points stand out. First, the highest densities are to be found in the public sector—coal, public utilities, railways, road transport, post office, health, education, and local and national government. Second, density increased in the great majority of industries; only in agriculture, cotton and other textiles, bricks and building materials, wood and furniture, construction, and distribution were there declines. The latter two, being large industries, deserve some comment. In distribution, the reason for the decline is likely to be related to the growing number of women in the industry's labor force, whereas in construction there has been an important movement towards self-employment, undertaken for income tax purposes. Third, there has been a significant impact of employment trends on total union membership and density. Several of the industries in which there was a high density in 1948, notably coal mining, rail transport, and cotton and other textiles, have declined radically in total employment, whereas many of the industries with rapid employment growth—insurance, banking and finance, and health are examples—have been those with low densities in 1948. Thus, although densities have increased in the latter industries, union membership has not grown by the same absolute amount as employment growth. To this extent, the redistribution of the labor force has been unfavorable for union membership growth.

This point is further illustrated by Table 2.8, which breaks down membership and density by sex and by manual and white-collar categories. Thus, male manual union membership has declined absolutely over the period, even though the density has increased, whereas although male

TABLE 2.7
Union Membership (in Thousands) and Density (in Percentages) by Industry in the United Kingdom, 1948 and 1974

	1948			1974		
Industry[a]	Labor force	Union membership	Density	Labor force	Union membership	Density
Agriculture and forestry	785.9	215.7	27.4	415.5	92.3	22.2
Fishing	37.7	14.9	39.6	12.2	7.4	60.5
Coal mining	802.7	675.3	84.1	314.0	302.1	96.2
Other mining	81.4	37.0	45.5	50.6	26.2	51.8
Food and drink	597.4	227.4	38.1	783.9	401.1	51.2
Tobacco	49.1	26.1	53.1			
Chemicals	426.8	127.3	29.8	483.6	247.4	51.2
Metals and engineering	3676.1	1837.5	50.0	4118.0	2862.7	69.4
Cotton and man-made fibers	395.2	276.6	70.0	596.7	243.8	40.9
Other textiles	533.3	180.4	33.8			
Leather	79.0	24.7	31.2	44.0	20.5	46.6
Clothing	429.1	145.5	33.9	345.8	207.7	60.0
Footwear	139.5	92.8	66.6	87.1	68.8	79.0
Bricks and building materials	172.2	70.1	40.8	171.9	69.4	40.4
Pottery	75.3	31.3	41.5	60.5	56.8	93.8
Glass	68.1	28.2	41.3	74.5	58.5	78.5
Wood and furniture	279.8	122.0	43.6	289.6	102.0	35.2
Paper, printing, and publishing	455.5	264.1	58.0	596.1	426.6	71.6
Rubber	97.9	48.5	49.6	127.2	71.1	55.9
Construction	1353.7	613.2	45.3	1428.8	388.1	27.2
Gas, electricity, and water	322.9	218.3	67.6	352.3	324.0	92.0
Railways	694.9	612.1	88.1	224.0	217.0	96.9
Road transport	490.6	295.0[b]	60.1[b]	468.3	445.4[b]	95.1[b]
Sea transport	120.8	108.0	89.3	90.6	90.3	99.6
Port and inland water transport	155.7	123.2	79.1	81.5	77.2	94.7
Air transport	32.1	13.0	40.5	79.8	74.7	93.6
Post office and telecommunications	353.2	283.4	80.2	509.7	448.1	87.9
Distribution	2167.9	325.3	15.0	2810.1	321.8	11.4
Insurance, banking, and finance	425.9	137.1	32.2	680.5	305.1	44.8
Entertainment and media services	238.4	95.7	40.1	189.6	123.0	64.9
Health	525.9	204.6	38.9	1175.2	715.8	60.9
Hotels and catering	708.1	n.a.	—	824.2	42.5	5.2
Other professional services	276.8	n.a.	—	470.2	17.6	3.7
Education and local government	1280.5	792.2	61.9	2752.4	2356.0	85.6
National government	724.1	480.6	66.4	623.7	564.5	90.5

Source: R. J. Price and G. S. Bain, "Union Growth Revisited: 1948–1974 in Perspective," *British Journal of Industrial Relations,* November 1976, p. 343.

[a] The following industries are not included in this table: miscellaneous transport services, other manufacturing (less rubber), business services (property owning, advertising and market research, other business services, central offices not allocable elsewhere), other miscellaneous services (betting and gambling, hairdressing and manicure, laundries, dry-cleaning, motor repairers, distributors, garages and filling stations, repair of boots and shoes, and other services). Union density in this heterogeneous group of industries was less than 3% in 1974; total employment was 2.4 million.

[b] These figures are substantially overstated since it has not been possible to disaggregate the membership of the Commercial Trade Group of the Transport and General Workers' Union into those employed by haulage firms and those employed by manufacturing concerns. Union membership among the latter group should be classified to the relevant manufacturing industry.

TABLE 2.8

Unionization by Sex and Major Occupational Group in the United Kingdom, 1948–1974

	Male					Female				
	1948	1964	1970	1974	Percentage increase 1948–1974	1948	1964	1970	1974	Percentage increase 1948–1974
Union membership (in thousands)										
White-collar	1,267	1,681	2,143	2,593	+104.7	697	1,003	1,447	1,629	+133.7
Manual	6,410	6,329	6,123	5,972	− 6.8	988	1,206	1,364	1,561	+ 58.0
Total	7,677	8,010	8,266	8,565	+ 11.6	1,685	2,209	2,811	3,190	+ 89.3
Union density (in percentages)										
White-collar	33.8	33.4	40.0	44.5	+ 10.7	25.4	24.9	30.7	32.6	+ 7.2
Manual	59.5	60.0	63.3	64.7	+ 5.2	26.0	32.6	35.2	42.1	+ 16.1
Total	52.9	51.4	55.0	56.9	+ 4.0	25.7	28.6	32.7	36.7	+ 11.0

Source: R. J. Price and G. S. Bain, "Union Growth Revisisted: 1948–1974 in Perspective," British Journal of Industrial Relations, November 1976, p. 349.

white-collar unionization has doubled, the density has risen by only 10%. Again, female membership has increased far more than density. The table thus reflects the considerable increase in the white-collar and female labor force, and also their increased significance within the trade-union movement.

There are of course other factors of significance in unionization. One is size of establishment. Although there are no direct figures, the indications are that this is one of the main reasons for low union density in construction, agriculture, and private sector services. Making certain assumptions, Price and Bain calculated that if establishments with less than 200 workers were excluded, union density in manufacturing in 1974 went up from 62.2 to 89.2%. Other factors that appear likely to have affected the propensity to unionize are the positive inducements of the rapid rate of price and wage inflation and the supportive legal climate and unemployment as a discouraging element.[8]

Structure

Since the turn of the century the number of unions has fallen from 1323 in 1900 to 488 in 1975, mainly as a result of amalgamations. This itself suggests a rapid growth in the average size of individual unions, but in addition union membership is disproportionately skewed towards the larger unions. As Table 2.9 indicates, over three-quarters of union members are in the 25 largest unions. Moreover, by no means all unions are members of the TUC. Table 2.10 shows that in 1975 only 111 unions were affiliated to the TUC, but these comprised some 87% of total union membership, with only 2 unions with more than 100,000 members, the Institute of Professional Civil Servants and the Police Federation, outside it, and the former of these has recently decided to affiliate. Table 2.10 also indicates the substantial changes in rank order even since 1946, with unions such as the Miners and the Railwaymen declining in size and several public sector and white-collar unions increasing.

The structure of British trade unionism is complex almost beyond description, largely owing to the overlay of successive economic and social developments on what was already by 1900 a quite intricate framework. The unions at that time were, however, more clearly recognizable within the three conventional categories of craft, industrial, and general unions. with the oldest of the first two groups dating back to the 1850s and the general, or at that time, laborers', unions dating back a mere decade or so. Unions were predominantly geared to particular occupations with some orientation to the "aristocracy of labor," a term that seems to have been

---

[8]For further discussion, see G. S. Bain and F. Elsheikh, *Union Growth and the Business Cycle: An Economic Analysis*, (Oxford: Basil Blackwell, 1976).

TABLE 2.9
Membership of Trade Unions by Size at the End of 1975

Number of members	Number of unions	Total membership (in thousands, to nearest thousand)	Total number of unions (in percentages)	Total membership of all unions (in percentages)
Under 100	73	4	14.9	.0
100–499	133	33	27.2	.3
500–999	52	37	10.7	.3
1000–2499	68	108	13.9	.9
2500–4999	44	144	9.0	1.2
5000–9999	30	200	6.1	1.7
10,000–14,999	11	129	2.3	1.1
15,000–24,999	17	327	3.5	2.7
25,000–49,999	20	664	4.1	5.6
50,000–99,999	15	1045	3.1	8.7
100,000–249,999	14	1995	2.9	16.7
250,000+	11	7264	2.3	60.8
Totals	488	11,950	100.0	100.0

Source: Department of Employment Gazette, November 1976.

TABLE 2.10
Unions with More Than 100,000 Members in the TUC, 1946 and 1975

1946 Congress[a]		1975 Congress[b]	
TGWU	964,000	TGWU	1,857,000
AEU	704,000	AUEW	1,427,000
GMWU	604,000	GMWU	883,000
Mineworkers	533,000	NALGO	542,000
Railwaymen	410,000	Public Employees	507,000
USDAW	274,000	EEPTU	414,000
Woodworkers	176,000	USDAW	352,000
Post Office Workers	144,000	ASTMS	351,000
Electricians	133,000	Teachers	264,000
Civil Service Clerical	122,000	UCATT (construction)	257,000
Tailors	118,000	Mineworkers	255,000
Public Employees	102,000	Civil and Public Servants	215,000
Shop Assistants	101,000	Graphical Trades	193,000
		Post Office Workers	190,000
		Railwaymen	172,000
		Health Service Employees	143,000
		APEX	137,000
		Boilermakers	129,000
		Post Office Engineers	125,000
		Tailors	116,000
		National Graphical Association	107,000
		Iron and Steel Trades	106,000
		Bank Employees	100,000

Source: TUC Congress Reports.
[a] Total TUC membership unions: 192. Total individuals: 6,671,000.
[b] Total TUC membership unions: 111. Total individuals: 10,363,000.

used from the middle of the nineteenth century to describe "certain distinctive upper strata of the working class, better paid, better treated and generally regarded as more 'respectable' and politically moderate than the rest of the proletariat."[9] This was most obvious in the case of the craft unions, but the industrial unions frequently covered only the leading occupation(s) in the industry, whereas the general unions represented conglomerates of specific occupations grouped together for joint administration.

As the century developed, all three groups of unions spread, the operative unions into more nearly true industrial unions, some of the craft unions into the ranks of the semiskilled and later the unskilled, and the general unions into such pockets of unorganized workers as were available, picking up small associations through amalgamation on the way. As new industries such as vehicles, chemicals, and various sectors of light engineering emerged, and older, established ones grew, so unions sought new members in an ad hoc and unplanned way, helped by loose jurisdictional boundaries. The result was a slowly stablizing structure in which anomalies and competition abounded. The development of white-collar unionization, largely in the postwar period outside the public sector, saw a new growth of specialized but multioccupational unions competing with older unions that saw an opportunity to move upward from a blue-collar base.

In all this the inherently competitive posture of the unions had to be balanced with the need for cooperation in relations with employers, especially at higher levels. Hence there grew up federations of unions for collective bargaining purposes, with single unions being represented on dozens of different bargaining committees. The monitoring of interunion relations, insofar as this was carried out at all, was done by the TUC and the union federations themselves. It was only as late as 1939 that the TUC enumerated a clear set of rules of behavior for affiliated unions. These so-called Bridlington rules provide criteria by which the TUC Disputes Committee may judge on interunion disputes. In essence they provide that no one who is or has recently been a member of any trade union should be accepted into another union without inquiry. Where inquiry shows that the member is under discipline, engaged in a trade dispute or in arrears with contributions, he should not be accepted. Further, no union should start organizing in any establishment a grade of workers in which another union has a majority of workers employed and negotiates wages and conditions for them, unless by arrangement with the other union. Although these rules set limits to interunion competition, and a mechanism for resolving dispute, they leave many difficult problems of jurisdiction and contribute little to rationalization of trade-union structure.

---

[9]E. J. Hobsbaum, "The Labour Aristocracy in Nineteenth Century Britain," in *Labouring Men: Studies in the History of Labour* (New York: Anchor Books, 1967), p. 321.

Until very recently the state played a very small part by comparison with most other countries. It had virtually nothing to do with union recruiting or internal organization, and its main contribution came in its sponsorship of Joint Industrial Councils in the 1920s. Even here the main effect was in the public sector, in which as employer it naturally had to play a more direct role.

Internal Administration

The internal organization and administration of British unions tends to be more dominated by lay members than is typical elsewhere. Thus, the Donovan Commission in 1968 discovered an average of 3800 members per full-time official, two or three times the ratio of other major industrial nations. The reasons for this have been partly financial; dues are also lower than in other countries and not infrequently lower in real terms than earlier in the century. The Donovan Commission reported that weekly contributions had declined from 1.02% of male average weekly earnings in 1938 to .39% in 1966. In 1970 the average contribution per member was £4.61 per annum or some 9p per week; the highest average contribution was £9.48 by the Railwaymen, the lowest £2.14 by the Bank Employees. Some 86% of all union income was from subscriptions; only one, the Dyers and Bleachers, obtained less than half its income from this source.

Although there has been a decline in the welfare benefits that were an important part of financial expenditure earlier in this century, they are still significant, and the average for all registered unions in 1970 was about a quarter of all expenditure. There has been a more than commensurate increase in administrative expenses, which rose from 41% in 1936 to 60% in 1970. Moreover, the pay of officials remains as always far from generous, and the back-up legal, research, and training services that unions might like to offer continue to be provided only on a skeleton basis. Finally, funds that could be used for strikes have also diminished over time in real terms, and most unions could not contemplate paying strike pay for any large group of members over an extended period. Only about 7% of expenditure was on strike pay in 1970, and the average per capita assets were only £14.51.

But finance has been only part of the reason for lay domination. Because of the lack of officials, because bargaining was traditionally carried out externally to the plant, because organization was based on the geographical area rather than the plant, and because of multiunionism, communications with and control over the membership in the plant has never been easy for the national union. The main link between plant and union in the first half of this century was the dues collector, whose role was defined by an organizer of the Workers' Union just before World War I in the following terms:

> It is to the Collector that the Union principally looks for the maintenance of the strength of the Union, in his shop or section of the shop. Upon the Collector rests the responsibility of advice in the first instance, in those emergency difficulties which occasionally spring up in even the best shops; and upon him frequently falls the duty of acting as spokesman for the others, in discussion with (the) Foreman or Works Manager.[10]

Shop stewards in the modern sense existed in some establishments, and more widely during World War I, but their power has increased enormously in the last two decades. The emergence of the plant as a major focus of bargaining after the mid-1950s highlighted the organizational vacuum in union organization at the lowest levels, to which unions themselves did not react. Instead, it was filled by the rise of the steward, who now occupies a more important role than in any other country. Almost by definition, since the role varies considerably, numbers cannot be precise; but an estimate by the Commission on Industrial Relations suggested some 350,000 in 1971, of which some 60,000 were nonunion workplace representatives. The steward did not, and indeed still does not appear in the rulebooks of most unions, but grew out of the need to deal with shop floor circumstances and to provide a leadership that the formal union organization in many instances could not give.

Plant organizations vary considerably in their independence from the union, but generally speaking the less developed the industry-level agreement, the greater the scope for local autonomy, whereas the greater the degree of centralization of bargaining, as for instance in most of the public sector, the greater the role of the full-time official in local affairs. Moreover, where several unions are represented, as in most engineering plants, it has been natural for them to come together to coordinate plantwide activities through shop steward committees. Thus, a body could come into existence that did not owe allegiance to, and was not directly controlled by, any single union. Indeed, it has not been unusual for workers in one union to come under stewards of another union. The position of the national union has also been made more difficult by the preference of employers to deal with shop stewards rather than the full-time official, who cannot be fully aware of the circumstances of the particular plant, and, perhaps more importantly, normally does not possess the same allegiance of the workers as the stewards. Employers, indeed, have further weakened the official's position by using him more as a fire–fighter and a disciplinary threat than as a normal part of the industrial-relations machinery.

The result has been that the average worker has tended to see the steward as the embodiment of the union and pay little attention to its larger activities. The apathy and instrumental attitudes of union members, com-

---

[10]*The Worker's Union Record,* January 1914, quoted in H. A. Clegg, *The System of Industrial Relations in Great Britain* (Oxford: Blackwell, 1970), p. 38.

mon in all countries, has perhaps had stronger repercussions in Britain than elsewhere as a result of the problems created by lack of organization and institutional structure at plant level.

The Trades-Union Congress

The position of the TUC as the central agency in the British labor movement has never been challenged since its origin in 1868; even though it encompasses a minority of all unions, it has always spoken on behalf of the labor movement as a whole. Its role has however changed, and three distinct periods can be identified.

The first was from 1868 to 1921, during which the executive body was the Parliamentary Committee, which as its name suggests, had as its primary function that of political lobbying. However, once the Labor Party had become the political counterpart of the union movement, and when bargaining had moved to the industry-wide and national stage around the World War I period, there was clearly a need for an industrial rather than a political orientation for the TUC. Thus, in 1921 the TUC adopted its modern structure of a General Council based on industrial groupings and serviced by a central secretariat. The intention was that it should coordinate industrial action, but apart from the General Strike of 1926 it did little of this. In practice the constituent unions preferred their autonomy, and during this phase, as in the first, were largely able to maintain it. Indeed, the unchallenged position of the TUC was in considerable part due to its lack of influence over the internal affairs of unions or collective bargaining. Several attempts to promote a more national union structure, by promoting industrial unionism for instance, met with little or no response. The third phase, dating from approximately the middle 1960s, has established a new and much more significant role for the TUC as the state has sought to impose constraints on union power through law and income policies. In the bargaining that has followed, the TUC has been not only the voice but the leader of the labor movement, fashioning income policies, constructing legislation, acting indeed as an arm of government vis-à-vis its own membership as for the economy generally and moving well away from the point where Windmuller could justify placing the TUC at the bottom of a list of national trade union centers in terms of their power over their affiliates.[11] Some commentators have indeed seen the rise in influence of the TUC as presaging the approach of a corporate state. However, although the power of the TUC vis-à-vis its affiliated unions and their members has undoubtedly increased compared with the two earlier phases, it should not be

---

[11]J. P. Windmuller, "The Authority of National Trade Union Confederations: A Comparative Analysis," in *Union Power and Public Policy*, ed. D. B. Lipsky, (Ithaca, N.Y.: New York State School of Industrial and Labor Relations, 1975), p. 102.

overestimated. Most TUC initiatives have been initiated within its own secretariat or within a small group of union leaders within the General Council, and their influence on votes at congress is far from absolute, whereas their control of events at plant level also remains tenuous, as we shall see in later discussions of income policy.

Union Relationships with the Labor Party

The origin of organized political action by the union movement dates from the founding of the TUC as a body that could work for legislative relief from judicial attacks on the concept of unionism. This was not in itself sufficient in spite of legislation in the 1870s, and further judicial attacks followed, culminating in the famous Taff Vale case of 1901. In 1900 a new body had been formed, the Labor Representation Committee, with a certain amount of union support, but as a result of Taff Vale as much as socialist convictions, many unions recognized the need for an explicitly working-class party.

The new party won 29 seats in the 1906 election and in the 1920s replaced the Liberals as one of the two major political parties. In the party, the union movement was from the start the major voting block and financial provider; it is indeed a further important distinction of the British unions that they created the socialist political party, whereas in most European countries the left-wing political parties sponsored the trade unions. Largely for this reason, the integral links between party and unions in Britain have remained stronger than elsewhere, although there have inevitably been periods of strain, not least in the last few years when the party in government has interfered in the industrial-relations system, traditionally the autonomous province of the parties to collective bargaining.

In spite of their potentially dominating role in the party, the unions did not try to dominate in practice until very recently; on the whole the unions took few initiatives and were a conservative force in policy determination within the party, with most of their block votes being used to reinforce the leadership against left-wing opposition. (It should be noted that unions affiliate separately to the party, and not for their full membership, since individuals have the right to opt out of a political contribution; some unions, mainly in the white-collar field, do not affiliate at all, and the result of these two possibilities for nonmembership is that only about half of all union members are affiliated through their unions.) Indeed, in the interwar Labor administrations the unions felt that they were not even adequately consulted by the Labor governments; this situation improved in the 1945–1951 and 1964–1970 administrations, but the major initiatives still come from what might be called the intellectual rather than the union side of the party. In the early 1970s, however, the unions were responsible for a considerable shift to the left in the Labor party; moreover, a Labor party-TUC liaison committee was set up to formalize more frequent contacts, and it was this body that was responsible for the conception of the "Social Contract," of which more will be said in discussing income policy. Nor did the unions attempt to use their strength to dominate the Labor party in the House of Commons, although some 40% of Labor MP's are nominated as candidates with the specific support of individual unions. But this "sponsored" group has never constituted a majority of the party in the Commons, except when it was at a very low ebb following the 1931 and 1935 elections, and many of those sponsored have had only limited links with the union backing them.

There have nevertheless been indications in recent years of a greater interest by unions in obtaining sponsored MPs, since the Parliamentary party has strongly discouraged interference with the independence of the individual member. The only occasion on which the trade union group has exerted any concerted influence was in rejecting the 1969 attempt of the Labor Government to introduce constraints on union bargaining activities.

It remains to state the ideology of the unions more explicitly. It has always been a mixture of socialist idealism and pragmatism, with the balance in favor of the latter at most times. In spite of the structural attachment of most unions to the Labor party, they have recognized the need to work with the government of the day, although there have always been some, sometimes amounting to a substantial minority, who have sought more direct methods. Although these latter have on occasion mounted important constitutional challenges, the majority of the labor movement has always been prepared to work within the existing economic and political framework. Indeed, insofar as a distinctive ideology has been present, it has been the collective bargaining ethos of voluntarism, rather than the political ethos of socialism, although the balance has swung more in favor of the latter in the 1970s.

EMPLOYER ORGANIZATION

Employers' Associations

In the early part of this century, employer associations played a significant role in the development of the industrial relations system, but they have declined in importance in recent years. Only the central body, the Confederation of British Industry, which was created out of three employer associations in 1965, has grown in stature. Few of the employer associations had any length of continuous life back in the nineteenth century. Most of them came into existence as reactions to the growth of unions and they were often even more temporary than those of the workers'. Only rarely did effective employers associations predate unionism—coal, iron, and shipping were examples of this. By 1900 most associations were still local or district-based, but in a few important cases national organizations had developed; in engineering and building, for instance, the great strikes of 1897–1898 consolidated the position of the associations and resulted in the setting up of national procedures. This was one of the first steps in the centralization of collective bargaining into the industry-wide "traditional" system. If the employer associations did not provide the major impulse in this direction, they were necessary preconditions for that system.

On the whole the British employer associations were less antiunion than those in other countries. During its early phase in the third quarter of the nineteenth century, unionism did not have the political connotations with which it later became associated; moreover, employers, like unions, were happy to take labor out of the sphere of competition by district bargaining, although they resisted any attempts to control their prerogatives at plant level. There were thus no determined efforts to destroy unionism, although there was often resistance to recognition. Nor was there the close liaison between politics and industry that has been common elsewhere. Most employers had a strong distrust of the state and they were just as much in favor of voluntarism as an ideology for industrial relations as the unions.

Since World War I, employer associations have tended to react to events and tried to maintain their existing organization rather than respond to change. Thus, the Engineering Employers' Federation had no direct membership for the huge multiplant companies that comprise much of its jurisdiction; rather the individual factories affiliated to local associations. On the employer side, this was a gap at least as large as the omission of the shop steward from union constitutions. On the other hand, the very looseness of association bargaining has been attractive to companies, which can engage in bargaining at both industry and lower levels. Thus, firms have generally retained membership, although some firms, often of American parentage, have always pursued their own personnel policies, and there has been a tendency for large firms to leave their associations in recent years. There are, nevertheless, more employer associations than unions. A survey in 1965 showed 1411, of which some 750 were autonomous.

Personnel Management

For much of this century professional personnel management at company or plant level has scarcely existed in Britain. Personnel management largely grew out of the welfare function within the company and had little to do with handling union–management relations, which, insofar as they were carried out at all at plant or company level, were the perquisite of line management. For the most part however, companies did not concern themselves with questions of industrial relations policy, preferring to leave these to the employers' associations. The increasing specialization of management, and more importantly the increasing need to coordinate industrial relations activities at the plant level, has greatly increased the numbers of personnel managers; thus the Donovan Commission noted that there were well over 10,000 in 1968, but it also noted that they were primarily concerned with day-to-day issues rather than policy. At the board of directors level it is increasingly common to have a director responsible for industrial relations, but they are still found only in a minority of firms. In a study carried out in 1969, Marsh found that two-thirds of multiplant companies in engineering did not have any director responsible for industrial-relations issues.[12]

COLLECTIVE BARGAINING

The Collective Bargaining Process

The collective bargaining process in its historical perspective in Britain revolves around the growth and decline of the "traditional" or "formal" system of industry-wide bargaining. One of the key factors in this process was the absence of any development of institutions at plant level either during the nineteenth century or during most of the twentieth century to date. At the turn of the century bargaining was basically at the district level within each industry. It was not necessarily formally constituted, for although there were some joint boards that had existed for two or three decades with formal relationships, in other cases the parties came together to resolve disputes on an ad hoc basis, and even wage rates might not be negotiated, although some form of agreement on wage movements or wage minima was general. (It should of course be remembered that agreements at this time often referred to a minority of workers even in the industries where bargaining took place.)

The scope of an agreement might not be wide by modern standards, but it covered a not insignificant range of topics: time rates, minimum earnings for pieceworkers, rates for overtime and shiftwork, the normal week, stopping and starting times, mealbreaks, the provisions and enforcement of the procedure for dispute resolutions, the changing of the agreement. In some industries topics of more direct relevance to the management of work might be included—the manning of jobs or machines, demarcation between occupations, rules for work sharing or layoffs, provisions for apprentices. These were also the general topic areas which were

[12]A. I. Marsh, "The Staffing of Industrial Relations Management in the Engineering Industry," *Industrial Relations Journal,* Summer 1971, p. 16.

incorporated into industry-wide bargaining; it was not until the development of more comprehensive plant-based agreements in the 1960s that the scope of written agreements was widened, although it should be added that informal plant-level arrangements could be, and increasingly were, made on other issues. Indeed, in several industries the settlement of disputes originating at plant level through procedures represented the core of the relationship; this was especially true in the industries related to engineering and construction, where it provided the first move towards a national relationship. It might not be feasible to set national wage rates in such industries, but rules of conduct could be general.

Thus, by the onset of World War I there was already a partial move towards industry-wide bargaining, both through the development of national procedural agreements and because in some industries (cotton spinning, tinplate, and footwear) district and industry coincided. World War I provided the major impetus to industry-wide bargaining. The rapid increase in unionization, and even more the inflation of the wartime period, put heavy pressure on the existing arrangements. There was a good deal of discontent, some of it expressed with revolutionary overtones, and the government was forced into action. On the one hand, it set up the Whitley Committee to examine the state of industrial relations with a longer-term perspective. On the other hand, it encouraged and sometimes enforced arbitration on an industry-wide basis, thereby bringing the various district organizations together into industry-wide structures.

The Whitley Committee suggested that bargaining should be pursued at three levels—industry, district, and plant, the last through the setting up of work committees. Some 73 new industry wide bodies, called Joint Industrial Councils, were set up in the 4 years 1918–1921, and were especially important in the public sector, but there was little response to the call to set up plant-based bodies. There had been a rapid growth of workplace-based, shop steward committees just before and much more during World War I, but employers were suspicious of them, and after the immediate postwar boom they largely died away. The new JIC's did not seriously consider them as an integral part of the industrial-relations structure. Employers were not willing to compromise their managerial prerogatives at plant level, and preferred to resolve disputes arising at this level through the industry-wide disputes procedure.

Thus by the early 1920s the major outlines of what has come to be called the "traditional" system was established. With it was associated certain underlying values that can be subsumed in the concept of voluntarism—flexibility, freedom from state intervention, mutual responsibility within the parties for the enforcement of decisions, and a recognition of pluralistic inter-dependence and legitimacy. The system operated with considerable success until the 1960s. It was dependent on control being held at the national level, and this in turn was dependent on the absence of power at the plant level. In the interwar period and immediately after World War II, when unemployment and the memory of it constrained shopfloor activities, this control was viable.

It ceased to be viable, however, with the continuation of full employment after 1945; not only did employers have to compete for labor in a way that had not previously been the case, but price increases had to be validated by government fiscal and monetary policy, giving rise to what Hicks perceptively called the "labor standard" for the currency.[13] In such an environment the long latent pressures from the shopfloor were able to express themselves, largely through the newly reemergent role of the shop steward. The result was that the vacuum in plant-level institutions became a serious omission as fragmented, ad hoc, uncodified bargaining at this level became the norm in some key industries. Wage decisions were increasingly made at plant level, the scope of bargaining was widened, the procedural structure became overburdened as many more disputes erupted, unofficial strikes became a manifestation of the increasing breakdown of the system, and the traditional values were often rejected by the shopfloor in favor of more direct, self-assertive action.

The Royal Commission on Trade Unions and Employers' Associations (the Donovan Commission), appointed in 1965 and reporting in 1968, found nevertheless that the parties themselves remained relatively satisfied with the system, because it gave them flexibility and self-government. The commission recognized that these were important benefits, but went on to say sternly:

> They can be condemned only because the benefits are outweighed by the short-comings: the tendency of extreme decentralization and self-government to degenerate into indecision and anarchy; the propensity to breed inefficiency; and the reluctance to change—all of them characteristics which become more damaging as they develop, as the rate of technical progress increases, and as the need for economic growth becomes more urgent.[14]

The Donovan analysis therefore pointed to the gap between the formal system of industry-wide bargaining and the increasing extent of informal plant-based bargaining. It argued that the latter was increasingly the reality with which the institutional structure must come to terms, and that comprehensive plant or company agreements, based on coherent management policies and backed by much improved procedural machinery, were necessary for reform. On the other hand, it argued that the introduction of legal sanctions would be both unworkable and unfair until these basic structural reforms had been made.

[13]J. R. Hicks, "Economic foundations of wage policy," *Economic Journal*, 65, 1955, p. 391.

[14]*Report of Royal Commission on Trade Unions and Employers' Associations 1965–1968* (London: Her Majesty's Stationery Office, 1968), p. 33.

The extent of structural change since Donovan has probably been greater than at any other time in the history of the system, but it has still fallen well short of what Donovan recommended. There has been a development in professional expertise on both the management and the union side, an extension of training, a widening scope of bargaining, and some spread of comprehensive agreements. On the other hand, industry-wide bargaining has not been displaced to the extent that trends of the middle 1960s might have indicated, and fragmented bargaining by work-groups, which Donovan thought should coalesce into plant-wide bargaining, still creates problems of differentials and comparisons. Procedures have improved at plant level, but from a very low base, and there is still little strategic thinking about the optimal institutional structure for the plant.

In this slow progress, there has been a lack of leadership and initiative by government or the central management or union organizations; voluntary restructuring has become a diminished priority, overshadowed by the more political confrontations on the national stage over law and income policy. Indeed, these latter have operated counterproductively by making it less necessary for managements to introduce changes, by making unions less receptive to them, and in the case of income policy, by narrowing the limits of bargaining. The plant therefore remains a major problem area.

In statistical terms, bargaining structure is a difficult concept to define and categorize, and little detailed information can be given for most of the century. However, in 1973, the Department of Employment's annual "New Earnings Survey" asked employers to categorize the employees for whom they were replying in respect of their collective agreement status. Basic results are given in Table 2.11, which shows that 83% of male manual workers were covered by some form of agreement, compared with 72% for manual females and about 60–65% for nonmanuals. The continued dominance of the national agreement is evident, with roughly 40% of male workers being covered by national agreement alone and almost half the female nonmanuals being covered in this way. By contrast, no more than 10% of manual workers are covered by company or local agreement alone, and even less in the case of nonmanuals. Further information analyzed by Thomson, Mulvey, and Farbman shows that public-sector coverage is higher than that in the private sector, averaging almost 90%, whereas in manufacturing, coverage ranged from a high of 84% for male manuals to a low of 47% for female nonmanuals. Above all, it should be noted that whereas the percentage of the total sample covered by a collective agreement was 71.8%, only 49.2% of the labor force was unionized in 1973. Thus almost a quarter of the labor force appear to be covered by collective agreements without being union members.

It remains to be asked how effective unions have been in achieving a wage premium over nonunion members. No historical evidence on this

TABLE 2.11

Percentage of Full-time Adult Workers Reported To Be Affected by Various Types of Collective Agreement

Agreement coverage (sample group)	All agreements	National plus supplementary agreements	National agreement only	Company, district or local agreement only	No agreement
Manual males	83.2	32.2	40.6	10.4	16.8
Nonmanual males	60.4	11.4	39.6	9.5	39.6
Manual females	71.7	25.2	36.4	10.1	28.3
Nonmanual females	64.8	9.2	48.1	7.6	35.2

Source: A. W. J. Thomson, C. Mulvey, and M. E. Farbman, "Bargaining Structure and Relative Earning in Great Britain," *British Journal of Industrial Relations,* July 1977.

subject is available, but the "New Earnings Survey" data have stimulated a good deal of research. The general conclusion is that unions in Britain do influence relative wages, possibly with a present-day differential of about 20% (though estimates differ). Local, district, and company agreements appear to confer a bigger premium than national agreements.[15]

Procedures of Conflict Resolution

Under the traditional system of collective bargaining the parties were insistent on pursuing their own remedies to disputes; it was one of the hallmarks of voluntarism that outsiders were not welcome as participants or as third-party neutrals. The essence of the autonomous system of the parties was the procedural structure whereby issues arising at plant level could be taken upwards in steps to industry level. In this there was no distinction between interests and rights disputes, and it was not intended that decisions concerning a particular factory should be relevant to other situations. Given the lack of written agreement or available precedent, it would have been difficult for the third-party neutral to have enough knowledge of the situation to make a properly informed judgment, or so the parties felt.

Some qualifications must be made to this argument. In the second half of the nineteenth century, there were numerous boards of arbitration and mediation, but they generally became transformed into collective bargain-

[15]For a full discussion, see David Metcalf, "Unions, Money Policy and Relative Wages in Britain," *British Journal of Industrial Relations,* vol. 5 no. 2 (July 1977): 157–175; A. W. J. Thomson, C. Mulvey, and M. Farbman, "Bargaining Structure and Relative Earnings in Great Britain," *British Journal of Industrial Relations,* vol 15 no. 2 (July 1977): 176–191, use data to measure the differential directly, rather than estimate it by econometric methods, and report a differential somewhat less than half the figure quoted by Metcalf.

ing bodies as the issues widened beyond wages and became more complex. There was, too, a movement within the TUC at the turn of the century to accept compulsory arbitration, but this died away when the unions won legal freedom for their activities in the 1906 Trade Disputes Act. In addition, the Ministry of Labor Conciliation Service has always been regarded as a useful supplementary means of bringing the parties together, just as the Industrial Court was a recognized mode of arbitrating, especially in the public sector. Again, when there were especially severe disputes, Courts of Inquiry, which offered solutions under the guise of presenting the facts to Parliament, could often save the face of the parties. Moreover, during both world wars, and for some time after the World War II, there were limited schemes of compulsory arbitration that the unions in particular felt to be very useful.

But these qualifications should not obscure the basic fact that the parties in general strongly preferred to settle their own disputes, they saw the state as having neither a right nor a role in imposing solutions, and in particular they wanted the law kept out. The norms by which the parties operated were nonlegal in nature and could not easily be translated into law; for instance, it was not until 1969 that there was anything like a definitive judgment as to whether a collective agreement was legally enforceable or not.

As the system fell into disrepute in the 1960s dispute procedures were among the most severely criticized of its features. Not only were these quite inadequate procedures at plant level, but the much-vaunted industry-wide procedures were increasingly overburdened and ineffective. The Donovan Commission's report of the disposal of cases by the final stage (Central Conference) of the engineering industry procedure in 1966 is illustrative, if extreme. The number of Central Conference hearings rose fom 113 in 1955 to 519 in 1966. Of the 519 in the latter years, 13 were withdrawn or not proceeded with, in 239 "failure to agree" was recorded, 85 were referred back, and 127 were "retained," often a polite euphemism for hoping that the issue would resolve itself. Given that the average time elapsing from the origin of the dispute to Central Conference was in the region of 3 months, it is hardly surprising that a settlement record of 55 cases out of 519 or just over 10% convinced many groups of workers that they would be better served by taking immediate and direct action.

Nor was it therefore surprising that improvement of procedures was given high priority in the commission's recommendations on voluntary reconstruction. A new agency, the Commission on Industrial Relations (CIR), was set up to induce improvements, but ran foul of union opposition to the Industrial Relations Act of 1971. Respect for formal procedures has improved since Donovan, although not markedly, but the main innovation has been the creation in 1974 of the Advisory, Conciliation, and Arbitration Service. ACAS is an independent agency controlled by a tripartite council of employer, union, and public members, and has subsumed the old Department of Employment Conciliation Service and the advisory side of the CIR, as well as various investigatory legal functions to be described later. Perhaps because of its independence, it has had remarkable success in its first 2 years. Conciliation and arbitration have both rapidly increased, arbitration several fold, bringing conflict resolution much closer to the American model of third-party intervention.

Patterns of Conflict

As in many countries, Britain's historical strike statistics fall into readily identifiable phases. Table 2.12 shows the main strike indices throughout the country. The first decade of the century was relatively peaceful in comparison to the turbulent 1890s, but this was merely a prelude to the most stormy period in British industrial relations, the 6 years up to and through World War I, and especially immediately after the war, culminating in the General Strike of 1926. Strikes during this period were lower in number than later in the century, but often long and bitter. Thereafter, partly as a result of better relations but mainly as a result of the Great Depression, there was a low loss of days due to strikes up to World War II. Industrial relations in World War II were much better than in World War

TABLE 2.12
Work Stoppages Caused by Industrial Disputes 1900–1975

Years	Number of stoppages per year	Total days lost per year (in percentages)	Days lost per 1000 employed
1900–1909	464	3,545	n.a.
1910–1919	911	13,248	n.a.
1920–1929	625	32,282	n.a.
1930–1939	637	2,979	n.a.
1940–1949	1,686	2,024	n.a.
1950–1959	2,115	3,252	n.a.
1960–1969	2,447	3,550	271
1970	3,906 ⎫	10,854 ⎫	740 ⎫
1971	2,228 ⎪	13,497 ⎪	1,190 ⎪
1972	2,497 ⎬ Average	23,816 ⎬ Average	2,160 ⎬ Average
1973	2,873 ⎪ 2,782	7,089 ⎪ 12,626	570 ⎪ 1,186
1974	2,922 ⎪	14,694 ⎪	1,270 ⎪
1975	2,263 ⎭	5,805 ⎭	—

Sources: *British Labour Statistics: Historical Abstract* (London: Her Majesty's Stationery Office, 1971). *Department of Employment Gazette,* Annual Series.

I, since there was much more effective union cooperation in the system of compulsory arbitration set up at the beginning of the war. The pattern of relative peace continued after the war and a modified system of arbitration was continued until 1959. During the first two decades after the war a notable feature was the high proportion of strikes in coal mining, which in some years represented three-quarters of the total number of strikes, although a much smaller proportion of the days lost.

But although the numbers of days lost remained at a moderate level up to the time when the Donovan Commission reported in 1968, other characteristics of conflict were becoming a source of concern. Some 95% of strikes were unofficial (not backed by the national union) and/or unconstitutional (in breach of procedure). The established resolution mechanisms, notably the industry-wide procedures, proved inadequate to deal with this type of strike. The problem was not the direct loss of man–days, but rather that strikes involving a small number of workers could affect the sequential production process and thus much larger numbers of workers in key industries. Strikes were also highly unpredictable: managers were cautious in introducing change for fear of the reaction, whereas unions seemed unable to regulate the behavior of their shopfloor members. It was thus the cumulative effect of these small-scale but damaging strikes that created the image of the "English disease."

In the 1970s there have still been many small unconstitutional strikes, but also a higher proportion of longer and national strikes. Some of these, such as the coal strikes of 1972 and 1974, have caused major national crises,

TABLE 2.13

Percentage Distribution of Stoppages and Working Days Lost by Cause, 1966–1974

	Number of stoppages	Number of working days lost
Pay-wage rates and earnings levels	54	82
Pay-extra wage and fringe benefits	3	2
All pay	57	84
Duration and pattern of hours worked	2	2
Redundancy questions	4	2
Trade union matters	8	4
Working conditions and supervision	6	1
Manning and work allocation	11	3
Dismissal and other disciplinary measures	12	4
Miscellaneous	—[a]	—[a]
Total	100	100

Source: Department of Employment Gazette, February 1976.
[a] Less than .5%.

TABLE 2.14

Incidence of Stoppages in Manufacturing Industry by Size of Plant 1971–1973

Plant size	Number of stoppages per 100,000 employees	Number of working days lost per 1000 employees
11–24	8.0	14.8
25–99	19.2	72.4
100–199	23.0	155.0
200–499	25.4	329.1
500–999	29.7	719.4
1000 or more employees	28.7	2046.1

Source: *Department of Employment Gazette,* February 1976.

and the loss of days due to strikes has increased several fold, with a particularly high incidence in the "off" years of income policies. As such, the challenge of the strike patterns of the 1970s to government policy is somewhat different but no less difficult to deal with.

Finally, it is instructive to examine some dimensions of disaggregated strike statistics, although unfortunately these do exist only for recent periods and not for the whole century. Table 2.13 shows strikes by cause for the period 1966–1974. As can be seen, pay issues account for most strikes and the vast majority of days lost, with strikes for other reasons being far smaller in scope and usually shorter in time. Table 2.14 indicates that the number of days lost through strikes is overwhelmingly a problem of larger plants, although numbers of strikes are much more evenly spread throughout the size ranges of establishment. Table 2.15 breaks down strikes by industry grouping and also illustrates that the incidence of industrial conflict is heavily skewed towards certain industries. Furthermore, investigation has shown that on average between 1971 and 1973—a period of above-average industrial unrest—95% of plants did not experience an industrial stoppage at all. Thus the "strike problem" appears on this evidence to be largely confined to a small number of plants, even in industries that have high aggregate levels of strike activity, and this suggests that the problems arise primarily from plant—specific rather than industry—specific factors.[16] Other recent statistics also indicate a considerable variation in strikes between the geographical districts in Britain, with the Liverpool area being the most susceptible to conflict, even after the effects of industrial structure are taken into account.

[16]"Concentration of Industrial Stoppages in Manufacturing Industries," *Department of Employment Gazette,* February 1977, pp. 111–115.

TABLE 2.15

Number of Stoppages per 100,000 Employees and Number of Working Days Lost per 1000 Employees by Industry Order, 1966–1973

Industry order (standard industrial classification 1968)	Number of stoppages per 100,000 employees	Number of working days lost per 1000 employees
1 Agriculture, forestry, fishing	.8	27.5
2 Mining and quarrying	60.2	4305.5
3 Food, drink and tobacco	10.9	198.1
4 Coal and petroleum products	12.2	243.4
5 Chemicals and allied industries	11.0	136.8
6 Metal manufacture	32.8	761.8
7 Mechanical engineering	30.5	623.5
8 Instrument engineering	13.2	292.3
9 Electrical engineering	20.2	721.4
10 Shipbuilding and marine engineering	47.7	1820.4
11 Vehicles	40.0	2105.3
12 Metal goods (nes)	19.6	283.7
13 Textiles	10.1	161.1
14 Leather, leather goods and fur	5.0	17.6
15 Clothing and footwear	5.0	90.1
16 Bricks, pottery, glass, cement, etc.	15.1	320.2
17 Timber, funiture, etc.	11.2	99.8
18 Paper, printing and publishing	6.6	104.9
19 Other manufacturing industries	18.6	516.9
20 Construction	18.6	538.1
21 Gas, electricity and water	3.7	139.5
22 Transport and communication	21.2	975.9
23 Distributive trades	1.6	6.5
24 Insurance, banking, finance and business services	.3	46.4
25 Professional and scientific services	.6	40.3
26 Miscellaneous services	1.1	9.5
27 Public administration and defence	2.6	130.9

Source: Department of Employment Gazette, February 1976.

THE STATE AS EMPLOYER

One of the salient features of the British economy and its industrial-relations system has been the growth in size and importance of state employment. Table 2.16 illustrates the growth of employment, although it should be recognized that part of it is attributable to the transfer of jobs to the public sector (e.g., as a result of nationalization) rather than the creation of new jobs. There have also been changes within the subgroupings, such as the transfer of the Post Office from central government to the public corporations between 1960 and 1970. The pattern, which is somewhat disguised as a result of such changes, has been for fairly continuous

TABLE 2.16

Public Sector Employment, 1901–1974 (in Thousands)

Year	Armed forces	Central government	Local government	Public corporations	Total public sector	Labor force	Public sector as a percentage of labor force
1901	423	160[a]	375[a]	—	958[a]	16,605	5.8
1911	342	271	660	—	1274	18,509	6.9
1921	475	508	976	—	1959	19,604	10.0
1931	360	441	1263	—	2064	21,256	9.7
1950	690	1102	1422	2383	5597	23,068	24.3
1960	518	1639	1821	1865	5834	24,178	24.0
1970	372	1533	2559	2016	6480	24,738	26.4
1974	345	1724	2844	1930	6843	25,112	24.1

Sources: The data for 1901–1950 are taken from M. Abramoritz and V. F. Eliasberg, *The Growth of Public Employment in Great Britain* (Princeton N.J.: Princeton University Press, 1957). Those for 1960 onwards come from *Economic Trends*, HMSO, London: annual series.

[a] Figures are approximate.

growth in central and especially local government, with health and education the primary contributors in the post-World War II period, but a decline in the public corporations, especially coal and railways. In addition to the headings shown in the table, there has recently been a rapid growth in the number of companies effectively owned by the state, such as Rolls–Royce and British Leyland, which are counted as part of the private sector for employment statistics, but which could more properly be designated as part of the public sector.

Industrial-relations institutions in the public sector are not too dissimilar from those in the private sector. In contrast to many countries, there are no specific legal arrangements dealing with the public sector, with the exception of groups such as the police, and until 1971, public utility employees. Bargaining is nevertheless much more centralized than for the private sector, and in the governmental sectors at least, comparability with the private sector is the main criterion of pay determination. This latter point has caused considerable difficulties with the operation of income policies in view of the time lags involved, and it has thus been hardly surprising that the public sector unions have been amongst the most vociferous opponents of income policy.

THE STATE AS REGULATOR

Before the 1960s

As has been noted in passing in several of the preceding sections, the role of the state was abstentionist throughout most of the century. There were two main reasons for this, (a) the strong desire for voluntarism and autonomy by the parties, and (b) the rejection of legal controls. In other countries, the pattern was for the state to establish rights for unions, and in exchange, to expect acceptance of a quid pro quo of legal controls. In Britain, however, the unions were strong enough to win for themselves an equal role in collective bargaining in many industries and a considerable presence in politics without the intervention of the state. For a very long time they rejected state assistance precisely on the grounds that it would compromise their independence. Moreover, they feared that legislation would be turned against them; they had seen the antagonism of the judiciary in the second half of the nineteenth century, and although they were able to obtain remedial legislation to curb the judiciary in the 1870s, and more especially in the Trade Disputes Act of 1906 and the Trade Union Act of 1913, there was suspicion of legal modes of action right into the 1970s. With this view employers largely concurred; not until the 1960s did they seriously consider asking for legislation to curb unions.

With these attitudes there was little that the state could do, even if it had wanted to, and generally it did not. The one piece of antiunion legislation, the 1927 Trade Disputes and Trade Unions Act, which was passed in the rather emotional reaction to the General Strike of 1926, was an aberration, not enforced by employers, and described by Ernest Bevin, the most powerful union leader of his day, as "more of an insult than an injury."

The state did nevertheless play a significant role, albeit a supportive one. A good deal of use was made of conciliation and arbitration in the period before and during World War I, and the leading conciliator at the Board of Trade, Sir George Askwith, became a well-known public figure. The efforts of the Whitley Committee of 1917 have already been mentioned as leading to a number of Joint Industrial Councils, but this was only one of four major attempts through conferences or committees to seek for joint labor–management action. But more generally, the only area where the state played an interventionist role was by setting up trade boards (later wages councils) to set minimum standards in industries where bargaining was not developed. Dating originally from the 1909 Trade Boards Act, over 50 councils were set up in industries covering some 3.5 million employees by the mid-1960s. The councils consist of equal numbers of employer and union representatives and three independent public members, one of whom is chairman, and can make proposals about pay and holidays that can then be embodied in an enforceable order by the relevant minister. Recent years have however seen attempts to phase out the councils in favor of more conventional machinery. A similar objective resulted in the Fair Wages Resolution of the House of Commons, imposing standards on government contractors, dating originally from 1893, with various modifications since then.

Recent Developments

The role of the state as regulator has changed radically in the last decade. The prior picture had been one of an evolutionary system in which the industrial parties were almost entirely autonomous and in which the state, played at the most an auxiliary role; encouraging and enhancing collective bargaining arrangements. That picture has now changed to one in which the state is deeply involved in most aspects of industrial relations in a search for ways of controlling the system. We have already dealt with one dimension of this new approach, that of inducing voluntary reconstruction in collective-bargaining institutions, but the other two modes of intervention that have been utilized, through law and income policy, have been much more controversial. Indeed, it would not be too much to say that the industrial-relations issues of the last decade have imposed an immense strain on social consensus and on more than one occasion have produced confrontations that have threatened constitutional stability. In this period, in Britain much more than in other countries, industrial-relations issues have thus become central economic and political issues.

Law

Although the Donovan Commission advised against the immediate imposition of judicial controls over bargaining behavior, the major political parties saw the Donovan proposals for voluntary reform as having too long a timescale in view of the nature of the problem. The Labor government's 1969 White Paper "In Place of Strife" put forward a range of proposals, several of which were unacceptable to the unions, notably a cooling-off period for unofficial and unconstitutional strikes. Legislation encompassing this proposal produced a threatened revolt from the Parliamentary Labor party and had to be withdrawn. Nevertheless, industrial-relations law was one of the major issues of the 1970 General Election, and the new Conservative government's first major legislative action was to pass the Industrial Relations Act of 1971, the first broad-ranging attempt in British history to bring the industrial-relations system under judicial control.

The act incorporated many features of the Americal legal structure, with unfair industrial practices, recognized bargaining agents, emergency provisions not unlike those of the Taft–Hartley Act, and the like. Its major provisions included the registration of trade unions; the enforceability of collective agreements, henceforth to be presumed to be intended by the parties to be enforceable; the limitation of legal immunities under the 1906 Trade Disputes Act, and the right to belong to or not to belong to a trade union, which effectively outlawed the closed shop, although not necessarily the agency shop. The attractions for the unions in the act, notably a right for unions to be recognized given adequate organization, and a right for individuals not to be unfairly dismissed, proved insufficient to outweigh the disadvantages.

The act was strongly opposed by the labor movement, and the great majority of unions refused to register under the act or to cooperate with its institutions. The Labor Party pledged itself to repeal the act at the first opportunity, whereas employers, with a few exceptions, made no real attempt to enforce the act by bringing cases. There were, nevertheless, several points of confrontation between the unions and the law, notably when five shop stewards were committed to jail for contempt of court in the *Midland Cold Storage* case. This precipitated a widespread sympathetic strike and the calling for a one-day general strike by the TUC, that proved that there was sufficient solidarity within the labor movement to enable defiance of the law to be successful, and thereafter the act fell into general disrepute.

When the Labor party took office in March 1974 after an election called to resolve another industrial relations issue, the miners' strike against the existing income policy, it announced another package of legislative measures, the product of the TUC-Labor Party Liaison Committee, and largely dominated by trade-union thinking. Its first measure, the Trade Union and Labor Relations Bill, primarily designed to repeal the 1971 act with the important exception of the unfair dismissal sections, was frustrated when the opposition in Parliament was able to push through provisions giving individuals the right to opt out of union membership in certain loosely defined circumstances. Thus, when the Labor Party obtained an overall majority in Parliament in another election in October 1974, it introduced an amendment bill to remove these provisions. However, this also ran into difficulties when, for the first time in over a quarter of a century, the House of Lords refused to accept a Commons bill, over the issue of press freedom. The result was a threat by the government to involve the Parliament Act by which the Commons can override the Lords, and a broader attack on the legislative role of the Lords, incidents that were again symptomatic of the importance of industrial relations in the political arena. The bill itself was duly passed in the following session.

The second plank of the Labor program was its basic replacement for the Industrial Relations Act, the Employment Protection Act of 1975, which created rights for individuals in the area of employment protection, and for unions in respect of the disclosure of information, recognition for collective bargaining, and consultation over redundancies. The act also established as statutory bodies the Advisory Conciliation and Arbitration Service and the Central Arbitration Committee, both of which had important roles in securing these rights in disputed cases.

Another feature of the act is Schedule 11, under which unions can claim as a right, payment for their members at the recognized level for the industry, or failing any recognized level, the general level for comparable employers in the district. Experience under this schedule is limited, since this part of the act was not immediately operative, but a significant number of cases have been successfully taken to the Central Arbitration Committee in 1977. Many of these first cases appear to be regarded as a way round the restrictions of pay restraint, and it remains to be seen whether under free collective bargaining Schedule 11 will have a significant role to play. There is no doubt of its capacity to prove important if unions wish to use it extensively.

One salient feature of the act is the absence of any of the restrictions on union behavior that had bedeviled the Industrial Relations Act and "In Place of Strife." Indeed the supreme principle of the Labor government is that no union or union member should under any circumstances what-soever be brought into conflict with the law, a reflection of the immensely strong historical antipathy between the courts and the unions.

As well as these two pieces of legislation, there have been several other important acts, which however relate more directly to individual rights and working conditions and hence are more appropriate for a later section, whereas the last major plank of the Labor program, industrial democracy, will be dealt with in the conclusions, since its perspective is oriented to the future, not the past or present.

We might categorize the new approach to labor legislation as essentially regulatory, where the Industrial Relations Act was in large part restrictive, and the prior philosophy abstentionist; the new approach is also more in keeping with European Common Market patterns. Why did the unions change their minds about the desirability of labor law, since this has been the dominant factor in the legislation? There are probably two reasons. First, after their success in defeating the Industrial Relations Act, the unions felt strong enough to ensure that favorable legislation would not carry a quid pro quo of restrictive controls. Second, in view of the clear need to control wages and thus accept the temporary inapplicability of free collective bargaining, the unions had to seek other approaches to benefits for their members. In creating the new body of law, paradoxically, the unions are diminishing, or at least narrowing, the role of collective bargaining, since several of the issues brought within the scope of law have traditionally been matters of bargaining.

Incomes Policies

A further point of challenge to the traditional system has come from the operation of the various incomes policies of the last 15 years or so. The primary function of these has been to control the inflationary wage pressures the industrial-relations system was felt to be producing, but a secondary objective of at least some of the policies has been to induce change in the system, notably through such strategies as the encouragement of productivity bargaining, involving the removal of restrictive practices in exchange for higher wages and conditions through collective bargaining. Again, there is insufficient space to do justice to either the provisions or the results of the policies, but a brief review is desirable, since Britain to a greater extent than any other country has used incomes policies as a central feature of overall economic management.

State intervention in wage determination began with enforced arbitration in the two world wars, accompanied by the direction of labor, and these were followed by a wage freeze in the period 1948–1950. This latter was hardly an incomes policy as the term is understood today. Although it tied wage increases to the growth of productivity, there were no guiding norms for increases or any mechanism to evaluate claims. No exceptions were made, and there was no mention of price or profit control. Nevertheless the TUC was acquiescent, in spite of complaints about the lack of prior consultation, until the policy was rejected at the 1950 Congress, largely on the grounds that there was no parallel control of profits.

The recent history of incomes policies was initiated by the Conservatives, with their "pay pause" of 1961–1962 and the setting up of a guiding agency, the National Incomes Commission. This was however a transient policy whose major effects were in the public sector. It was followed by a much more detailed policy between 1966 and 1969, when the Labor government set a series of specific guidelines with the National Board for Prices and Incomes as the interpretive agency. This was designed as a policy for the long-run growth and distribution of incomes, and provision was made for various exceptions to the guidelines, notably through productivity bargaining, which enjoyed a considerable vogue as a means of improving the efficiency of the industrial relations system, but which in retrospect produced few lasting benefits and more often provided a convenient loophole through which some groups, notably those engaged in decentralized bargaining, could avoid the rigors of the policy. Resistance to the policy grew as anomalies multiplied and festered, and by 1969 the government was ready to try an alternative approach, the ill-fated venture into legal reform to which we have already referred.

The Conservatives, in fighting the 1970 election, decried the value of incomes policies in general, but faced by the rapid rise in wages that followed the ending of the Labor policy, they were forced to reconsider their position. Initially, this was done informally by means of what became known as the "N–1" policy of successively lower rates of increase for major agreements in the public sector (i.e., that each agreement should contain an increase 1% lower than the previous agreement negotiated in the public sector). The private sector was exhorted to follow suit, but with little effect, and the result was to exacerbate the feeling of the public-sector unions that incomes policies were primarily directed at them.

This policy was effectively ended by a major challenge from the National Union of Miners with a long strike early in 1972 that resulted in an award of a 22% wage increase by a Court of Inquiry. The Conservatives then initiated unsuccessful talks with the TUC to try to obtain its cooperation, following which a statutory policy was introduced, with an initial freeze followed by specific limits in Stages 2 and 3, and operated through a machinery consisting of a Pay Board and a Price Commission, drawn largely, as with the Industrial Relations Act, from American experience. Ostensibly, compliance was good, although the results in terms of increases in the national wage bill fell well short of the objectives, but again, the National Union of Miners challenged the government with another major strike early in 1974. This resulted in much of industry being put on a three-day week, and even more importantly, the overt challenge to the government led to the calling of a General Election in February 1974, in which the electorate effectively repudiated the Conservative policy by returning a minority Labor government.

The incoming Labor government had explicitly rejected an enforceable incomes policy in favor of the "Social Contract," which had been developed jointly by the TUC and the Labor party in the year before the election. In this package the TUC would encourage wage restraint in exchange for various Government actions of a social and industrial relations nature, such as the passage of the legislative program already noted and the maintenance of price controls. The TUC first accepted the continuation of Stage 3 of the Conservative policy until this expired in the summer of 1974, then introduced its own guidelines, intended to provide wage increases in line with the increase in the cost of living. However, these were either ignored or misinterpreted and wage rates rose by some 30% during the period of "Social Contract Mark I."

In its document "The Development of the Social Contract" in July 1975, the TUC admitted that its existing policy was inflationary, and for the period of "Social Contract Mark II," up to August 1976, it proposed a flat-rate increase of £6 per week for all workers, except those earning more than £7000 per annum, who would get nothing. The Government, increasingly worried about the trend of inflation, gratefully accepted this proposal, and incorporated it almost verbatim into its own White Paper, "The Attack on Inflation." Indeed, it could be argued that this action of the TUC represented a pinnacle of trade-union power anywhere in the world, whereby a union movement effectively took responsibility for a major part of economic policy because its power to enforce such a policy was considerably greater than that of the elected government. This policy, largely because of its simplicity, was far more successful than most, even though it was ostensibly voluntary.

In April 1976 the government tried and partially succeeded in regaining the initiative in a budget that explicitly recognized the centrality of the

TABLE 2.17
Incomes Policies, Wages, and Prices 1965–1977

Period	Policy	Percentage of increases at annual rates	
		Weekly earnings	Retail prices
April 1965–June 1966	Norm 3–3.5%	7.6	5.1
July 1966–June 1967	Standstill to end 1966. Severe restraint to June 1967. Norm zero.	1.7	2.5
July 1967–March 1968	No norm but 4 criteria for increases—productivity, low pay, manpower demand, serious anomalies.	8.8	2.8
April 1968–December 1968	Ceiling 3.5%. Continuation of criteria.	7.9	5.5
January 1969–December 1969	Ceiling 3.5%. Continuation of criteria.	8.3	5.1
December 1969–June 1970	Norm 2.5–4.5%. Weakening of policy. Wider criteria.	15.8	8.2
June 1970–December 1970	No pay policy.	12.8	7.3
December 1970–December 1971	"N–1" policy.	9.4	9.0
December 1970–November 1972	"N–1" policy, but effectively broken by miners' strike early 1972.	17.0	8.5
November 1972–April 1973	Wage freeze.	8.4	10.4
April 1973–November 1973	£1 per head + 4%. Ceiling £250 per year. Average 7.5%.	14.8	9.8
November 1973–June 1974	7% or £2.25 per head, whichever greater.	17.1	19.9
June 1974–July 1975	Social Contract. Increases based on cost of living.	29.0	25.3
August 1975–July 1976	£6 per head up to £8500 annual income.	14.0	12.9
August 1976–July 1977	5%, £2.50 minimum £4 maximum.	8.8	17.6
August 1977–	Weak guideline of 10%, 12 month interval between settlements.		

Source: Department of Employment Gazette.

relationship with the unions by proposing to tie the level of taxation to the rate of wage increase to be negotiated with the TUC. In the event, it was agreed that the guidelines for the period from August 1, 1976 to July 31, 1977 should be an increase of 5% on total earnings for all hours worked with a cash minimum of £2.50 and a maximum of £4 per week.

Despite the wish of the government to extend the policy for a further year, growing opposition to wage restraint prevented this, and the sole concession was a hard won acceptance by the unions of a 12 month interval between negotiated wage increases. The government has also exhorted negotiators to reach agreements that overall will confine the rise in the national wage bill to 10%. Thus, as in 1969 and 1974, a reasonably firm income policy has been discarded in the face of union pressure, and it remains to be seen whether a return to free collective bargaining can be combined with moderation in wage settlements. Whatever the short-term result, the medium-term expectation must be that incomes and prices policies will reemerge in an updated form.

The problems of income policies are fully evident to British governments—anomalies abound, there are great difficulties in finding adequate sanctions, there is likely to be a wage explosion when the policy is relaxed, and so on—but in spite of these problems successive governments have returned to incomes policies as the only practical means of reducing wage pressures. Table 2.17 gives a crude indication of the aims and achievement of the various policies referred to above, but it should be borne in mind that there are difficulties in measuring the impact of policies, especially in view of the time lags involved.

WAGES

As with the labor force statistics, wage statistics need to be viewed in various different ways to provide an indication of trends over time—money wages, real wages, and distributional patterns according to industry, occupation, and sex. No full official series are available throughout the century, and extrapolations from point-of-time-based statistics are unsatisfactory for a number of well-recognized reasons. Even the better data of recent years can hide important aspects. Thus, for some categories of occupation or industry, for instance, differences within the group are likely to be as great or greater than those between groups. Again, both absolute and relative wages in an exceptionally inflationary period such as the present can change very rapidly, with a group like the miners imposing considerable short-term changes on the wage hierarchy, or, for that matter, the public sector as a whole reversing its traditional lag position vis-à-vis the private sector.

Money and Real Wages

Table 2.18 shows that for the period 1900–1970 money wages rose twenty fold, but also that there had been far from a smooth rate of increase. The figures need of course to be read in conjunction with the real-wage figures that indicate a three-fold increase, with most of the increase coming in the post-World War II period. According to E. H. Phelps Brown,[17] this compares unfavorably with France, Germany, Sweden, and the United States, all of which experienced at least a four-fold increase in real wages over the same period.

The first phase, before World War I, was a bad period for British labor. Money wages were rising very slowly from £58 per annum in 1900 to £63 per annum in 1913, whereas prices were rising rather faster, and the result was a drop in real incomes, of about 3%. After a period of relatively rapid growth in the last quarter of the nineteenth century, the frustrations thus aroused helped explain the labor unrest as World War I approached. Britain differed from other countries in undergoing this reduction in living standards, which was primarily attributable to stagnant productivity in a period of rising international competition. The explanations for this stagnation are more controversial, varying between the high proportion of capital being exported at one extreme and labor attitudes and union defensiveness towards change at the other.

Money wages rose rapidly in the inflationary climate of World War I, almost trebling by 1920 to some £172 per annum. After a sharp fall in the next 2 years, the picture was one of stagnation or slow decline until the late 1920s, caused by Britain's inability to adjust to the changed international economic conditions of the postwar period. In 1929 Britain was of course engulfed by the Great Depression, and wages went further down until 1933, since when money wages have never again been reduced. But prices were also falling during this period, and although real incomes remained at roughly its prewar level in the early 1920s, after 1927 there was a rise in real wages for those who were fortunate enough to be in employment. Indeed, by 1938 real wages were almost one-quarter above the figure fifteen years earlier.

World War II did not have the tensions or such rapid inflation as World War I. Nevertheless, money wages had just about doubled by 1947 as compared to 1938. Thereafter money wages rose steadily at a compounded rate of almost 7% to 1960. By the 1960s the industrial relations system, and wage inflation in particular, had been identified as a major economic problem, and successive governments felt the need to impose income policies. These did not keep wages to the desired level, and the

[17]E. H. Phelps Brown, "Levels and Movements of Industrial Productivity and Real Wages Internationally Compared," *Economic Journal,* March 1973, p. 67.

TABLE 2.18
Money and Real Wages in the United Kingdom, 1900–1970

Year	Annual money wages (in pounds) for male manual workers[a]	Index of real wages[b]
1900	£58	104
1905	56	100
1910	60	104
1913	63	101
1920	172	104
1925	122	113
1930	120	124
1935	117	131
1938	127	133
1947	266	160
1950	317	169
1955	465	191
1960	602	221
1965	847	256
1970	1191	301

[a] Money wages 1900–1960 are taken from E. H. Phelps Brown and M. H. Browne, *A Century of Pay 1968*, pp. 444–447. For 1965 the money wage figure relates to manufacturing only and is inclusive of holiday pay, from *British Labour Statistics, Historical Abstract* (London: Her Majesty's Stationery Office, 1971), Table 55. Money wages for 1970 are taken from the *New Earnings Survey and is also inclusive of holiday pay.*
[b] The real wages index is drawn from E. H. Phelps Brown, "Levels and Movements of Industrial Productivity and Real Wages Internationally Compared, 1860–1970," *Economic Journal*, March 1973, pp. 58–71. A break in the series occurs after 1955. 1890–1899 = 100.

result has been the most rapid peacetime inflation of wages for centuries, in spite of a rising trend of unemployment from the latter 1960s.

There have been two important components of this recent increase in money wages, other than inflationary pressures external to the industrial-relations system. One has been the extent of supplementary pay over the basic rate; whereas in the interwar period wage rates and earnings were roughly the same, by the mid 1960s in many industries earnings were something like double the industry-wide basic rate. High overtime was a main constituent in this gap, often designed to raise wages rather than perform strictly necessary work, together with the spread of payments by results systems, shift working, and supplementary plant-level basic rates, whereas the extent of this wage drift was increased by the continuous, ad hoc nature of the informal bargaining that spread rapidly in this period. Wage drift has however somewhat diminished in the 1970s as higher unemployment has reduced demand pressure, and as tighter income polices have dictated more emphasis on basic rates.

The second component has been the ability of powerful groups, especially in the public sector, to obtain very large increases in basic rates, partly to reestablish the group in what is seen by them as their rightful position in the wage hierarchy, partly to ensure that they obtain a significant increase in real wages, and partly to insulate themselves against an anticipated increase in both the rate and the level of inflation. This process has in many respects become self-reinforcing as groups have sought to leapfrog each other or follow the lead of the most powerful groups. Two examples are revealing: (a) the increase in weekly earnings of underground coal miners between April 1974 and April 1975 was 51.3%, more than double the rate of inflation; and (b) a much less aggressive group, nurses and midwives, by dint of a "catch-up" award, increased their earnings by 77% in the same period.

To sum up so far, real wages in the twentieth century have increased roughly three fold, but the improvements have been uneven in their incidence. The first quarter of the century produced little improvement, and although the interwar period improved matters, a large proportion of the labor force was out of work. Large improvements have therefore been left to the post-World War II period, although the rise in real wages was not nearly as fast as many of Britain's competitors'. Between January 1970 and January 1977 the index of average weekly earnings rose 178% whereas the retail price index rose 113%, indicating a further rise in real wages.

Wages are of course only one component in real incomes and these are very considerably influenced by the increasingly complex structure of taxes and benefits under fiscal policy. To examine the impact of these in any comprehensive way is well beyond the scope of this chapter. Direct taxation at the beginning of the century started well up the earnings hierarchy and

TABLE 2.19

Estimates of Redistribution of Annual Income for all Households (in pounds) by Taxes and Benefits, 1973

Original incomes	Impact of taxes and benefits
Under 381	+734
381–556	+605
557–815	+492
816–1193	+246
1194–1948	−10
1949–2560	−249
2561–3749	−570
3750+	−1360

Sources: Royal Commission on the Distribution of Income and Wealth, *Report no. 1* (London: Her Majesty's Stationery Office), Table 23.

TABLE 2.20
Dispersion of Weekly Earnings of Manual Men, 1886–1975

Year	Median earnings (in pounds)	Percentage of the median				
		Lowest decile	Lower quartile	Median	Upper quartile	Highest decile
1886	1.21	68.6	82.8	100	121.7	143.1
1906	1.47	66.5	79.5	100	126.7	156.8
1938	3.40	67.7	82.1	100	118.5	139.9
1960	14.17	70.6	82.6	100	121.7	145.2
1968	22.40	67.3	81.0	100	122.3	147.8
1970	25.60	67.3	81.1	100	122.3	147.2
1972	31.30	67.6	81.3	100	122.3	146.6
1975	53.20	69.2	82.9	100	121.2	144.5

Sources: *British Labour Statistics, Year Book 1973,* Table 45 (London: Her Majesty's Stationery Office), *Department of Employment Gazette.*

scarcely affected manual workers; now, however, it covers almost all those at work and is an important consideration in collective bargaining, although of course it is tied to personal and family circumstances and not to the job itself.

Table 2.19 shows that in 1973, when the average male manual worker in industry was earning about £2000 a year, the net impact of taxes and benefits on a household income at this level was a deduction of over £250; whereas low-income households received net additions of several hundred £s.

A further factor in real income is what has come to be called the social wage, in recognition that personal consumption is not financed entirely out of take-home pay. Indeed, as the TUC noted in justifying wage restraint under the Social Contract in 1975, for every £4 of personal spending financed privately £1 of spending is financed by the government; viewed in gross terms this amounted to £15 per week per head of the working population on the basis of current expenditure, or £19 per week if capital expenditure on projects such as hospitals and schools were included.

One final point in this section refers to the dispersion of earnings. In spite of changes in the wage hierarchy, many of which have been considerable in the last few years, there has been a remarkably even pattern of dispersion of earnings for manual men in the whole labor force for the century as a whole, and indeed going back into the nineteenth century as Table 2.20 illustrates.

Sex Differentials

In 1906, weekly earnings of manual women varied from 55% of the adult male rate in textiles to 37% in metals and engineering. The majority of industries paid around 40%. By 1975 the differentials had narrowed significantly according to the New Earnings Survey of that year. For all industries and services, manual female earnings were 58% of male, and coincidentally, the nonmanual differential was almost exactly the same. To some extent these differentials can be explained in terms of lower hours of work (5–7 hours weekly) and less opportunities for shift-work earnings (but many women are on payment by results schemes and derive a higher proportion of their earnings from this source than men.) The narrowing of the differential probably owes something to the secular growth in the demand for female labor—though of course supply has expanded enormously also. More recently, the Equal Pay Act of 1970, which was phased to come into full operation in 1975, has sought to ensure that men and women doing the same work are paid equal rates, whereas the Sex Discrimination Act of 1975 requires that employers should in no way discriminate against women, for example, in hiring or promotion. Although it is too early yet to determine the effects of the latter act, it is certain that the Equal Pay Act has been influential, particularly since equal pay adjustments were not to count against pay raises under the terms of the 1972–1974 income policy.

The evidence indicates that unequal payment is a much more important factor in explaining the gross (weekly) earnings differential between the sexes that is unequal occupational or industrial distribution. Chiplin and Sloane, from analysis of 1974 data, report that the gross differential is accounted for by differences in hours (13–15%), earnings differences (79%) and occupational distribution (5–7%). Age differences also have some independent effect, but this is again minor compared with earnings difference.[18] However, Nickell has recently shown that, whereas men invariably have higher *hourly* earnings in the prime-age bands than in the younger age groups, women between 25 and 44 years of age earn significantly less than their younger counterparts.[19] This seems to be explained by the overrepresentation of the older group in the low-wage, female-intensive industries, and in that respect the prospects of greater equality of female earnings will depend on the success of the Sex Discrimination Act as well as the Equal Pay Act, and on the development of a greater attachment to the labor force on the part of women.

Occupational Differentials

Over the century some occupations have disappeared, and new ones have taken their place. Others have the same title but the job content or

---

[18]B. Chiplin and P. J. Sloane, "Male—Female Earnings Differences: A Further Analysis," *British Journal of Industrial Relations,* vol 14, no. 1. pp. 77–81.

[19]S. J. Nickell, "Trade Unions and the Position of Women in the Industrial Wage Structure," *British Journal of Industrial Relations,* vol. 15, no. 2 pp. 192–210.

TABLE 2.21

Index of Male Earnings per Annum in Selected Occupations for Selected Years, 1911–1975

	1911–1913	1924	1935	1960	1975
Clerks	100	184	194	689	2736 (£2709)
Foremen	100	237	242	898	n.a.
Skilled workers					
Coalface workers	100	161	133	823	3459 (£3874)
Engine drivers	100	232	217	725	2810 (£3344)
Bricklayers	100	203	187	717	3186 (£2995)
Semi-skilled workers					
Bus drivers	100	178	204	510	3096 (£3313)
Bus conductors	100	204	218	674	4340 (£3125)
Shop assistants	100	145	136	587	2731 (£2267)
Agricultural laborers	100	171	185	1,067	4031 (£1935)
Unskilled workers					
Building laborers	100	221	201	763	3968 (£2579)
Male manual average	100	211	215	982	3715 (£2898)

Sources: G. Routh, *Occupation and Pay*; "New Earnings Survey, April 1975," *Department of Employment Gazette,* November 1975.

environment has altered dramatically. Adding this to normal problems of historical data and coverage, we are faced with formidable problems in trying to obtain a picture of the changes in occupation at differentials over the period. Table 2.21, however, gives some help.

The occupational wage hierarchy that existed prior to 1914 was on the whole coexistent with the social hierarchy. White-collar and supervisory jobs tended to rank above skilled manual workers, though the table shows some exceptions, followed by semiskilled and unskilled workers. In the interwar period, the white-collar occupations fared better than the manual groups, especially in the aftermath of the Great Depression. By 1960 the clerk had fallen well behind the skilled occupations and indeed was earning much less than the average male manual worker, in part an effect of the expanded educational system and probably most of all of the large scale use of women in clerical and office work. The greatest proportional increases over the period to 1975 were made by the low-skill, low-paid workers, indicating an overall tendency for differentials to diminish, an issue further discussed below.

Within the manual sector, even though overall patterns of dispersion have remained, there is less stability in relative earnings between groups. Table 2.22 shows the relationship between fitters and laborers in the engineering industry between 1914 and 1975. Differentials were at their highest before World War I, but were compressed sharply during the war and in the early 1920s, recovering slightly in the interwar period. Another

TABLE 2.22

Average Weekly Earnings of Fitters as a Percentage of Those for Laborers in All Engineering Industries, for Selected Years, 1914–1975

Year	Earnings
1914	165.4
1918	140.5
1923	138.3
1926	141.7
1930	144.2
1935	141.8
1939	147.9
1943	125.4
1951	127.1
1955	129.8
1960	135.1
1965	138.2
1970	137.5
1975[a]	129.6

Source: National Economic Development Office, *Engineering Craftsmen: Shortages and Related Problems,* Table B7 (London: Her Majesty's Stationery Office).

[a] Post-1975 figures are not directly comparable with previous years.

sharp compression occurred during World War II, followed by recovery to the mid-1960s, and a subsequent fall to near the historical low. The decline in differentials has also been found between skilled and unskilled in other industries and appears to be greater for payments by results workers than for timeworkers. This latter point is compatible with the growth of fractional and informal bargaining and the divergence of rates and earnings noted earlier.

The compression of skill differentials has been particularly rapid over the last 5 to 10 years, and there has been some speculation on the extent to which income policy has been responsible. Every policy statement on income since 1962 has made reference to the objective of improving the position of the less well paid, relative to the rest of society. In the 1960s successive policies provided "gateways" through the restrictions on grounds of low pay. In the 1970s considerable use has been made of the flat-rate increase, which tends to reduce percentage differentials. Thus the Department of Employment reports that in 21 out of 26 two-digit industries the ratio of the highest to the lowest decile of the pay distribution was reduced over 1970–1976, and similar evidence exists for occupations over 1973–1976 (though there is little evidence of compression of differentials *between* occupational categories.[20] Brown, in a study of West Midlands engineering plants during the 1972–1975 period, concludes that there was an unprecedented compression of skill differentials over this period, but argues that it did not occur primarily under the statutory policy, but rather under the relatively free collective bargaining of the voluntary Social Contract that followed it.[21] Yet, Hunter suggests that over the period 1960–1970 low-paid groups such as textile and agricultural workers did not improve their position relative to the all-industry average.[22]

Economic theory would lead us to expect a widening of differentials at the onset of a recession, either because employers raise them or because skilled labor is hoarded on account of the investment in its training. But the experience in Britain has been of sharply falling differentials at a time of rising unemployment. Perhaps the most likely explanation is that the high rate of inflation over the last few years has produced an increased willingness to accept flat-rate increases, both because inflation is believed to hit the lower paid hardest, and because higher-paid workers have experienced a form of money illusion due to slow adjustment of the conception of "fair" differentials in periods of rapid price inflation.[23]

Thus, although the role of income policy cannot be entirely discounted, it seems probable that the main explanation of the recent compression of differentials is due to inflationary conditions, whereas over the longer term the extension of education and training opportunities and the effects of technological change in reducing skill requirements in some occupations may also be a powerful influence.

It should also be added that there is associated evidence of recent narrowing of the manual–nonmanual differential, and managers have suffered badly relative to other groups. Table 2.23 shows movements in earnings for manual men and for various groups of managers between 1970 and 1975 at constant 1970 prices. It can be seen that there has been a significant decline in the incomes of managers, especially after taxes.

Industrial Differentials

The problem of unraveling changes in the interindustry wage structure is, if anything, more complex than that of occupational differentials. At the two-digit level, industries may have the same title as at the beginning of the century but their composition may have changed enormously. Fur-

[20]"Pay Differentials and the Dispersion of Earnings," *Department of Employment Gazette,* June 1977, pp. 593–599.
[21]William Brown, "Incomes Policy and Pay Differentials," *Oxford Bulletin of Economics and Statistics,* February 1976, vol. 58 no. 1, pp. 27–50.
[22]L. C. Hunter, "British Incomes Policy 1972–74," *Industrial and Labour Relations Review,* October 1975, vol. 29, no. 1. pp. 76–77.
[23]See Brown, "Incomes Policy," pp. 45–46.

TABLE 2.23

Movements in Median Salaries, Before and After Taxes, 1970–1975 (at constant 1970 prices)

	Manual men		Junior managers		Middle managers		Top managers	
	Before taxes	After taxes	Before taxes	After taxes	Before taxes	After taxes	Before taxes	After taxes
	Median earnings (in pounds)							
1970	1335	1099	1780	1424	6030	4222	14,000	7112
1973	1502	1235	1788	1434	6118	4264	12,886	6958
1974	1489	1193	1741	1358	5720	3717	11,822	5875
1975	1558	1200	1796	1351	5766	3459	11,982	5204
	Index							
1970	100	100	100	100	100	100	100	100
1973	113	112	100	101	101	101	89	98
1974	112	109	98	95	95	88	82	83
1975	117	109	101	95	96	82	83	73

Source: Royal Commission on the Distribution of Income and Wealth, *Report No. 3*, "Higher Incomes from Employment," Table 25.

Note: After taxes is computed on the basis of a married man.

thermore, technology will also have changed almost beyond recognition in many cases, new industries will have appeared and others will have declined in importance to the point of extinction. And, of course, the occupational composition of industries will have altered dramatically in many cases, as will the sex structure of the industrial labor force.

Yet there is some interest in knowing how the interindustry wage structure has behaved over time. Frequent reference has been made to the stability of the industrial wage structure, and the implications of such stability for the theory of wage and employment adjustment. Does stability imply the dominance of institutional pressures so that customary differentials remain despite changes in production technology and in products themselves? Or is the elasticity of labor supply among industries so great that very small wage adjustments are all that is necessary to generate the required reallocation of labor?

A full answer to these questions cannot be attempted here, but some tentative guidance can be given. Table 2.24 compares the ranking of average weekly earnings for adult male workers in 19 selected three-digit (Minimum List Heading) industries for 1906 and 1976. Not all the industries are absolutely identical in title, and some with the same title are subject to the qualifications mentioned above. The table is also deficient in that it excludes many important industries where data are simply not readily available for comparison, and it is always possible that if a fuller comparison could be made, it would produce different results. However, the evidence is that there are some industries that have retained their position in the wage structure over a long period of time: the public utilities, iron and

TABLE 2.24

Ranking of Average Weekly Earnings for Male Manual Workers, 1906, 1976: Selected Industries

Industry	1906 rank	1976 rank	Industry title in 1976 if different from 1906
Woollen and worsted	15	15	
Jute	19	19	
Lace	1	14	
Carpet manufacturing	16	10	
Boot and shoe (ready made)	12	17	Footwear
Gas	6	7	
Electricity supply	8	8	
Water supply	12	11	
Building trades	5	9	Construction
Iron and steel	2	3	Iron and steel (general)
Ship and boat building and repairing	3	6	Shipbuilding and repairing
Railway carriage and wagons	9	13	Railway carriages, wagons and trains
Electrical apparatus, telegraph apparatus, etc.	4	18	Telegraph and telephone apparatus
Grain milling	18	4	
Malting and brewing	17	5	
Sugar refining	14	1	Sugar
Tobacco, cigar, etc.	10	2	Tobacco
Porcelain, china, and earthenware	7	12	Pottery
Leather, tanning, and dressing	11	16	

Source: British Labour Statistics: Historical Abstract, London: Her Majesty's Stationery Office, 1971; and Department of Employment Gazette.

steel, woollen and worsted, and jute. Others have shifted position markedly, such as lace (down), grain milling, malting and brewing, and sugar refining (up). Overall, the rank correlation coefficient for the two sets of data is + .04, well below the 5% significance level and indicating considerable instability over the period.

This finding contrasts with other evidence (for larger numbers of industries) over shorter periods of time. Crossley reported a comparison of hourly earnings for 132 industries between 1948 and 1959 that yielded a rank correlation coefficient of + .87.[24] If this can be taken as showing declining stability in the wage structure as the time period is lengthened,

[24]J. R. Crossley, "Collective Bargaining, Wage Structure, and the Labour Market in the United Kingdom," in *Wage Structure in Theory and Practice,* ed. E. M. Hugh-Jones, North Holland, Amsterdam, 1966, p. 200.

one would expect to find explanations in factors such as changes in the size of the industrial labor forces, in productivity, and in the occupational mix. Thus, the decline of employment in lace making may explain the long-term decline in its wage ranking, whereas the declines in grain milling, malting and brewing, and sugar refining are likely to reflect rising productivity, with technical and occupational changes. Over the shorter run these changes will be less marked, and adaptations in employment size and in technology will be achievable with relatively minor wage adjustments. Thus Phelps Brown and Browne in a study of earnings and employment in British manufacturing industry over the decade 1948–1959 conclude that:

> Within a wide range the rate of (employment) growth of an industry seems to have imposed no particular requirements on the relative earnings it offered but outside that range it did. Yet even here it seems to have acted according to no continuous relation, by which the greater the expansion the higher the required rise in earnings, but only as a blanket negative— industries that are to expand by more than 30 per cent in a decade must not let their relative earnings fall; the forces that make industries contract by more than 5 per cent in a decade will seldom let their relative earnings rise.[25]

In conclusion, it is clear that although there is evidence of stability in the interindustry wage structure in the short to medium run, this is by no means complete, and in the longer term considerable changes are to be found, though even then some industries have retained their position in a rather remarkable way.

Regional Differentials

No comprehensive comparative statistics on regional earnings are available throughout the century, but Table 2.25 serves to show that there are significant regional differentials and that the structure is subject to change even over a relatively short period. Although the figures are for male manual workers, both the structure and the changes in it are similar for women and for nonmanual workers.

The Southeast generally has been, and remains, the highest paying region, but its differential over the lowest paying region was reduced from 13.6 to 11.9% over the period, in parallel with the tendency for other wage differentials to be compressed. It is notable that the Northern Region, Scotland, and Wales have all improved from a below-average to above-average level, whereas West Midlands has slipped below average. Underlying these differentials, there are of course differences in industrial and

[25]E. H. Phelps Brown and M. H. Browne, "Earnings in Industries of United Kingdom," *Economic Journal*, September 1962, p. 535.

TABLE 2.25
Indices of Weekly Earnings by Region, 1968 and 1976 (April):
Male Manual Workers

Region	1968	1976
Southeast	105.2	102.5
East Anglia	92.6	93.4
Southwestern	93.1	91.6
West Midlands	103.5	99.8
East Midlands	98.3	97.7
Yorkshire and Humberside	96.1	99.8
Northwestern	99.6	98.9
Northern	97.0	104.8
Wales	98.7	100.5
Scotland	95.7	101.7
Great Britain	100	100
	(£23.10)	(£65.10)

Sources: "New Earnings Survey, 1968," *Department of Employment Gazette.* "New Earnings Survey 1976, Department of Employment Gazette.*

occupational structure, but it is likely that other considerations are important. In particular, the level of labor demand certainly has an effect, and the relative decline of the Southeast and West Midlands—traditionally the low unemployment regions—can be attributed to a deterioration in their employment position. Conversely, the improvement in Wales, Scotland, and the Northern Region reflects a relative increase in employment levels, with the help of the government's regional policy (which is generally accepted to have strengthened after 1963).[26] Since the figures in Table 2.25 are for earnings, they will be particularly sensitive through overtime to changes or differences in demand, and this almost certainly goes a long way to reconcile the presence of a marked regional differential structure with the prevalence of national (industry-wide) wage rates.

CONDITIONS OF WORK

We deal in this section with the environments of work, including many features of what now constitute the concept of the welfare state. There have been three main periods of innovating activity in this area—under the Liberal government of 1906–1914, the Labor government of 1945–1951, and in the last decade or so, although of course other developments have taken place outside these.

[26]Barry Moore and John Rhodes, "Evaluating the Effects of British Regional Economic Policy." *Economic Journal,* March 1973, pp. 87–110.

In the nineteenth century a number of factory acts and related measures were passed, mainly governing the employment of women and young people and laying down standards of safety. At this time trade unions, which were (significantly) registered under the Registrar of Friendly Societies, carried out many of the welfare schemes in operation. The first major provision embodying twentieth-century attitudes towards security came in 1897 with the passage of a Workmens Compensation Act for accidents. The Liberal government of 1906 extended this and embarked on a number of measures that have been collectively called the birth of the welfare state. In 1908, old age pensions were provided for the first time and hours were regulated for miners and shop workers, and these were followed by the Trade Boards Act of 1909, which has already been mentioned in connection with wage councils. But the most important step forward came with the National Insurance Act of 1911, which had two separate parts, one dealing with health insurance, which was almost universal, and the other concerned with unemployment insurance, which was restricted to seven industries, covering only 2.25 million workers that were considered to be most susceptible to cyclical employment conditions. Both were run at least nominally on insurance principles, with accrued benefits as of right, with the health scheme operated by local insurance committees that paid the medical bills, and the unemployment side administered through Labor Exchanges and such trade unions as modified their own schemes to it. The unemployment scheme was oriented primarily to short-term unemployment, and when longer-term unemployment began to be significant early in the 1920s, the financing of the scheme began to break down. By the early 1930s, with several million out of work, means-tested public assistance was the only way to cope. In 1934 an Unemployment Act was passed that separated the insurance scheme proper from the problem of destitution and long-term unemployment relief by creating the Unemployment Assistance Board to take responsibility for those unemployed beyond the 26 weeks insured limit. The act also extended the coverage of compulsory insurance so that 14.5 million workers were covered by 1937.

The second major phase of creating the welfare state came with the Labor government of 1945–1951, but central to its approach was the seminal Beveridge Report of 1942. Beveridge envisaged a cradle-to-grave system of social security in return for a single weekly flat-rate contribution, covering various kinds of benefits—sickness, medical, unemployment, disability, death, pregnancy, retirement, and industrial injury. These were to be operated without recourse to a means test by a new Ministry of Social Security. By no means all these objectives were achieved, but in 1945 family allowances were introduced, in 1946 a comprehensive National Health Service Act was passed, in 1948 the National Assistance Act was passed to provide for the administration of poverty relief, and other aspects of the

Beveridge scheme were incorporated into related pieces of national insurance legislation. In practice the benefits did not keep pace with rising prices, so that the National Assistance scheme, intended only as a safety net for a small minority, became applicable to large numbers of insured people. But if Beveridge's principles were therefore not fully carried through, the major point of the report was, namely the responsibility of government for the maintenance of minimum living standards.

The third phase differs from the other two in that it has been less concerned with the provision of global financial provisions and more with the protection of individuals in particular employment circumstances. However, in the former area the National Insurance Act of 1966 extended the principle of earnings-related benefits and contributions, already in operation in respect of pensions, to unemployment, sickness, and industrial injuries. The major new pieces of legislation have had as their objectives the provision of security and the ending of discrimination at work. The Redundancy Payments Act 1965, already mentioned in connection with manpower policy, created a right to compensation after a 2-year qualifying period from the time an individual's job disappeared. The Equal Pay Act of 1970 was the other major piece of legislation of this type by the 1964–1970 Labor government; it set a 5-year period in which the pay of women should be brought up to that of men in equivalent jobs in the same establishment.

The Labor government that took office in 1974 did so with very explicit commitments to legislate as part of its side of the Social Contract with the unions. However, it was also happy to take over two partially passed pieces of legislation from the Conservatives. The Health and Safety at Work Act 1974 was in part a much-needed consolidation of the morass of previous legislation in this field, but it also created a new structure, the Health and Safety Commission as a policy-creating body to develop regulations in a wide range of areas, various general statutory duties for employers vis-à-vis their employees and the general public, and rights for union representation in this field. The Sex Discrimination Act 1975 was in many respects the sister of the Equal Pay Act, since it extended antidiscrimination legislation from pay and contractual conditions to the other areas of the employment relationship such as recruitment, training, and promotion as well as various nonemployment areas such as education and housing. Explicitly parallel to sex discrimination was race discrimination. After an initial act in 1968, the Race Relations Act of 1976 defined discrimination in terms of effects rather than motives and provided legal redress for the individual in the employment field through the system of industrial tribunals.

These pieces of legislation provided considerable new rights for employees, but in somewhat specialized areas. The main piece of general legislation was the Employment Protection Act 1975, already mentioned in terms of the rights it conferred on unions. Beyond this, the act further extended individual rights in unfair dismissal, in the area of the individual contract of employment and in provision for employee claims on the insolvency of employers: it also created *new* rights of guaranteed pay for short-term layoffs (but limited to £6 per day and 5 days per calendar quarter), time off work for any of four different reasons, and 6 weeks pay and a right to return to work for women workers in maternity. Taken in total the recent legislation provides a statutory basis for working conditions to a degree that is qualitatively far different from previous British experience, and under which government intervention in the working environment approaches general European Common Market levels.

A LOOK TO THE FUTURE

The traditional British system of industrial relations was unique among the developed nations in the extent of the autonomy of the parties and the abstention of the state. The last decade has seen a major change in this situation, and Britain is now more like most other countries, but still with some unique features. Attempts to control the industrial relations system have reached a point where the union movement has essentially been able to dictate the terms on which the state will intervene through the mechanisms of law and income policy. There are virtually no direct controls over the behavior of unions or work groups other than those that the unions themselves agree to, and most of the latent power in the system is still decentralized to an extent not found elsewhere. The new system has not been introduced without major political and economic confrontations, and still is by no means entirely assimilated or institutionalized. Nevertheless, the risk of confrontation appears to have diminished for the present, although still leaving certain open questions for the future.

The most immediate question is that of industrial democracy. The traditional mode of worker self-expression in Britain has been collective bargaining, with nationalization the means of pursuing socialist objectives. In 1973, however, the TUC issued a document entitled "Industrial Democracy," which became the focus of a Labor government commitment to pursue industrial democracy by having worker representatives on the board of directors of large companies. This new approach was in keeping with Britain's entry into the European Common Market that year, although the TUC did not see this as its primary reason for a change in policy. The government, having passed two major pieces of industrial relations legislation in keeping with the Social Contract, was rather less sure how to implement its commitment to industrial democracy, and appointed the Bullock Committee of Inquiry to give guidance. The Committee reported in January 1977, suggesting a formula of equal representation for worker and shareholder representatives, with a smaller group of directors to be jointly nominated by the two primary groups. The report however met with a storm of protest from employers, and indeed limited enthusiasm from unions, some of which would still prefer to pursue their objectives through the extension of collective bargaining. The government has promised legislation, but its ability to push this through in the present Parliament must be doubted in view of its perilous Parliamentary majority. Nevertheless, pressures both from within Britain and the obligations of Common Market policy seem likely to produce legislation in the not-too-far-distant future, although some compromise on the scheme suggested by the Bullock Committee may well emerge.[27] Even so, any legislation putting worker representatives on the board of directors will certainly create difficulties of implementation, not least in terms of the need for the various unions representing employees in a company to act together in nominating or electing worker-directors.

Looking into the somewhat longer-term future, two main issues stand out. The first is whether the unions can persuade themselves and their members that it is in their own interests to maintain a level of wage increases commensurate with international competitiveness. In spite of monetarist arguments, few people in Britain doubt that union power is great enough under a system of free collective bargaining to create continued difficulties for the British economy in an international context.

The second issue is the relationship between the union movement and the state. The chapter so far has indicated the ability of the unions to influence and in some instances to dominate national economic decisions and institutions. The question is therefore where this situation, if continued and extended, could lead. As has been pointed out, the nominal ideology of the unions is socialist, whether of a centralized or decentralized nature. However, there would seem to be reasons connected with the nature of unionism itself to doubt whether either of these variants of socialism will be actively pursued. Unions represent sectional interest groups whose views under the present structure are not capable of being expressed under either state centralism or workplace autonomy. They are on the other hand compatible with a market economy in which decisions are taken at several levels under a fairly direct degree of state domination. The unions have several actual and potential channels of influence: through the Labour party, both in the country and in Parliament; through government and quasi-governmental agencies, amounting to a tripartite direction of the economy between government, industry, and the TUC; and through companies themselves, via collective bargaining, planning agreements, and industrial democracy. An extension of this type of economy would point to a

---

[27]As reflected in "Employee Participation and Company Structure," *Bulletin of the European Communities,* Supplement 8/75, 1975.

framework of planning but still allowing a good deal of autonomy at lower levels, that might be defined more in terms of a corporate state than a socialist state. What is certain is that unions are no longer concerned solely with the narrow focus of the industrial-relations system, or rather that they have projected the industrial-relations system into the larger economic and political systems.

3. THE FEDERAL REPUBLIC OF GERMANY

HANS GÜNTER
GERHARD LEMINSKY

THE ECONOMIC, SOCIAL, AND POLITICAL ENVIRONMENT

The Federal Republic of Germany is a highly industrialized country that is now approaching the stage of the postindustrial dominance of the service sector. However, industry still contributes about 50% of the gross domestic product and employs nearly half of the labor force. It remains the main stronghold of unions and of employers' organizations. The present industrial-relations model originated mainly in, and is still predominantly conceived for, industry.

The evolution of the position of labor and of the industrial-relations system in Germany reflects changes in the wider economic, social and political environment. For the labor movement, two ideologies ran parallel for some time: (*a*) a revolutionary and international one involving the transformation of society according to Marxist ideas; and (*b*) a reformist and national view, seeking the improvement of the position of labor within the existing social order. Under the impact of environmental constraints and potentials, the latter eventually became the predominant orientation. It was consolidated with the democratic renewal and the economic prosperity of the post-World War II years in the Federal Republic of Germany, which functioned as a social stabilizer.

With the end of the reconstruction period and unprecedented growth, however, younger union leaders have become more critical of the social partnership ideology. Industrial relations thus tend to turn into a moderate consensus situation: no return to class struggle but a greater readiness to accept conflict over income shares and influence in society.

In the early 1950s, the growth rates reflected in part the restoration of capacities that had been destroyed during the war. The continuing high growth rates in the 1960s were sustained by export market successes and by

Labor in the Twentieth Century

the growth of the foreign labor contingent (after reduction in the influx of workers from the former German eastern territories and from the German Democratic Republic, which were important growth factors in the earlier postwar years). The first deviation from the continuous upward trend arrived with the 1966–1967 recession. The 1970s witnessed a substantial slowdown of the growth rates, which were affected by the worldwide recession by the middle of the decade.

In the countries of the European Community, the commission that directs the Common Market is slowly becoming an important source of power and authority in labor and social policy. For many years European economic integration advanced economic harmonization, whereas social conditions became further diversified despite, for example, the introduction of the free movement of labor. With respect to industrial relations, the influence of the community on Germany has thus far been small. This situation appears to be changing slowly with the adoption of a social action program by the community, which has produced, among other things, a directive on the protection of workers in the event of mass dismissals and on the protection of workers' tenure rights in cases of mergers and takeovers. A draft of the so-called Fifth Directive on the participation of workers in enterprises, and a draft statute for European companies was presented by the Community to the council on May 13, 1975. These tend to help equalize labor conditions in the member countries. The common economic framework provided in the community also stimulates the development of border-crossing social demonstration effects. It would appear, however, that the Federal Republic of Germany is more important as an exporter than as an importer of such models, since several of the community's initiatives incorporate characteristic features of German industrial-relations law and practice.

THE LABOR FORCE

Structural Changes

Changes by Economic Sector

As can be seen from Table 3.1, industry employs the largest part of the labor force at present and, according to recent labor force projections, is still expected to furnish more than 45% of employment in 1985. The growth of service employment, which should reach 50% by the same date, will be augmented by more than proportionate gains in the public sector. Since the mid-1960s, only the tertiary sector, and mainly the state sector,

TABLE 3.1

Labor Force by Major Economic Sectors (in Thousands)

Major economic sectors	1950	1955	1960	1965	1970	1974	1980[a]	1985[a]
Agriculture and forestry	5,189(25.8)[b]	4,450(19.5)	3,581(13.7)	2,876(10.7)	2,262(8.5)	1,932(7.4)	1,184(4.4)	966(3.5)
Industry[c]	8,431(41.9)	10,663(46.8)	12,497(47.9)	13,153(49.1)	12,973(48.8)	12,406(47.3)	12,721(46.8)	12,744(45.7)
Services[d]	6,455(32.3)	7,680(33.7)	10,014(38.4)	10,751(40.2)	11,347(42.7)	11,893(45.3)	13,249(48.8)	14,190(50.8)
All sectors	20,075(100.0)	22,793(100.0)	26,092(100.0)	26,780(100.0)	26,582(100.0)	26,231(100.0)	27,154(100.0)	27,900(100.0)

Sources: Bundesanstalt für Arbeit; *Überlegungen zu einer vorausschauenden Arbeitsmarktpolitik,* Nürnberg 1974, Table 6; and Bundesministeriums für Arbeit und Sozialordnung, *Arbeits und Sozialpolitik: Statistiken 1975,* Bonn, August 1975, Table 2.4.

[a] Projections.
[b] Numbers in parentheses indicate percentages.
[c] Industry includes: Energy and water, mining, manufacturing, and construction.
[d] Services include: Trade, commerce, transport, communications, banks, insurances, state, nonprofit organizations, and other services.

has been expanding.[1] Agricultural employment will continue its long-term decline.[2]

Although detailed statistics on intersectoral labor flows are not available, it is evident that agriculture constituted, during the postwar period, a labor reserve on which the other sectors, in particular industry, drew for much of their expansion. The agricultural labor force fell from one-quarter of the total in 1950 to about 7% in 1976, a dramatic structural change that hides a great number of adjustment problems and social costs. In its wake, the policy of agricultural subsidies developed in the Federal Republic, and elsewhere in Europe under similar conditions, has become an established feature of Common Market operations. It is now widely recognized as a form of "social policy" for the farmers.

Similar to tendencies in other highly industrialized capitalist countries, the postwar growth of the industrial labor force was accompanied by increasing concentration in larger production units.[3] This also had important effects on the evolution of the German industrial-relations model. Medium and large industrial enterprises are the main base of unions and employers' organizations, and the "ideal" situation of German labor–management relations is best approximated there. This is also true for the implementation of basic legislation, such as the Works Constitution Act. Specific features of the German model (e.g., the codetermination provisions) aim particularly at the large industrial enterprise.

At the same time, the substantial increase of service employment and the related growth of the salaried employee group, which also occurred in other sectors (in 1975, together with civil servants, this group comprised 49% of the "dependent" labor force[4] as compared with 29% in 1950[5]), have pushed typical white-collar concerns such as employment security, training, career problems, and participation very much to the forefront of industrial relations and social policy.

Recent research has formulated a number of reservations regarding the "three-sector theory" of labor force dynamics, which predicts that ser-

---

[1]Kommission für Wirtschaftlichen und Sozialen Wandel, *Wirtschaftlicher und Sozialer Wandel in der Bundesrepublik Deutschland*, Bonn, October 1976, p. 106.

[2]For a long-term historical survey of structural economic change in Germany, see Walter A. Hoffmann, *Das Wachstum der deutschen Wirtschaft seit der Mitte des 19. Jahrhunderts* (Berlin, Heidelberg, New York: 1966).

[3]See for instance, Norbert Koubek, "Konzentration in der BRD," in *Das Nein Zur Vermögensbildung*, ed. Karl H. Pitz (Reinbek: Rororo Aktuell, 1974), pp. 68–196.

[4]Wage earners, salaried employees, and civil servants as opposed to the "independent" labor force, namely, self-employed and family workers.

[5]Bundesministerium für Arbeit und Sozialordnung, *Arbeits- und Sozialstatistiken, 1976*, Bonn, December, 1976, Table 2.6.

vice employment tends to increase at the expense of agriculture, and to a lesser extent, of industry.

These reservations are of the following three types:[6]

1. The sectoral division of this analysis is too broad to be meaningful. The available statistical data are insufficient for this purpose.
2. Contrary to earlier assumptions, the tertiary sector (services) tends to become increasingly capital intensive with negative consequences for further labor intake into several tertiary occupations.
3. The thesis of an inevitable increase of services in total economic production is not sufficiently tested. The demand for services may reach saturation levels.

Rather than invalidating the three-sector thesis, these reservations point to important future labor problems and policy consequences. It has been rightly stressed, for example, that the service sector in the Federal Republic of Germany, and in other countries with a declining industrial work force cannot be seen as the automatic long-term employment alternative for workers made redundant by structural change. This would be even more the case if the tempo of this change increased. Studies for Germany do not seem to confirm this proposition. They find rather that the tempo of change in German economic structure was greater in the years between the two world wars and in the 1950s than in recent decades. This does not imply, however, that social problems connected with this change become necessarily smaller.[7] But, despite these reservations, the central future importance of the service sector, and in particular the employment opportunities offered by the state, has been stressed in various authoritative studies.[8]

Changes by Occupation and Employment Status

Persons employed independently (self-employed and family workers) accounted at the beginning of the 1950s for roughly 30% of the labor force in the Federal Republic of Germany. As a result of structural change and concentration, many self-employed and family workers, primarily from the agricultural sector, became wage earners or salaried employees. The reduc-

---

[6]Hans-Joachim Pohl, "Kritik der Drei-Sektorentheorie," in *Quintessenzen aus der Arbeitsmarkt- und Berufsforschung, 1968–1971,* (Erlangen: Bundesanstalt für Arbeit, 1972), p. 60.

[7]Hans-Jürgen Dinter, "Zum Tempo von Strukturwandlungen," in *Quintessenzen* aus der Arbeitsmarkt- und Strukturforschung, *ibid.,* p. 23.

[8]See for instance, Kommission für Wirtschaftlichen und Sozialen Wandel, *Wirtschaftlicher und Sozialer Wandel,* p. 160.

TABLE 3.2
Labor Force According to Occupational Status (in Percentages)

Year	Employees	Self-employed	Family workers
1950	68.7	15.9	15.4
1955	73.9	13.8	12.3
1960	77.1	12.7	10.2
1965	80.9	10.9	8.2
1970	83.4	10.0	6.6
1974	84.5	9.8	5.7
1976	85.0	9.8	5.2

Source: Bundesministerium für Arbeit und sozialordnung, Arbeits-und sozialstatistik 1977, Bonn, August 1977, Table 2.5

tion in the proportion of self-employed and family workers was less pronounced in industry and handicrafts. In trade and transport the number of persons belonging to both categories actually increased.[9] As a correlate, the proportion of employees[10] rose to 85% of the work force (see Table 3.2). This change has augmented the importance of the industrial-relations system as a regulator of work rules, labor conditions, and income for the population of the Federal Republic of Germany.

Despite these considerable modifications in labor-force structure, it is striking that the percentage of wage earners in the male labor force remained fairly constant (50–55%) during the past 90 years (Reich and Federal Republic). However, the percentage of female wage earners in total female employment dropped considerably.[11] It is understandable, therefore, that the question of the assimilation of wage earners into the salaried employee ranks continues to be a major concern in industrial relations and social policy. With respect to income, living standards, and partly values, a pronounced assimilation has taken place during the postwar period; but gaps persist in terms of fringe benefits social entitlements and position. The wage earner remains thus for industrial sociologists a distinct, relatively underprivileged category of worker in terms of social status and decision-making authority in the enterprises.[12]

The occupational change that occurred in the Federal Republic was

[9]Bundesministerium für Arbeit und Sozialordnung, Arbeitsmarktpolitik (Report of the Federal Government to the OECD), Bonn, 1974, p. 18.

[10]Wage earners, salaried employees, and civil servants (dependent labor force).

[11]Press and Information Office of the Federal Government, Gesellschaftliche Daten 1973, Bonn, 1974, pp. 86–87.

[12]Karl H. Hörning, "Der neue Arbeiter? Eine kritische Diskussion industriesoziologischer Untersuchungen," in Der "neue" Arbeiter. Zum Wandel sozialer Schichtstrukturen, ed. Karl H. Hörning, (Hamburg: Fischer, 1971), pp. 9–44.

TABLE 3.3
Employment According to Occupation (in Percentages)

	1950	1962	1970
Scientific, technical, and administrative occupations	6.0	7.5	10.3
Supervisory activities	2.0	2.5	2.3
Office occupations and related	11.2	15.1	18.3
Occupations in commerce	6.1	8.6	9.2
Service occupations	8.2	8.6	10.2
Occupations in agriculture and related	22.8	14.1	7.9
Producing occupations (industrial manual workers in large sense of word)	43.7	43.6	41.8
	100.0	100.0	100.0

Source: Werner Karr; Rudolf Leupoldt, *Strukturwandel des Arbeitsmarktes 1950 bis 1970 nach Berufen und Sektoren,* Bundesanstalt für Arbeit, Nürnberg, 1976, p. 14.

overwhelmingly a reflection of the changes in economic sector composition. Modifications of the occupational structure within economic sectors were of much less importance.[13]

In line with this observation, most of the employment reduction took place in agricultural and household service occupations, and the main increases were found both in technical industrial occupations (especially in metal manufacturing) such as assembly and production of electrical equipment, supervision of chemical processes, production and maintenance of tools and equipment for mass production, repairs of motor vehicles and machines; and in service occupations, including public administration. (The changes in the occupational labor force composition from 1950 to 1970 are summarized in Table 3.3.) Occupations specific to a single industrial branch and to the manufacture of traditional materials (for instance, wood and leather) also declined. Generally speaking, the number of occupations common to more than one industry has tended to increase. Subject to sufficient growth and mobility, occupational risks may thus diminish. But at the same time, the content of occupations appears to be changing more rapidly as a consequence of technological progress, which entails the need for more training and for retraining.[14]

[13]Friedemann Stoss, "Die Veränderungen der beruflichen Gliederung der Erwerbspersonen nach Wirtschaftszweigen in der Bundesrepublik 1950-1961," in *Quintessenzen,* p. 16.
[14]Bundesministerium für Arbeit und Sozialordung, *Sozialbericht 1970,* Bonn, 1970, p. 9.

TABLE 3.4
Labor Force Participation Rates by Sex
(Percentage of resident population)

Year	Total	Men	Women
1882[a]	41.9	60.6	24.0
1907[a]	45.5	61.1	30.4
1939[b]	51.6	67.8	36.1
1950	45.9	63.8	30.2
1955	48.2	65.7	32.7
1960	47.8	64.2	33.4
1965	46.1	61.9	31.9
1970	44.2	54.5	30.3
1973	43.5	57.8	30.5
1976	40.8	53.9	28.8

Sources: Press and Information Office of the Federal Government, Gesellschaftliche Daten 1973, Bonn, 1974, pp. 86–87; and Bundesministerium für Arbeit und Sozialordnung, Arbeits-und Sozial-Statistik 1977, Bonn, August 1977, Table 2.3.

[a] Territory of the German Empire.
[b] Figures converted to the territory of the Federal Republic of Germany.

Labor Force Participation Rates

Total labor force participation rates display a relative constancy over the last 90 years in Germany (see Table 3.4). In the postwar years, the rates for the Federal Republic increased up to 48.5% in 1957, but since then they show a steadily declining tendency.

The decline of the rates in the past 20 years can be attributed to three main factors: (a) decrease of the working-age population as a result of a changed age composition, (b) longer education of young people, and (c) introduction of flexible retirement age.[15] Taking into account demographic factors and various assumptions regarding schooling, retirement age, the possible mobilization of domestic labor market reserves, and the likely proportion of foreign workers, a slight increase of this activity rate is forecast for the coming years up to 1985.[16]

The rising participation rate in the 1950s was mainly due to a greater increase of the working-age population than of the total population as a result of the influx of refugees. An inverse relationship prevailed afterwards, that is, the total population increased more than the working-age

[15]Kommission für Wirtschaftlichen und Sozialen Wandel, Wirtschaftlicher und Sozialer Wandel, p. 85.
[16]Bundesanstalt für Arbeit, Überlegungen zu einer vorausschauenden Arbeitsmarktpolitik, Nürnberg, 1974, p. 27.

population. Furthermore, longer educational periods, mostly reflected in a lower activity rate for young unmarried women, made their influence felt.[17] The German figures are in line with the general experience that male participation rates are overwhelmingly determined by demographic factors: The bulk of the male working age population in practically all countries looks for work. Thus the male rate in Germany for the last 90 years remained near the 60% mark. On the other hand, the female rate in Germany and elsewhere is more dependent upon economic and cultural factors, in particular the ideas and attitudes regarding the place of women in society.

Women in the Labor Force

Economic and cultural change was clearly responsible for the increase of the female participation rate in Imperial Germany from less than 25% in 1880 to about 30% in 1907, a level that did not significantly change in the following decades. A rate of 30% also prevailed in the Federal Republic of Germany in the early 1950s, rising by 1960 to over 33% under the influence of the economic expansion, which provided more jobs for women. The rate then fell during 1960–1970 by about 3%, mainly because of the behavior of the unmarried women's rate (longer education). The low rate for 1976 should be influenced by the withdrawal of women from a depressed labor market. The participation rate of married women displays a marked long-term rise,[18] undoubtedly much a reflection of changing attitudes towards women at work.

Compared internationally, the present female participation rate in the Federal Republic of Germany is higher than in Italy or The Netherlands; similar to that in Austria, France, and Great Britain; but substantially lower than in the Scandinavian countries and in most of the Socialist Eastern European countries. German manpower policy is based on the premise that the not gainfully employed female working-age population is labor market reserve. But realistic policy must take into account sociological trends and societal attitudes, as well as economic requirements.[19] On the basis of demographic factors alone, the female rate could be expected to rise to approximately 41% in 1985.[20]

On an ideological plane, the provision of new employment possibilities for women is a declared goal in the interest of equality and justice, a goal in

---

[17]Bundesministerium für Arbeit und Sozialordnung, *Arbeitsmarktpolitik,* pp. 10–11.

[18]Bundesministerium für Arbeit und Sozialordnung, *Hauptergebnisse der Arbeits- und Sozialstatistik 1973/4,* Bonn, 1974, p. 15.

[19]Organization for Economic Cooperation and Development, *Manpower Policy in Germany,* (Paris: OECD, 1974), p. 107.

[20]Bundesanstalt für Arbeit, *Überlegungen,* p. 60.

which government and the social partners concur. Labor market research has isolated professional education as a key instrument for this purpose. Occupational opportunities and the willingness and ability of women to reintegrate into working life after the child-bearing age is, for example, significantly correlated with educational achievement.[21]

Another important labor market problem is the present concentration of women in a few occupational groups. As married women in particular have limited regional mobility, such a concentration is an obvious handicap for the increase of female employment.[22] The provision of more part-time jobs in a variety of sectors is often regarded as one countermeasure, in addition to the extension of crêches and full-time schools. Part-time employment of women increased substantially during the last decades (for example, by 42% from 1965 to 1971) and amounts now to about 20% of all female jobs.[23]

However, there are many disadvantages connected with the presently available part-time employment opportunities, such as low-skill requirements, little career development, and greater employment insecurity than is the case with full-time jobs. Therefore, the extension of flexible working hours is frequently regarded as a better solution for the improvement of employment opportunities for women than the further expansion of part-time work along traditional lines.[24] Certain official reports maintain, however, that the major persistent obstacle to the expansion of women's employment is the conservative attitude towrd women at work. A majority of the population, both men and women, are still reported to hold the view that gainful employment plays only a secondary role in a woman's life.[25]

The traditional roles ascribed to men and women lead indeed to an ambiguous situation for women in the labor market. Over the business cycle, women are recruited as additional workers or ousted from the labor force. Investment in the occupational training of women is therefore often regarded as a waste of resources. Although measures aiming at the reconciliation of the role conflict of women (professional role and household role) are certainly desirable as a short-term strategy, the more efficient long-term strategy for equality of women must be seen in the provision of better education and training. A greater participation of women in primary vocational training and in retraining is thus now advocated as an essential measure for the permanent improvement of the position of women in the

[21]*Ibid.*, p. 60.

[22]*Ibid.*, p. 61.

[23]*Ibid.*, pp. 122–123.

[24]Kommission für Wirtschaftlichen und Sozialen Wandel, *Wirtschaftlicher und Sozialer Wandel*, pp. 1026–27.

[25]Organization for Economic Cooperation and Development, *Manpower Policy in Germany*, p. 107.

labor market, including the reduction of earnings differentials between the sexes.[26]

The relative inadequacy of past policies for the promotion of women's work is evidenced by the observation that the proportion of women both in occupations in which they dominate (domestic workers, family workers, nurses, secretaries, textile workers) and in sectors where they are in a pronounced minority (machinery, construction industry) has not changed much during the last two decades or so. This means that the sex-specific labor market patterns remain very rigid despite considerable technological and organizational change, and that the trend for a more equal distribution of men and women in the labor force is not very strong.[27]

Foreign Workers

Germany has a long history of labor immigration, starting with intensified industrialization after national unification in the last three decades of the nineteenth century. As a complement to the large intraGerman migration from the eastern provinces to the industrializing regions in the west, Polish and Italian workers entered the industrial labor force in this period. In addition, a large contingent of seasonal workers from Eastern Europe regularly found temporary employment in agriculture. Thus, the percentage of foreign workers amounted to about 3% of the total labor force in 1907. It declined sharply during the years of the Great Depression.[28]

The World War II years saw a dramatic increase of the foreign labor component, partly as a result of forced-labor policies. As this period has an exceptional character, it is not relevant for the analysis of the long-term trends.

The postwar labor influx into the Federal Republic of Germany was correlated (accounting for some lags) with the growth phases of the gross national product.[29] In addition, special political and demographic factors were at work. By the end of the 1950s, the reconstruction period had come to an end, and full employment was reached in 1960 thanks to substantial investment and growth rates. During the same period, there was an influx of over 10 million refugees from the former eastern German territories, and of 3 million persons from the German Democratic Republic, a source that remained important until 1961, the year the Berlin Wall was built.

---

[26]*Ibid.*, p. 1025.

[27]Werner Karr and Rudolf Leupoldt, *Strukturwandel des Arbeitsmarktes 1950 bis 1970 nach Berufen und Sektoren* (Nürnberg: Bundesanstalt für Arbeit, 1976), p. 11.

[28]This paragraph largely follows the analysis by W. R. Böhning, *The Migration of Workers in the United Kingdom and the European Community*, (London: Oxford University Press, 1972), p. 33.

[29]Marios Nikolinakos, *Politische Okonomie der Gastarbeiterfrage Migration und Kapitalismus* (Reinbek Rororo Aktuell, 1973), pp. 48–49.

TABLE 3.5

Foreign Workers in the Labor Force

Year	Foreign workers (in thousands)	Percentage of labor force	Percentage of employees (dependent labor force)
1955	80	.4	.5
1960	279	1.1	1.4
1965	1119	4.2	5.1
1970	1807	6.8	8.1
1973	2498	9.4	11.0
1976	1925	7.7	9.0

Source: Bundesministerium für Arbeit und Sozialordnung, *Arbeits-und Sozialstatistik, 1977,* Bonn, August 1977, Tables 2.8 and 2.5.

Labor demands of German industry could largely be met by this exceptional development, so that the share of foreign labor was kept at a very low level until 1958. From the late 1950s on, economic growth could no longer be based on the extensive use of labor. It became dependent upon capital-intensive production methods and structural adjustments. A number of growth industries emerged and industrial concentration was accelerated. With the drying up of the German labor reserves, the foreign labor component rose steeply from 1958 to 1973, when it reached a peak of nearly 10% of the total labor force (11% of the dependent labor force—see Table 3.5). Growth industries and the large production units became the major areas of foreign worker employment.[30]

Despite variations in its magnitude and a declining tendency from 1973 on, a substantial proportion of foreign labor is now regarded as a permanent requirement of the German economy[31] even under the assumption of slower future growth. Some estimates suggest that the foreign labor component will be reduced to a stable level of 1.5 million by 1980.[32] This fact stands in striking contrast to the long-held official view that the Federal Republic of Germany is not an immigration country. Political and sociological reasons prompted this view and indeed, it can be argued that certain "tolerance limits" are being reached in industries and regions of heavy concentration of foreign workers. For these reasons, as well for cost–benefit calculations that take into account the social infrastructure requirements for foreign workers and their families, now militate in governmental deliberations for a stabilization, if not a reduction, of the

[30]*Ibid.,* pp. 45–63.
[31]Federal Institute for Labor *Überlegungen,* p. 75.
[32]Kommission für Wirtschaftlichen und Sozialen Wandel, *Wirtschaftlicher und Sozialer Wandel,* p. 167.

number of foreign workers.[33] A recruitment halt was announced in 1973, motivated by the deterioration of the economic situation, but this has not put a stop to illegal immigration.

Assimilation problems, housing conditions, and the prevalence of foreign workers in relatively low-skilled and low-paid jobs that are unattractive to domestic labor proclaim the danger of a foreign subproletariat, although considerable public and private efforts are being made to improve the situation. Increasingly, the integration of the foreign workers is seen as a problem of overall social planning, not only as a minority problem.[34]

The integration is complicated by the fact that there is a considerable number of foreign "target workers," that is, workers intending to return to their countries of origin with savings that would allow them improved professional or private positions. It has been found, however, that for various reasons most of these "target workers" stay longer than they first intended, or even indefinitely.

Since the foreign labor component varies with economic activity, it has played in Germany (and other capitalist European countries) a "buffer" role during periods of economic slowdown. This was true for the 1966–1967 recession, and is also the experience of the 1970s. Elements of this special labor market behavior include a falling number of new immigrants; backflow of labor to the countries of origin, resulting in an export of unemployment; and higher vulnerability of migrant workers to unemployment and underemployment. Foreign workers have often unemployment rates several times higher than German nationals. However, foreign labor is not a homogenous group in this respect. The difficulties are greatest for individuals and ethnic groups that immigrated last. Groups that have stayed for longer periods in Germany usually fare better.[35]

Foreign workers are sometimes considered as members of a secondary labor market for "marginal workers," in line with the dual labor market thesis (confronting "established labor" on one side with "marginal," more mobile, less qualified and insecure labor on the other). There seems to be a possibility that the influx of younger, more competitive foreign workers may have pushed certain groups of domestic workers (older, unskilled, and semiskilled) into such a secondary labor market.[36] In many instances, however, foreign workers constitute a noncompeting labor market group. Even in a recessionary climate, many vacancies created by the departure of for-

---

[33]H. Günter, *Note on Labour Migration and the Economy*, prepared for a Ford Foundation meeting, Paris, 5–6 April 1974, p. 3.

[34]G. Endruweit, "Akkulturationstheorien in der Gastarbeiterforschung," *Die Dritte Welt*, 1975, no. 2, p. 252.

[35]M. Nikolinakos, *Politische Ökonomie* p. 169.

[36]Günter Schiller, *et al.*, "Arbeitskräftewanderung als Herausforderung an Wirtschaftstheorie und Wirtschaftspolitik," in *Ausländische Arbeitnehmer und Arbeitsmarkt* (Nürnberg: Bundesanstalt für Arbeit, 1976), p. 11.

eign workers are not filled by domestic workers, who do not find the work sufficiently attractive. Unemployment and demand for certain types of foreign labor can thus exist simultaneously, which may stimulate the transfer of production facilities outside the country.[37] In addition, the approximately 500,000 vacancies created by an assumed reduction of the foreign labor force by 1980 cannot be seen in isolation. In particular, there is the possibility that during the same period, plants, mainly in manufacturing, will be lost as a consequence of rationalization measures and structural change in the international division of labor.[38]

Until the 1960s, Italian workers were the most important nationality of foreigners in the Federal Republic of Germany. In the 1970s, Yugoslav and Turkish workers dominate. They now account for more than 40% of all foreigners.[39]

Foreign workers are employed mainly in three sectors: iron and metal production and manufacturing, other manufacturing industries, and building and construction.[40] Little change has occurred in this respect over the past 15 years. The clustering in these three sectors also accounts for an uneven regional distribution of foreign workers in the Federal Republic. In striking contrast, another growth sector, services (with the exception of the hotel industry), has relied for its expansion mainly on domestic workers, possibly because of skill requirements.

Important for the general position of labor in the Federal Republic of Germany is the fact that the substantial increase of foreign workers during the past decades did not apparently alter long-term trends in real wages and productivity.[41]

LABOR POLICIES AND INDUSTRIAL RELATIONS

The Parties

The Changing Role of the State

In line with the neoliberal ideology prevailing in the early years of the Federal Republic of Germany, the primary function of the state was to guarantee security and order, and to intervene, in a compensatory way, to

[37]*Ibid.*, p. 15.
[38]Kommission für Wirtschaftlichen und Sozialen Wandel, *Wirtschaftlicher und Sozialer Wandel*, p. 167.
[39]Press and Information Office of the Federal Government, *Gesellschaftliche Daten 1973*, pp. 100–101.
[40]*Ibid.*
[41]Federal Institute for Labor, *Überlegungen*, p. 76.

prevent economic and social disruptions. Pushed by requirements of social management, and partly also as a result of changing conceptions of the role of government by the political coalitions in power, the state has taken, in recent years, a more and more active role in shaping economy and society. Steadily improved standards of social security have been introduced. Government has been made increasingly responsible (especially after the 1966–1967 recession) for the maintenance of full employment. An extended discussion has begun regarding new concepts of state interventions in the fields of industrial structure, investment control,[42] "frame planning," and innovating labor market policy. Many of these policies are controversial: Others do not fully satisfy any of the opposing parties, since they represent a delicate political compromise. This is the case, for example, with the extension of codetermination to all large enterprises by a law passed in March 1976. It was violently opposed by the employers, especially because of the possible equal influence of labor in decision making. But in the form adopted, which, as a result of pressures from the liberal Free Democratic party, does not give labor full parity in decision making, it was also disappointing to the unions. This is especially so since the law was pushed through by the Social Democrats, considered traditionally friendly to labor.

The changing role of the state has brought new areas of cooperation in industrial relations into existence, but also new conflicts, where the state entered areas thus far reserved to the labor–market partners, such as wage policy. This "double perspective" is one of the features characteristic of present industrial relations in the Federal Republic, a significant difference from the 1950s or the 1960s.[43]

The state considers itself the guardian of the public interest, but runs into a number of problems thereby. Experience proves that the concept of the public interest cannot be conceived in an abstract way, and it must be reconciled, for reasons of political viability, to the interests of articulate major groups. In Germany the promotion of economic growth by the state was for many years considered to be of national interest as a foundation for welfare, employment, and indeed the institution of the state itself. This tended to safeguard positions of management. But problems of environmental protection and distributive justice have led to a more critical evaluation of this goal.

In view of these and other problems, such as the relatively poor supply of public goods and services, tendencies toward concentration in manufacturing, unequal distribution of wealth, and regional and sectoral imbal-

---

[42]See, for example, M. Krüper, ed., *Investitionskontrolle gegen die Konzerne?*, (Reinbek: Rororo Aktuell: 1974).

[43]See in this context, Peter Marchal, *Gewerkschaften im Zielkonflikt*, Bonn (Stuttgart: Bonn Aktuell, 1972).

ances,[44] a longer-term view of public policy and planning has been recommended in a recent report by a Commission on Economic and Social Change appointed by the federal government.[45] The many possibilities for social groups to influence public decision making, together with the absence of specific long-term objectives for social development, are responsible, according to the report, for the concentration of public policy on the more obvious problems of particular groups. This has led in the past to a preference for short-term and reactive governmental measures.[46]

The gradual emergence of a longer-term public policy orientation can be seen from a number of measures introduced in the last 10 years, such as the adoption of medium-term financial planning in 1966, the Stabilization and Growth Act in 1967, the introduction of a mild income policy approach—the so-called "concerted action," and the creation of councils for problems of the business cycle (Konjunkturrat) and financial planning (Finanzplanungsrat). The industrial relations partners and the political parties have also begun to develop long-term ideas about desired economic and social change, of which the "orientation framework 85" of the Social Democratic party is the best known.

The Unions

Although a certain degree of trade-union pluralism has developed in the Federal Republic of Germany, despite great efforts to reach unity,[47] the unions organized in the German Confederation of Trade Unions (DGB)[48] are dominant in the field of collective bargaining as well as in politics. The confederation now has nearly 7.5 million members, or about 80% of all organized employees in the Federal Republic. It includes more than double the number of white-collar workers than the German Salaried Employees Union (DAG)[49] (with less than 500,000 members). The DAB has nearly as many members in the public sector as the Association of German Civil Service Officials (DBB)[50] (with about 700,000 members). A small number of workers are organized in a separate Christian Trade Union (CGD).[51]

The membership of the DGB rose from 5.5 million in 1950 to 7.4 million at the end of 1976, which was somewhat slower than the rise in total

---

[44]Kommission für Wirtschaftlichen und Sozialen Wandel, *Wirtschaftlicher und Sozialer Wandel*, p. 148.

[45]*Ibid.*, p. 41.

[46]*Ibid.*, p. 55.

[47]See Lutz Niethammer, "Das Scheitern der einheitsgewerkschaftlichen Bewegung nach 1945 in Westeuropa," supplement to *Das Parlament*, vol. 16/75, 19 April 1975, pp. 34–63.

[48]Deutscher Gewerkschaftsbund.

[49]Deutsche Angestelltengewerkschaft.

[50]Deutscher Beamtenbund.

[51]Christlicher Gewerkschaftsbund Deutschlands.

TABLE 3.6
Union Membership (DGB)

		Percentage of			
Year	Total (in thousands)	Female members	Wage earners	Salaried employees	Civil servants
1951	5912	17.1	83.3	10.6	6.1
1955	6105	17.2	82.6	10.5	6.9
1960	6379	17.1	80.6	11.3	8.1
1965	6574	15.7	78.4	12.7	8.9
1970	6713	15.3	75.8	14.7	9.5
1972	6986	16.0	74.3	16.3	9.4

Source: Press and Information Office of the Federal Government, *Gesellschaftliche Daten 1973*, Bonn 1974, p. 255.

dependent employment. It reflects very much the structural changes in the economy: marked reductions in unions of the primary sector, especially agriculture and mining but also industries such as textiles and leather; increasing membership in unions operating in the tertiary sector, for example, banking, insurance, public services, and in metal manufacturing. The proportion of blue-collar workers declined and white-collar members (including public service) rose proportionately (see Table 3.6).

Whereas the membership trend can be correlated with the evolution of the economy, the structure of German unionism must be seen in the context of the specific historical German situation. As in many other countries, the German unions were founded by political parties in the second half of the nineteenth century. In the course of industrialization, unions gained growing power. During the Weimar period after World War I, the Socialist unions were the most influential, followed by the Christian and Liberal unions. The democratic renewal after World War II offered the chance for a new start in unionism. The newly founded DGB was designed as a unitary organization to include members of all occupations and of all political convictions and creeds. This imposed a formal neutrality in relation to the political parties, contributing toward a certain "depolitization." But in practice, DGB objectives have more often coincided with those of the Socio-Democrats, and the Socialist faction is predominant in the confederation.

Heavy involvement of unions in politics was characteristic from the beginning of the labor movement in Germany.[52] The creation of unions

[52]For a fuller, but condensed, historic treatment of the German labor movement, see Helga Grebing, *Geschichte der deutschen Arbeiterbewegung* (Munich: *Deutscher Taschenbuch Verlag*, 1966). Other volumes dealing with this matter include Dieter Schuster, *Die deutsche Gewerkschaftsbewegung* (Kohlhammer, Stuttgart: 1973); and Hans Limmer, *Die deutsche Gewerkschaftsbewegung* (München: Olzog, 1966).

was initially forbidden by an interdiction of "coalitions" (political and interest associations), which was continued after the abortive March revolution in 1849. The abolition of this interdiction made it possible for the workers to found associations in the late 1860s. The initiatives for these union groups came from the political labor movement that they served.

Two groups of socialists were competing in the union movement in these early days. One, represented by Lasalle, was nationally oriented, and worked to solve the "social question" in association with the state. The unions founded under this tendency, organized in the general German Workingmen's Union (Allgemeiner Deutscher Arbeiterverein, founded in 1868), were mainly seen as instruments for a political movement demanding parliamentary democracy and equal voting rights, without much autonomy for the unions. The other group, represented by Bebel and Liebknecht, was of an international, Marxist orientation. In their view, unions were "schools for socialism," but they had different tactical tasks than the Social Democrat Labor party established in 1869, in their fight against capitalism.

During the following years, efforts were made to merge the two types of unionism, particularly after the amalgamation of the two socialist political groups in a unified Socialist Labor Party in Gotha, in 1875. This process was delayed after the adoption of antisocialist legislation (Sozialistengesetze) that outlawed the Socialist party (1878 to 1890). For political as well as practical reasons, the unions began to concentrate on day-to-day representation of worker interests, and although the antisocialist legislation was not directly aimed at them, their organizational and membership growth stagnated. In 1890, a federation (Generalkommission) of all socialist unions in Germany was created under the leadership of C. Legien.

Less important than the Socialist unions were the liberal trade unions, founded in 1868 (led by Hirsch and Duncker) with an explicitly antisocialist ideology. They acquired a strong position among white-collar workers. By the end of the nineteenth century, Christian unions were established, incorporating the social doctrines of both Catholic and Protestant churches and the ideas of the conservative political parties. They opposed the class struggle and advocated partnership of labor and capital.

This division into Socialist, Liberal, and Christian unions remained a characteristic of the German union scene until the end of the Weimar Republic.[53] Many of the typical features of present-day trade unionism in the Federal Republic of Germany can be traced back to the early conceptions of German unionism, in particular (*a*) the claim to represent not only their members, but the working class as a whole: (*b*) the idea that, in addition to furthering the day-to-day interests of the workers, unions should

---

[53]The period from 1919–1933, named after the town in which the national assembly met to write the constitution of the Republic.

press for structural changes in society: and (c) that the unions are basic institutions of a free democratic system. As a consequence, intervention by the state in the labor and social field is not to be distrusted, but is rather to be welcomed.

With the growth of the union movement up to World War I and the parallel growth of employer associations (dealt with in the following section), collective agreements grew in number. In 1874, the first collective agreement was concluded, covering printers. Despite resistance by employers, and also reticence by some unions, which feared too great an integration of workers into the capitalist system, the number of agreements in force was continuously increased until World War I. In 1907, there were more than 5000 collective agreements, covering nearly 1 million workers: by 1913 these figures had doubled. Although these agreements favored industrial cooperation, major labor conflicts also characterized this period, and in particular, a long and bitter strike of weavers in 1903, a miners' strike in 1905, and one of construction workers and dockers in 1910.

By 1914, the unions had strengthened and consolidated their organizations and had accumulated considerable financial means. In the eyes of most union leaders, this organizational achievement was an essential element for effectiveness and continuity. This explains why the unions in the following crucial years accepted many compromises in the interest of maintaining and further developing their organizational position, thus neglecting wider perspectives of social change, even after the revolution in 1918.

When World War I broke out, the attitudes of the unions were influenced by a wave of nationalism, and they accepted an agreement to refrain from all strike activity (Burgfrieden). Collectively agreed upon labor conditions were frozen at the 1914 level. In 1916, within the context of new legislation for the improvement of war production efforts, the unions won for the first time legal recognition as representatives of labor in works councils for blue- and white-collar workers. But as the war went on, the unions became more critical of such cooperation, and asked for improvements in labor conditions, reduction of working hours, better health services, and the creation of a labor ministry. This was partly an attempt to control the growing unrest of the workers evidenced in spontaneous strikes that were waged not only against bad working and living conditions, but also as a protest against union leadership and the Social Democratic support for official government policy. As a consequence of military service, union membership, which had reached a peak in 1913 of more than 3 million, fell to 1.2 million by 1916.

To facilitate the transformation of the war economy to a peacetime basis, and to restore soldiers to production, unions and employers established a joint central working group (Zentrale Arbeitsgemeinschaft) in 1918. However, their motives for cooperation differed. The employers wanted to save industry from revolutionary change and nationalization with the help of the powerful union organization committed to the idea of parliamentary democracy and reformist change. The unions, on the other hand, feared that the huge social problems created by the war could not be solved without the active assistance of the employers. In 1924 this alliance broke down.

Union membership rose considerably in the period of the Weimar Republic (2.8 million in 1918, 7.3 million in 1919, and 7.8 million in 1922), although it sank under adverse political and economic conditions—inflation and depression—to 4.7 million in 1930. Major institutional developments and union attitudes in the years between 1918 and 1933 foreshadowed present-day industrial-relations aspects of the Federal Republic of Germany, such as the institution of the works council (1920), collective agreements as the main regulatory instrument for fixing wages and working conditions, and the development of labor legislation to form a network of minimum social norms. The social security system, introduced in the Bismarck era, was considerably extended as of 1923; and in 1927, unemployment insurance was added. Most important for future development was the orientation of unions towards the concept of codetermination and the idea of economic democracy (Wirtschaftsdemokratie). It was formulated, particularly under the influence of Fritz Naphtali,[54] from 1925 on as a counteracting force to the capitalist system and consisted of three elements, namely, economic planning, nationalization, and participation of workers in decision making at all the various levels of industry. The concept of economic democracy went beyond the immediate interests of the workers. It was a concept of democracy for workers more than of democracy with the workers. Under prevailing conditions, it could be only partly implemented. Economic planning was never achieved. Apart from the institution of works councils, a preliminary national economic council was created that did not acquire much practical importance. The idea of nationalization was given up and the unions did not press for it, fearing to lose their autonomy in the process.

In sum, it can be said that during the period of the Weimar Republic (a) the unions confirmed their purpose as reformist organizations cooperating closely with the state, (b) the majority rejected radical thought and change, (c) several program elements, particularly the idea of codetermination, achieved little importance in the Weimar period but laid the foundation for significant developments after World War II.

The unions were dissolved in 1933 after unsuccessful attempts to secure their survival, including a plan in April 1933 to create a unitary organization. But it was the common resistance of leading unionists of all ideologies that created a basis of confidence that allowed a considerable

---

[54]Fritz Naphtali, *Wirtschaftsdemokratie, ihr Wesen, Weg und Ziel*, Berlin, 1928.

degree of unitary unionism after World War II,[55] with the exceptions noted earlier.

After 1945, the majority of the unions adopted the practice of "one industry—one union." Within the DGB setting, there are 16 industrial unions, each with jurisdiction over all blue- and white-collar workers, and even civil servants within their sector. The most powerful union in the DGB is the Metal Workers' Union (IG Metall) with about 2.5 million members representing more than one-third of the total membership of the DGB. In public service, the union for public services, transport, and communications (ÖTV)[56] with more than 1 million members, is the "pattern setter" for collective bargaining. The 16 DGB unions are autonomous, especially in collective bargaining, which at times poses problems for the authority of the center.[57] The sixteen industrial unions have district and local organizations. There is no full union representation of the "shop-steward" type in the enterprises, however. But the majority of the works councils, performing the main functions of inplant representation of workers, are overwhelmingly composed of union members. In addition, another union voice in the plants has been established in recent years through so-called "men of confidence," to whom more detailed reference will be made below.

The DBG is the most important union representative of the national level in the fields of labor legislation and policy. Nevertheless, the importance of the other unions in public life is greater than their membership figures might suggest.

The guidelines of DGB policy are decided at congresses held every 3 years. Between congresses, a "Committee of the Confederation" meets four times a year. The most important institution for current decision making is in fact the Executive Board of the DGB, comprising the 16 presidents of the industrial unions and the nine members of the managing council of the confederation. It holds monthly sessions.

The first program of the DGB was formulated at the Munich Congress in 1949. The new organizational structure adopted at this congress implied its independence of political parties.

The Munich program of 1949 renewed the idea of economic democracy inherited from the Weimar Republic. Except for codetermination in coal and steel (parity of capital and labor in supervisory boards, and labor directors in management boards), the DGB was unable to obtain the implementation of the other important elements of the previous program.[58]

[55]Helga Grebing, *Geschichte der deutschen*, p. 210.

[56]Öffentliche Dienste, Transport, Verkehr.

[57]Organization and structure of the DGB are described in G. Leminsky and B. Otto, *Politik und Programmatik des Deutschen Gewerkschaftsbundes* (Köln: Bund-Verlag, 1974), p. 453.

[58]See in this context, E. Schmidt, *Die verhinderte Neuordnung, 1945–1952* (Frankfurt: Europäische Verlagsanstalt, 1974).

In its place, the DGB adopted a short-term social action program with less controversial goals, such as increased real wages, reduction of hours of work, and increased social protection.

The Düsseldorf Congress of the DGB in 1963 adopted a new program that was greatly influenced by the demonstrated effect of the growth and full employment obtained under liberal economic policies. Thus, the unions further delayed their goals of fundamental change and listed within their priorities full employment, economic growth, and a fair distribution of income. However, they stressed even more strongly than in the past the right of workers to codetermine their working conditions. The new program did not drop the old aim of economic democracy, but it placed immediate emphasis on goals that could be achieved within the existing environment.

New problems have come up since, such as the qualitative effects of growth, changes in working conditions resulting from intensified competition and technological change, environmental problems, and imbalance of the public versus the private sector. The economic recession of recent years confronted the unions with unemployment, stagnation of real income, and new problems of social security. The changing role of the state, the growth of multinational companies, international trade, and structural problems in different economic sectors require a redefinition of some union concepts.[59]

The representation of the German unions in the economy and in society is closely connected with their history. They never considered themselves as only "business unions." One of the main features of trade-union ideology was the idea that the freedom and security of the working class could only be realized in a changed social order. They were strongly of the belief that political democracy is indispensable to industrial democracy. The unions accepted the republic created after World War I as their state, and acquired the habit of pressing for government regulation in the social and industrial-relations fields. It became a practice in the Weimar Republic to appoint unionists as labor ministers, and this practice was revived in the Federal Republic of Germany.

This tendency to call on the state may have fostered a certain legalistic approach toward industrial relations. In recent years, the unions have realized that this approach is not always favorable. Power relations in parliament brought about the enactment of some labor legislation to which the unions were opposed. The present codetermination legislation for all large enterprises is a case in point.

Aided by a large income from membership dues,[60] the unions have

---

[59]See in this context, G. Leminsky, *Die Zukunft der Gewerkschaften in der Wohlstandsgesellschaft,* prepared for an international workshop of the IG Metall, Oberhausen, 11–14 April 1972.

[60]See especially, Kurt Hirsche, *Die Finanzen der Gewerkschaften* (Düsseldorf: Econ-Verlag, 1972).

created and successfully run a number of commercial banks, housing societies, tourist agencies, and insurance companies. Some observers believe that the managerial experience thus acquired gives the unions a greater understanding of enterprise management.

The unions have an established place in the economy and in society. They are involved in all problems of the labor sector, from consultation on social legislation and the administration of social services[61] (often jointly with employers) to their influence on labor conditions through collective bargaining and codetermination. Present in all spheres of social life, they tend to see themselves as a "central part of the democratic infrastructure."[62]

However, their growing involvement in national decision making and management, in cooperation with government and employers' associations, is not always seen by union members as advancing labor's specific interests, particularly since the objectives agreed upon usually militate for wage restraint. The unions will thus have to make greater efforts to prove their continuing relevance. Many unionists also tend to feel that in national level decision making, unions share more responsibility than real power.

Employers

Perhaps more than in countries with a longer democratic tradition, economic efficiency is, in the Federal Republic of Germany, a prime stabilizing factor for the social and political order that was adopted after World War II. Maintenance of conditions considered essential for an efficient market economy, such as sufficient authority for decision making by managers, private ownership, and a favorable investment climate, have become widely shared values in Germany.

Viewed against this background, employers have a firm position in society and are powerful industrial-relations partners, not the least because refusals of concessions to unions can be presented as being in the general interest. Thus, employers tend to see themselves as the guarantors of a free, efficient society.[63] However, German employers, although often defending established positions, accept reformist change, if only in the interest of maintaining the present basic structure of society. Initiatives for change in social and industrial policies usually originate in the unions or in government, but the employers traditionally also take initiatives, especially in enterprise-level social policy, and have promoted the growth of innovations,

---

[61]For instance, social security.

[62]Heinz O. Vetter (President of the DGB), "Für ein neues Grundsatzprogramm des DGB," *Gewerkschaftliche Monatschefte* 4 (1976), p. 200.

[63]See for instance, Confederation of German Employers' Associations, *Fortschritt aus Idee und Leistung: Erklärung zu gesellschaftspolitischen Grundsatzfragen*, Köln, June 1975.

for example, the spread of wealth ownership by employees through collectively bargained savings schemes. Yet qualitative change modifying existing power relations usually meets with violent opposition on the employers' side. However, it is one of the strengths of the German industrial-relations system that both sides of industry usually adhere loyally to new obligations, once they are laid down.

The interests of employers in Germany are efficiently represented by their associations, if judged by the criteria proposed by one analyst,[64] namely, information to members, interest representation vis-à-vis the public authorities, participation in administering or creating social institutions, negotiations with unions, and information to the wider public.

The top organization of German employers for labor and social matters is the German Confederation of Employers' Associations (BDA)[65,66] to which an impressive number of sectoral and multisectoral associations are affiliated in industry, commerce, and agriculture (44 national sectoral associations and 13 regional multisectoral associations). This comprehensive membership makes the role of the BDA a difficult one. The BDA does not engage in collective bargaining, which is the function of its affiliates. However, it is important in providing information and guidance through its Collective Bargaining Coordinating Committee. Its major base is large-scale industry.

Ninety percent of all private enterprises in the Federal Republic of Germany (employing about 95% of the total work force) belong to an employers' association. Only a few of the big firms in such industries as coal, iron and steel remain outside.

Historically, employer associations in Germany, as in other European countries, were founded mainly as a response to the growth of the trade-union movement.[67] Two central employer associations were created in 1904 that amalgamated into one national association in 1913. The period after World War I saw a further increase in employer associations, in particular in the nonindustrial sectors, which had been neglected up to that time. During the Weimar Republic, the associations acquired a considerable degree of authority over their members.

The increased organization of both workers and employers contributed to a considerble institutionalization of industrial relations. Despite continuing divergence in political goals between labor and capital, cooperation

[64]Pierre Walin *Cinquante ans de rapport entre patrons et ouvriers en Allemagne,* (Paris: Colin 1970), vol. 2, p. 214.

[65]Bundesvereinigung der Deutschen Arbeitgeberverbände.

[66]Economic matters are within the competence of the Confederation of German Industry (BDI, Bundesvereinigung der Deutschen Industrie). This separation dates from the days of the Weimar Republic.

[67]Rosewitha Leckebusch, *Entstehung und Wandlungen der Zielsetzungen, der Struktur und der Wirkung von Arbeitgeberverbänden* (Berlin: Duncker und Humblot 1966), p. 15.

between unions and employers in practical operations benefited from these developments.

Like the unions, the employer associations were dissolved during the Third Reich period. A National Socialist "Labor Front" assumed social-welfare functions and the mobilization of workers for the goals of the state. The wage-setting role was taken over by the state trustee for labor matters (Reichstreuhänder für Arbeit).

The reorganization of employer organizations after World War II was a slower process than reorganization for the unions because of an initial reluctance by the occupying powers in the Western zones to reinstitute a liberal economy. Hampered by the restrictive directives of the military government, the top organization (BDA) was not founded until November 1950.[68] Like the unions, the employer association saw its task to be participation in the "construction of a social order, thus going beyond the role of a mere representation of interest"[69] making in this way an "active contribution to social peace."[70]

Membership in the German Confederation of Employers is still rising. This is partly a function of the increasing amount of technical services that the confederation and its member associations provide for the current operation of firms, such as legal consultancy, assistance in the application of labor norms and relations, and management development. Practically all German-headquartered multinationals, and all subsidiaries of major international firms operating in Germany, are members of an employer association. A prominent example of a nonaffiliated enterprise is Volkswagen, which is perhaps a special case since it was created as a state-owned enterprise. (At present 40% of its capital is in public ownership and 60% is in the hands of small private shareholders.) Overall, the influence of multinational firms on the policies of the confederation appears rather lower than their economic weight.

The advances made by organized labor in the last few years under the socialist–liberal governmental coalition, in particular the extension of codetermination in March 1976, are looked at with concern by many German employers.[71] Although the alleged danger of a "union state" is difficult to substantiate, there is little doubt that the balance of power between labor and capital is changing. The combination, in one person, of the

[68]Gerhard Erdmann, *Die Deutschen Arbeitgeberverbände im Sozialgeschichtlichen Wandel der Zeit*, (Berlin: Luchterhand, Neuwied, 1966), p. 231. (A comprehensive historical treatment of the development of employers' associations in Germany by a former managing director of the BDA.)

[69]*Ibid.*, p. 225.

[70]*Ibid.*, p. 351.

[71]See in this context Hanns Martin Schleyer (former President of the BDA), "Gewerkschaften aus der Sicht der Arbeitgeber", *Gewerkschaftliche Monatschefte*, (4/1976): 202–210.

functions of the BDA and BDI presidency was considered as the employers' first reaction to new conditions but has been abandoned again in 1978 with the election of a new BDA president. Fierce opposition has been shown against various union efforts to modify present industrial-relations features, such as their desire to have lockouts prohibited and to obtain the payment of unemployment benefits to workers indirectly affected by strikes.[72]

Labor Norms and Collective Bargaining

Labor Legislation

Traditionally, labor legislation has played an important role in Germany. In many instances, such legislation sets a framework for labor–management relations (e.g., the legislation on collective-bargaining principles and the Works Constitution Act of 1972, which defines the rights of workers and their representatives at the plant level and provides for co-determination rights). Statutory norms also provide a floor of minimum standards for conditions of work (hours, wages, vacations, dismissal procedures, and safety regulations). Despite the tremendous development of collective bargaining, unions still push for completion of the labor code, which is seen as a body of irreversible social rights. Collective-bargaining achievements are passed on to labor as whole in this way.

One of the most important regulatory laws for industrial relations in the Federal Republic of Germany is the Collective Agreements Act. It stipulates the autonomy of unions and employers, but regulates strictly the procedures for their interaction. There is a "peace obligation" during the term of an agreement—strikes or lockouts can only be called after its expiration. Legislation is also restrictive in other ways with respect to strikes. It legalizes only those strikes called by unions: strikes for political action, and sympathy and solidarity strikes are illegal. Many procedural matters must be taken into account in calling a strike, and it has to be preceded by conciliation efforts.

Because of rapid economic and social change, the juridical system plays an important role in interpreting and developing new labor norms. But it does not always satisfy all parties. The Federal Labor Court has, for example, stated that strikes and lockouts are equally acceptable forms of industrial strife, a position with which the unions do not agree. It has also ruled that collectively agreed advantages for union members only are illegal. The labor court furthermore decided that collectively agreed wage

---

[72]*Ibid.*

rates can only relate to minimum levels: they cannot determine the wages actually paid. In this way management retains the possibility of following an independent plant-oriented wage policy, feeding a "wage drift."

Labor legislation and the courts have limited the use of the strike weapon to the collective-bargaining context. In all other cases of conflict between management and labor, grievance procedures, arbitration, and court decisions must be invoked. For example, works council members must observe the obligation of peaceful cooperation in good faith: they are not allowed to call a strike. Because of the intricacies of labor laws and court decisions, legal training and consultancy has become an important part of the activities of unions, as well as of employers' associations.

Collective Bargaining

Collective bargaining in the Federal Republic of Germany has increasingly developed a "dual structure." The principal collective-agreement level is the industry. Industry agreements exist for various regions, and in rare cases they are concluded for the whole territory of the Federal Republic. In addition, it has become more and more the practice for works councils to adapt these agreements to the situation of individual firms by way of complementary plant-level bargaining. In profitable firms, they can often secure much better wage rates than those collectively agreed upon at the level of the industry. Full-fledged collective bargaining at the plant level is now the aim of several unions, particularly for large-scale enterprises. Not only is there opposition from employers, but there is also controversy among unions on grounds of solidarity and coordination by the central union organization. Despite these problems, there are an increasing number of industry- and region- wide agreements that include a so-called "opening clause" that specifically states the possibility of adapting the agreement to the plant level.

The customary wage agreements (with a usual duration of 12 months) deal with money wage rates and wage categories. More general agreements cover occupational classifications, wage groupings, and principles of job evaluation. A third main category includes the general frame agreements dealing with basic conditions of work, such as working time and days of annual leave. The last two categories are usually concluded for the entire territory of the Federal Republic (and the industry in question) and renewed every 3 to 4 years.

Furthermore, there are a great number of specific agreements relating to such matters as concilation or arbitration procedures, protection for workers against rationalization, and the rights of special "union men of confidence" (a kind of shop stewards) recently appointed in many firms in addition to the works council.

Collective agreements have often introduced new labor norms that later became minimum standards of labor law. A typical example was the introduction of the "social plan" idea in the German labor code. The "social plan," a package of protective and compensatory measures for workers made redundant, was first introduced in firms subject to the codetermination legislation for coal and steel on the basis of plant-level negotiation. It was then taken over by the industry and regionwide collective agreements. The fundamental idea was that management decisions prompted by economic and social change and carrying negative consequences for employment must be accompanied by a parallel "social plan," and this was provided for in the Works Constitution Act of 1972.

In the Federal Republic of Germany there are now approximately 10,000 collective agreements. About 2000–4000 are renewed every year. The conclusion, changing, or abolition of collective agreements are inscribed in a collective-bargaining register of the Federal Ministry of Labor and Social Affairs. The register can be consulted by anyone.

As in other European countries, some widening of the subject matter included in collective bargaining has taken place in recent decades. Although labor legislation still holds a prominent place in the setting of norms for labor relations and conditions, the importance of collective bargaining has tended to increase.

Incomes Policy

Incomes policy in the strict sense of the word does not exist in the Federal Republic of Germany. However, after the recession of 1966–1967, the government introduced as part of the Stabilization and Growth Act so-called "concerted action." It consists of occasional meetings under the chairmanship of the Minister of Economic Affairs to discuss problems of economic development in which employers, unions,and a number of other interest groups and various ministries participate. The government normally presents a tableau of the main economic data, which are reviewed by the participants and on which opinions are exchanged. Though no formal guidelines are issued, the power of public opinion, informed about these meetings, can act as a constraint, especially on wages policy. But views are very divided on this mild form of incomes policy, and it is usually conceded that not much coordination has been achieved since its inception,[73] although it is a tangible expressionof the social partnership idea. In 1977 the DGB withdrew from "concerted action" in retaliation for a BDA action at the Federal Constitution Court against the 1976 codetermination law.

---

[73]Rolf Seitenzahl, *Einkommenspolitik durch konzertierte Aktion und Orientierungsdaten* (Cologne: Bund-Verlag, 1974).

RESULTS OF INDUSTRIAL RELATIONS AND LABOR POLICY

In terms of systems-analytical language, this section deals with the "output" of industrial relations and labor policy in their interaction with the wider economic, political, and social environment. Only a few key indicators can be analyzed in this chapter. Those selected relate to employment and unemployment, conflict and consensus; wages, hours of work, and labor conditions; social security; and labor's position in decision making in the production process and in society at large.

Employment and Unemployment

With the influx of millions of workers into the Federal Republic of Germany, and the preference given in public policy to price stability after the currency reform of 1948, unemployment levels remained relatively high during the first years of the Federal Republic (Table 3.7). Despite unprecedented GNP growth rates, it took until the end of the 1950s to reach full employment. From then up to the middle of the 1960s, Germany experienced a long period of highly successful economic policy, when high-growth rates were combined with a very low level of unemployment and a comparatively high degree of price stability. This success did much to make the concept of the market economy and the social partnership ideology

TABLE 3.7
Unemployment

Year	Annual average (in thousands)	Percentage of total labor force
1950	1863.5	11.0
1955	1073.6	5.6
1960	270.7	1.3
1965	147.4	.7
1970	148.8	.7
1971	185.1	.8
1972	246.4	1.1
1973	273.5	1.2
1974	582.5	2.6
1975	1074.2	4.7
1976	1060.0	4.6
1977	1030.0	4.5

Sources: Bundesministerium für Arbeit und Sozialordnung, *Hauptergebnisse der Arbeits- und Sozialstatistik 1973/74, Bonn, 1974;* International Labor Organization, *Bulletin of Labour Statistics, Geneva,* 1978.

attractive to the unions. It included the acceptance of constant adjustment of labor to structural change. This "progressive" union attitude, however, was put to a severe test in declining industries (in particular coal mining); but ample alternative employment possibilities and public adjustment assistance attenuated the social cost of reconversion.[74]

The favorable employment trend in the Federal Republic was backed, to an important extent, by a strong foreign demand for German products, which was in turn furthered by an undervalued German currency during most of the postwar years.[75] The permanent export surpluses are indicative of the positive employment effects of foreign trade, although the direct effects of incremental exports are relatively small owing to the fact that most export branches are highly capital intensive.[76]

The period of continuous growth was interrupted by the recession in 1966–1967 (during which the GNP dropped temporarily by about 10%), causing a jump of the unemployment rate to over 2% in 1967. At the beginning of this period (1966), the Social Democrats joined a "great coalition" government with the Christian Democrats, who had been the dominant political force since the creation of the Federal Republic. It was superseded in 1972 by a government formed by the Socialists and the Free Democrats.

The 1966–1967 recession revealed that there were certain problem groups in the labor market, such as older and unskilled workers, subsequently called "groups under special attention in manpower policy."[77] Even in the ensuing upswing of activity, these groups suffered disproportionately from long-term unemployment. Increasing difficulties with the "magic triangle" of policy goals (high growth rates, high employment, and price stability) led to the acceptance by government of somewhat higher unemployment levels. New instruments for active economic and manpower policies were created between 1967 and 1969 under the impact of the earlier recession, including the Stabilization and Growth Act, the Employment Promotion Act, the Federal Training Promotion Act, and the Vocational Education Act. The role of the Federal Institute for Labor was much enhanced by this legislation, especially in the area of vocational training. Adults are now increasingly making use of their entitlement to financial assistance from the federal institute for purposes of further training and set-

---

[74]Hans Günter, "Trade unions and industrial policies in Western Europe," in *Industrial Policies in Western Europe* (eds. S. J. Warnecke and E. Suleiman, Praeger New York: 1975), pp. 93–117.

[75]Rüdiger Soltwedel, Dean Spinanger, *Beschäftigungs-probleme in Industriestaaten* (Nürnberg: Bundesanstalt für Arbeit, 1976), p. 121.

[76]Dieter E. Louda, *Aussenhandel und Beschäftigung* (Nürnberg: Bundesanstalt für Arbeit, 1976), p. 114.

[77]*Manpower Policy in Germany*, p. 95.

tling in. In 1971 more than 360,000 workers received such grants.[78] Skilled workers seem to benefit more from these efforts, in part because the schemes for unskilled workers are still unsatisfactory.

The recent unemployment rates of approximately 5% show both the limits of advanced labor market approaches in an internationally highly integrated economy such as that of the Federal Republic of Germany, and their strength. Several structural aspects of unemployment were rather successfully dealt with, including training and assistance to various marginal labor market groups. The maintenance of a substantial proportion of workers in short-time employment, thanks to public subsidies, is another result of labor market intervention. However, the solution of the major cyclical unemployment problems depends clearly upon the level of economic activity. As in the case of several other major industrial capitalist countries, Germany is reluctant to resort to large-scale fiscal and monetary policies to stimulate the economy. The present selective economic interventionism seems to be supported by labor, not the least because of a well-developed social security system that provides, on the whole, satisfactory assistance to jobless and short-time workers.

The continuing high unemployment level in the years 1975–1976 (on average more than 1 million) has recently led to doubts about the effectiveness of such special governmental programs as the plan to use 1.6 billion DM in 1977 to facilitate employment of long-term jobless, older workers, young workers, and women. A debate took place on whether more fundamental measures, including a reduction of hours of work, possibly at a reduced wage compensation, can bring a more adequate and permanent solution. Economic growth alone does not, in the present situation, guarantee full employment. With underutilized capacity, there is not much incentive for employers to undertake employment-creating investments. Competitive pressures lead rather to further rationalization. Thus, despite a GNP growth rate of nearly 6% (in real terms) in 1976, the unemployment level stagnated.

Conflict and Consensus

Avoidance of social conflict and its spillover into the political scene is a stated objective of the social partnership ideology. It capitalizes on the fact that orderliness ranks traditionally high in the value scheme of German society. There is little tolerance of industrial strife by the public.

Because of this element and a variety of institutional arrangements for the avoidance and delay of open conflict, as well as the union's desire to retain the strike as an ultimate weapon, the level of industrial conflict has

[78]*Ibid.*, p. 141.

TABLE 3.8
Industrial Disputes[a]

Year	Workers involved	Working days lost
1953	50,625	1,488,218
1954	115,899	1,585,523
1955	600,410	856,752
1956	53,467	1,580,247
1957	45,321	1,071,846
1958	202,614	782,254
1959	21,648	61,825
1960	17,065	37,723
1961	20,363	60,907
1962	79,177	450,948
1963	316,397	1,846,025
1964	5,629	16,711
1965	6,250	48,520
1966	196,013	27,086
1967	59,604	389,581
1968	25,167	25,249
1969	89,571	249,184
1970	184,269	93,203
1971	536,303	4,483,740
1972	22,908	66,045
1973	185,010	563,051
1974	250,352	1,051,290
1975	35,814	68,680
1976	169,312	533,696

Source: International Labor Office, *Yearbook of Labour Statistics*
Geneva, (selected years).
[a] Strikes and lockouts.

been very low in Germany during the past three decades.[79] But in addition to these constraints, the low level of conflict also demonstrated a considerable improvement of labor-management cooperation in the long-term perspective.[80]

As Table 3.8 shows, there was a relatively large number of strikes in the 1950s, predominantly in the metal industry. Also, 1963 stands out as a strike-prone year. Wages were among the main issues, but earlier strikes also involved putting pressure on the legislature when it was debating the codetermination law for coal mining and steel, adopted in 1951.

The ensuing period of social peace was suddenly interrupted in the fall

[79]H. Günter, *Future Industrial Relations: Federal Republic of Germany and Austria*, monograph prepared for a research project of the International Institute for Labor Studies, Geneva, 1972, pp. 12–13.

[80]Pierre Waline, *Cinquante ans de rapport*, p. 214.

of 1969 by wildcat strikes of unprecedented magnitude, especially in the iron industry. They were often interpreted as signals of greater alienation between union leadership and the rank and file. Contrary to a widespread belief, spontaneous strikes have always existed in the Federal Republic of Germany. However, they are usually relatively short and isolated events, quickly brought under the control of the unions. Therefore, although the 1969 movement does not signify a qualitative change, it stands out by its magnitude and side effects.

There is a consensus in most available studies that the inability of unions to adjust their wage policies to the rapid increase of production and profit after the 1966–1967 recession was a major reason for workers' discontent.[81] The unions were bound by collective agreements concluded under the influence of a depressed economy and of the government's desire to stimulate the economy through a joint effort with employers and unions.

The importance of the spontaneous strikes in 1969 in German industrial relations went much beyond their immediate impact. They induced unions to strengthen their leadership in various ways, for instance by pushing, often successfully, for enterprise-oriented bargaining, shorter collective agreement periods (reductions from 18 months to now generally 1 year), better grassroots organization, and access of unions to the plants. Facilitating such access was one of the principal legal innovations of the revised Works Constitution Act of 1972. By accepting such changes as well as by the "wage explosion" in 1970, employers attempted to reactivate the partnership approach. /

The statistics of labor disputes reflect a greater militancy in the 1970s. The year 1971 stands out with respect to working days lost. Official (i.e., union-supported) strikes dominate, and financial questions are among the main concerns. Again, there was a concentration of disputes in strongly organized sectors, such as the metal and chemical industries. The 1973 strike in the metal industry of North Wurttenberg–North Baden is considered by some an outstanding event, since it forced the conclusion of a collective agreement leading to considerable improvement in qualitative aspects of working life, such as longer rest periods, collectively agreed upon regulation of group incentive rates, and increased job security for workers over 55 years of age.

The incidence of spontaneous strikes has remained at a significant level in recent years, although generally speaking such work stoppages

---

[81]See for instance, M. Schumann *et al.*, *Am Beispiel der Septemberstreiks: Anfang der Rekonstruktion der Arbeiterklasse?* (Frankfurt: Europäische Verlagsanstalt 1971); and Heinz Markmann, "Les grèves spontanées de l'automne 1969 dans la République fédérale d'Allemagne," in *Les conflits sociaux en Europe*, ed. Guy Spitaels (Bruge: College of Europe, 1971), pp. 141–155.

remain isolated events. They have been analyzed as falling mainly into four categories: (*a*) warning strikes in support of official union claims, (*b*) reactions against wage settlements considered insufficient, (*c*) plant level conflict, and (*d*) action against actual or impending plant closures.[82] Foreign workers frequently take the initiative in spontaneous strikes, partly with group-specific claims[83] (for example, longer home leave). Purely political strikes are very rare events in the history of the Federal Republic of Germany.

Lockouts are a legitimate weapon in Germany and, as noted above, the conditions for their use are less restrictive than in a number of other European countries. Although their incidence is small and decreasing (as is the strike incidence) in the historical perspective,[84] the number of days lost reached substantial levels in conflict-prone years, such as 1963 and 1971, exceeding at that time the days lost because of strikes. One study concludes that the economic implications of lockouts tends to increase as a result both of economic concentration and the centralization of unions.[85]

Wages and Labor Conditions

Real weekly wages and real annual income have increased in the long run in the Federal Republic of Germany, very much in line with the evolution of productivity.[86] Labor's share of national income increased mainly as a result of the growing proportion of employees in the labor force (see Table 3.9).

The German data are in line with the general experience that in capitalist, industrialized countries, profits grow more rapidly than wages in the upswing, whereas the opposite applies in the downswing. Several efforts by German unions to widen permanently the wage quota through massive nominal wage increases failed, since employers were able to reestablish their shares through price increases. In addition, during most of the years in question, the unions usually included productivity evolution as an essential factor in their wage claims.

Changes in industrial wage differentials also reflect the dominant influence of productivity. Modifications in the ranking of earnings by indus-

---

[82]Eberhard Schmidt, "Spontane Streiks 1972/73," in Otto Jacobi *et al. Gewerkschaften und Klassenkampf: Kritisches Jahrbuch 1973* (eds). Fischer Taschenbuch Verlag, (Frankfurt: 1973), pp. 30–42.

[83]Walter Müller-Jentsch, "Die spontane Streikbewegung 1973," in Otto Jacobi *et al.* (eds). *Gewerkschaften und Klassenkampf: Kritisches Jahrbuch 1974,* (Frankfurt: Fischer, 1974), p. 52.

[84]See for instance, *Gesellschaftliche Daten 1973*, pp. 114–115.

[85]Rainer Kalbitz, "Die Entwicklung von Streiks und Aussperrungen in der BRD," in *Gewerkschaften 1973*, pp. 163–176.

[86]See for instance, Council of Economic Advisers *Annual Experts' Report 1966–1967*, (Stuttgart and Mainz: Kohlhammer), pp. 64–65.

TABLE 3.9
Share of Labor in National Income

Year	Percentage of compensation[a]	Percentage of compensation[b]
1950	58.4	65.5
1955	59.3	61.7
1960	60.6	60.6
1965	64.7	61.8
1970	66.7	61.8
1971	68.3	62.9
1972	68.6	62.9
1973	69.5	63.5
1974	72.6	66.3
1975	72.8	66.5
1976	71.2	64.8

Source: Bundesministerium für Arbeit und Sozialordnung, *Arbeits-und Sozialstatistik 1977*, Bonn, August 1977, Table 1.5.

[a] Percentage of compensation of employees in national income.

[b] Same percentage, keeping the proportion of employees in the labor force the same as 1960.

try followed changes in labor productivity, despite efforts made by powerful unions to keep top positions (for example, in mining which lost its leading position). Wage differentials between male and female workers and among skill groups fell during the last few decades, indicating that these are less dependent on economic variables and can thus be more easily shaped by the industrial-relations system.[87]

Hourly real gross wages in industry increased during the past quarter century more than 3.5 times, and weekly real gross wages by more than 3 times (see Table 3.10). This seems very impressive as compared with other Western industrialized countries: But if account is taken of the relatively low German wage level in 1950, the Federal Republic of Germany does not differ too much from the international average. This is even more true if a long-term perspective (1890–1899 = 100) is taken.[88] The gross annual earnings of German wage and salary earners were in 1975 among the highest in the EEC.[89]

[87]For a longer-term analysis of these differentials, see H. Günter, "Changes in Occupational Wage Differentials," *International Labor Review,* February 1964, pp. 136–155; and recent issues of *Statistisches Jahrbuch für die Bundesrepublik Deutschland,* published by the German Federal Statistical Office.

[88]See in this context, E. H. Phelps Brown, "Levels and Movements of Industrial Productivity and Real Wages Internationally Compared, 1860–1970," *The Economic Journal* 83, (March 1973), pp. 58–71.

[89]Bundesministerium für Arbeit und Sozialordnung, *Arbeits-und Sozialstatistik 1977,* Table 9.5

TABLE 3.10
Real Wages in Industry

Year	Hourly earnings	Weekly earnings
1950[a]	100.0	100.0
1955	128.9	130.5
1960	172.9	163.0
1965	236.8	219.0
1970	303.9	280.1
1971	321.0	289.9
1972	331.9	297.2
1973	343.2	307.3
1974	354.1	310.4
1975	359.9	305.9
1976	365.9	376.8

Source: Bundesministerium für Arbeit und Sazialordnung, *Arbeits-und Sozialstatistik 1977,* Bonn, August 1977, Table 5.4.
[a] 1950 = 100.

Together with indicators of changes in consumption patterns, with the equipment of households with durable consumer goods, and with expenditures for trips and vacations,[90] these data demonstrate the unprecedented increase of German employees' material levels of living. Nevertheless, the equipment of wage-earners' households is still much lower than that of other groups in the active population.

Net real earnings grew less than the gross figures because of a disproportionate increase of wage deductions. The average deductions for income tax and social security contributions amounted in 1965 to 17% for all wage earners and salaried employees. The present figure is approximately 30%.[91]

Collectively agreed upon hours of work in industry and public administration during the middle of the 1950s still averaged in the neighborhood of 48 hours per week for both wage earners and salaried employees. They fell by roughly 8 hours during the following 20 years to reach, in the early 1970s, the 40 hour mark.[92]

Both weekly hours paid for[93] (Table 3.11) and hours actually worked (Table 3.12) follow, in the postwar period, a similar declining tendency. Self-employed and hourly workers usually work longer hours than the

[90]See for instance, *Gesellschaftliche Daten 1973*, pp. 137–149.
[91]Götz-Ulrich Bischoff, "Die Entwicklung von Realeinkommen und Lohnabzügen," *Bundesarbeitsblatt* (Bonn: Bundesministerium für Arbeit und Sozialordnung, 1974), p. 464.
[92]Bundesministerium für Arbeit und Sozialordnung, *Sozialstatistik 1977*, Table 4.1.
[93]Including, in addition to hours actually worked, hours paid for but not worked, such as time corresponding to public holidays, paid leave, and paid rest periods.

TABLE 3.11
Weekly Hours Paid for in Industry[a]

Year	Men	Women	Men and women
1950	49.4	44.2	48.1
1955	49.8	45.1	48.6
1960	46.3	42.5	45.3
1965	45.2	41.3	44.3
1970	44.9	40.6	44.0
1971	44.0	40.4	43.2
1972	43.7	40.2	42.8
1973	43.5	40.2	42.8
1974	42.6	39.6	41.9
1975	41.2	38.3	40.5
1976	42.0	39.6	41.6

Source: Bundesministerium für Arbeit und Sozialordnung, *Arbeits-und Sozialstatistik 1977*, Bonn, August 1977, Table 4.4.
[a] Including construction.

other labor force categories. The hours of wage earners have been the lowest of all for many years.

The evolution of working hours is in the long run correlated with productivity, but obviously much less strongly than wages. This reflects a rather limited trade-off zone for workers. In other words, hours of work are largely conditioned by the exigencies of work organization so that real wage increases are much easier to achieve than shorter hours. On the other hand, increasing numbers of workers obtain flexible hours, especially in

TABLE 3.12
Weekly Hours Actually Worked[a]

Year	Self-employed	Family workers	Civil servants and judges	Salaried employees	Wage earners	All groups
1957	58.5	61.5	45.8	46.6	45.3	48.3
1960	56.9	57.4	45.1	46.1	45.0	47.5
1965	57.4	55.8	44.3	44.7	43.5	46.1
1970	57.0	48.6	43.4	44.0	42.9	45.2
1971	57.3	49.1	42.8	43.5	42.5	44.8
1972	57.1	45.9	42.5	43.2	42.0	44.2
1973	56.8	44.4	42.4	42.9	41.9	44.0
1974	55.9	44.6	41.7	42.3	40.8	43.1
1975	55.5	46.0	40.5	41.3	39.8	42.2
1976	56.0	46.5				42.5

Source: Bundesministerium für Arbeit und Sozialordnung, *Arbeits-und Sozialstatistik 1977*, Bonn, August 1977, Table 4.6.
[a] This table refers only to male workers.

administration and other white-collar occupations, and alternative working-time arrangements seem to have a great deal of future potential.[94] The evolution of working hours is an imperfect proxy indicator for the development of free time and its value to workers. This chapter does not have the space to elaborate on this point, for which time-budget surveys would be needed to shed more light on such elements as commuting time, training and educational needs, and changing habits and facilities for the use of leisure.

Another readily available indicator for the conditions of work are data on occupational disease and accidents. Their incidence has declined, on the whole, from 1950 to 1971,[95] but the total cost for their compensation has increased.[96] On the other hand, the rate of fatal industrial accidents in manufacturing has remained very steady over the last 25 years (.16 to .20 per thousand man years), and, even taking account of differences of statistical compilation, seems among the highest in Europe.[97]

Efforts have been made to obtain information on qualitative aspects of working life as a basis for public policy. The results of a recent study[98] show that about two-thirds of employees are satisfied with their present occupational activity. Satisfaction levels are correlated with education and income. Workers on incentive rates are less satisfied than those on time rates. Female workers are less satisfied than their male colleagues. As regards labor conditions, unskilled and semiskilled workers are less satisfied than other categories. The content of work is least satisfactory to young workers with little education. Men evaluate their career opportunities more positively than women (which is not surprising). Possibilities of codecision making, speed of work, workload, and provision of information are among the aspects with which workers are least satisfied. Increasing intensification of work as a consequence of rationalization and competitive pressure has been cited by the unions as requiring immediate attention in terms of humanization of work.[99]

Social Security

Germany has had a reputation for advanced social security programs since passage of the famous basic legislation in the 1880s during Bismarck's

[94]Bernhard Teriet, "Wochenarbeitszeit und Wochenarbeitszeitflexibilität," *WSI Mitteilungen* 2 (1976), pp. 105–114.

[95]*Gesellschaftliche Daten 1973*, p. 113.

[96]Bundesministerium für Arbeit und Sozialordnung, *Sozialbericht 1970*, p. 194.

[97]International Labor Office, *Yearbook of Labor Statistics 1977* Geneva, 1977.

[98]Based on an inquiry commissioned by the Federal Ministry of Labor and Social Affairs, see Axel R. Bunz *et al., Qualität des Arbeitslebens*, Institut für angewandte Sozialwissenschaft, Bonn, May 1974.

[99]See, Heinz O. Vetter (ed), *Humanisierung der Arbeit als gesellschaftspolitische und gewerkschaftliche Aufgabe*, Report of a DGB Conference, (Munich: Europäische Verlagsanstalt, 1974), pp. 16–17.

chancellorship (health insurance, 1883; accident insurance, 1884; old-age and invalidity insurance, (1889). Amendments to the original laws were subsequently made, including a major revision in 1911, introducing a uniform national insurance code. In the same year, survivor's pensions were added, sickness insurance was extended to farm workers, and salaried employees were covered by social insurance under a special scheme. In 1927 unemployment insurance was introduced, combined with a system of labor exchanges within a newly created national office for Employment Exchange and Unemployment Insurance (the forerunner of the present Federal Institute for Labor). During the Third Reich period, effective participation by the employers and workers in the administration of social security, introduced after World War I, was abolished. Certain improvements were made regarding female employees and children's allowances, and a new scheme for independent artisans was established.

The principal achievements in the post-World War II period were the linkage of pensions to the earnings of the active population (1957); the extension of social security to population groups other than dependent labor, particularly the creation of a state-subsidized scheme for farmers and the opening of the old-age insurance system to self-employed; the increase of preventive health insurance provisions; and, last but not least, the tremendous development of training and retraining.

The 1957 pension reform can be considered the most far-reaching in the history of German social insurance. Its essentially new feature was the departure from the principle of subsistence benefits and the adoption of the principle of the adjustment of economic status of the pensioner to the evolution of average active earnings.[100] Although this pension formula was compatible with the financial viability of the insurance scheme in a growing economy, a considerable problem has arisen recently that may possibly lead, among other things, to modified adjustment procedures[101] —practically a certainty in the coming 2 to 3 years. The maintenance of the pension formula was one of the promises of the Social Democratic party in the 1976 federal elections campaign, so pensions have become a very sensitive political issue.

Social security expenditures, in the restricted sense used by the International Labor Organization,[102] rose during 1950–1975 from 15 to 22% of gross national product.[103] According to the wider concept of the German so-called "Social Budget," which refers not only to public pension schemes

[100]For a detailed account of German social security developments, see Gaston V. Rimlinger, *Welfare Policy and Industrialisation in Europe, America and Russia*, (New York, London, Sydney, Toronto: Wiley, 1971), pp. 89–192.

[101]Achim Seffen, "Rentenversicherung, Kassenebbe," *Der Arbeitgeber*, 19 December 1975, pp. 1107–1108.

[102]For this definition, see *The Cost of Social Security* (Geneva: International Labor Ofrice, 1972).

[103]Bundesministerium für Arbeit und Sozialordnung, *Socialbericht 1976*, p. 122.

but also includes public training expenditures, promotion of employment, family and child allowances, savings subsidies, and occupational insurance schemes, the social expenditure quota reached nearly 32% of GNP in 1976.[104]

The rise in social expenditures, recently very much connected with the development of costs of health protection, is of growing public concern. In the longer-term perspective, this increase results both from the extension of social protection and the transformation of the age structure of the population. In the years to come, population trends will be characterized by a decline in the number of children and an increasing number of old pensioners.

In 1976, the gross pension of a typical employee with 40 years of contributory service amounted to about 47% of his gross average active earnings (net pensions to nearly 67% of his net active earnings).[105] A growing proportion of the cost of social security is being obtained through contributions from insured persons and employers. In addition, the state makes annual contributions to the social security scheme. Social security taxes for insured persons in the period 1950–1975 increased from 8 to over 12% of gross earnings.[106] Approximately 60% of employees are entitled to contracted or freely paid plant-based old-age pensions, in addition to the obligatory state scheme.[107] For them, a law adopted in 1974 establishes a statutory guarantee for these additional pension rights. It lays down minimum norms for plant-based pensions, including provisions ensuring the maintenance of entitlements in case of a change in the place of work. Thus, an important obstacle to labor mobility has been removed.

Despite the extension of the social security schemes to various population groups other than wage earners and salaried employees, the network of social protection still favors the latter traditional target group. Some individuals who were never economically active or were so only for short periods of time remain insufficiently covered. This is true in particular of many women. A recommendation has been made to create social protection for women, independent of the present schemes.[108]

Labor's Position in Decision Making

There is little doubt that organized labor has made great advances in the Federal Republic of Germany, acquiring decision making power in the social, economic, and political life of the nation. The spread of codetermi-

[104]Bundesministerium für Arbeit und Sozialordnung, *Arbeits-und Sozialstatistik 1977*, Table 7.2.

[105]*Ibid.*, Table 7.9.

[106]Bundesministerium für Arbeit und Sozialordnung, *Sozialbericht 1976*, p. 198.

[107]*Ibid.*, p. 35.

[108]Kommission für Wirtschaftlichen und Sozialen Wandel, *Wirtschaftlicher*, p. 26.

nation, by virtue of which unionists are now represented in the supervisory boards of all major German enterprises, is a particularly visible feature of this evolution. Although full parity with capital has not been reached (except for the coal and steel sectors, where it was established in 1951), past experience with minority representation of labor (one-third of the seats in the supervisory boards were reserved for labor representatives in all enterprises with more than 500 employees, falling under the provisions of the Works Constitution Act of 1972) tends to suggest that it also affects power relations.[109]

In the Federal Republic, the idea of participation is bound up with the representation of workers on the supervisory boards. In addition to the provisions of the Works Constitution Act and of the Codetermination Act for coal and steel, there is now a law under which employee representatives take half of the seats on supervisory boards in all enterprises with more than 2000 employees. However, the influence of workers is less than in the coal and steel industry, since the chairman of the board, normally elected by the share-holders, has a double vote in case of a tie.

In the unions' view, greater participation in decision making by workers and their organizations takes definite priority over participation of workers in productive capital, wealth, and profits. Despite this fact, provisions for "wealth acquisition" by workers now exist (as mentioned earlier) in a large number of collective agreements, covering more than half of the labor force. These schemes are overwhelmingly employer-financed: the contributions are exempt from taxes up to a certain annual level. The purpose of these measures is the promotion of a more equitable distribution of wealth, to be achieved in the long run. Considered by some people as a possible tradeoff for greater claims for participation in decision making, wealth formation by employees has not worked out this way and is apparently no longer a priority goal for the unions. This is even more the case since plans to establish a collective worker-owned and union-administered fund of shares (copied from schemes proposed in some Scandinavian countries, in particular Denmark) met with strong resistance from employers and some political parties. The political influence of the unions has also increased.

Most members of Parliament (Bundestag) are unionists, but usually not those in official positions; and in case of role conflict, union interests are usually given secondary consideration.[110] The unions are also well represented in the parliamentary commissions that precede most political decision making, in committees and consultative councils of various ministries, and in a multitude of other bodies of interest representation. But they are

[109]See for instance, *Mitbestimmung im Unternehmen: Bericht der Sachverständigenkommission* (Biedenkopf Report) (Stuttgart: Kohlhammer, 1970).

[110]Urs Jaeggi, *Kapital und Arbeit in der Bundesrepublik,* (Frankfurt: Fischer, 1973), p. 101.

confronted there with the equally important representation of employers.[111] For these reasons, the political system has still kept a great deal
of its independence. For example, employers could not prevent the instal-
lation of codetermination, and the unions have fought unsuccessfully for
the establishment of a national economic and social council.

Much headway has been made toward the goal of integrating the
worker in society. His class–consciousness has weakened in the process.
Recent attempts by leftist intellectuals and a few union leaders to revive the
concept of class for new labor strategies have had little result thus far. This
is all the more interesting since integration is still lowest at the workplace,
where task–determination by others, masked by functional requirements,
frequently continues. Perfect equality by right and, frequently, equality in
fact is attained mainly outside the workshop. Inequality of opportunity
remains great, however, because of low social mobility, among other
things.[112] Leading positions in the economy, in cultural life, and in administration are still filled to a considerable degree by members of rather
closed social groups.[113] Education, a strategic factor for greater social
mobility, is also still rather unequally distributed. The proportion of wage
earners' children among university students is low. The finding that the
floor of inequality has been raised, whereas many inequalities have not yet
been eroded,[114] seems to be largely correct for many important aspects of
social life.[115]

MAJOR CURRENT PROBLEMS

Many of the current problems of the Federal Republic of Germany
stem from the syndrome of reduced growth, continued rationalization, and
structural economic change. The longer-term structural aspects of these
phenomena have been studied by the Commission on Economic and Social
Change mentioned before.[116] In addition there have also been attempts to
isolate the possible longer-term repercussions of the economic recession.[117]

---

[111]*Ibid.*, p. 102.

[112]H. Leo Baumann and H. Grossman, *Deformierte Gesellschaft?* Soziologie der Bundesrepublik Deutschland (Reinbek: Rowohlt, 1969), p. 44.

[113]Ralf Dahrendorf, *Gesellschaft und Demokratie in Deutschland,* (Munich: Deutscher Tasch,
1971), pp. 233–280.

[114]Baumann and Grossman, *Deformierte Geselschaft,* p. 44.

[115]See in this context, Bundesministerium für Arbeit und Sozialordnung, *Einkommens-
und Vermögensverteilung in der Bundesrepublik Deutschland,* Bonn, 1976.

[116]See Kommission für Wirtschaftlichen und Sozialen Wandel, *Wirtschaftlicher und Sozialer
Wandel.*

[117]See, for instance, W. Klander, P. Schnur, "Mögliche Auswirkungen der letzten Rezes-
sion auf die Arbeitsmarktentwicklung bis 1990," *Mitteilungen aus der Arbeitsmarkt- und Berufsforschung* 3 (1976), 2378266.

The most immediate problem requiring action is undoubtedly the persistently high level of unemployment, which is all the more painfully felt since it contrasts strikingly with past years of full and overfull employment. Both in 1975 and in 1976, the Federal Institute for Labor registered, on the average, approximately 1 million unemployed and 750,000 short-time workers. Although there has been a slow reduction of this unemployment level, influenced by seasonal factors, the unemployment figure stood, at the end of February 1977, at 1.2 million, or 5.3% of the labor force. Several hundred thousand foreign workers have gone back to their native countries. Overtime work has been considerably reduced and there are at least 500,000 persons (especially women) who have not joined the labor force since they know that employment opportunities are missing.

There is a fair consensus among labor market experts that a massive bloc of unemployed may persist in the near future, even if economic growth should again reach higher rates. Increased capital intensity of production as a result of recent modernization and nationalization, and the possibility of making flexible use of the labor force potential by the abolition of short-time work and the increase of overtime instead of new recruitment make economic growth with little employment increase a plausible proposition. In the slightly longer-term perspective the situation is complicated by demographic trends. Additional employment possibilities have to be created to absorb a greater number of young people who will leave the educational system in the coming years. Therefore, the view that full employment cannot be restored in the next few years, using the traditional instruments of economic and labor market policies, has become increasingly accepted.

One new way of approaching the problem would be through particular measures for certain groups hit hardest by the recession. In breaking down the global unemployment figures, several target groups can be isolated that require selective policy approaches. These include workers with low skill qualifications, women, foreign workers, and young people under 20 years of age.

The unions are very concerned about these problems, the more so since they have no comprehensive solution to offer. They have started to look at the full cost of unemployment[118] and consider that it is higher than the cost of better education, training, retraining, and job creation (including public works) by which, in their view, much unemployment could be eliminated. Other possible approaches, such as the reduction of working hours, longer holidays, the generalization of educational leave, restriction of overtime work, and a decrease of the labor force participation rate

[118]See in this context also, S. Mukherjee, "Employment Crisis in Western Europe?," *Labour and Society*, 1976, no. 2, pp. 95–105.

through longer education and greater flexibility in retirement schemes, are also being studied.

Many of these approaches are now summarized under the concept of reducing the lifetime work period for the individual. The proposal to reduce the average working hours, made by DGB president Vetter as the "last resort"[119] to combat unemployment, is controversial among employers and some industrial unions as well.

It remains to be seen how much consensus can be found for devising concrete measures through legislation and collective bargaining. The present views of employers and unions differ considerably. In line with the "logic of the market economy," employers hold that government incentives for new investment coupled with moderate wage policies by the unions will eventually reestablish high employment. The unions, on the other hand, argue that generalized investment incentives will indeed produce greater economic growth, but also greater unemployment, since they would invite further rationalization measures. They, therefore, favor selective investment incentives and state action or subsidies for labor intensive activities such as housing construction, slum clearance, and social services. They also want the government to consciously develop further employment possibilities within its own administrative functions. Finally, they consider it essential not only to increase the demand for labor, but also to reduce its supply, especially through a variety of measures curtailing the lifetime work period referred to above.[120]

The government has thus far taken a middle position between the incentive approach advocated by the employers and the selective approach favored by the unions. The existing government program is a mixture of traditional growth incentives, labor market measures, and some selected policies of job subsidy, plus public works for the improvement of the social infrastructure.

As in many industrialized countries, working conditions are also among the dominant present issues in the Federal Republic of Germany. Such conditions as alternating night and day work and shift work, monotonous and repetitive work, assembly lines, and unfavorable factors in the work environment (such as noise or vibrations) have come under special scrutiny. The same is the case for the effects of work organization and technology on skill requirements, the content of jobs, and intensification of work. These "spill-over" problems of economic growth and modernization are difficult to evaluate in a precise way because of the lack of data. However, the available observations and studies support the con-

---

[119]See interview of H. O. Vetter in *Welt am Sonntag*, 2 January 1977.

[120]For a further development of employer and union points of view on employment policies, see respectively, R. Tittle, *Arbeit für alle aber wie?* (Köln: Bund Verlag, 1976); and U. Engelen-Kefer, *Beschäftigungspolitik* (Köln: Bund Verlag, 1976).

clusion that many of the deficient labor conditions cannot be compensated for through extended rest periods and leisure.

Considerable efforts are being made by government, unions, employers, and academic institutions to study these "quality of working-life problems" and to find solutions. Many employers have started to experiment with alternative forms of work organization with the aim of improving both labor conditions and productivity, although this trend is much less pronounced than in Scandinavia. Both the unions and the employers have made the problem of humanization of work the subject of several congresses.[121] The unions claim that the best policy instrument for obtaining progress in labor conditions is collective bargaining. Better protection against dangerous or repetitive jobs, minimum cycles of work for assembly line workers, and new criteria for wages, eliminating individual piece work, are among the specific goals of the unions. A further aspect is, in their opinion, more information, consultation, and codetermination by workers and works councils in the regulation of labor conditions.

Recently, legislation has been passed obliging firms to observe certain minimum conditions for the industrial environment, to recruit safety engineers, and to improve plant-level medical services. Under the government's "action program for a greater humanization of working life," experiments in new forms of work organization are being supported, including one by Volkswagen (started in the spring of 1976) to produce cars without assembly lines. It is clear, however, that the present period of unemployment is not propitious for a rapid improvement of labor conditions.

The government's action program adopted in 1974 is a complex of measures with special focus on workers' protection, shopfloor participation, reduction of hierarchical command structures, and the design and introduction of more humanized technologies and workplaces. It is supported by a comprehensive research program in the labor field. Since its inception, approximately 150 research projects have received financial support from the government. Research institutes as well as enterprises can apply for such assistance. The unions fear that some enterprises will actually get subsidies for research and experimentation on rationalization, rather than on humanization measures. They have succeeded in modifying certain conditions for the granting of state support for enterprises, which are in line with this preoccupation. On the whole, however, both employers and unions consider the governmental action program on the humanization of work an appropriate measure of state intervention in the labor field.

---

[121]See in this connection for instance, Heinz O. Vetter, ed., *Humanisierung der Arbeit als gesellschaftspolitische und Gewerkschaftliche Aufgabe,* and Association of the Metal Industries in Baden-Württemberg, *Plädoyer für eine humane Arbeitswelt* (Results of a Congress of the Association in Esslingen in 1973), Stuttgart, 1973.

Reform of education and vocational training are other dominant current issues, including new standards for in-plant training, instructors, technical colleges, and recurrent education. Some improvements were made through a vocational training law passed in 1969. Reforms of education and training must now take into account the lessons of the recent economic crisis. For the first time in many years, there is now an excess of school graduates over the number of apprenticeships offered by firms. Small firms can no longer use apprentices as a source of cheap labor since the introduction of stricter standards for training. Technology and organization have changed too, making in-plant training (the dominant German situation) a less effective instrument. Because of the prominence of in-plant training, the supply of apprenticeships is controlled almost exclusively by private firms, which overreacted to the depressed economic situation. The broadening of vocational training, better control, and more effective coordination between such training and the general educational system are among the issues of the current debate. The unions are pressing for greater participation in decisions on training and education.

Practically all current labor problems have, therefore, a close relationship to the development of industrial democracy and to the increasing influence of workers and their representatives in society.

The most controversial continuing issue is the extension of "parity codetermination." The idea of codetermination has marked German industrial relations during all the years after World War II. It is one of the major long-term concerns of the unions. They stress that "parity" codetermination (effective equal representation of labor) on the supervisory boards, and the inclusion of a labor director on the managing board, allow works councils and collective bargaining to function better.

The unions believe that only "parity" representation can guarantee a real democratization in industry. In their view, such codetermination could bring about a situation in which personnel and social policy matters acquire equal importance for management with financial, investment, and marketing problems. Codetermination also seems necessary to the unions because German collective bargaining focuses on the industry level and thus cannot take care of problems at the plant level.

"Parity" codetermination is, for the unions, the missing link in the existing network of participation arrangements. At the shopfloor and plant level, the works council represents the workers' interests, particularly in respect to personnel, social, and working conditions issues, but also as regards economic matters, as laid down in the 1972 Works Constitution Act. Worker representatives can, in the unions' opinion, effectively represent labor only if they are kept fully informed by the works council. The labor director has managerial functions, but he can carry them out only if he is backed by the labor representatives on the supervisory board.

In support of their view, the unions point to the positive experience with codetermination during times of difficult structural change in coal mining and steel. The employers hold, on the other hand, that codetermination and workers' representation on management boards is incompatible with collective bargaining and represents an attack on private property as well as on managerial efficiency.

The new codetermination legislation, which was passed in March 1976 and covers all enterprises with more than 2000 workers, constitutes a delicate political compromise. This law, to be implemented before the end of 1978, does not provide full parity of influence for capital and labor on the supervisory board. Formally, labor is equally represented on the supervisory boards (six labor representatives, of whom three can be unionists from outside the firm, and six representatives of the shareholders). But in cases of tie votes, the chairman of the supervisory board can cast the deciding vote. Since the chairman is always a representative of the shareholders, capital retains, in actual fact, the last word.[122] The influence of labor is further reduced because employees in managerial positions are entitled to elect within the labor quota a special representative to the board. The unions fear that this board member will be management oriented in reality. Other groups of employees can also elect their own representatives, so that labor solidarity could be endangered. In addition, there is no provision for the approval of a labor director by the employees, as in coal and steel.

The employers are also not satisfied with the 1976 legislation. They have misgivings about the near parity representation of labor, and also fear that the outside trade unionists who can sit on the supervisory board may have other loyalties. The functional prerequisites for efficient management for the benefit of all are, in their view, being sacrificed for an expansion of the power of the unions.[123] In June 1977, the president of the top employers' organization (BDA) lodged a complaint against the 1976 codetermination legislation, claiming that it was unconstitutional since it infringed basic, legally guaranteed ownership rights. This had rather negative effects on the unions' cooperation (as mentioned before).

The compromise formula in the new codetermination law, which does not replace the special legislation for coal and steel, is the result of the influence of the liberal Free Democratic party, the present junior partner in the government of the Social Democrats. The Free Democrats favored a formula that gives labor less than parity influence and provided for the special representation of employees with managerial functions. Both the employers and the unions will have to live with the "unloved" new legislation. One of the consequences for the unions could be that they might give

[122]For a full discussion of the new law, see Erhard Kassler, "Stationen zu einem ungeliebten Gesetz: Dokumentation und Information," *Das Mitbestimmungsgespräch* 1(1976): 3–15.

[123]"Mitbestimmungs-Entwurf bleibt unannehmbar," *Der Arbeitgeber*, 8 March 1974, p. 152.

more weight to independent action and less to legislative approaches, which, as the new codetermination law indicates, are not always satisfactory to them. At the same time they continue to maintain the goal of full parity codetermination in their program.

Finally, the financial problems of the social security system dealt with earlier must be mentioned as another major current labor problem.

The present crisis has revived an intense debate about the role of the state in the economy. This is illustrated by the discussion of the most pressing short-term needs, the reduction of unemployment and the reattainment of full employment. Although the government maintains that social reforms are being continued,[124] it has become obvious that the reattainment of economic growth is a precondition for the satisfactory functioning of the industrial-relations system and for the solution of many current, as well as long-term, labor problems. The "zero-growth ideology", which in the Federal Republic of Germany, as elsewhere, has won many followers who are concerned with the preservation of the environment, is losing its attraction. These concerns are being articulated now about more specific projects, for example, the popular resistance to the proliferation of nuclear power plants. Despite the many conflicting developments, the need for continued reformist change to prevent revolutionary disruption remains, in the foreseeable future, a common denominator of all major parties to industrial relations and labor policy.

---

[124]See, for instance, interview with Chancellor Schmidt in *Der Spiegel*, 5 April 1976 no. 15.

4.   FRANCE

FRANCOIS SELLIER

INTRODUCTION

France in the eighteenth century was the most populous and one of the most economically developed countries of Europe. But in the nineteenth century it was the first country where, long before the others, a decline in the birthrate appeared. Industrialization, despite an early start, did not take on the rapid development that one observes in England and in Germany. Agriculture, favored by good geographical conditions, but still more by protective tariffs, employed a very sizable part of the population until 1946. One may wonder whether this importance of agriculture—combined with the weakness of industry and the precocious development of the tertiary sector—is explainable mainly by economic causes or by political causes.

Among the political causes, the importance of which is revealed by protective tariffs, one might mention the political fear of the development of the working class, long considered a "dangerous class." The revolutions of 1789, 1830, and 1848, and especially the revolution of the "Commune de Paris," have associated "workers" with "revolution" in French political history. This connection doubtless explains in part the late establishment of collective agreements. One must also attribute this backwardness to the very slow development of management organization; the state long remained the main partner of the labor unions. It still is today, to a considerable degree.

Between 1945 and 1970, an era of rapid industrialization began. At the same time, rapid population growth took place, which, though not lasting, was sizable, as compared with the past. These two facts have introduced into France a dynamism that affects all the elements of society, including the system of industrial relations.

Labor in the Twentieth Century

THE ACTIVE POPULATION AND
WAGE EARNERS

The study of the active French population can begin from a point of view that is productive for the analysis of the system of industrial relations, by emphasizing certain factors that have influenced it. In as much as these characteristics are specific to France, they allow one, in a comparative study, to determine the role—or, on the contrary, the absence of the role—of the environment in the formation and evolution of industrial relations. In essence, it is a question of seeking out how the social relations of industrialization are realized through transformations of the activity of the population.

The factors that have made France exceptional, from this point of view are

1. The long period of demographic stagnation connected with the appearance of low birthrates at the beginning of the nineteenth century
2. The importance over a long period of the use of foreign manpower
3. The heavy labor-force participation of women

All of these factors suggest a permanent scarcity in the labor market, particularly of qualified manpower.

Demographic Stagnation and Rates of Activity

The growth rates of the total population and of the population of working age have long been the lowest of all industrial countries. These rates, which had dropped between the first and the second halves of the nineteenth century, rose again only after World War II, and for the population of working age, since the 1960s, as indicated in Table 4.1

It should be observed that the natural growth of population alone would not have allowed these rates to be reached. The percentage of foreigners in the total population, always sizable since 1921, has continued to increase, passing from 4.6 to 7.5% in 1931 and to 8% in 1968. A large proportion of them belonged to the population of working age.

Table 4.2 breaks down the rate of total population growth into natural growth and growth attributable to immigration. It is clear that immigration, except during the Great Depression and immediately after World War II, has played an essential role. During the latest period shown in the table (1962–1968), the lesser importance of immigration is due to the repatriation of a million Frenchmen from Algeria, most of whom arrived in 1962. Since 1975, the French government has stopped immigration and has even offered departure subsidies to unemployed immigrants.

This characteristic of the French working population helps explain the

TABLE 4.1
Average Annual Rates of Population Growth, 1896–1975

Period	Total population	Population of working age (15–64)
1896–1913	.2	.2
1913–1929	.2	.2
1929–1938	.2	−.4
1938–1949	−.1	.2
1949–1963	1.0	.5
1963–1969	.9	.8
1968–1975	.8	.9

Sources: J. C. Toutain, *"La Population de la France de 1700 à 1958,"* *Cahiers de l'Institut de Science Économique appliqée,* Supplément no. 133, Séries AF, 3 (January 1963): 130; *Les Collections de l'Insee* (Institut National de la Statistique et des Etudes Études Économiques), Série D.52, p. 95.

high rate of women's participation in the labor force at the beginning of the century; the scarcity of manpower had pushed them, more than in other countries, to work not only in agriculture and in the services, but in industry as well. In Great Britain, the rate of female participation was only 25% at the beginning of the century; it remained stable until the last years between the world wars, then rose to 31% in 1961. In France, on the contrary, given the high level reached at the beginning of the century, the rate diminished regularly from 1900 to 1962, but it was still as high as 35% in 1921 and 30% in 1954. Toward 1960, the overall rates of female participation were relatively close in France, Germany, and the United States. From 1962 on, the rates of female activity in France rose again, in accordance with the trend that is observable in all the industrial countries (see Table 4.3).

The high level of female participation at the beginning of the century and its diminution until 1962 can be explained by the importance and progressive decline of agriculture, because the rates of female activity in the country are higher than in the city. It is estimated that 20–25% of the decline in the overall rate of female activity between 1901 and 1962 can be imputed to the reduction of the agricultural population.[1]

The evolution of the rate of female activity and the belated nature of its recovery can also be explained by changes in demographic policy. Children's allowances have always been a characteristic feature of the French social security system, put into effect in 1932. But this "birthrate" policy was progressively attenuated beginning in the 1950s.

[1] J. J. Carré, Paul Dubois, and Edmond Malinvaud, *La Croissance Française* (Paris: Editions du Seuil, 1972), pp. 66 *ff.*

TABLE 4.2

Components of Population Growth, 1896–1975 (Average Annual Percentage Increase)

	1896–1911	1921–1931	1931–1936	1946–1954	1954–1962	1962–1968	1968–1975
Natural growth rate	1	2	.5	7.5	6.5	6.5	6
Growth rate attributable to net immigration	1	5	–.5	1	4.5	3.5	2
Growth rate of total population	2	7	0	8.5	11	10	8

Sources: J. J. Carre, Paul Dubois, Edmond Malinvaud, *La Croissance Française* (Paris: Éditions du Seuil, 1972) p. 59; *Les Collections de l'Insee,* Série D52, p. 11.

TABLE 4.3

Rates of Participation of the Total Population, by Sex 1901–1975 (in Percentages)

	1901	1906	1911	1921	1926	1931	1936	1946	1954	1962	1968	1975
Men	67	66.5	67	70	69	68	64	66	62.5	58.5	55	52.5
Women	36	36	35.5	35.5	33	33	30.5	32	30	27.5	28	28.4

Sources: Carré, Dubois, Malinvaud, *Croissance Française*, pp. 68–69; *Les Collections de l'Insee*, Série D.52 pp. 100, 156.

Since 1962, the rise of the rate of female activity has been substantial. For married women, the rate of participation rose from 32.4% in 1962 to 40% in 1975. This increase is very clear for the young. For the age class of 17–25 years, the participation rate of married women was 43% in 1962, 50% in 1968, and 61% in 1975. This phenomenon is related to the falling birthrate.

There appears to be a causal connection between the increase in the level of education of women and their propensity for work; the higher the level of education, the greater the activity. In the age class 20–24 years, the participation rates are 36% for married women with no diploma, 65% for those having an apprenticeship certificate, and 75–78% for those having the baccalaureate or a diploma higher than the baccalaureate.

Finally, the increase in the percentage of white-collar jobs has favored married women's tendency to work, as they tend to occupy this type of position. The rate of female employment in white-collar work rose from 52% in 1954 to 64% in 1975. However, after a decline between 1954 and 1968, from 22.7 to 20.4%, the share of females in the total labor force rose again to 22.4% in 1975.[2]

Participation rates for the extreme ages, both for men and for women, have fallen. This diminution is observable, moreover, among men (the statistics are less reliable for women, due to uncertain classifications in agriculture) for all age groups except 25–34 years, the rate for which remained unchanged from 1901 to 1968 at 96%.

The most remarkable reduction is for the 15–24 year group, and for those 65 years old and over. The first is a recent phenomenon, dating from 1962, and the latter goes back to the interwar period (see Table 4.4).

Partition by Sectors and Industries

The evolution of the distribution of the active population into sectors is shown in Table 4.5. An interesting fact emerging from these data is the

[2]Robert Salais and M. G. Michal, "L'Activite des Femmes Mariées," *Economie et Statistique* (September 1971):27; Laurent Thévenot, "Les Catégories Sociales en 1975," *Economie et Statistique* (July–August 1977):3.

TABLE 4.4

Changes in the Labor Force Participation Rates for Two Age Groups of Males, 1901–1968
(in Percentages)

	1901	1906	1911	1921	1926	1931	1936	1946	1954	1962	1968
15–24 years	—	—	86.5	87	86.5	87	81.5	81	81	74.5	64
65 years and over	60	60	60	61	55.5	53.5	47.5	48	34.5	25	16

Source: Carré, Dubois, Malinvaud, *Croissance française*, p. 66.

slow growth of industry up to 1954 (construction and public works included). There is a near identity of the figures for 1913 and 1954. The
comparison is even more striking for manufacturing alone; the labor force
actually declined between 1913 and 1954, and particularly between 1929
and 1954. Further, the level of industrial labor force of 1929 will not again
be exceeded.

Three remarkable facts must be underlined in this area. First, there is
the considerable importance right at the beginning of industrialization, and
maintained over a long period, of the textile and food industries. Second,
there was the precocious and relative importance of service activities, and
more specifically of noncommercial activities (administration, the army,
and domestic services). Third, the agricultural sector remained large until
quite recently.

TABLE 4.5

Distribution of the Working Population by Major Sectors (in Thousands, Percentages in Parentheses)

	1913	1921	1929	1938	1954	1968	1975
Agriculture, forestry, and fishing	7,450 (37.4)	9,000 (41.4)	6,600 (32.5)	5,900 (31.4)	5,030 (26.1)	2,950 (14.6)	2,060 (9.3)
Industry and construction	6,720 (33.8)	6,600 (30.7)	7,430 (36.6)	6,060 (32.3)	6,870 (35.7)	7,850 (38.9)	8,167 (37.2)
Industry without construction	5,760	—	6,310	5,280	5,550	5,850	6,100
Services and transportation	5,730 (28.8)	6,030 (27.9)	6,270 (30.9)	6,800 (36.3)	7,350 (38.2)	9,350 (46.5)	11,473 (53.5)
Total	19,900 (100)	21,720 (100)	20,300 (100)	18,760 (100)	19,250 (100)	20,150 (100)	21,700 (100)

Sources: Carré, Dubois, Malinvaud, *Croissance française*, pp. 120–123; M. Cahen, "Evolution de la Population Active
en France Depuis 100 Ans," *Etudes et Conjonctures*, (May–June 1953): 250; "Enquête sur L'emploi (Population Active au Sens du Recensement," *Les Collections de l'INSEE* (Série D.42): 30, 34.

Role of Low-Wage Industries and Importance of the
Female Working Population

In the late 1800s, nearly half the active population in industry was concentrated in textiles (48.8% in 1872). In 1921, and still in 1931, the textiles and the food industries occupied nearly one-third. These workers were largely female. The proportion of women workers in these two industries was 90% in 1906, 80% in 1921, and 50% in 1954.

This characteristic of French industrial development is linked with the slowness of industrial concentration. The segment of the population employed in large enterprises (more than 500 employees) compared with the population employed other than in home industry (enterprises of more than 10 salaried workers) remained remarkably stable from 1906 to 1966, at about 30%.

The Continued Importance of Agriculture and the
Rural Exodus

In 1921, the French agricultural population was relatively more numerous than in 1913, comprising 41.4% of the total active population. It employed 2.84 million wage earners, nearly one-third of the agricultural population. The largest decrease occurred between 1946 and 1968. In 20 years, the agricultural population fell from 7.5 million to 3 million. The number of agricultural employees declined still more rapidly than the total: from 1.9 million in 1936 to 1 million in 1954, and to less than 400,000 in 1975.

Thus, an important flow of workers of rural origin continued to feed the secondary and tertiary labor force. This flow was all the more important in that the birthrate among farmers was higher than that of urban dwellers, and a large number of the children of farmers and agricultural workers left the country. The average number of children per family, for individuals born between 1882–1916 was 2.28, but was 2.83 for farmers and 3.0 for agricultural employees. The departure rate of children rose from the first to the second period, and the rate was always higher for wage earners' families than for farmers' families (farm owners or tenant farmers).

Importance of the Tertiary Labor Force

Many scholars have stressed the slowness of industrial development in France in the second half of the nineteenth century. A comparison between France and Germany puts into perspective the relatively slow development of industrial employment in France and the early growth of the tertiary sector. In 1938, the percentage of the labor force employed in the tertiary sector (36.5) exceeded the percentage employed in the secondary sector (32.3), whereas agriculture still employed 31.4%. The lead of service employment was taken during the Great Depression and continues with the rapid growth, from 1936 to today, of civil service and other services.

However, after World War II, partly under the influence of the Common Market, rapid industrialization took place in France. The high growth rates of the national product, the liberalization of trade in Europe, the incentives provided by the state through the Commissariat of the Plan de Modernisation, had positive effects on the development of industry, so that from 1954 to 1975, while the total labor force increased by around 2 million, the number of employees in industry increased by nearly 1 million.

The Social Structure of Employment

At the beginning of the century and still after World War I, more than one-third of the labor force was agricultural. Today the proportion in services and transportation exceeds 50%. Along with this occupational transformation went transformations of the social structure. First, the proportion of salaried employees increased in relation to that of workers. Second, among salaried employees, the proportion of upper-level employees increased. Third, the number of professionals (e.g., doctors, lawyers) greatly increased, especially after 1960. Finally, among wage earners, the proportion of employees in the public or nationalized sector, who often benefit from a permanent employment status, has increased.

The proportion of blue-collar workers in the nonagricultural active population remained almost unchanged over a long period (55% in 1901 and 54% in 1931), but by 1975 it had declined to 41.6%. However, it should be pointed out that the recent downward trend has been accompanied by an increase in the absolute number of blue-collar workers whereas, from 1931 to 1962, there was an actual reduction. This illustrates the emphasis on industrial growth in postwar France.

The distinction between blue-collar and white-collar employment needs clarification. In fact, among non-blue-collar workers it is necessary to distinguish ordinary employees from what are traditionally called in France the "cadres," a management category that is founded partly on a hierarchical criterion, but also on a functional criterion. In addition to these categories of salary earners, there are groups of individuals whose social status is relatively high, but who are not employed by firms; these groups include professionals, as well as employers in small commercial or industrial enterprises. The diversity of change among these occupations (see Table 4.6) indicates the rapidity of the social transformation that has taken place in France since World War II.

TABLE 4.6
Annual Percentage Change in Selected Occupational Categories,
1962–1975

Total active population	+ .9
Farmers (owners or tenant farmers)	−5.6
Agricultural workers	−6.1
Individual employers in industry and commerce	−1.9
Liberal professions and upper management	+5.6
Middle-level management	+4.7
Salary earners	+3.6
Blue-collar workers	+ .9
Domestic service employees	+ .9
Other	− .1

Source: *Économie et Statistique,* (July–August 1977): 5.

For certain high-level categories, the rate of change over the period 1954–1968 has been calculated, and is shown in Table 4.7. The rapid relative increase in the higher categories brought about an improvement in the chance of raising one's occupational status, although the opportunity remained unequal among the various categories. Social origin has retained a major effect on the future status of children. More than 40% of sons whose fathers fill a position in management or in the professions enter the same occupation. This figure remained stable between 1953 and 1970. In all other cases, except for ordinary white-collar workers, for sons whose fathers had a status inferior to that of higher management or professional, the probability of reaching a higher status rose.

In spite of this progress, the obstacles to social mobility remain large and are perceived as an injustice. Since 1971, the government, through a

TABLE 4.7
Rate of Change of Selected High-Level Categories of the Labor Force, 1954–1968

	Labor force (in thousands) 1968	Percentage increase from 1954 to 1968
Professionals	166.8	+ 39
Doctors	84.4	+ 40
Teachers, members of the literary and scientific professions	209	+155
Engineers in private industry	136.8	+ 68
Higher administrative management (private industry)	275.2	+237
Higher management in the public sector (technical, administrative, and judicial)	222.1	+ 42

Source: *Economie et Statistique* (October 1975): 18.

law on occupational retraining, has encouraged enterprises to facilitate the acquisition of new skills by their employees. But thus far the opportunities have been utilized more by individuals of relatively high status than by workers.

Public versus Private Employment

The importance of the distinction between public and private employment lies in statutory differences with respect to employment security and other social programs, particularly in the area of pensions.

In July 1972, the number of employees of national and local governments was estimated at around 2.9 million. But from the point of view of employment security, 250,000 nonpermanent employees should be excluded, as well as 100,000 part-time employees. There remain about 2.5 million employees with widely differing ranks and salaries, but all benefiting from similar advantages. They form approximately 12% of the total active population and 13.5% of the active nonagricultural population. The public employment percentage remained stable from the beginning of the century until 1931 (the army is included in these figures), but a rapid increase from 1936 to 1972 was due particularly to the growth of the educational system.

Another notable change in the social structure of employment, not measured by the figures on public employment, arose out of the policy of nationalization followed in 1936 and 1945. The employees of the railroads, the electricity and coal-mining industries, and, to a lesser degree, the banks and insurance companies, have benefited from employment guarantees and other social amenities not available to most wage earners.

This discrimination introduces considerable complexity in the labor market, for the differences of status and contract render comparisons difficult. Supplementary social benefits are generally more prevalent in the public and nationalized sectors, particularly in the area of pensions, where either the retirement age is lower, the amount of the pensions higher, or both. However, salaries are often higher in the private sector. Since 1950, miners and postal workers have waged the longest strikes, either in attempts to make up a lag in the wage level (miners, 1963), or to maintain retirement advantages (postal service, 1953).

The complexity of the labor market has increased particularly since 1946, when entire industries (e.g., railroad, electricity) or large businesses (e.g., Régie National des Usines Renault [Renault] and saving banks) were nationalized. Wages and fringe benefits are different in each of these nationalized sectors. Some of them (e.g., Renault) have employment conditions that are not very different from large enterprises in the private sector; others (e.g., electricity) have rules that are very close to those in the civil service. Some of them (e.g., coal mines) have seen their employment di-

TABLE 4.8
Employment in the Public Service and Nationalized Industry, 1931–1972 (in Thousands)

	1931	1936	1972
Railroads		422	270[a]
Coal mines		107	100
Water, gas, and electricity		107	166
Banks and insurance companies (nationalized)			200[b]
Total: nationalized sector		329	736
public service	1,313	1,433	2,500
Total: statutory employment	1,313	1,952	3,236
Nonagricultural labor force	13,907	13,044	18,500
Percentage of public and nationalized employment	9.6	13	17.4

Sources: Annuaire Statistique de la France, (1966): 114; *Annuaire Statistique de la France,* (1976): 71.
[a]This figure is from 1973.
[b]This is a rough estimate.

minish, while others (e.g., Renault) have seen it grow. But employment in a nationalized firm is generally regarded as a considerable advantage. This is why it is interesting to observe the evolution of the ensemble formed by public and nationalized employment, which is sometimes called "statutory" employment in France.

The rapid growth of statutory employment, as shown in Table 4.8, has affected employee perception of the most desirable type of employment. The evolution of industrial relations since 1945 has been strongly influenced by this perception, particularly in the area of employment guarantees, which has become an objective of union demands in the private sector, as well as in the public sector, as a result of the growing number of "auxiliaries" who are not, at the time they are hired, entitled to all the benefits of the "titular" employees.

THE TRADE UNIONS

The principal difficulty in determining the importance of trade unionism arises from the uncertainty of membership figures—the only source for such figures being the unions themselves. Another difficulty results from the growth of unionism among higher-level employees ("cadres") after World War II. The nationalization of the railroads in 1936 and the mines, electricity, and five commercial banks in 1946 brought about a strong trend toward organization.

The relevant data for the pre-World War II period are shown in Table 4.9, from which it is clear that the growth of union membership came in bursts. Table 4.10 presents similar data for postwar years with the dif-

TABLE 4.9
Nonagricultural Blue-Collar Workers and Union Membership, 1913–1933 (in Thousands)

	1913	1920	1922	1930	1933
Nonagricultural blue-collar workers[a]	3500	5200[b]	5200[b]	6300 [b]	6300 [c]
Union members	1000	2000	1200	600	800
Percentage of union members	28	38	23	9.5	12.5

Sources: J. C. Toutain, "La population de la France de 1700 à 1958," Tables 61, 62, 63; J. D. Reynaud,
    Les Syndicats en France (Paris: Editions du Seuil, 1976), vol. 1, p. 140, vol. 2, p. 140; G. Caire,
    Liberté Syndicale et Developpement Economique (Geneva: International Labor Office, 1976), p. 52.
   [a]The dates are those of the census taken at the date nearest to that for which the number of union members is available. For 1913, the figure of the 1906 census (3385) was raised to 3500.
   [b]This figure is from 1921.
   [c]This figure is from 1931.

ference that the base is not blue-collar workers, but all nonagricultural employees. Again, the fluctuating nature of union membership is apparent.

Until 1972, except in unusual periods, the percentage of union members did not exceed 25 and was often lower. This traditionally low percentage was exceeded after both world wars and at times when there were hopes among workers for great political changes (e.g., the creation of the Soviet Union in 1917, the electoral victory of the Popular Front in 1936, and the national liberation in 1946). These phenomena of union growth and decline appear in other countries, but in France they seem to depend more on political events than on economic circumstances.

The law of December 1968 (Code de Travail, Article 412-1-17), which provides a basis for the establishment of local unions in enterprises with more than 50 employees, has contributed to the growth of union power and to the influence of unions in works councils. The laws on vocational training and participation (to be discussed shortly), which give the works councils a role in their application, have also contributed to the same end.

A measure of union influence, as distinct from union membership, is

TABLE 4.10
Number and Percentage of Union Members Among Nonagricultural Employees, 1936–1972

	1936	1946	1954	1962	1972
Nonagricultural employees	8,800	9,900	11,000	12,700	10,000
Union membership	4,000	5,000–6,000	2,500[a]	2,200[b]	4,000
Percentage of union membership	45	50–60	23	17.3	25

Sources: *Données Sociales, 1974*, p. 22; J. D. Reynaud, *Les Syndicats en France*, vol. 1, p. 140, vol. 2, p. 194.
   [a]This figure is from 1955.
   [b]This figure is from 1961.

furnished by the proportion of companies in which a local union section has been established. In 1969, this was 21.9% of all enterprises with more than 50 employees. By 1975, the proportion had risen to 46.3%. The absolute figures were as follows:

Companies subject to the law	37,000
Companies having one or several local unions	17,000
Companies having a CGT local union	11,000

The growth of union influence between 1970 and 1975 is confirmed by the increasing number of companies in which a works council has been elected. The percentage rose from 30 in 1966–1967 to nearly 60 in 1972–1973. The progress was mainly in middle-sized companies. There has thus been a spread of union influence, which, until recently, had been limited to large companies and to certain industries. The industrialization in the period 1950–1970 may be at the core of this tendency, which has been reinforced by the slowdown of economic growth and strong social tensions that have been engendered since 1968. As for the large companies, they are nearly all "organized," as Table 4.11 shows, although since the 1970s the growth of local unions has been strongest in medium-sized enterprises.

Union influence can also be estimated using the statistics of works council elections. Workers who vote for a union list do not necessarily belong to that union. By their votes, however, they express an attitude and a preference. This indicator provides an upper bound for the influence exerted by unions.

Let us first consider participation or abstention in employee voting. We compare the percentages of votes obtained by the large, traditional union organizations—Confédération Générale du Travail (CGT), Confédération Française Democratique du Travail (CFDT), Force Ouvrière (FO), Confédération Française des Travailleurs Chrétiens (CFTC), and Confédération Générale des Cadres (CGC)—with the sum of (*a*) abstentions and (*b*) the votes obtained by nonunion representatives or by other unions, organizations that are suspected of being supported by employers, and that are, in any event, characterized by rightist tendencies. The data appear in Table

TABLE 4.11
Percentage of Companies, by Size, Having One or Several Union Locals on July 1, 1975

50–149 employees	35.3
150–299 employees	61.8
300–1000 employees	79.5
1000 and above	96.4
Total	46.3

Source: Travail Informations, *Notes du Ministère du Travail*, 27 (1977): 3.

TABLE 4.12
Abstentions and "Nonunion" Votes in Works Council Elections

Year	Percentage of abstentions	Percentage of votes for "nonunion" candidates or for "other" unions	Total
1967	27.8	15.5	43.3
1968	26.5	10.3	36.8
1969	28.3	19.0	47.3
1972	27.7	13.7	41.4
1973	29.3	17.1	46.4

Source: Yves Delamotte and Jacques Dussiot, Les Elections aux Comites d'Entreprises, *Revue Française des Affaires Sociales* (1974): 146.

4.12. Union opposition or abstention varies between 40 and 45% of all employees.

In the nationalized industries, where the participation of union members on the representative personnel committees gives them a special function, abstentions are lower than in the private sector, but are not negligible: in 1968, about 16%[3] as opposed to 26% in the private sector. In the civil service also, abstentions are low, on the order of 15%.

Let us now examine how union influence is distributed among the six principal federations of labor, including a union organization that is specifically for management, the CGC. Included in the data in Table 4.13 are only the votes of the private and nationalized sectors, without the important civil service.

The CGT clearly dominates the picture in the large private companies and in the nationalized industrial sector. In the latter, the FO is more important than the CFDT, but the CFDT received more votes than FO in the large companies. The influence of the large federations is less strong, on the average, in small and medium-sized companies, where some employers try to organize works councils through nonunion lists. But nearly half of all employers still avoid the legal obligation to establish councils.

Union influence is growing, particularly in the non-blue-collar categories, and even among management employees. It is in the nationalized industrial sector that the influence of the large traditional unions, and especially of the CGT, is strongest. The concentration of workers in this sector lowers the cost of organization. In addition, the official roles accorded the unions give them much greater authority than in the private sector. This is also the case in the civil service.

[3]See Gerrard Adam, "La Représentativité des Organisations Syndicales," reproduced in J. D. Reynaud, *Les Syndicats en France* (Paris: Editions du Seuil, 1976), vol. 2, p. 119.

TABLE 4.13
Percentage Distribution of Votes among Labor Federations

	Nationalized industrial sector, 1968	Private sector, all enterprises, 1972	Private sector, enterprises with more than 1000 employees, 1972
CGT	59.1	44.1	55.2
CFDT	15.8	18.9	23
FO	10.6	7.6	8.5
CFTC	6.5	2.6	3.1
CGC	2.5	5.6	4.5
Others	6	21.2	5.7

Sources: *Revue Française des Affaires Sociales* 1 (1974): 146; J. D. Reynaud, *Les Syndicats en France*, vol. 2, p. 119.

Trends in Unionism

In 1895, the formation of the CGT temporarily gave a lead to the partisans of a separation between trade-union action and political action. In 1906, there was a compromise between the revolutionary anarcho–syndicalists and the reformists. The Congress of Amiens gave the CGT a "charter," which based union action upon the class struggle. At the same time, however, it recognized the importance of the "daily task of protest . . . for the effectuation of immediate improvements." These original tendencies retain a certain importance for union ideology today: the distrust of collective agreements and the fear of not being able to control anarchist tendencies among the workers.

On the eve of World War I, the conversion to reformism of the secretary general of the CGT, Leon Jouhaux, gave preeminence to that tendency. The nomination of Jouhaux, in 1914, as "delegate of the nation," and the demand in 1916 for social provisions in the peace treaty proposals, marked a change in the attitude of the CGT, which until then had been opposed to any cooperation with the government.

The CGT also reinforced its organizational structure. As early as 1906, the principle of industrial unionism, the grouping of all workers of one industry into one union, whatever their occupations, was adopted and craft unionism was condemned.

Just after World War I, communist groups appeared and attempted to apply the principles of Leninism to unionism. A split occurred in 1921. The communist minority left the CGT and founded the Confédération Générale du Travail Unifiée (CGTU). The two were reunited in 1936 under the pressure of the appearance of fascism and nazism, and of the economic crisis resulting from the Great Depression. In 1939, the announcement of the Nazi–Soviet pact resulted in exclusion of the communists. Reunification took place once more in 1944. But power within the CGT had changed: In 1939, 10 federations out of 30 were directed by the communists; in 1944, the number had risen to 21. At the 1946 Congress of the CGT, the communists gained a majority. A new split occurred, again under the pressure of political events (the Marshall Plan, the Cold War) and economic circumstances (austerity policies related to the reconstruction effort). It marked the birth of the FO, a minority group in the CGT that formed its own organization.

A Catholic union was formed in 1919, with its strength mainly among white-collar workers. Under the influence of the Catholic social-action movement, particularly the "Christian working youth," Catholic unionism greatly extended its influence among blue-collar workers during the social crisis of 1936. Regarding itself at first as a Catholic organization closely tied to religious leaders, the union gradually threw off its parochial links and, in 1947, proclaimed its independence with respect to "all exterior political or religious groups." It progressively abandoned the traditional Catholic doctrine of cooperation between employers and workers in order to emphasize the necessity for negotiation and strikes.

As far as principles and programs are concerned, the principal changes that have occurred in the French labor movement since the 1950s involve the evolution of the former Catholic Confédération Française des Travailleurs Chrétiens. In 1964, a socialist group in the Federation gained on control and recreated it as the CFDT. Even before this date, however, but particularly since 1968, the CFDT, which is the second largest federation in number of members, emphasized socialist and anticapitalist positions in class–struggle terminology, but from a viewpoint opposite to the "democratic centralism" of the communist model, which characterizes the CGT. The CFDT now bases its program on the idea of workers' self-government, at the work place and in the plants.

In the two other blue-collar organizations, the CGT and the FO, the changes were less important, indeed negligible, at least as far as principles are concerned. However, the events of 1968, the extension of the political and labor struggle to students, and more generally, the arrival at working age of a large number of young people (in France, the baby boom took place between 1946 and 1955) had profound effects on all institutions, companies and unions included, in the sense that the authority of established leaders was reduced.

Even before the transformation of the Christian federation into the CFDT, a trend toward a more general economic orientation had gradually appeared. The term "democratic planning" had been adopted, and meant that the union was to influence all economic decisions. Criticism was aimed at the free play of market forces, as well as at the tendency, anarcho-syndicalist in origin, of refusing all cooperation with the state. This was the period in which "flexible planning" still had great prestige in France and was regarded by all, except the communists, as an essential means toward economic growth and social rationality. But it was after the events of 1968, and for the first time at its 1970 convention, that the CFDT chose to "replace capitalist, technocratic society with a socialist democratic society."[4] This new society was to be founded on three principles: (a) self-government, (b) ownership in common of the means of production and exchange, and (c) democratic planning.

The next important change was the adoption of a position favoring class unionism and the affirmation of the class struggle. This resulted in a vocabulary very similar to that of the CGT, characterized by absolute anticapitalism. On both sides one speaks of mass or class unionism; both uphold the class struggle and condemn profits. This convergence of anticapitalistic language, moreover, was very quickly accompanied by a labor alliance between the CGT and the CFDT for unity of action, in order to promote concrete demands. At first, the alliance stood up poorly against the pursuit of separate interests. It was reconstituted in June 1974, and continues to exist today, although the CFDT prefers to limit action in common to the struggle for specific demands, and hesitates to participate in demonstrations against general economic policies of the government. However, alongside the common anticapitalist language and the alliance for concrete action, differences of principle remain. The sharpest difference concerns the appropriate attitude toward the state.

For the CFDT, involvement in socialism means an affirmation of the principle of union independence of political parties, even in a "new socialist and democratic society." The CFDT argues that not only is political action for gaining power not the responsibility of unions, but also that, even should a democratic socialist government come to power, no unvarying support should be given it. This is a principle fundamental for the new CFDT: mistrust of political power and the state, including the Socialist state. For the CGT, on the other hand, the state, as soon as it becomes socialist, must be considered an ally of the workers and generally receive their support.

As conceived by the CFDT, the new society will need not only a socialist state, but also a transfer of power to the workers not only through self-management at the workshop level, but in all intermediate political and economic institutions as well. This power will be derived from free elections and will be capable of eventually opposing that of the state.

The CGT responded to the CFDT proposal of "transfer of power to the workers in all intermediate political and economic institutions" by elaborating a proposal for the transformation of the organizations of economic democracy that exist at present: the economic and social council, the

---

[4]*Syndicalisme, Hebdomadaire CFDT,* 1291 (1970):23; emphasis added.

industrial commissions of the commissariat of the plan, the administrative councils of the nationalized companies, and the works councils. The suggested changes would result, in fact, in giving the CGT the stronger influence in these organizations.

The Economic and Social Council is at present a national advisory assembly composed of representatives named by the large professional and economic interest groups (e.g., employers, unions, etc.) and of experts named by the government. The CGT proposes that in a reorganized council, the unions would have a greater influence, each union having a voice proportional to its members. The experts would no longer be named by the government, but in part by the professional groups. Economic and social committees in the various regions of the country would reinforce actions of the national council. In the commissariat of the plan, the sector commissions (by industry and sector) would no longer be constituted, as they are today, by governmental decision, but according to criteria that would give the unions and political parties greater weight than that of the employers and the government. Similar principles would give the unions a decisive weight in the councils of the nationalized companies. For the works councils, the number of representatives for each union would be proportional to votes received. In 1974, for example, the method of voting only gave an average of 40% of the seats to blue- and white-collar workers of the CGT, whereas it received 50% of the votes, and often more in the large companies.

The traditional attitude of all the French unions on organization of the enterprise is refusal to participate in economic and social decisions (e.g., choice of workers to be laid off for economic reasons). However, their programs provide for a strengthening of the rights of works councils, particularly in preventing layoffs. The unions also plan to influence investments, but from the point of view of their location and effects on employment. The CFDT wants to give workers the possibility of participating in the choice of company management, but it is implicitly understood that the union would retain all of its right to criticize and to strike.

This negative union attitude is quite common. Even the FO is clearly hostile to codetermination. The social doctrine of the FO is much more inspired by unionism in the United States. In fact, this federation places collective bargaining above all else. Bargaining implies a situation in which the social actors recognize their different interests and bring about compromises through negotiating and possibly striking. According to the FO, the European plans for worker codetermination would lead the union toward integration with the company. The FO argues that it is not possible to bargain with management and at the same time to participate in managerial decision making. This is why, on the appearance of an official report on company reform, the FO contested the proposal in the report to allow the presence of employee representatives, with the right to vote, on boards of directors, for "economic democracy can only be the result of free and permanent union intervention and pressure."[5]

Another aspect of the principles on which the social program of the FO is based is the refusal to countenance any incomes policy, that is, intervention of the state in the free play of bargaining between social partners. The FO, however, is in favor of establishing contacts with the government on social and economic questions. In addition, it participates in the deliberations of the commissariat of the plan, but it is clearly opposed to any tripartite decision making.

In spite of their great doctrinal differences, the three large French labor unions are close to one other on industrial democracy questions. All refuse codetermination. All are against incomes policies. Only the vocabulary differs. What the FO calls "integration with the company" (codetermination) or "compromise with the state" (guidelines), the CGT and the CFDT term "class collaboration." All prefer a works council where employee representatives have only a consultative role to one that has the right of determination, but also the obligation of social peace. Social peace, moreover, is rejected in collective bargaining by the CGT, and generally by the CFDT, but not by the FO, which here again joins with American union ideology in recognizing the possibility of collective agreements that are binding upon the signatories.

When it comes to broaching European problems, the FO, which belongs to the International Confederation of Free Trade Unions, insists on the importance for the new Federation of European Trade Unions of preserving "the great principles of liberty and independence which gave life to the founding organizations coming exclusively from the ICFTU and which joined together for a major task: the construction of the European Community." One can easily understand its opposition to the attempts of the CGT to enter the European labor federation. The FO also insists on the necessity of abandoning certain aspects of national sovereignty in order to fight unemployment and inflation.

The CGT, which belongs to the Communist World Federation of Labor, decided in October 1975 to consider as its priority in international action the political problems of Western Europe, and its request for affiliation with the Federation of European Trade Unions is the most important of these questions. The CGT does not plan to modify its view of the Common Market, which it regards as an organization entirely dominated by capitalist interests and an "economic relay station of American multinational companies"[6] through West Germany. But it wants to adapt itself in its contacts with other European unions to the situation in each country, "tak-

---

[5]Force Ouvrière, *Mensuel de la Confédération Force Ouviere,* June 1976, p. 9.
[6]See *Le Peuple, Organe Officiel Bimensuel de la CGT,* 992 (15 June 1976):24–25.

ing into account the evolution of the class consciousness of the workers."[7] Leaving aside divisive questions, it is a problem of adopting on an international level a line analogous to that which the CGT calls "unity of action" on the national level: without putting into question the principles, to unite with other unions to achieve specific demands. For example, the fight for reducing the work week would be supported. On the other hand it will refuse anything that resembles acceptance of sacrifices to be made by employees in an economic policy of "saving capitalism," such as incomes policies.

This policy of broad cooperation and flexible alliances is facilitated by the economic crises. The CGT emphasizes the fact that the European unions grouped in the Federation of European Trade Unions are making demands very close to its own. There is also convergence with the Economic and Social Council on the reduction of the work week, the retirement age, investment control, and freedom to bargain. At the second Conference of European Unions in 1976, including most of the unions of Europe, the CGT suggested the organization, on the European level, of permanent work groups on questions of working conditions. For the CGT, "the main question is to know whether the European labor movement wants to resolve the problems laid down, especially that of action, in class terms."[8]

In opposition to the Common Market, the CGT proposes a Europe of "cooperation," not only between developed and underdeveloped countries, but also among the various states of Western Europe. The CGT wants the World Federation of Labor to have "a more concrete approach to West-European problems" and to adopt a strategy peculiar to these countries; in this, it is in agreement with the Italian communist CGIL.

Thus, one sees an impending change in union politics. Even the CGT cannot do without a positive European orientation. This development cannot be dissociated from political developments in France and Italy, where there was the possibility of the participation of communist parties in coalition governments along with the socialist parties, which favor the building of Europe. In this case, it would not be possible for the CGT to be entirely against Europe. "The Europe of cooperation" would permit greater tactical opportunities.

The CFDT continued to belong to the World Confederation of Labor after dropping the term *Christian* in 1964 (it has since left the confederation). On the European level, it still belongs to the Federation of European Trade Unions. It sees in the Common Market "the Europe of business" and not "the Europe of workers." From this point of view, its position is close to that of the CGT. But, it has much more hesitation in declaring it-

[7]*Ibid.*
[8]*Ibid.*

self for any particular European strategy. However, in 1977, the CFDT took a very critical position with respect to the World Confederation of Labor.[9] This international organization, according to the CFDT, is incapable of exerting any influence on the international level, particularly with respect to multinational companies. The CFDT proposed that the unions of the World Federation become involved in a unitary policy and join the international labor secretariats.

In addition, the CFDT seeks, along with the Federation of European Trade Unions, a coordination of union action on a European scale, particularly for employment. It advocates the development of a new continental labor organization, including the International Confederation of Free Trade Unions, the World Federation, and other organizations.

The development of the principles of the French unions' programs, particularly that of the CGT—which is more open to cooperation with unions of different political leanings—and the CFDT—made more radical by the enonomic crisis and unemployment—was related to the development of European communism and to the impending possibility of cooperation between socialists and communists in the government of France. What has been said about conflict of principles on relations between a socialist state and the unions, on the one hand, and on proposals for modifying the procedure for naming representatives to the works councils, which would give a dominant influence to the CGT, indicates that there is still intense competition between the two federations. Hidden temporarily by mutual declarations of cooperation, this competition recovered all its strength after the 1978 elections, in which the leftist parties failed once more.

Europe will be one of the stakes in this competition. If serious proposals for controlling the activities of the multinationals (including greater employment security) were made by the European community and the United States it is probable that the CFDT would revise its present anti-European radicalism. Its positions would then be fairly close to those of the FO.

COLLECTIVE BARGAINING

The Process of Bargaining

The collective agreement, an institution that is now more or less general for workers in the private sector, is, in fact, a relatively recent phenomenon in France. Here again, one observes the great waves associated with social crises or unusual events, which have but an ephemeral existence. It was only in the period 1950–1955 that there opened up a phase of negotia-

[9]*Syndicalisme, Hebdomadaire CFDT*, 1652 (1977):21; *Syndicalisme, Hebdomadaire CFDT*, 1672 (1977):17.

tion on the industry level that progressively covered most of the private sector permanently.

It is remarkable that before World War I, and even between the two world wars, collective bargaining played a negligible role in the determination of working conditions and wages. Law, on the contrary, had great importance. Even today, the scales fixed by collective agreements for entire industries have only a limited importance at the company level. On the other hand, the minimum wage set by the public authorities, which is applicable to only about 5% of workers, has a direct influence on most workers.

In our view, the traditional importance of the law in the determination of working conditions can be attributed to the late development and to the weakness of employers' organizations. It takes two to negotiate. Labor unions were not unimportant in France before 1914. They had about 1 million members in 1913, grouped into more than 5000 local unions. Since the number of industrial workers was around 3.5 million, roughly 26% were unionized workers.

In this period, however, collective bargaining existed only in the mining and printing industries, which are geographically very concentrated (the first in the north, the second in Paris), and in which the employers had an obvious interest in organizing in order to avoid "whipsawing." But, in general, the organization of employers was poorly developed, at least insofar as relations with the labor unions were concerned.

The first associations of employers, organized at the end of the Second Empire (1860–1870), were originally oriented toward tariff protection for industry. This was the main role of the Association for National Labor, dominated at first by the textile industries, then by the Comité des Forges (a group in the iron and steel industries). Its main objectives were lobbying for tariff laws and the creation of cartels for dividing up the markets. A confederated employers' organization, oriented not only toward commercial and economic policies, but also toward social policies, appeared only in 1919. This confederation was set up, moreover, at the demand of the state, which wanted a partner for economic and social problems, particularly for the application of the law of 1919 on collective wage agreements. On the other hand, the labor unions had created a unified confederation, the CGT as early as 1895.

The structure of the employers' federation created in 1919 was weak, and the organization had little authority over its members. The case was the same for individual industry organizations. It was not until 1936, with the social crisis and the intervention of the state in solving it, that employers' organization was strengthened, mainly under the influence of the Union des Industries Minières et Métallurgiques (UIMM). The UIMM is still, along with the Union des Industries Textiles and the Union des Industries Chimiques, the most important of the employers' negotiating organizations.

It is interesting that the two dates (1919, 1936) that saw development of employers' organization correspond to two periods of social crisis and of state intervention. And this was also the case in 1968. The general strike of that year resulted in state intervention favoring the conclusion of an agreement between the employers and the unions on the level of the national federations. The social crisis of 1968 gave rise to an important reform of the structure of employers' organization: Interregional links were strengthened and the national federation was given real negotiating power that could be exercised in opposition to its industry members under certain circumstances. A political policy of social action, openly favorable to collective bargaining was adopted.

State action in the area of industrial relations has been manifested in three different ways:

1. At the time of arbitration during great social crises
2. By introducing laws leading to the setting up of procedures for negotiation or for settling conflicts
3. By its action as employer in the nationalized sector or in the civil service

In addition, special mention must be made of the role of the state in determining the minimum wage.

State intervention goes back to the period before World War I, and first appeared in the years 1880 and 1890. At that time, state agents in the local areas, the *préfets*, always intervened in serious conflicts, at times, it is true, to quell them, but often to induce employers to negotiate and raise wages, or to promote arbitration. In long and violent strikes, it was possible for the regional representative in the National Assembly to intervene, or even a minister of the national government. This was the case, for example, at the time of the Creusot strikes in 1899, when Prime Minister Waldeck-Rousseau himself arbitrated the conflict.

In all the big social crises, the government intervened in order to settle conflicts whose intensity and violence could have had serious political consequences. The two most notable cases are the Matignon Agreement of 1936 and the Grenelle Agreement of 1968. The term agreement was openly disputed in 1936 by the employers, who spoke of a *"diktat."* In both cases, it was a question of government intervention for the purpose of obliging employers to negotiate on economic demands that were often excessive, but also with respect to union rights, which were more justified, such as the 1968 recognition of the right to organize union locals in the enterprise.

Even apart from these cases of crisis arbitration, the state's function in ordinary arbitration in the private sector is not negligible. This was the case from 1937 to 1939, through a 1937 law on mandatory arbitration. Today, compulsory arbitration no longer plays any role. But the opposing sides can have recourse to a mediator, according to a definite legal procedure. The decision of the mediator is not binding, but, since 1971, the side that rejects this decision must denounce it explicitly. However, this procedure is not often used.

More important is the practical role played at the company level by labor inspectors. Although legally the inspectors have only the function of checking up on the application of laws and collective agreements, the unions often have recourse to them in case of disputes with the employers, and their intervention can aid in the solution of a conflict. When a dispute becomes very serious, it is not unusual for the unions to involve local or national public officials in order to raise the conflict to the political plane.

The legal recognition of unions (1884) came long before World War I, but it was only recognition of the right of association, and not the right (implying an employer obligation) to bargain. The very notion of the obligation to bargain has always met with strong opposition from the courts, and it was only in 1971 that a law was enacted providing for penalties against the party that would not answer a demand for bargaining.

World War I led to serious agitation in the factories, and the Russian Revolution created a new political climate. France had not yet adopted the principle of collective agreements. Even the legal idea of nonindividual contracts was contested. A law of March 1919 on collective contracts first created the legal possibility of collective agreements between labor unions, on the one hand, and employers or associations of employers on the other. A large number of agreements, including mainly wage clauses, were negotiated. These agreements covered entire industries. Their duration was indeterminate. Price increases should have resulted in readjustment of the wage scales, but in fact, employers refused demands for revision, and the agreements rapidly fell into disuse. It must be added that the agreements applied without distinction to all employees—union members or not—a fact that did not contribute to the strengthening of the unions.

The political and social crises of 1936 resulted in new legislative action in the areas of collective bargaining, arbitration, and union rights in the enterprise. For the first time, agreements could be extended by ministerial decision to companies that were not members of the signatory employers' organizations. This compensated for the organizational weakness of these associations.

The law also provided for a certain number of subjects that an agreement would have to cover, such as hiring, apprenticeship, wages, and hours, in order to encourage the parties to establish an internal labor-law code contractually. However, since legislation was already highly developed in certain of these areas, the main objective of the agreements continued to be the determination of wages. The same phenomenon as in 1919–1920 occurred: Inflation rapidly rendered the contractual rates null and void.

However, the laws of 1936 had set up an arbitration procedure for the adjustment of wages. The arbitrators were chosen by the parties from lists established by the civil authorities and were composed of neutral persons endowed with social prestige. These arbitrators were very active, and their decisions on wage adjustment were generally well accepted. They were particularly preoccupied with determining wage increases that would compensate for price increases and take into account the number of worker's dependents. Thus, during this period when the electoral victory of the parties of the left and the increasing threat of war had created a national consensus, conflicts were generally settled by means of compulsory arbitration, a procedure in which the decisions could be appealed to a Superior Court of Arbitration. In 1937–1939, the social consensus was sufficient to make arbitration acceptable. It was not yet sufficient for the process of negotiation to continue on its own. Moreover, it was legally interrupted in 1939 with the declaration of war.

Until 1949, wages were theoretically controlled by ministerial decision both as to level and differentials. After the war, when economic activity picked up again, these decisions were easily circumvented by assigning workers skill levels that were higher than the ones they actually processed. The administrative system of wage determination became more and more incapable of controlling the labor market, and freedom of wages was reestablished in 1949.

As early as 1946, a new system of national industrial collective bargaining had been instituted by law. But, because of concern about inflationary pressures, wages were excluded from negotiation. As a result the law was little applied, not only because of the wage exclusion, but because it imposed only one level of negotiation: the national level, by industry.

A new collective bargaining procedure, which included the negotiation of wages, was established by a 1950 law on collective agreements, and it is still in force today in its general principles. This law repeated the 1936 distinction between ordinary agreements and agreements liable to extension, which is most important in activities like agriculture, textiles, or commerce where there are many small companies over which the employers' organizations have little authority. The law contains a restrictive definition of "representative" unions, tending to prevent the organization of company unions, without, however, adopting the rule of the majority and of exclusive representation, as in the United States. It allows the conclusion of agreements at all levels, including that of the enterprise, but the principle of the superiority of industry agreements over company agreements remains.

Levels of Negotiation

The levels of negotiation vary according to geographic division (nation, region), industry (all industries, one industry, one company), and substance (general conditions, particular clauses such as vacations, other fringe benefits, wages). Industry agreements are sometimes national, as in petroleum, chemicals, and construction; and sometimes regional, as in iron and steel. In construction, the national agreement excludes wages, which are determined on the regional level. In nearly all of the large companies, there are general agreements on pensions and vacations, and on occasion, on such special matters as hours paid to union representatives beyond the minimum hours allowed by law or national agreement. A 1971 law gives equal status to enterprise and industry agreements in order to encourage negotiation at the enterprise level.

Negotiation on the national level for the whole of industry and commerce ("interprofessional") has developed considerably. It was at first a matter of agreement on such fringe benefits as pensions and unemployment compensation. Then this type of agreement was applied to additional problems, in particular to training and refresher instruction, employment guarantees in cases of industrial reconversion, equalization of blue-collar and white-collar benefits, the possibility of early retirement with immediate payment of full pension, and employment classifications. Collective bargaining at all levels has greatly increased since World War II, and France is no longer very different in this respect from a country such as Germany.

However, one must emphasize certain characteristics that distinguish French collective bargaining from that of other countries. Agreements are generally concluded without a definite term; there is thus no date for renegotiation stipulated in advance. Nor is there the obligation of industrial peace during the application of the agreement. These characteristics are interdependent. The result is that strikes are often the most practical means of renouncing an agreement. Competition between unions tends to favor this procedure. However, there are signs that evolution toward a less anarchical procedure is taking place.

Collective bargaining was installed with great difficulty because of the resistance of employers' organizations and the lack of legally determined representation for workers. Legal recognition of unions as organizations having negotiating power was obtained only in 1968. De facto recognition had already been secured in nearly all large companies for some time. But until then, the only workers legally recognized as official representatives were elected employee representatives and members of the works councils. They had no specific bargaining rights, but only the right to present local demands and consult on the economic situation of the company. The works council itself is an organization presided over by the employer. The legal recognition of the unions in the company, although belated, was important, since a channel of negotiation was established. Elected representatives and works council members, as well as the representatives named by the unions, theoretically cannot be laid off by the employer.

Wage Bargaining

In analyzing collective bargaining in France, it is necessary to distinguish between negotiation of general clauses on working conditions and negotiation of wages. For the former, it is clear that collective bargaining has made great progress, to the point where one can say that today nearly all the wage earners of large-scale industry are covered by a collective agreement—around 90% in metallurgy, for example. Not only is the rate of coverage high, but revisions and improvements have been frequent for the past 10 years, especially through multiindustrial agreements.

The problem of wage bargaining, especially in a period of economic expansion and rising prices, poses rather different problems. Here, it is a question of a procedure for regular adjustments. As has been pointed out, French wage agreements are of indeterminate duration and do not include any obligation to bargain. The most serious obstacle for wage agreements is the tendency of employers to put off action and, correlatively, the tendency of the unions to demand rapid revisions. The result is that wage change depends, on the one hand, on instructions given to employers by their associations, and, on the other, upon union pressure exerted within the enterprise.

As already noted, wages in the private sector were determined in 1937 and 1938 by compulsory arbitration, and between 1939 and 1949 by ministerial decision. It was only with the 1950 law on collective wage agreements that wage bargaining became free. The same law decreed a legal minimum wage and a procedure for adjusting its level.

The significance of a legal minimum wage depends on its level relative to the average wage. If it is much lower, its influence is slight. In France, the relative level has varied in different periods. From 1950 to 1970, the minimum wage was determined by the general price level. Since real wages tended to vary with national income, the minimum wage diverged progressively from the average real wage, and influenced it less and less.

Consequently, social crises occurred that obliged the government to raise the minimum wage considerably: between 1954 and 1955, the minimum was raised 25% over a few months. Such jumps immediately influenced the entire wage structure. This is why, beginning in 1970, the legal system of readjustment of the minimum wage was modified. Not only does it vary with the price level, but at least once a year, it is adjusted according to the annual increase in average hourly wages for all industry.

We have already noted the role of the state as arbiter of wages in the private sector from 1937 to 1939. It is now necessary to describe its role in nationalized sector wage determination, and its efforts to introduce collective bargaining into the public sector.

It was again at the time of a social crisis that the determination of wages in the nationalized industrial sector (mines, electricity, and railroads) was revised. In 1953, a miners' strike was called because of an alleged wage lag for miners as compared with the private sector. A commission of experts, named by the government, established the validity of this lag and proposed a considerable increase in the miners' wages, which was granted. The government later appointed a commission charged with examining the general problems of the state as employer. The report of this commission opposed the arbitrariness of the state's wage decisions and proposed that negotiation with the unions be increased. Mixed wage-study commissions were set up and negotiations took place on the criteria for wage increases. Agreements were signed in the nationalized industries. These have a definite term and must be renegotiated periodically. A tacit no-strike accord for the duration of the agreement was effectuated, particularly in the electricity industry.

It is a paradox that collective agreements on real wages have been concluded in the nationalized enterprises, which are relatively independent of the constraints of the market, and are subsidized by the state, whereas such agreements are still rare in the private sector.

The system of agreements in the nationalized companies is fragile, however, and has not stood up well against the great inflation of the 1970s. The state's effort to implant such a system, an attempt that also covered the civil service, is interesting in that it provided a model for private companies, but thus far in vain. In 1971–1973, efforts by private employers' organizations to stimulate negotiation on wages within enterprises encountered strong resistance from employers in the medium-sized companies.

However, a movement toward negotiation at the enterprise level is beginning to take shape in the large companies. A first wave of company agreements occurred after 1955 in imitation of Renault and affected only about 100 companies. After 1968, there was a new wave, larger than the first. This marked a clear increase in the propensity to negotiate at the enterprise level. The phenomenon of "waves" renders uncertain the evolution that one may expect in the future. But the reinforcement of enterprise unionism, on the one hand, and the institutionalizing of negotiation, on the other, may help to explain recent developments and can be seen as signs of permanent change in the French system of industrial relations.

Strikes

The irregularity that has already been noted in the rise and fall of unionism is also reflected in strike movements, caused by the great upheavals in national political life. However, it is necessary to distinguish between two categories that may have different determining factors: ordinary strikes and waves of strikes. Any observer of strike statistics in France is struck by the occurrence, every 10 or 20 years, of such waves, some of which (1936,1968) were of such magnitude that they could not be measured statistically. They coincide with events in the political arena and are only slightly influenced by union organization. An exception occurred in 1906, when strikes for the 8-hour day took place under the leadership of the CGT.

Strike waves appear clearly in:

1893:   3,175 thousand workdays lost

1902: 4,675 thousand workdays lost
1906: 9,439 thousand workdays lost
1919–1920: 15,478 and 23,112 thousand work days lost
1930: 7,209 thousand workdays lost
1936: general strike
1947: 23,361 thousand workdays lost
1968: general strike

Although based on statistics of workdays lost, this list is not very different from that obtained by Shorter and Tilly,[10] based on the number of strikes and strikers. These authors define a strike wave as the situation in which the number of strikes and the number of strikers for a given year exceed the average of the preceding 5 years by more than 50%. According to this criterion, they found 1890, 1893, 1899–1900, 1904, 1906, 1919–1920, 1936, 1947–1948, and 1968 to be strike wave years.

The character of the waves of 1919–1920, 1936, 1947–1948, and 1968 is clear; it may be defined as an exceptional spread of strikes to a large number of companies of all sizes, to all regions, and to all industries under the influence of a national event of great political significance, often accompanied by economic recession.

If these waves are disregarded, there is relative invariability of lost workdays, resulting from two opposite trends: an increase in the number of strikes and strikers, and a decrease in the length of strikes. The relevant data are shown in Table 4.14.

Strikes in France are caused by two major factors. The first is primarily economic, arising particularly when circumstances increase the employers' ability to pay, whereas the second is political and is facilitated by economic recession. With the reduction of the length of strikes, their symbolic aspect takes on more importance than the economic cost sustained by the protagonists.

The decline, until 1974, of the ratio between lost workdays and the number of nonagricultural workers results both from the reduction of the length of strikes and from the increase in the number of workers. This decline, moreover, is understated, since strikes after World War II tended to spread to white-collar employees in the private sector, especially in commerce and banking. Thus, until 1974 the average strike cost per worker, and even per striker, fell considerably. Strikes became a generalized expression of labor discontent.

However, the economic crisis of 1974–1976 reinforced the tendency to strike. The rise in the strike coefficient was due not only to the size of the strikes, but also to the drop in the number employed. Since 1968, and

---

[10]Edmond Shorter and Charles Tilly, *The Shape of Strikes in France 1830–1960* (Cambridge: Cambridge University Press, 1974), p. 107.

TABLE 4.14

Average Annual Working Days Lost Due to Strikes during Periods
without Strike Waves

	Lost working days (millions)	Lost working days per 1,000 nonagricultural workers
1907–1913	3193	.49
1921–1935	3430	.47
1948–1967	3021	.43
1969–1974	3203	.41
1975–1976	4000	.60

Source: Données Sociales, 1973, p. 50.

especially since 1974, there have been some long, hard and costly strikes, generally during recessions, to protect employment. This marked a transition from the symbolic or admonitory strike to the resistance strike, despite the precariousness of financial aid from the unions to the strikers.[11]

The dominant characteristic of the French scene remains the brevity of the average length of the strike and the frequency of short strikes. However, it is not difficult to determine what the function of this type of strike is, and how it is linked to the system of collective bargaining. In a country like France, where wage agreements are concluded for an indeterminate period and where the tactics of employers generally consist in not taking the initiative for their renewal (the word, *"attentisme,"* or "waitism," has become common usage), it is almost necessary for strikes to be used as a signal for the reopening of negotiations.

WAGES AND WORKING CONDITIONS

Changes in the length of the workweek constitute not only an important element in assessing living conditions, but also tell us something about the bargaining strength of employees. In a country like France, where the active population was stagnant for so long, strong resistance on the part of employers to the reduction of working time could be anticipated.

L. A. Vincent has attempted to estimate the length of the workweek since 1896.[12] He notes that the facts are not known before 1931, except for

[11]In the private sector, some strikes end with an agreement providing for a partial wage payment for strike days; the frequency of this practice is not known. Union strike funds are not widespread except in the CFDT, and there they are modest. Unions appeal to worker solidarity in collecting aid for striking workers, rather than relying on cash reserves.

[12]L. A. Vincent, "Population Active, Production et Productivite," *Etudes et Conjoncture* (February 1965):73 *ff.*

the mines. For the period preceding 1931, he estimated the workday by the relationship between daily wages and hourly wages in a number of occupations, based on investigations carried out by mayors and conciliation boards. For the period after 1931, he corrected the data from Ministry of Labor enquiries in order to take small companies into account (companies with fewer than 100 employees before 1946, and 10 employees after 1946).

The first struggles were for the reduction of the length of the workday for women and children.[13] In 1882, a proposal for limiting to 10 hours the workday for women and children was adopted by the French Chamber, but rejected by the Senate. In 1889 the Senate again rejected a proposal limiting the workday to 11 hours for children younger than 18 years, and for women. Finally, in November 1892, a law was enacted establishing a maximum of 11 hours for women and 10 hours for minors under age 16. This law, which had many exceptions, was poorly enforced. Before World War I, working days of 12 hours were common for men and even for women.[14] In the mines, a 1905 law set the normal length at 8 hours, and limited the maximum length of the workday to 9 hours. As for the workweek, a 1906 law made a weekly day off a general requirement. But in these cases, it is difficult to say to what extent the laws were enforced.

The reduction of the workday was a union demand that motivated the great strikes of 1906 and 1918–1919. A 1919 law, installed the 8-hour day and the practice of giving Saturday afternoon off. It was once again the strikes of 1936, in the revolutionary atmosphere that followed the electoral victory of the Popular Front, that forced the adoption of the 40-hour week and a 2-week paid vacation, but war and postwar events intervened. In 1976, paid vacations of 4 weeks were generalized and some collective agreements provide for an additional week of winter vacation.

Data on annual workhours from 1890 to 1963, by subperiod, are shown in Table 4.15. Before World War II, the decline in the working year occurred in jumps—between 1913 and 1919, and between 1929 and 1936—under the pressure of union demands that were strongly politicized. On the other hand, the reduction between 1963 and 1973 was obtained contractually and gradually.

In addition to paid vacations, employees have the possibility of paid time off in order to acquire supplementary training. Members of works councils and shop stewards, as well as secretaries of union locals, have the right to special-training leave with pay.

[13]Madeleine Guilbert, *Les Fonctions de la Femme dans l'Industrie* (The Haig: Mouton, 1966), pp. 56 *ff.*

[14]Madeleine Guilbert thinks that the trend toward reducing the length of the work day for women slowed the increase in their employment in certain occupations. *Ibid.*, p. 58.

TABLE 4.15

Hours Worked Per Year in Industry, 1896–1973

	1913	1929	1938	1949	1963	1973
Index by subperiod	96 (1896=100)	892 (1913=100)	83 (1929=100)	112 (1938=100)	101 (1949=100)	95 (1963=100)
Average number of hours worked per annum	3000	25000	2000	2100	2100	1950
Index of hours worked (1913=100)	100	82	66.6	70	70	65

Sources: Carré, Dubois, Malivaun, *Croissance Française*, p. 127; *Annuaire Statistique de la France*, 1976, p. 74.

TABLE 4.16
*Percentage of Unemployed among Wage Earners and in the Total
Active Population*[a]

	Wage earners	Active population
1896	3	1.4
1901	3.5	1.6
1906	2.6	1.2
1911	1.8	1
1921	5.1	2.7
1926	2.2	1.2
1931	4	2.2
1936	8.5	4.5
Average 1896–1926	3	1.5
1946	1.2	.7
1954	2.5	1.5
1962	1.7	1.2
1968	2.8	2.1
1975	5.0	4.5
Average 1946–1975	2.6	1.9

Source: Carré, Dubois, Malinvaud, *Croissance Française*, p. 82.
[a]Figures are based on 87 departments for the years 1896–1911
and 89 departments for the years 1921–1975.

Unemployment and Earnings

Estimates of unemployment from 1896 to 1975 are shown in Table 4.16. In analyzing these figures, one can either take a long-term perspective (1896–1975), or a medium-term perspective (1921–1936; 1946–1975). Over the long period, there was a reduction of unemployment among wage earners. This conclusion is strengthened by the fact that the figures are closer to the actual situation after 1946 than earlier, particularly before World War I. In 1900, Pelloutier observed unemployment of from 25 to 40% for the year 1894 in the construction industry and described in detail the unemployment of intellectuals.[15] As for the unemployment rate in the active population, the statistical trend shows an increase. But this increase may be a statistical illusion, owing to a decline in the relative importance of the agricultural sector.

A medium-term perspective provides different results. During the periods 1921–1936 and 1946–1975, the situation changed from a very favorable state of employment to a state of serious unemployment. Since 1965 in particular, there has been a worsening of the unemployment rate. This is due to a number of structural causes, such as (*a*) rapid growth of the proportion of the labor force in employee status, (*b*) an increase in the rate

[15]Fernand Pelloutier and Maurice Pelloutier, *La Vie Ouvrière en France* (Paris: Maspero, 1975), pp. 276–287.

of female labor force participation, (c) the rapidity of technological change, and (d) the consequent obsolescence of skills. But at the end of the period, there was also a decline in the investment rate. It should also be noted that since 1968, there has been an improvement in the statistics, linked to the strengthening of the placement organization l'Agence Nationale pour l'Emploi.

Although while the number of unfulfilled job requests (corrected for seasonal variation) fluctuated roughly between 100,000 and 150,000 between 1949 and 1966, continuous growth brought it to 400,000 in 1972–1973 (2.5% of the active population), and to 1 million in 1976. The unemployment situation has become an important element in the French social and political climate. The protection of employment has also become a theme of conflict that is legitimized by public opinion.

Earnings

The results of earnings calculations are affected by choice of the unit of labor and a number of other factors such as indirect wages, the skills chosen (the wages of the unskilled have risen more than those of skilled), and the region under consideration (wages in the provinces have risen more than those in Paris). We adopt the choices made by A. Tiano[16] in his estimates, which were themselves based on estimates of J. Fourastie and C. Fontaine[17] for wages, and on J. Singer-Kerel[18] and the Institut National de la Statistique et des Etudes Economiques for prices.

The series chosen were as follows: For nominal wages, the statistics on direct average hourly wages in the Parisian metallurgical industry were used, corrected for the disparity in growth between Paris and the provinces, and for the progressive increase in indirect (social) wages. The periods have been divided up variously, on the basis of the possibilities allowed by the available statistics (see Table 4.17).

If one were to use the corrected hourly wage figures, real wages rose by a factor of 1.89 from 1892 to 1960. But the lowest figure, 1.20, is not an abstraction. It is valid for skilled unmarried workers in the Parisian metalworking industry. For the period 1920–1960, the results are more favorable. Though when one turns from real hourly wages to annual earnings (direct and indirect), the increase is not as great because of the reduction in hours worked per annum.

It is interesting to study two particular periods in more detail: 1938–1952 and 1962–1973. Table 4.18 contains annual data on real wages for the

---

[16]See F. Sellier and A. Tiano, *Economie du Travail*, 2nd ed. (Paris: PUF, 1971), pp. 296*ff*.

[17]J. Fourastie and C. Fontaine, *Documents pour l'Histoire et la Theorie des Prix* (Paris: Colin, 1958).

[18]J. Singer-Kerel, *Le Coût de la Vie à Paris de 1840 à 1954* (Paris: Colin, 1961).

TABLE 4.17
Percentage Increase in Real Wages, 1892–1960

	1892–1960	1920–1960
Average direct hourly wages (for metallurgy in Paris)	20	51
Corrected to take account of differences between Paris and the provinces	51	88
Corrected to take account of indirect wages	89	37
Correct to take account of indirect wages, on an annual basis	36	47

Source: F. Sellier and A. Tiano, *Économic du Travail* (Paris: PUF, 1971), pp. 310–311.

former period. What appears is the effect of the war on real wages. The level of 1938 was attained only 20 years later. This initial level was already low due to the impact of the Great Depression. It also appears that the increase in the length of the workweek, because of the strong economic expansion of the 1950s and 1960s, allowed weekly earnings to rise more than hourly earnings.

Beginning in the 1960s, and particularly from 1965 on, expansion continued; but the conventional length of the workweek decreased, and the trend toward rising unemployment appeared. It is interesting to observe

TABLE 4.18
Index of Real Direct Earnings, 1938–1962 [a]

	Hourly earnings	Weekly earnings
1938	151	133
1949	100	100
1950	100	101
1951	109	111
1952	115	117
1953	121	122
1954	129	137
1955	139	143
1956	146	152
1957	154	161
1958	150	155
1959	153	158
1960	160	167
1961	168	176
1962	172	182

Source: INSEE, *Annuaire Statistique de la France,* 1966, p. 431.
[a] 1949=100.

TABLE 4.19
Indexes of Real Hourly and Weekly Earnings,
1962-1973

	Real direct hourly earnings	Real direct weekly earnings
1962	100	100.
1969	132	134
1970	138	134
1971	145	140
1972	152	144
1973	161	151

Source: Annuaire Statistique de la France, 1975,
p. 519.

from the data in Table 4.19 that during 1962–1973, when real earnings increased considerably, weekly earnings rose less than hourly earnings. In 1965, the length of the workweek was still 45.6 hours. It fell to 43.4 hours in 1973.

During the depression of 1974–1977, the length of the workweek fell again. Real hourly earnings continued to rise by about 4% per year from 1974 to 1976 in spite of inflation, but real weekly earnings were stable. In 1977, the public authorities managed to stop the increase of real hourly earnings at the same time as a slight increase in the length of the workweek improved weekly earnings. It seems certain, however, that the end of the era of rapid growth of real wages has been reached.

Wage Differentials

The structure of French wages, compared with that of other European countries, is marked by two opposing characteristics. On the one hand, the wage spread between the sexes seems to be less than elsewhere. This is shown by the relationship between average hourly wages of men and women for various European countries, in Table 4.20. On the other hand,

TABLE 4.20
Ratio of Male to Female Gross Hourly Earnings for
Industrial Workers

	Germany	France	Italy	Netherlands	Belgium
1964	1.48	1.32	1.40	1.84	1.55
1971	1.43	1.28	1.30	1.70	1.48

Source: J. J. Silvestre and J. J. Bouteiller, "Wage Structure in
France: The Problem of Wage Hierarchy," The International Journal of Social Economics, 2(1974): 177.

TABLE 4.21
*Ratio of Average Direct Hourly Labor Costs Between Nonmanual
and Manual Workers, Manufacturing Industry*

	Germany	France	Italy	Netherlands	Belgium
1969	1.56	2.01	2.03	1.64	1.79

Source: J. J. Silvestre and J. J. Bouteiller, "Wage Structure in
France," p. 181.

the wage spread between blue-collar and white-collar workers seem generally higher in France than elsewhere, except for Italy (see Table 4.21).

As for the wage differential among skill levels, the statistics of the
European community for 1966 show that the ratio of the wages of a skilled
worker to the wages of an unskilled worker in manufacturing is higher in
France and Italy, than in Germany, Belgium, or The Netherlands.

These results can be best explained by the scarcity of manpower that
long constituted a bottleneck to French economic development. This shortage encouraged immigration and provided a bonus for the labor reserve
of women. On the other hand, the same shortage of manpower gave an
advantage to skilled workers.

For 20 years these differentials remained relatively stable, as Table
4.22 shows. There the wages of the different categories of male wage
earners are compared to those of women. The comparison does not take
into account the different lengths of the workweek, which explains the
larger differential than that shown in Table 4.21. The decline in the differential after 1958 can be explained by rapid industrialization, the growth
of employment, the relative increase in the number of nonmanual em-

TABLE 4.22
*Indexes of Change in the Earnings of Various Categories of Male Employees Relative to
those of Female Wage Earners, 1952–1971* [a]

	Blue-collar workers (women)	Blue-collar workers (men)	White-collar workers	Middle management	High-level employees
1952	100	148	199	301	572
1958	100	156	182	319	635
1963	100	153	176	313	608
1967	100	154	176	325	654
1971	100	143	175	295	595

Source: Michel Freyssenet, Francoise Imbert, and Monique Pinçon, *Les Conditions
d'Exploitation de la Force de Travail 1945–1975* (Paris: Centre de Sociologie
Urbaine, 1975), p. 141.
[a] Female workers = 100.

TABLE 4.23
Indexes of Increases in the Purchasing Power of
Average Weekly Earnings and Average Monthly
Income of a Family with Two Children

	Average weekly earnings	Average monthly income
1949	100	100
1950	101	102
1952	117	113
1953	122	118
1954	132	125
1955	143	130
1956	152	137
1957	161	145
1958	155	137
1959	158	135
1960	167	140
1961	176	147
1962	182	151
1964	195	159
1965	200	162
1966	207	165
1967	213	166
1968	222	172
1969	237	175
1970	245	178
1971	254	183
1973	278	203
1974	286	203

Source: Freyssenet, Imbert, and Pinçon, *Les Conditions d'Exploitation*, p. 129.

ployees, and the increasing difficulty of filling the least skilled jobs. Industrialization in rural areas had as one of its purposes the counteracting of these difficulties, but it was unable to prevent the relative rise of the lowest wages. Since 1971, this movement has accelerated, in part as a result of a policy of increasing the minimum wage.

Combining the statistical series on prices, wages, and length of the workweek from 1949 to 1974, yields the data in Table 4.23. In order to take into account transfer payments to families, we have added an index of the monthly income of a family with two children, living in Paris, receiving, in addition to the average earnings of a blue-collar worker, the various social benefits available to such a family, as well as the relevant tax reductions. It can be seen that real direct-work earnings have increased considerably more than total earnings including payments. For a family with two children, as a matter of fact, family allowances have lost much of their absolute and relative importance. As for direct weekly earnings, they have continued to grow, except in 1958, a year of economic crisis and political upheaval.

Physical Working Conditions

Aside from the length of the workweek, it is difficult to evaluate changes in physical working conditions objectively. Physical and mental stress depend on the work environment, the machinery used, and the rhythm and organization. One reason for the improvement of working conditions is the decreasing importance of certain industries. This is the case for female labor in textile factories, which are still important, but much less so than formerly; and of male labor in the coal mines. Silicosis, one of the most serious of occupational diseases, is becoming less frequent.

The reduction of the workweek and increased wages are linked to a growing trend toward economizing labor by accelerating its rhythm. There are few indicators of these changes, but the frequency, and particularly the seriousness, of work-related accidents are in part results of this phenomenon. Among the available indicators, I cite only the number of serious accidents per 1000 employees, and the number of fatal accidents per 1000 employees, noting, however, that these figures understate the real situation, since they are related to the total labor force falling under the scope of social security (blue-collar and white-collar workers in industry and commerce), whereas the relative number of blue-collar workers, who are more subject to the risk of accidents, has fallen.

From 1954 to 1974, the number of serious accidents, resulting in the payment of benefits, rose from 64,000 to nearly 120,000; the number of deaths due to work-related accidents from 1643 in 1950 to 2117 in 1974 (accidents in transportation excluded).

A study by the Institut National de la Statistique et des Etudes Economiques[19] showed a clear relationship between the frequency of work-related accidents and the length of the workweek. Since an increase in economic activity not only prolongs the length of work, but also leads to the employment of manpower that is still not very accustomed to industrial labor, particularly immigrants, the risk of accidents increases. Immigrant workers, who constituted 3.4% of the active population in 1973, suffered 22.3% of serious accidents.

Among the factors that may result in the greater arduousness of labor, one may single out night work and alternating shifts. As for piecework, it is an indicator of pressure intended to increase labor intensity.

The frequency of blue-collar shift work doubled between 1957 and 1974 (from 14.3 to 31.3%) in manufacturing. The steel, textile, and paper

[19]*Donnees Sociales, 1973,* p. 47.

TABLE 4.24
*Percentage of Workers Paid on the Basis of
Piece Work, France*

Workers	Percentage
All skills	
Men and women	14.6
Women	24.0
Semiskilled	
Men and women	15.4
Women	28.4

Source: Élisabeth Vlassenko, "La Structure des
Salaires dans l'Industrie. *Les Collections
de l'INSEE,* Série M. 43–44, p. 147.

industries are those in which this frequency is highest (respectively, in 1974, 77%, 50%, and 52%). It is in systems of three or four shifts that work can be most difficult. They involved only about 3% of all workers in 1974. But the importance of systems of alternating shifts (rotating schedules) was greater: They affected about 20% of the workers. This type of work is harmful to health as well as to family and social life.[20]

Other modes of work organization result in a high degree of physical or psychological tension, for example, assembly line work, which, when defined very strictly, involves nearly 10% of all manufacturing workers. Twenty-five percent of workers in the shoe, clothing, automobile construction and parts industries, and 22.5% in the pharmaceutical industry, work on an assembly line. This type of work is practiced more by women than by men: 51% of assembly line workers are women, whereas women represent only 22% of the blue-collar population. These figures cover only blue-collar workers. However, "scientific" modes of work organization are penetrating the tertiary sector.

As for systems of wages based on output, historical statistical data are not available in France, where this type of remuneration seems to be relatively less common than in other countries. However, an October 1974 study by the Common Market yielded the results shown in Table 4.24.

In conclusion, it may be said that economic progress has been more beneficial to the health of French workers through the higher standards of living it has allowed than through the working conditions it has brought about. The development of world trade contributes to the deterioration of working conditions in a country, at least during periods when the comparative advantage for that country's industries is on the decline, (for example, in France, textiles, leather, shoes, and electronics). These industries often

[20]Workers on alternating shifts suffer more than others from gastric troubles and nervous disorders.

employ workers who are young, under conditions that rapidly wear down their working capacity:

> In electrical engineering, female workers are often younger than thirty, almost always younger than 40 years old. After that age, the decrease of visual acuity renders them incapable of the tasks of micro-assembling and microtooling. On automobile assembly lines, few semi-skilled workers are older than forty partly because of posture fatigue which that implies.[21]

Inasmuch as international competition is an on-going process, which eliminates the most poorly situated industries, and constantly attacks new ones, there exists always, for this reason alone, a fringe of workers with difficult working conditions. Thus, on the fringes of industry, a long-term improvement of physical working conditions may not occur. Even deterioration is not to be excluded, due to the nature of technical progress: the increased speed of machines, often linked to their power, may worsen exposure to sound and to vibration.

The social and political tensions caused by these factors are reduced when the country can recruit foreign manpower from poor countries. For a long time workers from rural areas filled these jobs. The disappearance of the rural reserves necessitated calling on the young, the women, and foreigners. An improvement in working conditions would make industrial jobs now turned down by indigenous manpower more attractive. Less arduous industrial work would avoid the present exclusion from the active population of persons suffering from minor handicaps. Labor presents a problem for most modern industrial societies that they have not yet resolved: that of a new balance between the political exigencies of full employment and the social exigencies of improvement in working conditions.

One last aspect that is important for the evolution of the system of industrial relations remains to be examined: the change in the structure of employment.

The first thing to note is the reduction of independent work and the growth of wage-earning employment, and therefore of the importance of the social relationship of subordination and authority, which, on the economic level, result in the growing importance of bargaining demands as the normal method of increasing pay. The second concerns the change in the structure of the wage-earning population itself. Is there a larger relative number of *skilled* wage earners today than there was formerly? On the supply side, the spread of education raises average ability, but it does not necessarily raise the proportion of best qualified individuals. On the demand side, has the structure of jobs changed so that a larger proportion of them involve high skill classifications?

---

[21]Commissariat General du Plan, Comite Emploi et Travail, *Preparation du VII Plan* (Paris: La Documentation Francaise, 1976), p. 133.

It is difficult to give a precise statistical answer. A slight growth in the proportion of skilled workers among manual workers, from 1954 to 1972, seems probable, though it is only clear between 1962 and 1968 (32.5% in 1962 and 38.5% in 1968). Nonetheless, it is possible that over a longer period, the proportion of skilled workers is fairly stable. Technical progress both creates and destroys skills. Just as it eliminates some occupations, it constantly creates new ones.

Social Welfare Programs

One of the most obvious favorable changes that has occurred in the condition of blue-collar workers, and wage earners in general, over the past 50 years, is the introduction in 1930–1932 of social security, with three different programs: health insurance, family allowances, and old-age pensions. The risk of work accidents was covered as early as 1892 (from 1858 for employees of the state and local governments). Family allowances are one of the oldest forms of social transfer, which could be explained by the low birth rate of the French population up until World War II, relative to other European nations, and particularly Germany. The first family allowances were established during World War I for government employees. They were extended to the private sector in 1932, then to independent workers in 1961 (farmers) and 1962 (craftsmen, businessmen, independent professions). But while they were being extended, economic growth made them less necessary by greatly increasing workers' income. In addition, the baby boom had temporarily reassured the public authorities about the fertility of the French family.

French family allowances provide a special payment to nonworking mothers with more than one child, in addition to an allowance paid to wage earners based on the number of children, when there are more than two. This allowance, long paid without relation to family income, was discontinued in 1971. It is now paid only to those having low incomes. This reform is one of several that tend to differentiate family benefits so as to focus primarily on low-income families.

Compulsory health insurance was first extended to wage earners in 1930, and then to the entire population in the 1960s. The system functions on the basis of the reimbursement of around 75% of the amounts paid to doctors or pharmacists, who are nearly all engaged in private practice. Mutual societies often supplement the payments and ensure free and direct access to public and private hospitals. The financing of health insurance is based on employer and employee contributions.

Up until 1955, wage earners in France had no unemployment insurance. The unemployed received only a small welfare allowance. This system still exists, but it is now supplemented by insurance financed by employers and wage earners, and subsidized by the state. Various combinations of benefits have developed. In 1975, they permitted 90% of an employee's wages to be guaranteed for a year, if he were laid off for economic reasons. This plan benefited around 12% of the unemployed; 120,000 persons out of a million.

Compulsory old-age insurance was installed in 1930. The amount of the pension is low. But since the 1950s for management, and the 1960s for all wage earners, supplementary retirement agreements have been concluded between unions and employers. The pensions paid under these systems, added to the pensions of the compulsory system, provide about 70% of preretirement income after age 65. Since the depression of 1974–1976, in order to relieve unemployment, subsidized contractual systems were established which afford the same benefits to wage earners who retire at age 60.

THE FUTURE OF THE SYSTEM OF INDUSTRIAL RELATIONS

One of the questions that you may now be posed concerns the future ability of trade unions to organize the majority of wage earners on a permanent basis. It has often been said that the politicization of the unions and the divisiveness that results from it are incompatible with a large membership. However, French experience in unionism in the civil service, in the nationalized companies, and even in the large private companies, where membership rates are high, shows that political division does not necessarily impede organization when the unions fill important practical functions such as participation in advisory commissions on personnel evaluation, and negotiation for wage increases at the enterprise level.

The real question is whether the French system of industrial relations will be able to overcome the vicious circle of nonrecognition and radicalism. The strength of the principle of employer autonomy in the area of personnel management and the trend toward unilateral decisions in the enterprise can be explained in part by the radicalism of trade unions. A situation in which unilateralism and radicalism mutually sustain one another is very harmful.

But there is a possibility of change. This is what seems to be indicated by the experiments in bargaining at the end of the 1960s in the public and nationalized sectors, where, until then, the principle of unilateral decisions had predominated. Some experiments in consultation and flexible negotiation in private firms have also appeared in France since the 1960s. They suggest a greater degree of union recognition by employers; they also favor the solution of conflicts by the parties themselves, and they tend to promote collective bargaining. It is true that the French unions have up until now been reluctant to commit their members, partly because of the absence of collective agreements of fixed duration. The solution to this problem is not facilitated by the pressure put on trade unions by small groups of activists.

The increase in unemployment since the late 1960s, and its rapid growth since 1974, tends to reduce the bargaining power of the workers. But at the same time, progress toward recognition of the unions at the enterprise level and the growing tendency toward bargaining increase the functional authority of the unions. Can this growth of authority lead to union acceptance of bargaining on employment and wages within the framework of a growth-oriented economy? This is one of the most important questions for the years to come. The answer that will be given also depends on the degree of cohesiveness among employer associations and on their authority over their members. There does seem to be a trend toward increasing this authority. The strengthening of organizations of wage earners and employers, on the one hand, and the greater difficulty of achieving economic growth and full employment, on the other, may force the French system of industrial relations to move toward renunciation of the vicious circle of union radicalism and unilateral decision making by employers.

5. JAPAN

TAISHIRO SHIRAI
HARUO SHIMADA

INTRODUCTION

This chapter has two purposes: One is to provide an integrated view of the evolution of the Japanese labor market and industrial relations in order to understand their dynamic character, and the other is to acquaint the reader with basic statistical data relating to labor force, wages, and union activities in the historical process of Japan's industrialization since the turn of the century.

Japan is set apart from Western nations both in distance and in terms of its cultural, social, and linguistic structure. And yet, in view of the increased economic and political interdependence of nations today, it is imperative for us to promote a more correct and balanced understanding of the structure and working of the social, economic, and political systems of the respective countries with each other. Analysis of industrial relations, an integral subset of the total societal system of a country, can serve as a key to approach this goal.

It seems to us, however, that the state of Western literature on Japanese industrial relations in not only insufficient in terms of its scope of analysis but also involves some bias in its content—particularly in the sense that the expressed views are still somewhat unduly dominated by the preoccupations of social traditions and unique cultural legacies. In hope of developing a more balanced understanding of the evolutionary character of Japanese industrial relations, we will try to put forth some alternative, historical interpretations of the dynamic development of Japanese industrial relations in the first part of this chapter.

Although statistical data are mostly self-explanatory, we have prepared separate sections that are devoted either to giving some systematic comments on statistical data or to giving historical descriptions of the subject.

Labor in the Twentieth Century

The major subjects of these sections are: labor force, wages, and labor movements.

INTERPRETING JAPANESE
INDUSTRIAL RELATIONS

Japanese Industrial Relations—Are They Misinterpreted?

Introduction

It is a common mental procedure to build a stereotype to help express or remember something. But once a fixed notion is established, it often becomes difficult to develop one's thoughts beyond it. And in this respect, the Westerners' conceptualization of Japanese industrialist relations, which is to some extent shared by the Japanese as well, is not an exception.

Japanese industrial relations have not been a major focus of Westerners' attention until relatively recently. Characterized as a strange culture with peculiar traditions, Japanese experience was simply alien and did not appear relevant to Westerners' interests. But the pattern changed markedly when Japan began a phenomenal economic growth in the mid-1950s.

The interest of foreign observers grew increasingly keen because Japan presented a unique case of Western-type economic development among nonWestern nations. They wanted to know why only Japan, among all other Asian countries, was able to industrialize herself as quickly and effectively as she did. Why was Japan able to sustain a pace of growth unprecedented even by Western industrialized nations? What are the reasons that made this achievement possible?

Of particular interest were such questions as how the traditional elements of an Oriental society and the rigorous logic of industrialization were assembled together in Japan to realize such a high pace of development. Were the historical and cultural peculiarities associated with the traditional Japanese society deterrents against, or accelerators of, industrial development?

To an important extent, answers to these questions were suggested by some of the foreign observers and endorsed subsequently by eminent Japanese scholars and experts. By the early 1960s there already existed a widely accepted notion of a peculiarly Japanese social system that presumably explained the questions of Japanese economic development. The system consists of three major elements that are uniquely Japanese: lifelong employment, length-of-service reward systems, and enterprise unionism.

Composed heavily of, or, in part, even generated within, the cultural legacy of premodern Japanese society, these elements nevertheless allegedly served economic purposes effectively by providing a high degree of commitment of the workforce to the employer, a sense of security and satisfaction to the worker, and industrial peace and cooperation within the enterprise community. In other words, the values of traditional society matched marvelously with the rigorous logic of modern industrialism.

As the sustained rapid economic growth of the 1960s attested to the workability of this system, at least in the sense that it was not incompatible with rapid technological and economic changes, the concept of an industrial relations system composed of these three unique elements was firmly established as the stereotype notion of Japanese industrial relations and prevailed widely among inside as well as outside observers.

The notion is seemingly so complete and self-evident that, once established, it tends to blind the eyes of new observers. Caught up by this notion, one may overlook the signs of change or forget that the system itself has been constantly modified in the historical process of its formation. Moreover, this notion tends to overshadow many suggestive and insightful research findings on the workings of Japanese industrial relations and the labor market. In fact, as a result of such research findings, the stereotype has been criticized and modified in the past. But the basic idea of the stereotype still seems to survive and enjoy a surprisingly broad popularity.

To the extent that this notion is a good approximation of the facts within a limited aspect of industrial relations during a limited period of time, it certainly serves as a useful piece of knowledge. But to facilitate an understanding of the whole complex of the systems and to provide more accurate predictions for their future, it is necessary to develop a more comprehensive and better balanced understanding of the evolution and functioning of Japanese industrial relations systems. In this chapter, we will attempt to advance historical explanations of some of the leading features of Japanese industrial relations, with a hope to fill this gap. Before we begin our discussion, however, let us briefly review selected literature in this field.

A Brief and Selective Review of the Literature

Among the pioneering works of Westerners, the first book that called forth remarkably broad repercussions, among Westerners as well as Japanese, was James C. Abegglen's *The Japanese Factory: Aspects of Its Social Organization,* which appeared in 1958.[1] This is a tightly organized report of the author's research into a limited number of large Japanese plants.

Motivating Abegglen's research were the questions "How may Western modern industrial technology be fitted into a nonWestern context?" and

---

[1]James C. Abegglen, *The Japanese Factory: Aspects of Its Social Organization* (Glencoe, Ill.: Free Press, 1958).

"What kinds of adjustments must take place to integrate this technology and the local people into an effective industrial unit?"[2] To capture the difference between the Japanese way of adjustment and the Western methods clearly, the author used American organizational arrangements as a comparative reference. To him, Japanese practices appeared in sharp contrast to American counterparts in some of the basic aspects of a factory organization.

In terms of employment relationship, he writes in an oft-quoted paragraph:

> At whatever level of organization in the Japanese factory, the worker commits himself on entrance to the company for the remainder of his working career. The company will not discharge him even temporarily except in the most extreme circumstances. He will not quit the company for industrial employment elsewhere. He is a member of the company in a way resembling that in which persons are members of families. . . .[3]

Of the wage system, he observes:

> recompense in the Japanese factory is in large part a function of matters that have no direct connection with the factory's productivity goals. . . . It is not at all difficult to find situations where workers doing identical work at an identical pace receive markedly different salaries, or where a skilled workman is paid at a rate below that of a sweeper or doorman. The position occupied and the amount produced do not determine the reward provided.[4]

And he says the following in summation:

> The importance given to education, age, length of service, and similar factors in the total wage scale means that the worker is heavily penalized for job mobility and strongly rewarded for steady service. Taken together with the factors involved in recruitment, it will be seen that labor mobility is virtually nonexistent in the Japanese system. What is rewarded is the worker's loyalty and a deep commitment to the firm.[5]

Confronted with all the peculiarities of the Japanese system, he makes the inevitable analogy that "the Japanese factory seems family-like in its relations," and he advances the hypothesis that it is a "consistent and logical outgrowth of the kinds of relations existing in Japan prior to its industrialization."[6] More specifically, he maintains that the observed relations may be seen as a rephrasing of the feudal loyalties, commitments, rewards, and methods of leadership in the setting of modern industry.

[2] *Ibid.*, p. 3.
[3] *Ibid.*, p. 11.
[4] *Ibid.*, p. 67–68.
[5] *Ibid.*, p. 68.
[6] *Ibid.*, p. 130.

The loyalty of the worker to the industrial organization, the paternal methods of motivating and rewarding the worker, the close involvement of the company in all manner of what seem to Western eyes to be personal and private affairs of the worker—all have parallels with Japan's preindustrial social organization.[7]

In his interview research in the mid-1950s, Abegglen did not see or appreciate the economic effectiveness or efficiency associated with Japanese factory organization. Indeed, he pointed out repeatedly the immobility of the workforce, the lack of cost-consciousness, and the nonrelation of wages to skill and efficiency factors as all implying a noneconomic and somewhat irrational organizational behavior. What was most striking to him, however, was the fact that modern technology was absorbed and digested in the Japanese industrial organization without altering the basic organizational character of Japan's feudal society.

But as the Japanese economy demonstrated remarkable growth year after year, the mood of evaluating Japanese industrial relations has shifted gradually from merely indicating that they are not incompatible with rapid growth to showing that they are congenial with, or perhaps even conducive to, growth, Whereas most Japanese scholars and practitioners have been critical of the kinds of peculiarities pinpointed by Abegglen, condemning them as symptoms of the backwardness of Japanese capitalism, Japan's tremendous economic growth has caused an increasingly greater number of Japanese to revise their view in favor of the peculiar Japanese system. Whether the Japanese system was a cause or an effect of rapid growth is as yet an unresolved question. But the general notion that remarkable economic success and semifeudal social relations coexist quite compatibly in Japan prevailed widely among foreign observers in the early 1960s.

As an outcome of research on comparative industrial relations, four American scholars characterized Japan as follows:

> Because industrialization was originally sparked by a dynastic elite, the idea of paternalistic concern for the welfare of subordinates is strongly rooted in Japanese management. Although the government has intervened to regulate the manager in the field of labor relations, it has nevertheless given strong encouragement to the paternalistic approach. Until recently, the labor organizations have been fairly weak at the enterprise level, and they have made only minor inroads into the area of managerial authority.[8]

And they go on to describe the system of lifelong employment:

> Industrial employment commonly has involved a life commitment to a single firm. Indeed, the non-temporary Japanese worker has been as

[7]*Ibid.,* p. 132.

[8]Clark Kerr, John T. Dunlop, Frederick H. Harbison, and Charles A. Myers, *Industrialism and Industrial Man* (Cambridge, Mass.: Harvard University Press, 1960), p. 131.

bound by custom to his employer as if he were in the closed circle of a preindustrial tribe. He would not think of seeking alternate employment, nor would his employer ever try to dismiss him. He has permanent membership in the enterprise.[9]

In these passages we can see a common understanding of the Japanese industrial relations as strongly paternalistic, reinforced by such elements as permanent employment and weak or docile enterprise unions. As Japan's economy grew vigorously during the 1960s, Japanese practitioners, and to some extent scholars as well, began to feel that these peculiarly Japanese elements, which had been regarded so far as quasi-feudal, were in fact conducive to economic efficiency. Indeed, the president of the Federation of Employers' Associations has described the practice of lifetime employment, length-of-service reward systems, and enterprise unionism as the "three sacred treasures" of Japanese industrial relations. Through these developments, the stereotype concept of Japanese industrial relations with three "special" elements has been firmly established and shared widely by both Western and Japanese observers.

It is important to note, however, that this line of thought is not the only interpretation of Japanese industrial relations, even within relatively limited samples of Western literature.

One should bear in mind that in the same year as the publication of Abegglen's book, Solomon B. Levine's *Industrial Relations in Postwar Japan*,[10] an important contribution to the study of Japanese industrial relations, was also published. This is indeed the most comprehensive report on the structure and working of Japanese industrial relations that has ever appeared in Western literature. But to the extent that Levine qualified carefully both universal and particular elements, structural and behavioral characteristics, as observable in Japanese industrial relations in the mid-1950s, and expressed them in a reasonable balance, the book gave, in spite of its reliable description, a somewhat less appealing impression to readers when compared to the sweeping generalization of Abegglen.

Several years later, a powerful assault was made against Abegglen's thesis from an economist's point of view by Koji Taira. His provocative articles were eventually consolidated in the form of a book, *Economic Development and the Labor Market in Japan*.[11] The major point of Taira's criticism is that the seemingly paternalistic labor management system in the Japanese factory originated, not in feudal relations in the preindustrial society, but rather from a rational economic calculus by employers in a phase of

[9]Kerr et al., *Industrialism*, p. 146.
[10]Solomon B. Levine, *Industrial Relations in Postwar Japan* (Champaign, Ill.: University of Illinois Press, 1958).
[11]Koji Taira, *Economic Development and the Labor Market in Japan* (New York: Columbia University Press, 1970).

modern industrial growth. By carefully documenting the fact that paternalistic labor–management emerged as late as World War I as a rational reaction of employers of major corporations to a chronic shortage of skilled workers and the resulting high turnover rates or low commitment, he denounced Abegglen's hypothesis, arguing that if it were true there should have existed industrial paternalism from the beginning of Japan's industrialization, of which there is no evidence. Taira further contends that, from the earliest stage of industrialization, the Japanese labor market has been quite flexible in such a way that neoclassical economic analysis applies quite well. In all, he demonstrated persuasively that the peculiar character of Japanese industrial relations is not so much a carry-over of the feudal society as a rational economic choice of employers.

Still another powerful criticism of Abegglen's thesis is contained in Robert Cole's highly informative and insightful report of his observation of Japanese factory workers, *Japanese Blue Collar: The Changing Tradition.*[12] Based on observations made while he was living in a workers' town and working in two factories—a small diecasting workshop in the downtown area and a medium size auto parts plant in the suburbs—he describes and analyzes intensively the actions and attitudes of workers, as well as the informal rules of the workshop. Quite unlike what Abegglen described as "family-like" relations, he discovered in almost every aspect of factory life elements of competition, conflict, power politics, and rational calculus, which show up, however subtly, in a different way under the different institutional setting of a Japanese factory. His report of his rich factual observations presents an eloquent critique of Abegglen's generalization.

In addition to these provocative books, a number of research studies have been published in English which help to deepen and enrich Westerners' information on Japanese industrial relations.[13] These reports provide much more accurate information on the structure and working of Japanese industrial relations than was available in the 1950s, even allowing for ongoing changes in industrial relations themselves. In spite of all these developments, a review of recent literature would nevertheless leave the reader with the impression that the influence of the "sacred treasures" is still dominant, though to somewhat less extent and in a more elaborated manner than Abegglen's original version.

[12]Robert E. Cole, *Japanese Blue-Collar: The Changing Tradition* (Berkeley, Calif.: University of California Press, 1971).

[13]Alice H. Cook, *Japanese Trade Unionism* (Ithaca, N.Y.: Cornell University Press, 1966); Robert Evans, Jr., *The Labor Economics of Japan and the United States* (New York: Praeger, 1971); Ronald Dore, *British Factory—Japanese Factory: The Origins of National Diversity in Industrial Relations* (Berkeley, Calif.: University of California Press, 1973); K. Okochi, B. Karsh, S. B. Levine, *Workers and Employers in Japan: The Japanese Employment Relations System* (Tokyo: University of Tokyo Press, 1973); Robert M. Marsh, and Hiroshi Mannari, *Modernization and the Japanese Factory* (Princeton, N.J.: Princeton University Press, 1976).

Recently two interesting works have been published on Japanese industrial relations: One is a lengthy paper written by Walter Galenson and the other a short monograph by the secretariat of the OECD.[14] These two papers share many commonalities in their background factors: Both authors are not so-called Japanologists, although they have deep interest in Japan; both papers are based on careful and extensive reading of existing literature on Japan; and both authors conducted interview research in Japan for several months. In other words, one may safely regard these two pieces of analysis as good representative samples of well-informed interpretation of Japanese industrial relations, which can be of great use to nonspecialist Western observers.

In terms of analysis, the two papers generally agree with the exception of one very important point. Both papers are in general agreement in describing and assessing the functions of the employment and reward systems, enterprise unions, and labor–management relations. But in terms of evaluating the viability of the Japanese industrial relations system, the two papers differ sharply.

To Galenson, a major factor in Japan's long delayed enrichment of social welfare facilities, relative to its level of economic development, is the Japanese labor unions' lack of power, which has made them unable to secure a fair share of the increased national resources for the working class. The failure of unionism in this respect, he thinks, will undermine the social and political stability of Japan. Based on this judgement, he suggests:

> Movement toward a Western labor market model is optimal for the future social stability of Japan. In saying this, we are not unmindful of unique elements in Japanese culture that may make complete covergence impossible. Present circumstances must be viewed in the context of the historical legacy, which has endowed the social system with many traditional elements. . . . Nevertheless, we feel that Western labor market organization has a good deal to offer in helping curb authoritarian tendencies in government and management and in providing consumption patterns that are more favorable to lower-income groups.[15]

The OECD's report stresses the role performed by what it calls the "fourth pillar," in addition to the aforementioned three sacred treasures, as an important factor in integrating the whole system and making it operate viably. Briefly, the fourth pillar may be expressed as "social norms within the

[14]Walter Galenson and Kōnosuke Odaka, "The Japanese Labor Market," in *Asia's New Giant: How the Japanese Economy Works*, eds. H. Patrick and H. Rosovsky (Washington, D.C.: The Brookings Institution, 1976). OECD, *The Development of Industrial Relations Systems: Some Implications of Japanese Experience* (Paris: Organization for Economic Cooperation and Development, 1977).

[15]Galenson, *Japanese Labor Market*, p. 670.

enterprise." The norms have three features: the enterprise as a community, the vertical relationship and reciprocal obligations, and the consensual system of decisionmaking. To the OECD the most influential factor that may well erode the stable basis of the traditional system of the four pillars is the change in the attitudes and values of young workers. Allowing for the possible impact of such changes, the report still predicts:

> This nation, renowned for its pragmatic adaptability, will find it possible to assimilate what seems to be the more individualistic and relaxed style of the new generation into the traditional structure that has helped to make the economic success story of the last 25 years. Some of the pillars of the present system may undergo change in the meantime and transition may not be painless but the result could be an even stronger and socially responsible structure than before.[16]

In view of the many similarities between these two papers, both in terms of background factors and of focused issues, this sharp difference in their conclusive evaluations is striking. If both papers captured the structure and working of the Japanese system accurately, a disparity of this magnitude on such an important point, namely the viability and stability of the Japanese system, would not have emerged. Therefore, either one of them is mistaken or both of them have erred in opposite directions. At any rate, this difference seems to suggest that there are considerable errors or biases in their analysis.

Although it is nearly impossible to pinpoint where and how such erroneous assessments or judgments were made, we suspect that the undue prevalence or popularity of the stereotype notion of Japanese industrial relations is perhaps responsible. By saying this, we do not mean that these authors have been preoccupied with, or excessively influenced by, the stereotype notion. Indeed, they both tried to go beyond this notion, and through logical exercise they came out with radically different, but quite unique, suggestions. But rather, what we are saying is that they made their assessments, too bravely perhaps, on the basis of information inadequate for such global predictions. But we do not mean that their means of data collection were deficient. As we noted earlier, their assessments are based on the most extensive reading of the existing literature in the Western languages. In other words, it is implied that so far the kind of information needed for an overall assessment of Japanese industrial relations has been lacking. And we suspect that this lack of information is closely related to the undue popularity of the stereotype. And, perhaps, the dominance of the stereotype concept in turn has blunted research efforts needed to collect more relevant information.

---

[16]OECD, *Development of Industrial Relations Systems*, p. 33.

What Has To Be Done?

It has been suggested that the types of information that are currently available in the existing literature are not adequate to draw overall predictions as to the future outcomes of Japanese industrial relations, as was attempted by Galenson and the OECD. The question arises then, as to what kinds of information we need to fill this gap?

Before enumerating what we ought to have, let us first examine what we already have. A review of existing Western language literature will show that we already have a sufficiently large amount of information on the systems of employment and compensation, how these systems are made up and how they work, as well as on the structure and functions of the enterprise unions, their leadership, finances, administration, and so on.[17]

A review of the literature would also convince one that not all Japanese workers enjoy employment tenure throughout their lifetime as the term "lifetime employment" connotes. Instead, only some categories of workers—less than half of the total employed—enjoy relatively stable employment status until they reach the age of compulsory retirement, which is between 55 and 60. Other categories of workers have a much less stable employment status: Among them are female workers, workers in small firms, temporary workers, subcontract workers, seasonal and part-time workers, and so forth.

On the aspect of compensation, whereas it is true that wages and salaries are differentiated primarily with age, length-of-service, and educational attainment, many studies have shown that the Japanese wage differential structure is not as irrational as Abegglen has asserted, when viewed from the standpoint of economic efficiency. Moreover, ample information is now available that shows that Japanese enterprise unions, quite unlike American company unions of the 1920s, do bargain vigorously in economic issues, as demonstrated by widespread wage negotiations. It is also known that enterprise unions themselves are a stiff restraint against employers who attempt to discharge member workers. In short, the existing literature gives us a much more accurate and realistic understanding of Japan's industrial relations than Abegglen's simplistic generalization of what are called the three sacred treasures.

With so much information available, how is it that there are such vastly different predictions as to the future course of Japanese industrial relations as Galenson's and the OECD's? It appears to indicate that the seemingly rich information is still not adequate for an accurate assessment of the stability and viability of the Japanese system. Although Galenson correctly captured

---

[17]Dore, *British Factory—Japanese Factory;* Galenson, *Japanese Labor Market;* and the Organization for Economic Cooperation and Development, *Manpower Policy in Japan* (Paris: OECD., 1973).

the structural and functional characteristics of enterprise unions, he never-theless failed to appropriately capture the values and attitudes of workers; the goals of unionism; the sense of achievement, fulfilmnt, disenchantment and frustration in the institutional setting of Japanese industries. This is probably a result of the lack of relevant data. Also, although the OECD paid much attention to values of workers, as exhibited, for example, by its extensive research and attitude surveys, the conceptualization of the fourth pillar is too optimistic and hypothetical. It apparently underestimates the forces of frustration and dissatisfaction, residing explicitly or implicitly at various levels of the industrial-relations structure, and their possible ties with political and ideological elements. To put it differently, Japanese workers are not as disappointed in and detached from enterprise unions as Galenson asserts, nor as self-actualized in happy and harmonious relations with employers as depicted by the OECD. Not only can one characterize the nature of industrial relations typologically, but one must recognize that the dominant nature itself may well change. Indeed, conflict and congru-ence, stability and instability in industrial relations are essentially dynamic phenomena, specified by a complex of factors that constantly unfold and diminish in the historical process of evolution.

Viewed in this way, the data available from the existing literature are in fact too limited to enable someone to conceptualize the dynamics of indus-trial relations adequately. Many of them are the reports of one-time sur-veys, or of research covering only a short period of observation, and often of a limited segment of the industrial society, from which generalization is not warranted. Historical research, on the other hand, often lacks analysis. Taira's work is a notable exception in this respect. But its viewpoint is unfortunately too one-sidedly anchored in market analysis and not really helpful in inducing insights into other important elements and forces that also involve in and generate the dynamics.

In our view, there are two major areas of research that have so far been relatively underdeveloped in the Western-language literature of Japanese industrial relations: (a) conflict and conflict resolution process, and (b) his-torical evolution process of unionism and industrial relations. Note, how-ever, that these areas have not been ignored. Instead, these are the problem areas that have attracted much attention. Those who are impressed by the "harmonious" relations in Japanese industry were necessarily interested in the former area, whereas those who emphasized the legacies of preindus-trial society inevitably concentrated on the latter area. But it is our conten-tion that neither area has been given sufficient analytic or systematic treat-ment. Although harmony and conflicts have been much discussed, the discussions have been largely impressionistic.[18] Although much has been

---

[18]There has been little systematic and rigorous analysis of the working of Japanese labor–management relations in the framework of conflict and conflict resolution processes.

accomplished in describing historical chronologies, little effort has been made to capture the evolutionary process analytically.

In this chapter, we shall attempt a first step in bringing progress to these areas, especially the latter, historical analysis. With the hope of provoking constructive discussions, we will present our hypothetical views on three aspects of the historical evolution of Japanese industrial relations: unionism, manpower development, and the role of the government.

Unionism and Its Achievements

Introduction

In evaluating the achievements that the Japanese labor movement has made so far, due consideration should be paid to two major factors: (a) the short history of Japanese unionism relative to that of Western nations, and (b) the set of environmental constraints that have surrounded the development of the Japanese labor movement.

The history of Japanese unionism is short compared to that of other advanced industrial countries. Before the end of the World War II, most of the unions that existed had won some form of recognition but did not perform collective bargaining functions. After the war, the labor movement picked up momentum and has grown spectacularly.[19] However, up to 1955, it had to go through difficult years of recovery and reconstruction in a defeated and devastated country. The political and economic situations in these years were not so favorable as to permit unionism to develop its full-fledged function. It was only after the start of spectacular postwar economic growth in the mid-1950s, which exerted a significant impact on the supply–demand balance of the labor market, that the Japanese unions occupied a favorable position from which to exercise their bargaining power vis-à-vis the government and the employers.

Another factor to be considered is a set of environmental constraints under which the labor movement was initiated and developed. By constraints we mean not only the "market context or budgetary constraint," "power context," and "status of actors" as conceptualized by John T. Dunlop, but also what might be termed the "cultural context or ideological

For instance, the fact that documents and records of the decisions of the Central and Regional Labor Relations Commissions have hardly been exploited by Western observers, who discuss much about the "harmony" in Japanese labor-management relations, indicates how nonsystematic and impressionistic their methodologies are to tackle the question which they propose to analyze.

[19] M. Sumiya, "The Emergence of Modern Japan" in Okochi et al., Workers and Employers in Japan (Princeton University Press, University of Tokyo Press, 1974), Chapter 2.

constraint."[20] This factor is particularly important for a non-Western society like Japan with its old and unique cultural traditions. For most Japanese, including the workers themselves, who were deeply rooted in the traditional value system of the society, the idea of "industrial democracy" was simply alien. Therefore, the process of adjustment naturally took a long time and was not without painful experiences.

In view of these two factors, which have been circumscribing union development in Japan, one may reasonably maintain that the poor evaluations of the achievements of Japanese unions in contrast to those of their Western counterparts may not be easily justified. To be sure, one may point out many anachronisms or defects associated with Japanese unions, but these are relatively minor when compared to the significant achievements they have made. Among the achievements worth noting are the: (a) rapid and steady expansion of union membership, (b) expansion of collective bargaining both in scope and dimensions, (c) general improvements in employment conditions such as wages, hours and fringe benefits, (d) institutionalization of employment security workers, (e) enlarged participation of workers in management decision-making, (f) formation of countervailing power against the conservative government, and (g) elevation of the status of workers in the social hierarchy.

Elements of Prewar Unionism

To understand the characteristics of current unionism and to capture appropriately the significance and implications of the achievements that the Japanese union movement has attained during the course of its development, it is necessary to have some knowledge of several notable characteristics associated with the prewar union movement. They are (a) leadership of intellectuals, (b) close linkage between unions and political parties, (c) ideological strife among unions, (d) employers' policy toward unionism, (e) emergence of enterprise unionism in large establishments, and (f) lack of legal protection for unionism.

Leadership of Intellectuals The leadership of the union movement in prewar Japan was largely provided by intellectuals imbued with some sort of reformist or revolutionary ideas. The first attempt to organize Japanese labor unions with the aim of performing a similar function to that of Western unions was made in 1897. One of the leaders of this early movement was Fusatarō Takano who was profoundly influenced by the American idea of craft unionism, and advocated an ideologically moderate unionism for skilled workers, concentrating on education and mutual help.

---

[20]John T. Dunlop, *Industrial Relations Systems* (Carbondale, Ill.: Southern Illinois University Press, 1958), Chapters 3 and 4.

The government, however, could not tolerate even such a moderate movement and virtually prohibited any social movement under the Public Peace Police Law in 1900. The revival of unionism was also initiated by intellectuals, such as Bunji Suzuki, a Tokyo University graduate who organized Yūaikai (Friendly Society) in 1912, which later developed into Rōdō Sōdōmei (General Federation of Labor), and Toyohiko Kagawa, a Christian evangelist. The movement was also joined by many leftist university students who performed active roles, mainly ideological, in the union movements. As unions grew, a new type of leader emerged, men who had risen from the blue-collar ranks. Most of them had developed their roots in the right-wing unions, unions that finally came together to establish the Nihon Rōdō Kumiai Kaigi (Japanese Congress of Trade Unions) in 1932, a federation which covered 80% of all union membership. Nevertheless, the leadership of intellectuals continued to exert a significant influence, particularly among leftist and middle-of-the-road factions.

Close Linkage between Unions and Political Parties   In the social and political climate of prewar Japan, which was antagonistic to the labor movement, the unions tended to associate closely with such political groups as the anarcho–syndicalists, socialists, and communists. Influence of anarcho–syndicalists was very strong in the labor movement prior to the Great Earthquake of 1923 and led to a bitter confrontation with socialist led Sodomei. However, with the assassination of Sakae Osugi, the prominent anarcho-syndicalist leader, amid the disorder caused by the earthquake, the strength of the syndicalists quickly faded away.

A new confrontation between socialists and communists developed with the introduction of universal suffrage in 1925. Rightist socialist, leftist socialist, and communist factions closely associated themselves with political parties, which aggravated the internal strife within the labor movement.

Ideological Strife among Unions   The prewar union movement and the socialist, communist, and other so-called proletarian political party movements were so closely tied together that a split in the parties immediately resulted in a union split and vice versa. This pattern of relationship between unions and political parties, with its highly ideological features, was basically inherited by the postwar labor movement and undermines union solidarity to this day.

Employers' Attitude and Policy Toward Unionism   With very few exceptions Japanese employers were generally hostile toward unionism. The very idea that workers would organize themselves and engage in concerted actions against employers was simply unacceptable to them. This notion was also shared by the government. Employers would like to handle their employee relations as a master-servant relationship within the pseudo-familial community of a particular enterprise, and they had strong feelings against the intrusion of union movements.

Emergence of Enterprise-Unionism in Large Establishments   In the 1920s, the works council, a form of employee representation encouraged by employers and the government, spread among many of the large public and private corporations. Leftist unions attempted in vain to convert such organizations into bona-fide unions. There was also a tendency among workers of large firms to organize themselves within the confines of the enterprise they belonged to. Such large corporations developed a complex internal labor market within which the so-called "*nenko*-system" or a set of rules that govern the allocation of labor force and the distribution of rewards was developed. Outside unions found it increasingly difficult to organize employees of such enterprises.

The unions developed after World War I may therefore be roughly classified into the following types: (*a*) craft and industrial unions, organizing mostly workers in small- and medium-sized firms. (The only exception in this category was the Japan Seamen's Union, a large industrial union that was able to take advantage of the open labor market and the common training system of the government-run schools.) And (*b*) vertical unions, which are equivalent to the enterprise unions in the post-World War II period, except that they were unions organizing, quite unlike their post-World War II counterparts, almost exclusively blue-collar employees. The status differentiation between blue- and white-collar employees was too high a barrier to organize both of them into the same union.

In the early 1930s, the vertical unions are estimated to have constituted nearly half of all union membership. Most of them, however, had been forced to dissolve shortly before the war. They were then re-organized as *Sampo,* a patriotic labor organization during the war, but after its end they were quick to revive as enterprise unions.

Lack of Legal Protection for Unionism   Before the end of World War II there was no legal protection for unionism in Japan. Instead, there were laws and administrative ordinances that either oppressed or restricted union activities. The most oppressive law was the Public Peace Police Law of 1900—Article 17 of this law made union activities illegal. This article was repealed in 1925 under the liberalistic atmosphere that was created after World War I. Attempts were also made to give some protection to workers' rights to organize and to bargain collectively; several trade union bills were introduced in 1926 and 1931. However, none of them were passed; instead, the Labour Dispute Mediation Act was enacted in 1926. The political tendency for liberalism was soon to disappear as Japan became more involved in military expansionism from 1931 on, leaving ever decreasing room for the legal protection of unionism.

Structure and Functions of Postwar Enterprise Unionism

Immediately after the end of World War II in August 1945, union organizations mushroomed quickly throughout the country, as we will review in detail later. This amazing growth was in part encouraged by a series of crucial legal reforms, such as the Trade Union Law (1945), the new Constitution (1947), and the policy of the Supreme Commander of the Allied Powers (SCAP) all of which favored unionization, and was in part necessitated by the dire necessity of workers to protect their economic lives in the devastated land.

Except for a few organizations, almost all the unions organized during this period were enterprise unions or more correctly "enterprisewide" unions. Ever since the abrupt emergence of postwar unionism, the enterprise union has been the most popular form of the basic unit of union organization. According to a survey of union organizational forms conducted by the Ministry of Labor, enterprise unions accounted for approximately 90% of the unit unions and 80% of total union membership during the postwar period. Let us therefore examine in some detail the structural and functional characteristics of this type of union.

The features of enterprise unions are (a) membership eligibility is confined to the regular employees of a particular enterprise; (b) in general, both blue and white-collar employees are organized in a single union; (c) the functionaries of the union are regular employees of the enterprise who are assigned to union business—they are paid by the union but retain their employee status. (Like many locals of industrial unions in the United States, enterprise unions in the private sector in Japan rarely have professional leaders.) And (d) the sovereignty of unions almost exclusively rests at the level of enterprise unions.

While many enterprise unions affiliate with industrywide federations, they have retained their independence, and the controlling or regulating power of the federal organizations over them has been quite limited. Along with the development of *shuntō* (i.e., the united unions' spring wage offensive, which will be discussed later), the authority and control of federal organizations has noticeably increased in recent years and the dependence of enterprise unions on federal organizations for various services has also increased. However, unions are still largely decentralized with the enterprise unions retaining their administrative autonomy.[21]

For example, enterprise unions have complete freedom from the con-

---

[21]For trade-union structure, see Solomon B. Levine *Industrial Relations in Postwar Japan* (Urbana, Ill.: University of Illinois Press Urbana, 1958). Chapter 4.

trol of upper organization to make vital decisions. They can make and change their constitutions, elect their own officers and functionaries, initiate strike actions and terminate them. Of particular importance is their autonomy in financial matters. Enterprise unions freely decide the amount of union dues as well as the proportion to pay to the federal organization. The industrial federations, the local councils, and the national centers to which enterprise unions affiliate decide their monthly per capita assessment. However, it is up to the enterprise union to register the number of members who should pay the required per capita. Unions tend to under-register in order to pay less to the federal organization, although this practice has been improving noticeably as the leadership and authority of the latter has become more established.

Actually, Japanese labor unions are relatively rich. The average amount of regular monthly dues per member was ¥872 in 1972. The Ministry of Labor estimated that in 1971 the figure increased to ¥1600 in 1975, representing about 1.3% of a workers' average regular monthly earnings. It should be remembered that beside regular monthly dues the Japanese unions generally collect contributions for strike benefits, for compensation for victimization, and for the unions' own welfare services.[22]

Therefore, the total amount of members' contributions is considerably higher than it would at first appear and is becoming very close to that of American unions. Moreover, because of enterprise unionism, their income stability is highly secured. The check-off system for collecting union dues is very popular, but even without it unions are generally in a favorable position to collect dues at the workshop level because of the freedom of union activities within plants or establishments.

There is a problem, however, with the inefficient way union money is spent. Because of the autonomy of enterprise unions, unions have to finance their management and activities almost on their own. They have to provide and support full-time functionaries and employees from their own budgets. Actually, the ratio of full-time union officials to the number of union members is very high in Japan, providing one full-time functionary for about every 500 members at the level of enterprise unions, perhaps higher than American industrial unions. The administrative expenses of enterprise unions are generally so high that they cannot afford to pay much to their federal organizations, usually no more than 10% of regular union dues on an average. This distributive pattern of union finance certainly undermines the strength of unions as a whole and circumscribes the scope and dimension of union activities.[23]

---

[22] According to a survey of union dues conducted by the Institute of Social Problems in Asia, the average monthly union dues was as high as 2,400 yen, roughly more than ten U.S. dollars. However, the unions covered by this survey are of relatively large size as compared with those covered by the survey by the Ministry of Labor.

[23] cf. Jack Stieber, *Governing the U.A.W.* (New York: Wiley, 1962), pp. 92–93.

Rationale of Enterprise Unionism

To foreigners, enterprise unionism may appear to be a strange form of workers' organization. For most professional labor leaders in prewar Japan, particularly those of Sōdōmei who resumed their activities right after the end of the war, the rapid spread of enterprise unionism was also unexpected and unwelcome. Moreover, most scholars have been more or less critical of this type of unionism and many of them have even identified this type of union with the "company union" as conceptualized in the United States. Even many incumbent leaders of today's unions often criticize enterprise unions and advocate industrial unionism such as that developed in the United States and West Germany.

However, it cannot be overemphasized that this form of union organization has been that of the workers' own choosing. To be sure, quite a number of unions existed during the occupation that were organized on the encouragement or even the initiative of management. However, in most cases these were largely a result of the ignorance or inexperience of the workers in organizing and managing unions. Unquestionably the overwhelming majority of unionists voluntarily associated themselves into this form of organization.

For Japanese workers the enterprise union was the only, and most natural, form of organization because their basic common interest as industrial workers had been formulated within an individual enterprise. This is particularly true in large enterprises where the basic conditions of employment, including wages and welfare facilities, are determined within their highly structured and self-contained internal labor markets. Even most workers in medium- and small-enterprises, where internal labor markets are much less structured, tend to organize themselves primarily into enterprise unions because they find it is the most workable way of forming and maintaining their unions.

Still another important factor that characterizes Japanese enterprise unions is the active participation of white-collar workers with their blue-collar counterparts. In the midst of the devastation and the miserable conditions of living that existed at the end of World War II, it was necessary not only for blue-collar, but also for white-collar workers to fight through the crisis by joining unions. Except in industries such as coal-mining, where the status differentiation between blue-collar and white-collar workers was too distinct to organize both into a single union, white-collar workers continued to join enterprise unions together with blue-collar workers. This turned out to be advantageous for Japanese unionism by maintaining a steady growth in membership throughout the postwar period without being adversely affected, unlike some other industrial countries, by changes in industrial structure, technology, and manpower development.

White-collar workers, on the other hand, provided an important resource of union leadership. The intellectual white-collar leaders in the postwar era, unlike their prewar counterparts, came largely from the ranks of the employees of the company. Among them, however, two major types are identifiable.

One is the dissatisfied and leftist inclined white-collar leader. There had been in prewar Japan a rigid status differentiation, not only between blue-collar and white-collar workers, but among the latter themselves. This status differentiation was particularly distinct within big enterprises, both private and public, as well as in the civil services. Those white-collar workers who did not have a college-level educational background, graduates from non-first-class universities, those who had been hired at an irregular time of the year, those who were not eligible for promotion for one reason or another, all of these more or less dissatisfied white-collar employees often took the leadership of the union movement, inspired by radical or revolutionary ideas such as communism or leftist socialism. This type of intellectual leadership characterized the movement of Sanbetsu-Kaigi (Congress of Industrial Unions) right after the war, as well as in some unions in the public sector, which has continuously constituted the major strength of *Sōhyō* (General Council of Trade Unions in Japan) the largest national center at present.

On the other hand, it also frequently happens that white-collar employees with more realistic ideas and stronger identification with the enterprise they belong to take the leadership of enterprise unions. In many private large corporations, union leadership was assumed by those white-collar employees with advanced educational backgrounds and promising prospects for entering the managerial elite. There have been many cases where, during prolonged strikes, the latter type of leadership has taken over from that of the former type by forming a break-away union (the so-called *daini kumiai*, or "second union")—a symptom of the organizational frailty of enterprise unionism.

At any rate, the intellectual, white-collar leadership unquestionably provides enterprise unionism with greater expertise in formulating union policies than would otherwise be available, but it also produces many ideological conflicts among union officials and their membership.

Union Goals and Achievements

In discussing the goals and achievements of postwar unionism, we would like to emphasize particularly the following two aspects: (*a*) the unions' goal and orientation toward egalitarianism, and (*b*) the employment security of member workers.[24]

---

[24]For the concept of egalitarianism and hierarchy in the Japanese cultural context see Edwin O. Reischauer, *The Japanese* (Cambridge, Mass.: The Belknap Press of Harvard University Press, 1977), pp. 157–166.

One of the basic characteristics of the union movement in postwar Japan was its strong orientation to egalitarianism. Reflecting the dissatisfaction, as well as the aspiration, of workers who had been regarded and treated unduly low in the prewar "status society," most of the union demands after the war were strongly tinted with egalitarianism. One of the most popular union targets at that time was "democratization of management," by which was meant, among other things, the abolition of the status system within enterprises, or at least the drastic narrowing of differentials between employees of different status in terms of wages, salaries, and welfare facilities. Non-elite white-collar employees concurred with blue-collar workers in such demands. For example, when wages were negotiated an increasingly greater weight was put on such determining factors as age, seniority, and number of dependents, so that wage or salary differentials between different trades or occupations within an enterprise tended to be narrowed at the expense of the more highly educated white-collar employees. At present, for the overwhelming majority of Japanese unionists, leaders and rank-and-file alike, the word "democracy" is a synonym for "equality," so that it is often quite difficult for a particular group of workers, such as skilled trades, technicians, and professionals, to insist on their sectional interests and be recognized as legitimate policymakers of the unions to which they belong. Another example that should be noted is that unions have demanded and successfully acquired biannual bonuses for every regular employee irrespective of his status within the enterprise. In prewar Japan, blue-collar and low-status white-collar employees received a sum of money twice a year in addition to their regular pay, but this was totally different from the biannual bonuses given only to white-collar employees with advanced educational backgrounds that were, in effect, a kind of profit-sharing.

This egalitarian orientation of Japanese unionism has been consistently maintained. Structural changes in the labor market in recent years, particularly the shortage of young blue-collar workers and the over-supply of college and university graduates, have tended to validate the unions' egalitarianistic demands. One of the notable achievements of the Japanese union movement is that the "salary status" of blue-collar workers has been remarkably reinforced.

Another important goal of the Japanese union movement has been the employment security of member workers. Indeed, employment security has been more important than mere improvements in wages and hours. It is true that Japan is an industrial society in which the dismissal of workers is the hardest decision that management must face. Workers, once hired as regular employees, are expected to commit themselves to the firm and to cooperate with other members for the maintenance and prosperity of the enterprise. Employers, on the other hand, try their best to avert dismissals, even at the cost of financial disadvantage. This is the employment practice that has been more or less strongly established among large- and middle-sized firms.

This employment practice is widely known in the Western world as a peculiar Japanese labor practice that is strongly bound by cultural traditions. It means that an employee would not think of leaving his employer, and the employer in turn would not even try to dismiss him under the system of "lifetime commitment."[25]

The facts are quite contrary to this misleading conception. Japanese employers do dismiss workers, and they have exercised their discretion to do so whenever they have found no other alternative. Of course, the employer tries to keep the valuable manpower that he has developed through the firm's internal training system. Another important factor behind the employer's reluctance to discharge large numbers of employees is the anticipated costs he will have to bear in case of the union's resistance. This is one of the major reasons why most large corporations, with their large-scale labor redundancies, did not take the step of mass discharge during the prolonged recession of 1973–1976.

Although Japanese unions are moderate in such industrial actions as slowdowns and strikes, once a dispute concerning mass dismissal occurs, they fight most bitterly, often causing protracted work stoppages that continue for hundreds of days. There have been many examples in the postwar period, especially in the late 1950s when redundancy dismissals frequently took place in the process of reconstruction of the economy under recurrent recessions after the Korean War.

Unions fight fiercely against dismissals because employment security is regarded as a vested right of regular employees, and thus a dismissal is a betrayal of employees' trust in management. Moreover, the fact that under the *nenkō* system discharged workers can rarely obtain jobs with rewards equivalent to those that they enjoyed in their former employment tends to intensify the situation. Discharged workers incur great losses, not only in terms of wages but also fringe benefits such as pensions, retirement allowances, and paid vacations, which have been so formulated as to encourage long-term commitment to a particular firm. If workers have little transferrable skill, like coal miners, their resistance against dismissal becomes desperate. The energy revolution in Japan in the early 1960s brought about a battle in some coal mine areas in 1960 and 1961.

Eventually employers may formally win the disputes. However, the costs involved and losses entailed are great, and often irretrievable. The repeated experience of such prolonged and bitter strikes against discharge has made Japanese employers in general very cautious and reluctant to attempt a mass discharge. Instead, they tend to adopt the less drastic

---

[25]Kerr, C., Dunlop, J. T., Harbison, F., and Myers, C., *Industrialism and Industrial Man* (Cambridge, Mass.: Harvard University Press, 1960), p. 172.

methods of manpower curtailment through shorter hours, attrition, transfer, and the voluntary resignation for premium severance pay. In Japan it is taken for granted that employers should assist those employees who have resigned to find new and suitable employment.

In this way, the unions' efforts for the employment security of members has certainly so entrenched the practice of long-term employment that employers can hardly infringe it arbitrarily. To be sure, one cannot find any collective agreement clause that explicitly refers to the long-term employment security of employees. Nevertheless, this practice has been increasingly taken for granted by not only the parties but by society as a whole.

The employment security that unions pursue is not confined to protection from discharge. In the process of rapid economic growth, although the number of cases of mass discharge has been reduced appreciably, cases of intraplant and interplant transfers have increased substantially, as a result of technological change and industrial relocation that often adversely affected workers' interests and employment opportunities. Issues relating to transfers such as wages, housing, transportation, education, and incurred expenses have been increasingly taken up in union–management negotiations and have resulted in better protection of the workers' interests.

Manpower Development and Japanese Industrial Relations

Introduction

The objective of this section is to discuss our second point of emphasis, namely, the impact of manpower development strategies adopted in a relatively early stage of industrialization, which, whether intended or not, played an important role in forming the peculiar characteristics of current Japanese industrial relations.

A brief summary of the points of discussion is in order: The first half of this section describes how manpower strategies have been developed by entrepreneurs, as well as by the government, in response to the given environmental constraints, especially of labor market conditions in an early phase of industrialization. The latter half elaborates the notable characteristics of Japanese industrial relations that have been affected most significantly by such manpower development strategies.

By examining the relationship between demand–supply conditions in the market of skilled labor on the one hand and the reactions of employers on the other, we have concluded that the seemingly "paternalistic" labor management system in modern large corporations is rooted in an economically rational response of employers to the severe shortage of desired types of labor. This system, which became prevalent during the interwar period, contained as an integral part the scheme of intrafirm training and promotion. In making such private manpower strategies work effectively, the role of the government was also crucial in developing modern industries and public educational systems, and in providing basic technical training through military service.

The latter half of the discussion is devoted to specifying the relationships between conspicuous characteristics of Japanese labor–management relations and manpower development strategies. In particular, three points are discussed (*a*) the system of internal training and promotion that has resulted in the emphasis on integration within the corporate community, since workers can find a source of common interest only within the same firm; (*b*) the process of skill acquisition that has been internalized within a firm, committing workers to rely more on the firm, and (*c*) the principle of egalitarianism that has been stressed since the end of World War II by enterprise unions.

Strategies of Manpower Development: A Rational Choice
under Market Constraints

Manpower development has been a keen and persistent need that Japan has faced from the very beginning of her industrialization. The strategies of manpower development adopted and pursued by employers, as well as by the government, were simply the results of their rational reactions to the given needs and constraints.

One of the most basic and perhaps the most important, factor that determined the type and course of manpower development strategies was the structure and condition of the labor market. Since the Japanese economy was largely agrarian in the last quarter of the nineteenth century, there existed only a very small free-labor reserve that could be mobilized for industrial work. Although considerable ambiguities remain associated with the statistical estimates of employment in these years, the proportion of agricultural employment to the total is estimated to be on the order of 70–80% (see Tables 5.1 and 5.4).[26]

More important than this statistical view are the characteristics of employment behind it. The existence of a large volume of agricultural labor did not necessarily mean that a large pool of potential labor was available for the newly developing nonagricultural industries. Because substantial improvements in agricultural productivity had been made in the preceding

---

[26]There is a rather large difference between Umemura's estimates of around 70% and Ohkawa's and Nakajima's estimates of around 80%. The paucity of reliable original data is the major obstacle for estimation of this period.

periods, there is good reason to believe that the employment conditions of the bulk of agricultural labor force were sufficiently above the minimum subsistence level.[27] There is also reason to suspect that many of the farm households were engaged not only in agricultural production, but also in manufacturing and commerce.[28] And to the extent that these supplementary activities were inextricable from the principal activity of farm households, there was in fact less labor available from agriculture for use in modern industries that might at first appear.

This may give some readers the strong impression that the Japanese economy went through an epochal structural change at some stage of economic development, say around the late 1950s, going from a condition of unlimited labor supply à la Lewis to one of labor shortage. This thesis was put forth most clearly by Minami.[29] What this notion implies is that the Japanese economy was able to enjoy unlimited supplies of labor during the period prior to the time when the economy passed a certain crucial stage of structural change. Although there is controversy as to when in the process of economic development such a structural change took place, it is implied that at some early stage of industrialization the supply of labor was limitless or very elastic.

On the contrary, what our earlier discussion noted is that the supply of labor was quite inelastic, at least in the short-run, even from the very beginning of Japanese industrialization. To put it more strongly it may be suggested that Japan passed the stage of development with unlimited supplies of labor, if it existed at all, long before she entered the period of modern industrialization in the mid-nineteenth century. The outspoken proponent of such a view is Taira.[30]

We are neither in the position, nor are we prepared, to referee these conflicting views.[31] But it is important to note, aside from the question as to whether or not the Japanese labor market was of "neoclassical" nature, that there are ample records and materials to suggest that in the early phase of industrialization employers had difficulty securing the desired amount and quality of labor force. Moreover, because of the shortage of industrial labor relative to demand, employers suffered from high turnover and the low commitment of workers, particularly of the skilled groups. This phenomenon was not limited to the early phase of industrialization. Employers

---

[27]Koji Taira, *Economic Development and the Labor Market in Japan* (New York: Columbia University Press, 1970).

[28]Mataji Umemura, "Sangyō-betsu Koyō no Hendō: 1880–1940" [Changes in Employment by Industrial Sectors: 1880–1940] *Keizai Kenkyū* [Economic Studies] 24, no. 2 (April 1973): 108.

[29]Ryōshin Minami, *The Turning Point in Economic Development: Japan's Experience* (Tokyo: Kinokuniya Bookstore Co., Ltd., 1973).

[30]Taira, *Economic Development*.

[31]Minami, *Turning Point in Economic Development;* and Taira *Economic Development.*

have recurrently encountered severe shortages of the desired types of labor, from 1915 to 1919, when the Japanese economy was booming under the impact of World War I; in the late 1930s and early 1940s, when industrial production expanding rapidly in the shift toward a wartime economy; and in the 1960s and early 1970s, when the economy was climbing the steep path of miraculously rapid economic growth. In other words, employers have suffered from labor shortages whenever increases in labor demand were greater than increases in supply during phases of rapid economic expansion. In these periods wages rose rapidly, usually with a narrowing of their differentials, as will be considered later in detail.

These cyclical fluctuations have given at various phases important impulses to employers and workers to modify their policies and attitudes. A most significant development in the Japanese labor management system took place during the World War I boom, and its impact has determined the basic nature of labor–management relations in subsequent periods. To express the change in brief, employers, particularly of large corporations, public as well as private, in selected industries where reliance on skilled labor was relatively high, began to institute the intrafirm training system as an integral part of the newly developed labor-management system.

This important innovation in the labor-management system did not take place all at once, but was gradually adopted by different branches of industry. In some industries, such as iron and steel, shipbuilding, and machine manufacturing, attempts to build such a system were made before World War I. One may note in this respect the leading role played by the government-managed, or public, corporations such as naval shipyards and iron and steel mills, where attempts to establish internal training systems started even before the turn of the century. But the number of such corporations was very small, and they were more of an exception than a rule in the general climate of labor–management policies prevailing before World War I. It was only after the end of the war that the system of internal training and promotion spread broadly among a number of large corporations and was accepted as a crucial part of the complex of labor-management systems.

This innovation was a rational reaction of employers to the labor market constraints at the time. Since a reserve of skilled labor suitable for modern industries was virtually absent at an early stage of industrialization, employers had to secure necessary labor services from the scarce supply of indigenous craftsmen whose skills were applicable or transferable to modern industries. These skilled workers were not only few in number, but often qualified to work with modern technology. Moreover, much of the labor-management function was controlled by master craftsmen, who distributed jobs and rewards among their clients. In effect, the employer managed labor problems only indirectly, through the hands of these master craftsmen. Whereas the supply of such skilled labor had been consistently scarce throughout the period of growing modern industries, the abnormal increase in demand during World War I aggravated the labor shortage until employers were constantly plagued by high turnover, rapid attrition, worrysome absenteeism, low commitment, and sometimes even dishonest infringement of labor contracts by workers.

Faced with such disturbances, it was only natural that employers wished to establish a training system and a framework of labor management under their own control. Aimed not only at building the desired amount and quality of labor force through internal training, the direct labor–management system was planned to secure an uninterrupted flow of efficient labor services by assuring the commitment and loyalty of employees through a variety of wage and nonwage means. Included among these means were housing, education, recreational facilities, health care, loans and credits, employer involved mutual-aid systems, recruitment, manning and promotion policies, and allowances and retirement-pay systems that were designed to induce the stronger commitment of workers to the firm.

It should be added that similar developments in labor–management practices in the direction of enriching the nonwage or "paternalistic" aspects had been achieved somewhat earlier in the textile industry, where dependence on skilled labor was not as high as in the metal-related industries. Although emphasis on skill development may be different, these developments in labor-management practices have also occurred basically for the same reason, namely, to secure the needed amount and intensity of labor services.

In general, it must be clear that the seemingly paternalistic labor-management system in Japanese industries finds its origin basically in the rational economic calculus of entrepreneurs in response to economic constraints in the first quarter of this century. The very emergence of the "paternalistic" labor–management practice in modern industries in this period precludes the hypothesis that the major explanatory variable that characterizes Japanese labor–management relations is the traditional values in premodern Japanese society.[32]

Equally important, side by side with the active role played by employers was the role of the government in manpower development in its broad sense. It was often with the help of governmental policies and government-initiated programs that the manpower development strategies of private industry worked effectively. For our concerns, three types of achievement deserve mention: (*a*) initiation of modern industry and the within-industry manpower development programs, (*b*) development of the

---

[32]Robert E. Cole, "The Theory of Institutionalization: Permanent Employment and Tradition in Japan." *Economic Development and Cultural Change* 20 (October 1971): 47–70.

public education system, and (*c*) development of manpower resources by the military.

The first point has already been touched upon in our discussion of the initiation of internal training systems in government-managed factories in heavy industries. Moreover, it should be added that to promote rapid diffusion of modern industry, the government sponsored a number of plants and corporations at the initial stage of industrialization, which were later transferred to private industrialists. But a more fundamental factor that helped the rapid diffusion of modern technology and the broad proliferation of industrial skills was the development of an effective public education network throughout the country. Only through a highly developed educational system promulgating modern industrial knowledge could a labor force with the necessary degree of sophistication and discipline be created from the largely agrarian population. Furthermore, the impact of military training should not be dismissed. In addition to its principal purpose, the military also provided both technical training and rigorous mental and physical discipline to young potential workers.[33]

Although the direct-control system of labor management with a built-in training function was established and spread among a good number of large corporations after World War I, its prevalence was still limited to a minor portion of the entire economy. In the interwar period of 1920s and 1930s, in contrast to the late 1910s, excess supply generally prevailed in the labor market. However, this system of labor management, which was born in the period of labor shortage, did not lose its effectiveness. It appears that the system was reinforced rather partly because of the increased commitment of workers to the firm under the ingrowing threat of unemployment and partly because skilled labor was still in short supply, probably owing to the appreciable technological progress in this period, as exemplified by remarkable development in the electric power and chemical industries.

By the late 1930s, when demand for labor began to expand rapidly again, it seemed that the system had developed its roots firmly in the soil of the corporative community of large enterprises. The experience of *Sampō* (an association of employees dedicated to serve the purpose of the nation through enhanced industrial activity) during the war reinforced employee solidarity within a firm rather than undermining it. The system continued throughout the Japanese industrial world, except for the sector of small firms, alongside the rapidly growing enterprise-union movement.

---

[33]In many heavy-industry plants such as, for example, steel mills and military arsenals, an employment practice was adopted whereby the employer gave initial training to young workers, and then, after their return from two years of military service, promoted them to full-fledged employees.

Impact of Manpower Development Strategies on Japanese
Industrial Relations

In the preceding discussion, we have ascertained that the manpower development strategies adopted by both employers and government as rational reactions to economic constraints and labor market conditions early in the twentieth century played a crucial role in formulating the innovative "paternalistic" labor-management system, which has had a profound impact on the basic characteristics of Japanese labor-management relations. However, we have not elaborated which facets of labor-management relations were influenced most significantly and in what way.

Among the various notable features associated with Japanese labor-management relations, there are three outstanding items that we would like to underline: (a) emphasis on integration of the corporate community within an individual enterprise, (b) inward orientation and commitment of workers to the firm, and (c) egalitarianism. Historically, all of these characteristics have been formed in close connection with the strategies of manpower development in the process of industrialization.

It is important to note, however, that those who planned and initiated manpower-development strategies do not seem to have had any particular intention to steer labor-management relations in order to foster such characteristics. When Japan's long seclusion was broken in the mid-nineteenth century, she found herself in the midst of the menacing major powers of the world. It is not surprising that under such circumstances the new Meiji government put the highest priority on building quickly both military power and the economic base needed to sustain it. The most pressing task, therefore, was to industrialize the country. Manpower development was an important prerequisite to achieving this goal. Rapid accumulation of capital and an efficient and docile labor force were all that the government and industries needed. No labor movements that might interfere with the desired pace of capital accumulation were welcomed. The government and the industrialists would not have thought much beyond this, at such an early stage of industrialization, in terms of forming industrial relations. Indeed, whereas on the one hand the government quickly established one of the most developed educational systems in the world in order to develop a skilled labor force, on the other hand it consistently oppressed labor movements. Japanese industrial relations nevertheless developed their peculiar characteristics as the dynamic process of industrialization proceeded, and prevailed widely, after World War II. They were the unexpected outcome of industrialization and manpower development strategies.

The first notable feature of Japanese labor-management relations, namely, integration within the corporate community, is closely related to two factors: (*a*) manpower development strategies that prevailed in the interwar period, and (*b*) post-World War II unionism. As discussed earlier, there was hardly any basis for integration of employees, especially among blue-collar workers, during the early period of industrialization when firms were dependent on a highly mobile labor force, managing them only through indirect control. It was only after the development of intrafirm training and direct labor-management systems that employees began to be integrated within the confines of individual enterprises. The system of internal training implies that the process of skill acquisition by workers, which had been left largely to spontaneous learning in the external labor market, is now internalized within the structured organization of a firm. As the internal training system develops, a routine pattern of employment and allocation of labor force also develops. The firm recruits workers who need not have any skills from external labor markets, trains them within the firm, allocates them to places within the firm where they were fitted in, promote them whenever vacancies emerge that are suitable for them to fill, and retires them when they reach a certain age. Unlike the systems used in the past, in this system the firm maintains complete control throughout the process. This is a typical picture of the working of the "internal labor market."

Incorporated into such a system, workers can find sources of common interest solely within individual firms and are cut off from external sources of possible unification. To the extent that active unionism had been ruled out of large firms prior to World War II, such isolation and segmentation of workers was inevitably reinforced. In other words, workers within a firm were integrated around the common interest conditioned basically by the internalization of the skill acquisition process, and this has become an important characteristic of Japanese labor-management relations. However, blue- and white-collar employees were rarely integrated before World War II because they shared little interest mutually. The impact of postwar unionism was crucial in extending the scope of integration to encompass blue- as well as white-collar workers within the same corporate community.

The second point, namely, the fact that employees are inward looking and committed to an individual firm, is also deeply related to the scheme of intrafirm manpower development. That is, under the system of internal training and promotion the occupational career of a worker would have to be enclosed within the internal labor market of a firm, with slim possibilities of development outside the firm. This would naturally oblige workers to commit themselves to a particular firm throughout their careers, since it is optimal for them to stay on in a firm rather than to change employers. This tendency was reinforced during the interwar period under the increased pressure of a slack labor market. Although labor turnover increased again during the late 1930s under the influence of a wartime economy, the basis of a worker's commitment to an individual firm has not been seriously eroded.

To put it another way, the worker in effect vests his basic and most essential property with the firm, his capacity to perform a job. He owes both his skill and his job to the same firm. He cannot therefore claim his job property right independently of his firm. This characterizes the economic basis of enterprise unionism in the postwar period.

The third point, egalitarianism, is largely the result of postwar union movements. Although one could trace the roots of some form of egalitarianism back to feudal communities, what made egalitarianism in its highly generalized form, encompassing a wide range of workers from managerial employees in the office to rank-and-file operatives on the shop floor, actually work was the vigorous union movements that flamed up right after World War II. The movements were encouraged by the then highly Japanized notion of "democracy," that is, outright egalitarianism across the board. Let us quickly add here, to avoid possible misunderstanding, that this egalitarianism prevails among so-called "regular" blue- as well as white-collar employees and does not extend to cover nonregular or temporary workers.

This may be interpreted, perhaps, as a massive and explosive reaction to the rigid status system that had governed society and industry during the prewar period. Since discussion of unionism is left to later sections of this chapter, let us here merely point to some notable impacts of egalitarianism on postwar labor-management relations.

The most significant impact was the fact that blue-collar workers have come to be treated practically on an equal basis with their white-collar counterparts in terms of employment, pay, and other fringe benefits, as far as they are regular employees of the same company. Blue-collar workers can enjoy an approximately equivalent degree of employment security as the white-collar workers enjoy. Although it is easy to grant such employment security to all employees in periods of expanding demand for labor, it becomes infeasible when demand shrinks. The economically rational firm, therefore, has to have some form of safety valve, such as workers employed on a temporary basis. Curiously, enterprise unions do not claim that "egalitarianism" covers such a stratum of workers. Egalitarianism has been important in uniting employees regardless of their occupational status, but only to the extent that they are "regular" employees of the company. In terms of wages, too, equalization has proceeded considerably, both in terms of salary status and wage rates. The peculiarity of the length-of-service reward system is found not only in the periodical increment in wages, but also in the small variance of wage rates given in regard to length of service and age. This narrow dispersion of wages for workers of the same age and length-of-service group is not unrelated to the persistent emphasis on egalitarianism by union movements. In addition, the role of age in determining the earnings of workers grew in importance after the war, partly as a result of the strong demand of unions for what they called "living wages" that meet the minimum life-cycle needs of working families.

To sum up, institutional and behavioral characteristics of Japanese industrial relations today have been created historically under the strong influences of manpower strategies developed in the interwar period and the egalitarianism of enterprise unionism after World War II.

The Role of the Government

Introduction

Throughout the whole process of industrialization in Japan, the government played the leading role in the field of labor. Three aspects of this will be discussed here: (*a*) the development of manpower resources, (*b*) the protection of workers and employment conditions, and (*c*) the labor unions and collective bargaining. Insofar as manpower development is concerned, the government has been on the whole successful in meeting the manpower requirement for the progress of industrialization. The core of the government's manpower policy has been a broad approach to education at various levels. But in the field of worker protection, including social security measures, the government's policy and achievements lagged behind the level of other industrialized countries in the prewar period. However, after the war, many remarkable improvements were made in this regard. It was only after the war that the government took positive steps toward encouraging a free labor union movement. But, the relationship between the government, which has continuously been in the hands of the conservative party, and the unions in the public sector has been characterized by protracted controversies that are yet to be solved.

Development of Manpower Resources

For the Japanese government after the Meiji restoration, it was of paramount importance to transform the traditional feudal society into a modern industrial state in the shortest possible period of time. One of the government's basic strategies for achieving this goal was the development of manpower resources through rapid spread of primary education among the people. Four-year education was made compulsory in 1874 and was extended to 6 years in 1908. The people responded to the policy with enthusiasm, so by the beginning of the twentieth century, the rate of males aged 6–10 years enrolled in school reached 95% and that of females, 90%. The government, both central and prefectural, also played a more prominent role in providing education at the secondary and advanced levels than did private institutions. Besides general education, the government also ran various vocational schools and colleges for such industries as railway, shipping, fishery, postal, and telecommunications.

It is also noteworthy that access to those government-run educational institutions was completely open to any male with the ability to pass the entrance examination and to manage the expenses. The tuition in these schools, colleges, and universities was generally low relative to the general level of income and even free in the case of teachers' colleges. This fact contributed greatly to the social mobility of the people and made Japanese society more competitive than that of most of European countries.[34]

After World War II, the system of national education was drastically changed by the pressure of the American occupation forces. Compulsory education was extended to 9 years and a coeducational system was widely introduced. New universities and colleges sprang up to meet the increased demand of young people for higher education. In 1960, among the total number of school graduates, the proportion of those from junior high schools was 53.4%; from senior high schools 37.4%; and from colleges and universities, 9.3%. In 1975 the corresponding figures were 9.2%, 57.9% and 32.9%, respectively. As the overwhelming majority of the newly founded colleges and universities were private institutions, most of them inadequately staffed and financed, the general degradation of the quality of education at this level was inevitable. With the stagnant economic growth caused by the oil crisis in 1973, the oversupply of college or university graduates has become a new problem in the labor market, the full impact of which is not yet fully realized.

On the other hand, the shortage of skilled blue-collar workers has been acutely felt, particularly among middle- and small-sized industries. As in prewar Japan, the vocational training of workers has been largely dependent on inplant training by individual enterprises. However, the government has played a more active role than in the past in the field of vocational training and retraining of workers, in order to enlarge employment opportunities for the rapidly increasing number of aged workers, displaced workers, and handicapped workers. The Vocational Training Act of 1969 helped enlarge the institutions for vocational training and retraining. In 1975, the number of trainees in the Public Vocational Training Institutions directly administered by the Ministry of Labor amounted to more than 200,000. Not only is the training at these facilities available free of charge, but the trainees get allowances from the government for training to help support themselves during the required period of training.

[34] About the highly egalitarian nature of the Japanese educational system see Reischauer "The Japanese," pp. 167–169.

Protection of Workers and Regulation of Employment
Conditions

Prewar Development   As a latecomer among industrialized societies
and handicapped by its dependence on trade with foreign countries, Japan
had to face considerable difficulties in developing legal protection against
inferior employment conditions and abusive labor practices for its workers.
The Meiji government officially started preparation for the enactment of a
factory law to protect workers as early as in 1882, but it took nearly 30 years
before the Factory Law was enacted in 1911, and implementation of the law
was further delayed until 1916. Employers and their organizations bitterly
opposed the legislation because they feared it would undermine the traditional master–servant relationship that existed between employers and
employees, as well as the international competitiveness of Japanese industries. In response, the government emphasized the necessity of a factory
law in order to improve the national health, which was vital to the maintenance of a viable defense force. At that time there were very few trade
unions that could voice their demands for the Factory Law. As a result, the
coverage of the law was quite limited because of the exemption of factories
employing less than 30 workers (later 15 workers). Also, the level of the
legal protection provided by the law was not satisfactory. In substance,
only women and minors were protected from long hours and night work.
For adult-male workers, very little protective regulation was provided, except for the principle of employer liability for industrial accidents and occupational diseases befalling workers. This provision of employer liability
was further elaborated in the enactment of the Workmen's Accident Compensation Insurance Law in 1931.

With the outbreak of World War I, the Japanese economy achieved an
unprecedented prosperity through the development of heavy and chemical
industries. The structure of the labor force was gradually changing toward
the preponderance of male factory workers over female workers. Urbanization continued, with its resulting impact on the working population's way
of life. It was under such changing circumstances that the Russian Revolution of 1917 and, more significantly, the so-called "rice riot" of 1918 engendered nationwide social unrest. The government was compelled to consider the introduction of social legislation to ease the tension. Also, Japan's
election to a permanent seat in the International Labor Organization (ILO)
as a member of the governing body contributed to the promotion of social
legislation. In 1922 the government enacted the Workers' Health Insurance Law, which was enforced in 1927.

However, faced with massive unemployment caused by the Great Depression, the government failed to introduce compulsory unemployment
insurance, mainly on the grounds that in Japan the practice of voluntary

payment of allowances to retiring and dismissed workers had already been considerably developed and that if an unemployment allowance became a vested right of workers through an insurance scheme it would produce lazy workers. Moreover, the absence of a national network of employment exchanges at the time would have prevented the effective operation of an unemployment insurance scheme.

As a substitute for unemployment insurance, the government attempted in 1935 to introduce a provident fund scheme to provide statutory retirement benefits for discharged workers. Employers strongly opposed the plan because of its compulsory application, which was contradictory to their traditional policy of voluntary benevolence for the workers' welfare. However, as a result of the political unrest that eventually led to the Sino–Japanese War in 1937, employer organizations softened their opposition, and the government enacted the Retirement Provident Fund Law in 1936, which was incorporated into the Welfare Pension Insurance Law in 1944. During the war, although legislation for the improvement of employment conditions remained almost at a standstill, there were further developments in the field of social insurance, such as the national Health Insurance Law of 1938 and the Seamen's Insurance Law of 1939.

All in all, however, in prewar Japan the government's policies for the protection of workers and for the betterment of employment conditions in the course of industrialization tended to lag behind economic growth mainly because of wide differentials in employment conditions necessitated by the existence of a large number of medium and small-sized firms.

Postwar Development   The enactment of the Labor Standards Law in 1947 was a momentous step in Japanese industrial history. The law established standards for wages, hours, overtime, rest, vacation, sick leave, sanitary and safety conditions, elimination of contract labor, and a one-month advance notice of discharge. The standards provided were on the whole as high as those of the most advanced industrial nations.[35] In order to administer the law, the Labor Standards Bureau was established within the Ministry of Labor, with the ministry's nationwide network of regional and local inspection offices to enforce the law and to police the actual conditions in plants and factories. Since the labor standards laid down by the law were beyond the capacity of the war-devastated Japanese economy, there was considerable agitation for revision of the law. Particularly because of the "dual structure" of the Japanese economy, there was a strong feeling that the requirements of the law were too severe for small- and medium-sized firms. There were a great number of cases in which the law was blatantly violated. Employers' organizations persistently advocated amendment of the law

---

[35]Ronald Dore evaluates the standards as "more generous than in any other capitalist country." Dore, *British Factory—Japanese Factory*, p. 116.

and the government presented the problem to the Central Labor Standards Council for its deliberation in 1952. Since then some minor revisions of the law have been made, but they did not result in a substantive lowering of labor standards. Japan's rapid economic growth and its increasingly acute labor shortage since the 1960s have reduced the employers' effort to revise or weaken the law. Instead, the government has made the provisions of the law more substantial than in the past. For example, the Minimum Wage Law was enacted in 1959 as a separate-law from the Labor Standards Act. Another example is the enactment of the Industrial Safety and Sanitation Act of 1973, some of whose provisions were originally included in the Labor Standards Act.

Labor unions in Japan have played a watch-dog role by organizing "shop-floor inspection" committees or "disclose the law-violation" drives. At the same time, the unions have continually opposed the attempts, either by the government or the employers, to lower the legal standards. Instead, they have put pressure on the government to improve the standards to the level of the most advanced countries. For example, they asked that a 40-hour, 5-day week and national flat-rate minimum wages be incorporated into the Labor Standards Law.

The government has promoted the introduction of the 5-day week since 1970. At the same time, it urged the extension of the compulsory retirement age in private industries from 55 years of age to 60. However, because of the wide differentials in employment and working conditions that still exist at various levels, and because of a growing shortage of employment opportunities for aged workers under the stagnant economic growth since 1974, the acceptance of both the 5-day week and the extension of the retirement age have not been as extensive as was hoped.

Important legislation in the field of employment stability was passed right after World War II. The Employment Stability Act, Unemployment Insurance Act, and Unemployment Allowance Act, all of which were enacted in 1947, helped the government to cope with the increasing social unrest caused by mass unemployment right after the war and in the succeeding period of reconstruction.[36] Also, the unemployment insurance scheme, which is operated under the sole control of the central government, contributed greatly to the manpower readjustment that was necessary because of technological and structural changes in industry during the course of the economic growth of the 1960s. Because of the low rate of unemployment that persisted for a long time, revenue has continuously exceeded expenditures, which enabled the government to introduce measures to cope with such displaced workers as coal miners, employees of the

---

[36]For labor legislation in post-war Japan, see Toru Ariizumi, "The Legal Framework, Past and Present" in *Workers and Employers in Japan* eds. Okochi, Karsh, Levine (Princeton University Press and Tokyo University Press, 1974).

American military and naval bases, and textile workers. The Employment Promotion Corporation, which has played an important role in the field of employment stabilization and vocational training, was established in 1961 with its funds being provided largely by the special fund of unemployment insurance.

In view of the rapidly deteriorating employment situation since the oil crisis of 1973, the government revised the Unemployment Insurance Law into the new Employment Insurance Law in 1975. One of the most noteworthy improvements brought about by the revision of the law was the introduction of a system called the Employment Adjustment Subsidy, whch aimed at minimizing the possible incidence of unemployment. Employers who are forced to layoff their employees temporarily because of deteriorating economic conditions would get a subsidy that amounts to half of the wages paid to the laid-off workers in the case of large firms, and two-thirds in the case of small- and medium-sized firms. In Japan, "layoff" does not mean a temporary release from employment, but a temporary release from actual work while retaining an employee status. In this way the Employment Adjustment Subsidy system functions as an effective instrument for the reduction of open unemployment.

Since the oil crisis of 1973, with its adverse effect on the employment situation, labor unions have become more concerned than before about the improvement of employment insurance and other social security measures.

Beginning in 1974, labor unions started to organize the "people's *shunto*," or spring struggle, not only for organized workers but for unorganized and particularly for socially underprivileged and handicapped people, to force the government to take steps for social improvement. The revision of the Employment Insurance Law with its related measures was at least partly the result of direct negotiation between unions' national centers and the government. Through the same process the old age pension schemes have been remarkably improved since 1973. However, the percentage of national income devoted to social security expenditures in Japan has long been less than that of other advanced countries. This condition is largely a result of the facts that (a) the age composition of the Japanese population and of the labor force is relatively young, (b) Japanese pension schemes have a shorter history than those of other advanced countries, so that disbursement by the schemes has been relatively smaller. With the rapid aging of the Japanese labor force recipients of pensions are rapidly increasing. As a result the proportion of pension disbursement in national income is expected to rise. In addition, the average level of pension has been improving in recent years. In 1977, for example, under the government administered Workers Welfare Pension Insurance Scheme, those who have 28 years of contribution get a little more than 100,000 yen a month (roughly equivalent to 420 dollars) and those with 20 years of contribution get about 80,000 yen (roughly 330 dollars), which can be said to be almost as high as that of the advanced countries of Europe.

Government Policy toward Trade Unionism and Collective
Bargaining

As mentioned above, there was no law to protect trade unions or the workers' right to engage in trade-union activities in prewar Japan. Instead, there were various oppressive laws and administrative ordinances that finally resulted in the demise of labor unions right before World War II. Abiding by the principles of the Potsdam Declaration, the American occupation forces encouraged a free union movement. Keeping pace with the rapid spread of unionism right after the war, the first Trade Union Law was enacted in December 1945, and enforced on March 1, 1946. The law was revised in 1949 in order to ensure more strongly the independence of the unions from employer's intervention. The law guaranteed the workers' rights to organize, to bargain collectively, and to engage in concerted actions such as strikes, all of which were later confirmed in the new Constituton. The Trade Union Law was patterned after the Wagner Act (1935) of the United States, introducing the concept of unfair labor practices of employers. In order to protect unions from such employers' practices, the law established tripartite labor-relations commissions, composed of labor, management, and public representatives. The commissions were established on two levels: A Central Labor Relations Commission in Tokyo and Local Labor Relations Commission in every prefecture. The commissions' task is roughly two fold. One is to examine unfair labor practces, another is to prevent or solve labor disputes according to the provisions of the Labor Relations Adjustment Law, which was enacted in September, 1947. The commissions were to adjust labor disputes through conciliation, mediation, and arbitration at the request of either or both of the parties involved, or ex officio in an emergency case. The Labor Relations Adjustment Law, on the other hand, prohibited workers engaged in safety maintenance work from striking, and workers in public utilities were required to submit disputes to mediation 30 days prior to any strike, which was later changed to 10 days notice.

Originally the Trade Union Law was applied to every worker, including those in the public sectors, such as civil servants and employees of national enterprises, except policemen and firemen. However, after the abortive nationwide general strike on February 1, 1947, the SCAP (Supreme Commander Allied Powers) adopted a firmer attitude in dealing with the then communist-led union movement. Then, after the extensive disputes waged by the National Railways Union and the Postal Services Union in the spring of 1948, SCAP issued a letter to the government in

July of the same year, announcing its intention to deprive public employees of the right to strike. The government issued Ordinance No. 201 pursuant to the request of SCAP's letter prohibiting strikes and other acts of protest by public employees and denying the principle of wage determination by collective bargaining in public employment. Moreover, in December 1948, the government transformed the government-operated railways, the tobacco monopoly, and later the telephone and telegraph industries into public corporations. In 1952, together with five additional national enterprises—the Postal Services, the National Forestry Agency, the State Printing Bureau, the Mint, and the Alcohol Monopoly—these public corporations were placed under the newly enacted Public Corporation and National Enterprise Labor Relations Law. The employees covered by the law were prohibited from engaging in strikes, and their right to organize and to bargain collectively was also restricted. Similar legal changes were enacted for civil servants, both national and local, whose right to bargain collectively was either denied or more restricted than employees of public corporations.

In this way, workers in the public sector came to be covered by laws different from the Trade Union Law. For wage determination and dispute settlement for employees of the public corporations and national enterprises, a tripartite commission, the Public Corporation and National Enterprise Labor Relations Commission, was founded. For wage determination of national civil servants, the National Personnel Authority was established and for that of local civil servants, a similar agency was established in every prefecture.

The fact that the workers in the public sector were placed under different laws than the Trade Union Act, which was applied to workers in private industry, has exerted a significant impact on industrial relations in Japan as a whole. It has considerably hindered the development of united action and solidarity among workers in the public and private sectors. Incidentally, the unions in the public sector are giant unions that constitute the major force of Sōhyō, the largest national center (constituting almost two-thirds of its membership). For example, Jichirō (All Japan Prefectural and Municipal Workers' Union with 1.197 million members in 1976), Nikkyōso (Japan Teachers' Union, 643,000), Kokurō (National Railway Workers' Union, 247,000), Zendentsū (All Japan Telecommunication Workers' Union, 292,000), Zentei (Japan Postal Workers' Union, 202,000), and Dōryokusha (National Railway Locomotive Engineers' Union, 47,000) are among the largest and most powerful unions in Japan. These unions have to negotiate with the government directly or indirectly, since wages and other working conditions are for the most part determined by legislation, which is a highly political decision. As a result these unions are more active politically and are more inclined to be involved in political power struggles than unions in the private sector. Although these unions are deprived of the right to strike they have often waged strikes and are subject to severe governmental disciplinary actions, such as the discharge, suspension, or reprimand of union leaders. The dispute between the unions in the public sector and the government was placed before the ILO in the early 1960s in connection with the ratification of ILO Convention No. 87 on freedom of association. Ratification, with its relevant legal amendments, was made in 1965, but it failed to improve the situation. Unions in the public sector persistently continued their struggle to recover their right to strike, culminating in 8-day consecutive strikes by the National Railway Workers' Union and the National Railway Locomotive Engineers' Union in November 1975. The strike failed to solve the problem, which has been turned over to several investigatory commissions established by the government, without reaching any workable solution so far.

Collective Bargaining and Incomes Policy

Insofar as collective bargaining in private industries is concerned, the government has taken a position of noninterference with the autonomy of the parties, although if an employer rejects collective negotiations with a union without proper reason, a labor relations commission can order him "to comply with a demand of collective bargaining in good faith." The Trade Union Law gives collective agreements a higher legal status than individual contracts or work rules set by firms for their employees. Once a collective agreement is formulated and signed by a union and an employer, the provisions concerning the treatment of workers are legally binding. Any individual labor contract that does not meet the standards set in the collective agreement, or any work rule laid down by the company that is incongruous with the provisions in the agreement, is invalid. Since most collective agreements are negotiated and concluded between an enterprise union and its responding enterprise, there is little cause to necessitate the involvement of governmental agencies. Even in cases of protracted and bitter strikes the government has generally taken a neutral position and let the labor relations commission take appropriate actions for adjustment. Unless violent action on a mass scale takes place, as it still does sometimes, particularly in the sector of medium and small industries, the use of the police force is frowned upon.

With this general principle of avoiding direct involvement of or interference by the government in wage negotiations in the private sector, there has been little room for the introduction of an incomes policy in Japan. Actually, incomes policy in the formal sense of the word has never existed in Japan. It is true that during several years around the time of the 1973 oil crisis, the possibility or desirability of introducing an incomes policy was seriously discussed. It was at this time that the wage rate increase by *shuntō* (labor's spring wage offensive), as well as consumer prices, accerelated. The wage rate increase by *shuntō* was 15% in 1972, 20% in 1973 and 32.9% in 1974 (see Table 5.23), all of these figures exceeding the rate of productivity increase in the same years. The corresponding rate of consumer price increase was 5.3%, 16%, 21.7%, suggesting the impact of wage increases on price inflation. The government was very cautious in announcing any intention of introducing an incomes policy, but it committed the deliberation of the matter to expert commissions appointed by the prime minister. The commissions reported back in the negative, mainly because, as they saw it, Japanese enterprise unions do not have a strong enough position in the labor market to raise wages more than is appropriate. Unions were of course against the introduction of any incomes policy, not only because it would undermine the freedom of collective bargaining, but because they felt the union drive for wage increases was not the cause but the result of price inflation. Employers were also generally against the introduction of an incomes policy because they feared that it would lead to governmental control over pricing and profit distribution. Therefore, it was almost impossible to get the national consensus indispensable to the introduction of an incomes policy. What the government could do was simply call for the parties involved in wage negotiations to exercise self-restraint in order not to aggravate the ongoing inflation. Actually, in the wake of the worst and most protracted recession since 1955, brought about about by the oil crisis, and in the resulting adverse effect on employment opportunities, the rate of wage increase by *shuntō* leveled down to 13.1% in 1975, 8.8% in 1976, and 8.8% in 1977.

Concluding Observations

We do not pretend that we have developed a comprehensive or systematic analysis of Japanese industrial relations in the four preceding sections. We have simply tried to advance an interpretation of the development of industrial relations in the historical process of Japan's industrialization.

In conclusion, let us set forth some speculative comments on the meaning and prospects of currently pressing issues in the Japanese labor market and in industrial relations. In discussing these issues, we will try to put them in a long-term perspective as an extension of our discussion in the preceding sections.

Among many other factors, we may point to three outstanding exogenous variables that are deemed to exert critical influence on the current and prospective course of the Japanese labor market and industrial relations. They are (*a*) a slower pace of expected economic growth, (*b*) the rapid ageing of population and labor force, and (*c*) the increasingly larger proportion of college graduates in the labor force. Let us examine each of these factors in turn.

Following the oil crisis of 1973, the Japanese economy, as the economies of many other oil importing countries, was caught up in a serious stagflation. The rate of growth of real GNP fell to minus 1.3% in 1974 and in 1975 it recovered slightly, reaching 2.4%. After having experienced the drastic impact of the oil crisis, the Japanese economy is now returning to a more normal path of economic growth. But this growth path is, as many experts predict, quite different from the one that the economy had experienced for the preceding two decades. Although the prospective economic growth of an average annual rate of around 6% for the coming decade is not at all meager compared with those of other industrialized nations, it is nevertheless not surprising that this abrupt shift of the long-term growth path from world renowned "miraculous rapid growth" gives rise to many social and economic problems, especially in view of the fact that the structure of the economy, the institutions of industrial society, and the pattern of people's behavior and expectations have all been formulated and molded on the assumption of very rapid economic growth.

The second factor is the rapid ageing of the labor force. Since the 1950s, decreasing birth rates and the declining trend of mortality, have caused the average age of the Japanese population to increase rapidly. With this change in the age structure of the population, labor force is, and will be, ageing rapidly for a few decades to come. The remarkable speed of the ageing of the Japanese labor force is illustrated by the fact that the proportion of male workers age 45 to 64 to the total male labor force is expected to increase by 10 percentage points, from 24% in 1970 to 34% in 1980, whereas the equivalent proportional increase of the age group took about 40 years, from 1920 to 1960, both in the United Kingdom and the United States.

The third factor is a massive increase of the number of college graduates in the labor force. The ratio of college and junior college graduates to the total of new entrants into the labor market was 20.4% in 1970, 34.2%. in 1975, and is expected to be 40.6% in 1980.

With these changes taking place exogenously, it is anticipated that several serious issues will be intensified in the labor market and in the sphere of labor-management relations.

One such problem is the increased difficulty of securing jobs for aged workers. In sharp contrast to the market for young workers, the job market for aged workers has been consistently very loose. Since most employers discharge elderly workers when they reach the compulsory retirement age of 55 to 60, older workers have to find second jobs even though their working conditions will be much inferior. Many aged workers who are looking for jobs are either not old enough to get pensions or for some reason have not joined social insurance programs. Even though social security benefits are available, there still exists a large group of elderly workers who for various reasons need jobs and more income in order to earn a living.

Although employment of older workers has been relatively difficult, even at times of rapid economic expansion, under the present system of employment, it is anticipated that the difficulty will be aggravated with the slowing down of economic growth. There is an increasing concern that widespread underemployment may emerge again, concentrated now among the older workers of the labor force. In short, given the present system of employment, especially in large firms, changes in two of the exogenous variables, the slowing down of economic growth and the ageing of the labor force, will intensify the problems of unemployment or underemployment of aged workers and consequently augment the difficulties associated with maintaining their economic lives.

The other pressing issue is the rapid increase in the number of college graduates in the labor force. To the extent that the organizational hierarchy is more or less fixed, the employers cannot supply a sufficient number of jobs suitable for college graduates. This is likely to give rise to frustration and dissatisfaction on the part of these college educated employees. Since there exist within a company many more qualified employees, at least in terms of a college degree, than the number of supervisory or managerial posts, school degrees have lost their meaning as a certificate for promotion. Employers must find other ways of differentiating workers in order to make the corporative organization work effectively.

Still another issue is related to the power of Japanese unions. Since the mid-1950s, Japanese unionism has made appreciable progress in terms of reinforcing collective-bargaining functions and mutual coordination among unions, through the enthusiastic experiences of *shuntō*. In contrast to the vigorous and successful *shuntō* movements throughout the 1960s and up to the beginning of the 1970s, the tone changed significantly after the oil crisis. Some observers contend that Japanese unions were able to act vigorously only in the tight labor market of the period of rapid economic growth. If this is indeed the case, then one might anticipate that the unions' bargaining power would diminish with the slowing down of economic growth. What, then, have the unions gained through the lengthy and painful course of the unionization process?

This has been a brief review of some of the focal issues at the present time. One may note that there are two features common to these topics that many currently consider most pressing. Those features are (*a*) the institutions of the labor market and industrial relations are too rigidly fixed, and (*b*) estimates of future economic growth have been based on the standard that was regarded as normal in the last decade or so.

We take a different point of view. In the long run, the seemingly rigid institutions may well change, say in the next 10 to 20 years. And what was regarded as normal may no longer be normal under changed institutions and expectations.

For example, it would not be unreasonable to speculate that employment of elderly workers will be improved in the future as a result of contemplated changes in employment practices that would be more favorable to elderly workers, governmental policy interventions, and changes in age-earnings profiles in the direction of flattening the slope. Indeed, with changes in labor market conditions, the age-wage profile has flattened considerably in the last decade and a half as will be shown in a later section (and Table 5.18). Consequently, it is possible that employment of young workers and new entrants into the labor market will be adversely affected. In fact, labor market conditions in the 1930s caused young workers and college graduates to suffer from insufficient demand. Moreover, viewed in a long-term perspective, less steep age-earnings profiles and a looser labor market for young workers than at present might perhaps be a more normal condition of the Japanese labor market.

Similarly, given the current systems of employment, promotion, and allocation of workers within the internal labor market of a firm, the increased number of college graduates in proportion to total employees will certainly give rise to difficult problems of adjustment in labor and personnel management. Sooner or later, employers will have to discard sheer educational attainment as an instrument of stratifying and differentiating employees and find other alternatives. Changes are already becoming visible in many business corporations. There is no special reason why educational attainment has to remain the crucial variable in differentiating employees' economic and organizational status when nearly half of all employees are college graduates. To the extent that people differ in their innate and acquired abilities, and the employer finds some way to differentiate workers accordingly, the corporate organization will operate effectively without reliance on school diplomas as a means of status stratification.

Japanese unionism, on the other hand, will inevitably be faced with new challenges under new circumstances. The search for alternative means of intrafirm stratification of employees will certainly be incompatible with the principle of outright egalitarianism, which has been the principal goal and achievement of postwar unionism. The slowing down of economic growth would make it increasingly difficult to provide employment security for all member workers. Compared to these problems, acceptance of only modest wage increases in *shuntō* is a much more amicable option for the unions. A real test of union strength will take place if economic conditions deteriorate to the point that outright egalitarianism and employment security for all regular employees (and union members) cannot be economically maintained.

HISTORICAL AND STATISTICAL REVIEW OF THE LABOR MARKET AND INDUSTRIAL RELATIONS

Labor Force

This section is devoted to a review of statistical data relating to the labor force. The several sets of statistical data that will be reviewed describe historical changes in the magnitude of the labor force and its structure.

Long-Term Trends in Employment

Let us first take a look at movements over time in the aggegate labor force. Although systematic data are readily available for the post-World War II period from the *Rōdōryoku Chōsa* (*Labor Force Survey*) and the *Kokusei Chōsa* (*Population Census*), the primary data obtainable for the prewar period are fragmentary and not consistent. Therefore, we have to rely on experts' estimates for the prewar period.

Of the several series of useful estimates that are available, we have listed three made by Umemura (Table 5.1) and Nakajima (Tables 5.2, 5.3, and 5.4). Table 5.5 presents rates of change in the size of the employed population for 5-year intervals calculated from these estimates. Since data on the labor force, that is, the portion of the population who are capable and willing to work, are not available consistently for the pre-World War II period, we will use estimates of employed population in place of labor force.

When we look at the movement of the aggregate number of employed population since the end of the nineteenth century, we find on the one hand that there is an appreciable secular trend of increase for a long period of time, and on the other that the pace of the increase has fluctuated in swings of nearly two decades.

The long-run trend of increase, from the turn of the century up to 1940, is shown by Umemura's estimates, for example, as an increase of from 24.4 million to 32.5 million or approximately 33% (see Table 5.1).

Nakajima's estimate (see Tables 5.2 or 5.4) is 24.8 to 32.3 million. During this period, these three series of estimates exhibit a satisfactory degree of conformity. According to the Umemura's estimates, the pace of the long-run increase seems to be accelerating somewhat during this period; rates of increase for successive decades were 4.5%, 6.5%, 9.2% and 9.7%, respectively.

For the postwar period, we have labor force data, thanks to the initiation of the *Labor Force Survey* in 1948 by the Bureau of Statistics. From 1948 to 1975, the size of the labor force increased from 36.2 million to 52.8 million (see Table 5.6). But to see the postwar increase on a comparable basis with the prewar data, we need to look at employed population instead of the entire labor force. Nakajima's estimates, presented in Tables 5.2 or 5.4, serve conveniently for this purpose since his postwar estimates were adjusted to be consistent with the prewar data. These estimates, which use census data as a base, for 1950 and 1975, respectively, are 36 and 53 million. The pace of the increase in working population during the postwar period is visibly much higher than in the prewar period. Employed population has increased by 22.4% during the 1950s and 19.1% during the 1960s. In other words, the long-run trend of acceleration in the increase of working population has continued to the postwar period with much greater strength. But the trend appears to have been virtually terminated or to have sharply changed its tone since 1970. The growth of working population has become markedly moderate in the 1970s and is expected to continue to be moderate, though with some swings, for the foreseeable future, mainly for demographic reasons.

Compared to these periods after the beginning of the 20th century, the picture prior to the turn of the century is much more obscure, chiefly because of the paucity of reliable data. Nakajima's estimate for 1880 is 19.4 million. In sharp contrast, however, Umemura's is 21.9 million for the same year.

Umemura's finding has a rather important implication in understanding the structure and working of the Japanese labor market. The very high rates of increase in employment in the 1880s and 1890s, as implied by Ohkawa's and other earlier estimates, are puzzling, since it is not entirely clear why employment increased so rapidly when economic conditions were not particularly good. By reducing the rates of employment increase in these years substantially, Umemura's estimates present a more reasonable picture; employment increased only sluggishly when economic conditions were not good and increased rapidly in booming years.

This leads us to our next point, cyclical swings in the rates of change in the aggregate magnitude of employment. Let us note once again, before commenting on the statistical data, that both secular and cyclical movements in employment relate closely to an important topic of structural change in the labor market that was discussed earlier. The question was to discern when the Japanese labor market reached the stage of full-employment. This point is important not only in analyzing economic development in terms of the timing of the "take-off," but also in the context of industrial relations in evaluating the bargaining power of unions.

A very simplistic interpretation would be that Japan reached a state of full-employment at some stage in her history, say in the late 1950s, and would suggest that labor supply was elastic prior to that stage, but became inelastic after that. Needless to say, changes in the rate of increase in employment alone cannot be an indication of the elasticity of labor supply. To identify changes in the elasticity, we would first have to discern changes in

TABLE 5.1

Employment by Major Industrial Sectors[a] and Sex—Umemura's Estimates (in Thousands)

Year	Total (both sexes)			Males			Females		
	Total	Agricultural[b]	Nonagricultural[c]	Total	Agricultural[b]	Nonagricultural[c]	Total	Agricultural[b]	Nonagricultural[c]
1875	2147	1559	588	1232	853	379	915	706	209
1880	2188	1564	623	1256	855	401	931	709	222
1885	2234	1565	669	1296	855	441	938	710	228
1890	2304	1564	741	1348	853	495	957	711	246
1895	2372	1548	824	1393	836	557	980	713	267
1900	2438	1585	853	1435	867	568	1003	719	285
1905	2498	1582	916	1492	865	627	1006	717	289

	Total (both sexes)				Males				Females			
	Total[e]	I[f]	II[g]	III[h]	Total[e]	I[f]	II[g]	III[h]	Total[e]	I[f]	II[g]	III[h]
					Series A[d]							
1906	2506	1671	377	358	1499	933	262	275	1007	738	114	83
1910	2548	1638	413	390	1537	921	285	298	1011	717	128	92
1915	2631	1562	494	445	1618	893	350	335	1012	668	144	110
1920	2713	1434	632	523	1687	821	428	387	1026	613	203	136
					Series B[i]							
1920	2726	1439	636	527	1699	825	432	391	1027	614	204	136
1925	2811	1406	640	635	1783	800	460	474	1028	606	180	161
1930	2962	1465	627	721	1903	821	474	549	1059	644	153	172
1935	3121	1445	698	824	2025	822	530	625	1096	623	168	199
1940	3250	1452	836	758	1975	724	635	528	1276	728	201	230

Source: M. Umemura, "Sangyōbetsu Koyō no Hendō, 1880–1940" [Changes in Employment by Industrial Sectors, 1880–1940] *Keizai Kenkyū* [Economic Studies] 24, no. 2 (April 1973): 107–116.

[a] The numbers employed by industrial sectors were estimated by extrapolating the numbers obtained from the Population Censuses of 1920 and 1930 for the desired periods, using the data of occupational breakdown of the death statistics obtained from the Survey on Causes of Death.

[b] Agriculture and forestry.

[c] All industries except agriculture and forestry.

[d] The number of Japanese living in mainland Japan at midyear.

[e] Includes a sizable number of individuals who are not classifiable according to industry and so is not the total of I, II, and III.

[f] Agriculture, forestry, and fishing.

[g] Mining, construction, manufacturing, gas, electricity, and water supply.

[h] Commerce, transporation, public service, and other services.

[i] All the inhabitants of mainland Japan as of October 1 of each year.

TABLE 5.2

The Number of Employed Persons, 1880–1975—Nakajima's Estimates (in Millions)

Year	Employed persons	Year	Employed persons	Year	Employed persons	Year	Employed persons
1880	19.40	1905	25.61	1930	29.55	1955	39.59
1885	21.05	1910	26.21	1935	31.26	1960	44.05
1890	22.50	1915	26.60	1940	32.26	1965	47.95
1895	23.72	1920	26.73	1945	—	1970	52.45
1900	24.75	1925	28.14	1950	35.99	1975	52.98

Source: Hideo Nakajima, "Wagakuni Shūyōsha no Sen-zen Sen-go no Suii" [Changes in the Number of Employed Persons in Pre and Postwar Periods in Japan] *Rōdōtōkei Chōsa Geppō* [Monthly Review of Labor Statistics], November 1976, pp. 1–15.

TABLE 5.3

Ratios (in Percentages) of Employed Population to Total Population (in Thousands)

Year	Total population	Employed population	Ratio
1875	35,316	17,532	49.6
1880	36,649	19,397	52.9
1885	38,313	21,051	54.9
1890	39,902	22,502	56.4
1895	41,557	23,721	57.1
1900	43,847	24,751	56.4
1905	46,620	25,614	54.9
1910	49,184	26,214	53.3
1915	52,752	26,604	50.4
1920	55,963	26,734	47.8
1925	59,737	28,142	47.1
1930	64,450	29,549	45.8
1935	69,254	31,259	45.1
1940	71,933	32,263	44.9
1945	72,147	n.a.	n.a.
1950	83,200	35,990	43.3
1955	89,276	39,590	44.3
1960	93,419	44,050	47.2
1965	98,275	47,950	48.8
1970	103,720	52,450	50.6
1975	111,288	52,980	47.6

Source: H. Nakajima, "Wagakuni Shūyōsha no Sen-zen, Sen-go no Suii" [Changes in the Number of Employed Persons in Pre- and Postwar Periods in Japan], *Rōdōtōkei Chōsa Geppō* [Monthly Review of Labour Statistics], November 1976, pp. 1–15.

TABLE 5.4

Employment by Major Industrial Sectors, Total of Both Sexes, 1875–1975—Nakajima's Estimates

Year	Employed persons (in thousands)				Compositional ratios (in percentages)			
	Total	Primary	Secondary	Tertiary	Total	Primary	Secondary	Tertiary
1875	1733	1515	72	146	100	87.4	4.2	8.4
1880	1940	1636	116	188	100	84.3	6.0	9.7
1885	2105	1700	168	237	100	80.8	8.0	11.2
1890	2250	1741	221	288	100	77.4	9.8	12.8
1895	2372	1756	274	342	100	74.0	11.6	14.4
1900	2475	1747	330	399	100	70.6	13.3	16.1
1905	2561	1714	391	457	100	66.9	15.3	17.8
1910	2621	1655	449	517	100	63.1	17.1	19.7
1915	2660	1574	505	581	100	59.2	19.0	21.8
1920	2673	1467	559	646	100	54.9	20.9	24.2
1925	2814	1469	584	762	100	52.2	20.7	27.1
1930	2955	1471	600	884	100	49.8	20.3	29.9
1935	3126	1476	708	942	100	47.2	22.6	30.1
1940	3226	1439	844	943	100	44.6	26.2	29.2
1945	—	—	—	—	—	—	—	—
1950	3599	1748	784	1067	100	48.6	21.8	29.6
1955	3959	1629	925	1405	100	41.1	23.4	35.5
1960	4405	1439	1280	1686	100	32.7	29.1	38.3
1965	4795	1185	1530	2080	100	24.7	31.9	43.4
1970	5245	1016	1778	2451	100	19.4	33.9	46.7
1975	5298	740	1812	2746	100	14.0	34.2	51.8

Source: H. Nakajima, "Wagakuni Shūyōsha no Sen-zen Sen-go no Suii" [Changes in the Number of Employed Persons in Pre- and Postwar Periods in Japan], *Rōdōtōkei Chōsa Geppō* [Monthly Review of Labor Statistics], November 1976, pp. 1–15.

demand for labor and then to examine changes in market wage rates. If an increase in demand was accompanied by an increase in supply without increasing wage rates, then one could infer that labor supply was elastic. But if an increase in demand was accompanied by an increase in supply only to such an extent that substantial increases in wages were induced, then one could conclude that labor supply was inelastic. Although we are not prepared to make any empirical test of such a question in this chapter, we nevertheless seek a partial answer by reviewing employment fluctuations. The other side of the coin are the changes in wage rates. This aspect of the problem will be examined later.

Cyclical Changes in Labor Force Employment

During the 1880s, particularly in the earlier part of the decade, economic conditions were depressive partly as a result of the deflationary

TABLE 5.5
Estimated Changes (in Percentages) in Employed Population[a]

Five-year intervals	Umemura	Nakajima
1875–1880	1.9	11.9
1880–1885	2.1	8.5
1885–1890	3.1	6.9
1890–1895	2.9	5.4
1895–1900	2.8	4.3
1900–1905	2.5	3.5
1905–1910	2.1[b]	2.3
1910–1915	3.2	1.5
1915–1920	3.1	.5
1920–1925	3.1	5.3
1925–1930	5.4	5.0
1930–1935	5.4	5.8
1935–1940[c]	4.1	3.2
1950–1955	—	10.0
1955–1960	—	11.3
1960–1965	—	8.9
1965–1970	—	9.4
1970–1975	—	1.0

Sources: Umemura's estimates computed from Table 5.1; Nakajima's estimates computed from Table 5.2.

[a]Employed population includes not only employees but also self-employed and unpaid family workers.

[b]The figure for 1905–1910 of Umemura's estimates is the figure of the estimate for 1906–1910 multiplied by the factor of 1.25.

[c]Data are not available for the periods 1940–1945 and 1945–1950.

TABLE 5.6
Employment by Major Industrial Sectors, Total of Both Sexes, 1948–1975

	Employed persons (in ten thousands)				Compositional ratios (in percentages)			
Year	Total	Primary	Secondary	Tertiary	Total	Primary	Secondary	Tertiary
1948[a]	3460	1695	824	786	100.0	49.0	23.8	22.7
1950[a]	3503	1778	807	886	100.0	50.8	23.0	25.3
1955	4090	1536	997	1557	100.0	37.6	24.4	38.1
1960	4436	1340	1242	1854	100.0	30.2	28.0	41.8
1965	4730	1113	1507	2109	100.0	23.5	31.9	44.6
1970	5094	886	1791	2409	100.0	17.4	35.2	47.3
1975	5178	658	1823	2688	100.0	12.7	35.2	51.9

Sources: Office of the Prime Minister, Bureau of Statistics, *Labor Force Survey,* Annual Report (selected years).

[a]Figures for 1948 and 1950 are unadjusted for the 1967 revision of survey method. The figures for 1950 are the average of the first half of the year.

policy of the government. According to Umemura's estimates, as shown in Table 5.5, increases in employment were moderate but the pace of the increase was gradually accelerating from the end of the 1870s toward the end of the 1880s. In the 1890s, when economic conditions recovered, employment kept increasing at a moderate pace; close to 3% every 5 years.

Around the turn of the century, the Japanese economy was caught in a persistent recession that was caused at least partially by the adoption of a gold-standard system. Although aggregate employment showed a modest increase in the decade around the turn of the century (see Tables 5.2, 5.1, 5.4, and 5.5), the increase in the nonagricultural sector was slowed considerably, in contrast to the agricultural sector, which increased appreciably. This implies that owing to a lack of job opportunities in urban areas, male workers were obliged to secure employment in agriculture.

Industrial activities began to flourish around 1910 and the economy enjoyed an unprecedented boom during the latter half of the decade 1910–1920 under the impact of World War I. Employment is manufacturing industries and mining increased remarkably during this time.

Employment in the primary-industry sector declined sharply, implying a massive mobilization of the working population from the primary to the secondary, and also in part to the tertiary, sectors of the economy.

In the 1920s, however, the economy was trapped in a worldwide depression. Employment in the secondary industry sector ceased to grow, and as the monetary crisis deepened the economic depression, it even recorded a sizeable decline. In contrast, agricultural employment declined at a much slower pace in the early part of the 1920s than in the previous period and even grew considerably, absorbing the labor force squeezed out of nonagricultural sectors, later in the decade.

While total employment remained stagnant under the depressive conditions of the economy during the 1920s, we should not overlook the fact that employment in some sectors increased substantially, as in the chemical and public utility industries, and in the public and commercial sectors.[37]

Whereas employment in the secondary industry sector as a whole increased only .6% in the first half of the 1920s and decreased by 2% during the latter half, chemical industry employment increased by 12% and 23% for the same periods. Public utility industries that supply gas, electric power, and water increased their employment by more than 50% during the latter half of the 1920s. Much of this increase was accounted for by the remarkable expansion of the electric power industry. The outstanding growth of the chemical industry was simply a consequence of development

---

[37]Our discussion of sectoral changes in employment here is based upon the data presented in M. Umemura, "Sangyō-betsu koyō no Hendō: 1880–1940 (Changes in Employment by Industrial Sectors: 1880–1940)," in Keizai Kenkyū (Economic Studies), Vol. 24, No. 2 (April 1973), p. 110.

in the power industry. The chemical industry was not the only beneficiary. The impact spread broadly and deeply into the economy by accelerating the shift from steam engines to electric motors in various branches of industry. In spite of the generally depressed outlook during this period, the economy was preparing itself for subsequent growth. Other developments that deserve consideration are the continuous growth in the public and commercial sectors. The major source of growth in the public sector was the expansion and enrichment of public educational programs. The content of the growth of the commercial sector is not very clear.

During the 1930s, employment, particularly in the secondary industry sector, grew remarkably. The increase was especially pronounced in the latter half of the decade, as the economic effects of military actions in China grew more prevalent. Indeed, with enormous increases in demand for metal, machinery, and chemicals, these industries developed enormously, and the entire economy was industrialized rapidly and thoroughly during this period. By 1940, the proportion of agricultural employment had decreased to less than 45%, whereas secondary industry employment had grown to as much as 26% of the entire employment in the economy (see Tables 5.1 and 5.4). Taking the industrial distribution of employment such as this as an indicator of the degree of industrialization, it took about a decade after World War II for the Japanese economy to regain the level of industrialization that had been achieved in 1940. Given the fact that it was only in 1933 that the number of male factory workers surpassed the number of their female counterparts, the rapid industrialization of the 1930s and early 1940s must have greatly intensified the labor shortage, particularly of skilled male workers. Moreover, with increasingly large numbers of young men drafted into military service, the wartime labor market may well have reached, at least temporarily, the state of super full-employment, with a large amount of unfilled excess demand.

In the postwar period, the aggregate number of employed persons increased at much faster rates than in the prewar period, as shown by Table 5.5. But this rapid increase appears to have ceased around the beginning of the 1970s.

The size of the labor force continued to grow rapidly during the 1950s and 1960s. This was an important factor in supporting the very rapid economic growth. During the 1950s, the labor force increased by nearly 2% a year, and in the 1960s at a rate higher than 1% (see Table 5.7). The expansion was especially rapid for several years in the mid-1950s and also in the mid-1960s.

Since the beginning of the 1970s, the pace of labor force growth has dropped sharply, to below 1% annually. This is not a temporary phenomenon. Based on predictions of demographic trends, labor force growth in the foreseeable future will continue to be less than 1%, which is much more

TABLE 5.7

The Size of the Labor Force, 1950–1975 (in Millions)

Year	Total	Male	Female
1950[a]	36.16	21.93	14.23
1955	41.94	24.55	17.40
1960	45.11	26.73	18.38
1965	47.87	28.84	19.03
1970	51.53	31.29	20.24
1975	52.77	32.94	19.83

Source: Office of the Prime Minister, Bureau of Statistics, *Labor Force Survey*, (selected years).

[a]The data for 1950 are based on the population age 14 and older, whereas data for 1955 and thereafter cover only those age 15 and older. The data prior to 1953 are unadjusted for the 1967 revision in the survey method, so that they are not directly comparable with the other data.

moderate than the rates observed in the 1950s and 1960s. Quite unlike the postwar experience, when the economy enjoyed abundant supplies of young labor up to the end of 1960s, the economy is now faced with a set of new problems associated with the rapid ageing of the labor force.

To conclude this review of the changes in employment and labor force for the postwar period, let us emphasize among other things that there were more or less regular cyclical swings in the rate of changes in employment, and also in labor force to some extent, with peaks in the 1910s, 1930s and 1950s. Against these changes in employment, the response of the other dimension of the labor market, namely wages, is a question which will be examined in the next section.

But before proceeding to the next section on wages, let us review some other relevant data, in order to understand changes in labor supply and the structure of the labor force.

Labor Force Participation Ratios

For the prewar period, we unfortunately have no data on labor force participation ratios. Instead, we have some estimates of the ratio of the employed population to the total population (see Table 5.3). The ratio of employed population to total population increased steadily until the end of the nineteenth century, and then decreased up to the time of World War II. After the war, it increased continuously until 1970 and then began to decline until quite recently. The sizable increase before the turn of the century is not affected by the problems we discussed in connection with the Umemura's estimates. Using the Umemura estimates of employed population, the trend for this early period is reversed. The secular decline from the beginning of the twentieth century until 1940 reflects the trend of the significant decline of the agricultural working population from 70% down to 44%. In the postwar period, despite the massive reduction of the agricultural population since 1950, the ratio of employed to total population increased until around 1970. This is a result of the joint effects of many factors. One of the most important was the remarkable decrease in birth rates during the 1950s, which reduced the proportion of the population younger than working age and consequently made the proportion of the employed population appear larger than it would otherwise have.

Let us now take a look at labor force participation ratios for the postwar period (see Table 5.8), which is a much better measure of labor supply behavior than the ratio of employed to the total population. The aggregate labor force participation ratio increased slightly during the 1950s and then declined steadily from the beginning of the 1960s. The seeming increase until the end of the 1950s is due in part to the fact that the data prior to 1953 are unadjusted figures of the old survey method that are not directly comparable with the subsequent data. But the slightly increasing, or at least stagnant, trend of the ratio is still observable for several years after 1953. This is the net result of negative income and positive substitution effects of labor supply as revealed by microanalyses, in addition to the effect of compositional changes in the labor force.

Since the end of the 1950s, we find that the aggregate ratio has consistently declined, from around 70% in 1960, down to 63% in 1975. Obviously, this decline has been largely the result of the substantial reduction

TABLE 5.8
Labor Force Participation Ratios, 1950–1975
(in Percentages)

Year	Total	Male	Female
1950	65.5	83.2	49.3
1955	70.8	85.9	56.7
1960	69.2	84.8	54.5
1965	65.7	81.7	50.6
1970	65.4	81.8	49.9
1975	62.9	81.1	45.8

Source: Office of the Prime Minister, Bureau of Statistics, *Labor Force Survey, Annual Report* (selected years).

in the aggregate female participation ratio that has taken place in the 1960s and early 1970s. This decline reflects not so much changes in the labor supply behavior of the female population as the significant decline in the proportion of agricultural employment in the economy during this period. The ratio of male labor-force participation also exhibits a modest decline. The steadily increasing trend for higher education among the young and the slightly decreasing labor-force participation rates of the aged population have been principally responsible for this downward tendency.

TABLE 5.9
*Average Monthly Hours Worked per Worker,
Manufacturing Industries*

Year	Total hours worked	Overtime hours
1925	256.5	n.a.
1930	241.2	n.a.
1935	250.2	n.a.
1940[a]	254.7	n.a.
1945	—	—
1950	189.0	14.7
1955	198.0	18.3
1960	207.0	25.0
1965	191.8	16.7
1970	187.4	19.0
1975	167.8	9.1

Sources: The data for 1923 and 1938 were originally obtained from Office of the Cabinet, *Rōdō Tōkei Yōran* [Handbook of Labor Statistics] (selected years). For 1939 through 1941 the data are from Office of the Cabinet, *Rōdō Tōkei* [Labor Statistics: Report of Monthly Survey of Labor Statistics] (selected years). For 1942 through 1944 the data are from Office of the Cabinet, *Rōdō Maigetsu Tōkei* [Monthly Labor Statistics] (selected years); the postwar data of 1947 through 1975 were taken from the Ministry of Labour, *Maigetsu Kinrō Tōkei* [Monthly Labor Survey] (selected years).

[a] All the prewar data were quoted from Nihon Tōkei Kenkyūjo [Japan Institute for Statistics], *Nihon Keizai Tōkei-shū* [Collected Statistics of Japanese Economy] (Tokyo: Nihon Hyōron Sha, 1958), pp. 288–291. The prewar data of monthly hours worked were calculated by the authors by multiplying average daily hours and average days worked per month.

Hours Worked

Another important factor that determines the magnitude of labor services is the length of working hours per worker. Table 5.9 presents average monthly hours worked per worker in manufacturing industries for the period from 1925 to 1975. The number of hours worked per month has declined remarkably over a long period of time, from the high of a 250- to 260-hour level in the prewar period down to a 170-hour level in 1975.

A close examination of the pattern of fluctuations during the prewar period would not make much sense, unfortunately, since the prewar data shown in this table were collected from various sources, which are not necessarily identical in measurement. It should also be borne in mind that the full-fledged Labor Standards Act, which was enacted shortly after the war, is responsible, along with demand conditions in the economy, for reducing the length of working hours in the postwar period substantially lower than in the prewar period.

The postwar data, taken from the *Monthly Labor Survey,* are consistent and reliable. The length of working hours in manufacturing industries reported in this survey has been declining secularly since the beginning of the 1960s; regular monthly hours worked, that is, total monthly hours worked less overtime hours, declined by more than 23 hours during the last 15 years. This sizable reduction has been attained chiefly through the increased number of annual and weekend paid holidays. Although regular working hours have been reduced persistently, total monthly hours worked fluctuate as economic conditions change. The observed cyclical fluctuations (see Table 5.9) are accounted for largely by fluctuations in overtime hours, which consisted of 6 to 12% of total monthly hours worked. Although these cyclical fluctuations are unavoidable, the general long-term trend for further shortening of working hours is nevertheless likely to continue.

Unemployment

Thus far, we have reviewed statistical data relating mainly to employment. The discrepancy between employment and the labor force is unemployment.

For the prewar period, we have only scant information about unemployment. The scarcity of unemployment data makes it very difficult to assess the size of the labor force for the prewar period. Table 5.10 presents an example of such limited and fragmentary information for the 1930s. The aggregate rate of unemployment rose to and remained at around 6% for a few years early in the 1930s, or the years immediately following the Great Depression, and then went quickly down to around 3% toward the end of the 1930s as economic conditions recovered, stimulated by expansion in war-related demands. It is interesting to note in Table 5.10 that

TABLE 5.10
Estimated Unemployment Rates, 1929–1938 (in Percentages)[a]

			Wage earners	
Year	Total	Salaried employees	Day laborers	Other workers
1929	4.54	3.86	7.67	3.52
1930	5.25	3.91	9.08	4.16
1931	6.68	4.65	11.34	5.50
1932	6.38	4.94	10.88	4.91
1933	5.11	4.01	10.24	3.25
1934	4.80	3.88	9.89	2.92
1935	4.52	3.82	9.34	2.72
1936	4.08	3.58	8.43	2.41
1937	3.38	3.17	6.97	1.90
1938	2.73	2.57	5.94	1.55

Source: Unemployment Survey of the Ministry of Welfare, quoted from Office of the Cabinet, Bureau of Statistics, *Rōdo Tōkei Yōran* [Handbook of Labor Statistics] 1939, pp. 60–61.

[a]Estimates of unemployment rates are based on monthly surveys of a limited sample size of population on the order of 7 to 8 million. Unemployment rates listed in the table are for December of each year.

there was a large differential in unemployment rates between day laborers and other wage earners, suggesting the simultaneous existence of a large labor reserve of unskilled laborers and a relative shortage of skilled labor.

Table 5.11 presents figures on unemployment for the postwar period. Both the number of persons and the rate of unemployment prior to 1953 are much lower in comparison to subsequent years. But this is largely due to the old method of the labor-force survey for this period, and direct comparisons before and after 1953 are not very meaningful. Allowing for this difference, we can still find a significant reduction in the rate of unemployment during the postwar period, especially between the 1950s and the 1960s.

When we trace the rate of unemployment defined as a fraction of the total labor force, it has varied from around 2% in the 1950s down to 1% in the 1960s, where it has persistently stayed until recently. In 1975, the rate increased again close to 2%, and in 1976 went above that level. But when we compute the unemployment rate using the number of employees as a denominator, the figures in the 1950s are more than doubled. This is because a large number of self-employed and unpaid family workers actually in the labor force in the 1950s were eliminated from the denominator. Taking this structural difference into account, one might say that the difficulty of getting a job for an urban worker was more severe in the 1950s than in

TABLE 5.11
Unemployment, 1948–1975[a]

Year	Unemployed persons (in ten thousands)	Unemployment rates (in percentages)		Year	Unemployed persons (in ten thousands)	Unemployment rates (in percentages)	
		U/L[b]	U/E[c]			U/L[b]	U/E[c]
				1961	66	1.4	2.7
				1962	59	1.3	2.3
1948	24	0.7	1.9	1963	59	1.3	2.2
1949	38	1.0	3.1	1964	54	1.1	2.0
1950	44	1.2	3.5	1965	57	1.2	2.0
1951	39	1.1	2.8	1966	65	1.3	2.2
1952	47	1.2	3.3	1967	63	1.3	2.1
1953	75	1.9	4.5	1968	59	1.2	1.9
1954	92	2.3	5.4	1969	57	1.1	1.8
1955	105	2.5	5.9	1970	59	1.2	1.8
1956	98	2.3	5.1	1971	64	1.2	1.9
1957	82	1.9	4.0	1972	73	1.4	2.1
1958	90	2.1	4.2	1973	67	1.3	1.9
1959	98	2.2	4.4	1974	72	1.4	2.0
1960	75	1.7	3.2	1975	99	1.9	2.7

Source: Office of the Prime Minister, Bureau of Statistics, Labor Force Survey, Annual Report (selected years).

[a]Figures for 1948 through 1952 are unadjusted for the 1967 revision of survey method. Data for 1948 through 1952 are based on the population aged 14 and above, whereas data for 1953 and thereafter are based on those aged 15 and above.

[b]Number of unemployed persons divided by the total labor force.

[c]Number of unemployed persons divided by the number of employed persons.

the mid-1970s, even though the ratios of unemployment to the total labor force are similar.

Postwar Structural Changes in Labor Force

In an earlier section we discussed alternative hypotheses about structural changes in the labor market. One important view, as proposed by Minami, maintains that the Japanese labor market has undergone a major stage of structural change since the end of the 1950s, going from conditions characterized by unlimited supplies of labor to those dominated by labor shortage. Whether or not this hypothesis is true, the Japanese labor market experienced enormous changes in the distribution of the labor force among the different industrial sectors, occupational categories, and employment status during the phenomenal economic growth that took place in the mid-1950s and was accelerated during the 1960s. In closing this section on labor force, then, let us briefly mention these changes.

TABLE 5.12

Employment by Major Occupational Categories, 1955–1975 (Male and Female)

Year	Total	Specialists	Managerial workers	Clerical workers	Sales workers	Agricultural workers	Miners	Transportation and communication workers	Operatives and skilled workers	Laborers	Service workers
						Employed persons (in thousands)					
1955	4090	190	90	370	543	1503	30	71	1074		219
1960	4436	220	91	499	596	1322	32	100	1279		298
1965	4730	238	131	636	615	1094	19	177	1236	229	354
1970	5094	295	134	755	662	880	11	232	1511	218	387
1975	5178	361	204	815	731	651	9	234	1564	147	454
						Compositional ratios (in percentages)					
1955	100.0	4.6	2.2	9.0	13.3	36.7	.7	1.7	26.3		5.4
1960	100.0	4.9	2.1	11.2	13.4	29.8	.7	2.3	28.8		6.7
1965	100.0	5.3	2.8	13.4	13.0	23.1	.4	3.7	26.1	4.8	7.5
1970	100.0	5.8	2.6	14.8	13.0	17.3	.2	4.6	29.7	4.3	7.6
1975	100.0	7.0	3.9	15.7	14.1	12.6	.2	4.5	30.2	2.9	8.8

Source: Office of the Prime Minister, Bureau of Statistics, Labor Force Survey, Annual Report (selected years).

TABLE 5.13

Total Employment by Major Occupational Categories[a], 1920–1940

Year	Total	Agriculture	Fishing	Mining	Manufacturing	Commerce	Transportion	Public service	Domestic service	Unclassifiable
					Employed persons (in thousands)					
1920	2663	1413	56	42	530	319	104	114	2	53
1930	2962	1414	55	25	570	448	111	204	78	57
1940	3248	1384	54	60	813	488	136	219	71	22
					Compositional ratios (in percentages)					
1920	100.0	53.1	2.1	1.6	19.9	12.0	3.9	5.4	0.1	2.0
1930	100.0	47.7	1.8	0.8	19.2	15.1	3.7	6.9	2.6	1.9
1940	100.0	42.6	1.7	1.8	25.0	15.0	4.2	6.8	2.2	0.7

Sources: Office of the Prime Minister, *Population Census*; Showa Dōjinkai, *Wagakuni Kanzen Koyō no Igi to Taisaku* [Significance and Policies for Full-Employment in Japan] (Tokyo: Shiseido, 1957).

[a] Does not include population under military service.

TABLE 5.14

Employment Status of Workers in All Industries, 1920–1975

Year	Number of persons (in ten thousands)				Compositional ratios (in percentages)			
	Total	Self-employed	Family workers	Employees	Total	Self-employed	Family workers	Employees
1920	2654	886	984	784	100	33.4	37.1	29.5
1930	2930	958	1025	948	100	32.7	35.0	32.3
1940	3216	846	1024	1346	100	26.3	31.8	41.9
1950	3572	1011	1297	1265	100	28.3	36.3	35.4
1955	4090	1028	1284	1778	100	25.1	31.4	43.5
1960	4436	1006	1061	2370	100	22.7	23.9	54.3
1965	4730	939	915	2876	100	19.9	19.3	60.8
1970	5094	977	805	3306	100	19.2	15.8	64.9
1975	5178	932	626	3612	100	18.0	12.1	69.8

Sources: The data from 1920 to 1940 were obtained from estimates based on Office of the Prime Minister, *Population Census*, (selected years) quoted in Showa Dōjinkai, *Wagakuni Kanzenkoyō no Igi to Taisaku* [Significance and Policies for Full-Employment in Japan], 1957. The data from 1950 to 1975 were taken from Office of the Prime Minister, *Labor Force Survey, Annual Report* (selected years).

Changes in the distribution of the labor force (or employment) among the different industrial sectors of the economy were explained earlier when we discussed cyclical changes in employment. Therefore suffice it to say here that after restoring the prewar level of industrialization in the mid-1950s, as indicated by the pattern of the intersectoral distribution of the labor force, the economy went through much more drastic changes in the structure of employment during the subsequent two decades. That is, the proportion of employment in the primary sector declined from nearly 40% in 1955 to less than 13% in 1975; whereas employment in the secondary sector increased from 24 to 35% and from 38 to 52% in the tertiary sector (see Table 5.6).

This drastic change in the intersectoral employment structure has apparently promoted changes in the occupational distribution of employment too, as seen in Table 5.12. Specialists, managerial workers, clerical workers, service workers, and transportation and communication workers are occupations that have grown notably. The number of agricultural workers, service workers, and transportation and communication workers and operatives has shown a moderate increase, whereas unskilled laborers have declined appreciably. Table 5.13 also provides limited data on the occupational distribution of employment taken from three censuses between 1920 and 1940. During these two decades we can trace the impact of industrialization as represented by the increasing number of manufacturing industry workers and the decreasing number of agricultural workers. But the prewar scheme of occupational classification was so close to industrial classification that little information may be obtained from the prewar data in terms of changes in occupational structure as such.

The impact of the rapid economic growth in the postwar period is also clearly visible in the distribution of employment classified by employment status. Table 5.14 shows that, in contrast to rapid reductions of self-employed and family workers, the number and proportion of workers with employee status has increased remarkably. Although many self-employed and family workers were engaged in farming, it is suspected that the rest constituted an important part of massive under-employment in urban areas during the stagnant economic conditions prior to the mid-1950s.

Wages

This section will review several aspects of wage statistics: trends, cyclical swings, rate of changes, differentials by occupation, skill, age, sex, and firm size, and negotiated wage increases.

Long-Term Trends and Movements in the Level of Wages

Tables 5.15 and 5.16 present long-term statistics for wages. Data for the prewar period are covered by Table 5.15, which shows the average

TABLE 5.15
Estimates of Wage Rates and Their Changes, 1885–1940

Year	Average daily wage rate (in yen)	Index[a] Money wage	Index[a] Real wage	Index[a] Consumer prices
1885	.14	10.4	32.1	32.4
1890	.13	9.7	28.8	33.7
1895	1.7	12.7	36.9	34.4
1900	.26	19.4	40.0	48.5
1905	.29	21.6	39.3	55.0
1910	.41	30.6	53.1	57.6
1915	.46	34.3	59.1	58.0
1920	1.40	104.5	7.26	144.0
1925	1.55	115.7	87.9	131.6
1930	1.42	106.0	101.5	104.4
1935	1.35	100.8	100.8	100.0
1940	—	—	—	—

Source: Kazushi Ohkawa, et al., *Chōki Keizaitōkei* [Estimates of Long-Term Economic Statistics of Japan Since 1868], *No. 8. Prices* (Tōkyō: Tōyō Keizai Shinpōsha, 1967); Comprehensive Wage Series by Occupation (Series A), p. 243 and Price Indexes, p. 134.
[a] 1934–1936 = 100.

daily wage rates for periods from 1885 to 1935, money and real wage indices, together with a consumers' price index. The wage data are all averages for male and female workers for manufacturing industries. Table 5.16 covers the postwar period from 1950 to 1975. The table contains average monthly cash earnings; average hourly wage rates; indices of

TABLE 5.16
Estimates of Wage Rates and Their Changes in Manufacturing Industries, 1950–1975[a]

Year	Average monthly cash earnings (in thousands of yen)	Average hourly wage rate (in yen)[b]	Index Money wage	Index Real wage	Index Consumer prices
1950	9.1	48.3	12.7	33.2	38.3
1955	16.7	84.4	23.2	44.2	52.5
1960	22.6	109.3	31.1	54.9	56.6
1965	36.1	188.2	50.3	65.6	76.7
1970	71.4	381.3	100.0	100.0	100.0
1975	163.7	975.7	230.3	133.6	172.4

Sources: Wages: The Ministry of Labor, *Monthly Labor Survey;* Consumer's Price Index: Office of the Prime Minister, *Statistical Survey of Retail Prices.* Selected years of the annual reports.
[a] Wage data are for regular employees of establishments with 30 employees or more in manufacturing industries.
[b] Hourly wage rate is computed by dividing average monthly cash earnings by average monthly hours worked.

money, and real wages, and consumers' price. The wage data in this table are also averages for both sexes for manufacturing industries.

During a prewar period of 50 years, which is covered by Table 5.15, the money wage rate increased appreciably along a long-term secular trend. This trend of increase was, however, not without fluctuations. The rate varied most obviously during the interwar period of the 1920s and the early 1930s. Another feature is that the level of money wage rose rapidly in times of war, as in the late 1890s during the Sino-Japanese War, a few years in the first decade of the 1900s during the Russo-Japanese War, 1914–1919 during World War I, and toward the end of the 1930s (and probably in the 1940s) shortly before (and during) World War II.

In sharp contrast to the prewar period, the upward movement in the postwar money wage rate has been steady. Indeed, since 1947, when data were first made available, money wage rates have never decreased even for a short time. There are three phases of major money wage increases: (a) an abnormal inflationary period right after World War II, (b) the first few years of the 1950s under the impact of the Korean War, and (c) a lengthy period of spectacular economic growth during the 1960s and the first half of the 1970s.

Real wages have not increased as much and as steadily as money wages. They fluctuated cyclically in almost every decade, without much improvement until early in the twentieth century. But since 1910, real wages have improved substantially. During the interwar period of depressed economic conditions, real wages made their most substantial improvements, thanks primarily to a general decline in consumers' prices. The prewar peak in the real wage rate was reached in 1931, at the bottom of the Great Depression.

After World War II, real wages increased steadily, with only one exceptional decline. Improvements were particularly appreciable for a few years right after the war, in the mid-1950s, around 1960, in the latter half of the 1960s, and in the first few years in the 1970s.

Changes in Wage Differentials

The basic reason for studying changes in wage differentials is that the movement of wage differentials is the clearest expression of the operation and structure of the labor market.

The data presented in Tables 5.17 and 5.18 provide us with some clues with which to make assessments of this question. In Table 5.17, three series of wage differentials are presented: differentials between the daily wage rates of industry and agriculture, of skilled and unskilled occupations in the building industry, and of male and female factory workers. The differential ratios are based on 5 year moving averages of the relevant wage series. In all three series of differentials, the ratio is the percentage of the higher wage relative to the lower wage, while patterns of fluctuation in the

TABLE 5.17
Movement of Wage Differentials, 1885–1955 (in Percentages)

Year	Industry–agriculture	Skilled–unskilled	Male–female
1885	136	151	—
1890	138	145	—
1895	129	150	—
1900	131	153	—
1905	135	158	205
1910	137	164	206
1915	132	160	207
1920	121	141	186
1925	118	153	221
1930	146	165	249
1935	176	167	304
1940	115	—	273
1945	—	—	239
1950	187	146	232
1955	219	147	239

Source: Koji Taira, "The Dynamics of Japanese Wage Differentials, 1881–1959" (Ph.D. dissertation, Stanford University, 1961), pp. 226–234.

differentials are obscure prior to the turn of the century, the movements in the three differentials have become reasonably synchronized since the beginning of this century. Differentials widened visibly in the 1910s, early in the 1930s, and around 1950; and narrowed significantly in the late 1890s, around 1920, and in the late 1930s, and presumably in the 1960s (not shown in the table).

Similar movements may be seen, too, in the wage differentials among various skilled and unskilled occupations as presented in Table 5.18. The selected occupations in the table are: the skilled occupations of carpenter, typesetter, shoemaker, and blacksmith; and the unskilled occupations of male nonagricultural day laborer, male and female agricultural day laborers, and female cotton weaver. In order to show the widening and narrowing of the wage differentials, the wages of one of the skilled occupations are indexed at 100 and the rest are expressed in percentages relative to that occupation. Whereas the wage differentials between carpenters and other skilled occupations move irregularly, the differentials between skilled and unskilled occupations show systematic movements within business cycles of approximately two decades. The regular changes are particularly pronounced in the differentials of male day laborers, both industrial and agricultural, and of carpenters. The differentials reported in the table widened in 1910 and in the 1930s, and narrowed in 1895, 1920, and 1939.

The observed changes in wage differentials, particularly those between

TABLE 5.18
Wage Differentials for Selected Occupations (in Percentages), Selected Years
1895–1956

Year	Carpenter	Typesetter	Shoemaker	Blacksmith	Day laborer Male	Agricultural day laborer Male	Agricultural day laborer Female	Cotton weaver Female
1895	100	71.9	96.9	90.6	68.8	59.4	34.4	37.5
1900	100	64.8	87.0	88.9	68.5	55.6	35.2	37.0
1905	100	70.0	95.0	91.7	68.3	53.3	33.3	21.7
1910	100	63.8	83.8	86.3	66.3	48.8	30.0	33.8
1915	100	72.6	86.9	82.1	65.5	54.8	34.5	35.7
1920	100	76.3	80.9	83.2	76.7	55.0	35.1	n.a.
1925	100	75.8	79.9	75.2	71.5	50.7	40.6	32.6
1930	100	94.4	85.5	86.4	65.5	45.8	34.5	34.5
1935	100	114.5	93.8	126.4	68.9	44.0	33.7	37.8
1939	100	86.9	81.3	118.3	73.5	68.7	55.6	31.7
1952	100	124.4	93.2	114.7	n.a.	42.2	33.4	32.8
1956	100	126.6	85.4	123.4	n.a.	n.a.	n.a.	34.8

Sources: The data up to 1920 are obtained from Office of the Prime Minister, Bureau of Statistics, *Rōdōtōkei Yōran* [Handbook of Labor Statistics] selected years of annual reports, the data for 1925 through 1939 are from the Ministry of Commerce and Industry, *Chingin Tōkeihyō* [Wage Statistics] selected years of annual reports, and the post-World War II data are from Tokyo Chamber of Commerce, *Shokushu Betsu Chingin Tōkei* [Wage Statistics by Occupation] selected years of annual reports.

skilled and unskilled occupations, are consistent with the cyclical movements of the changes in employment that we have reviewed in the section on labor force. That is, when employment increased in the growth phases of the economic cycles, wage differentials narrowed. And conversely, periods in which wage differentials widened are also the periods when employment decreased during depressed economic conditions.

The many dimensions of wage differentials suggest important implications for the structure and working of the labor market. In what follows, we will examine some selected aspects of wage differentials: age, sex, production versus nonproduction categories of work, and size of establishment. Although all of these types of differentials could be cross-classified, we will examine each type of differential in turn, partly to save space and partly because cross-classifiable data do not exist for the prewar period.

The age–wage differential is an important type of differential that has attracted much attention in Japan. The data for selected years since 1927 are presented in Table 5.19. In Japan, the wage differential by age is quite large. It is believed, and to some extent supported by statistical evidence, that it is considerably larger than in many of the Western industrialized

TABLE 5.19

Indexes of Wage Differentials by Age for Production Workers, in Manufacturing Industries, 1927–1973[a]

(Age 20–24 = 100)

Age	1927	1933	1936	1938	1948	1958	1960	1965	1970	1973
				Males						
12–13	30	27	29	34	—	—	—	—	—	—
14–15	37	36	37	41	57[b]	52	52	58	59	60
16–17	52	65	65	66						
18–19	72				71	74	75	76	81	80
20–24	100	100	100	100	100	100	100	100	100	100
25–29	125	128	124	118	126	137	133	124	127	121
30–34	142	149	145	131	148	170	167	144	144	142
35–39	154	164	161	142	163	191	189	158	151	146
40–44	159	175	174	149	166	207	208	169	160	155
45–49	157	182	181	151						158
50–54	151	182	181	143	145	172	170	159	149	164
55–59	129	131	138	111						118
60+	109	109	109	93	106	—	—	106	100	92
				Females						
12–13	46	50	58	62	—	—	—	—	—	—
14–15	61	63	69	75						
16–17	79	83	86	91	75[b]	69	73	80	79	85
18–19	92				89	85	88	91	91	94
20–24	100	100	100	100	100	100	100	100	100	100
25–29	102	108	110	103	109	116	111	101	100	100
30–34	104	114	115	102	117	109	105	96	90	86
35–39	104	117	117	98	127	105		94	90	85
40–44	103	119	118	98	121	106	101	94	92	92
45–49	99	121	121	94						90
50–54	94	113	113	86	111	98		94	91	98
55–59[a]	86	92	94	77						98

Sources: The data from 1927 to 1938 were obtained from Office of the Prime Minister, Bureau of Statistics, *Rōdōtōkei Jitchi Chōsa* [Survey of Labor Statistics] (selected years), and 1948 to 1973 are from the Ministry of Labor, *Chinginkōzō Kihontōkei Chōsa* [Basic Survey of Wage Structures] (selected years). Quoted from unpublished data compiled by Ryohei Magota, prepared for the Japan Wage Research Center, Comprehensive Seminar on Wages, 1975.

[a] Wages include various allowance payments. The data up to 1938 are daily wages and the data for 1948 and thereafter are monthly wages.

[b] The age bracket 14–17 in the post-World War II period corresponds to all ages younger than 17.

[c] The data for females 60 and older were deleted from this table.

nations. That is, the age–wage profile is much steeper in Japan than in Western countries.

A number of hypotheses have been posited to explain this phenomenon: the heavy reliance on intrafirm and on-the-job training, the emphasis placed on compensation to pay for the necessary expenses of a worker and his family during his life-cycle, the nonstandardized nature of technology, and the exploitation of young workers. It climbed steeply in the early 1930s and 1950s, and flattened in the 1920s, late 1930s, and 1960s. The wage profile was influenced by demand-supply conditions in such a way that when the labor market slackened, it got steeper, whereas it flattened when the labor market tightened.

Let us shift our attention to the behavior of wage differentials by sex and also by production versus nonproduction workers. Data for the years from 1955 to 1975 are reported in Table 5.20. During these two decades, both types of differentials narrowed secularly. The percentge of a male production worker's wages to those of male nonproduction workers increased from 62.2 in 1960 to 76.0 in 1975, a substantial decrease in the differential. Similarly, for female workers the equivalent differential narrowed as shown by increase from 67.9% in 1960 to 73.8% in 1975. For the same type of work, wage differentials by sex have narrowed appreciably during the same period.

Wage differential by firm size is another notable feature of Japanese wage structure. Large firms pay substantially higher wages to their workers than small firms, and this type of differential is considerably larger than in the United States.[39] Table 5.21 shows the changes in wage differentials by size of establishment for the years 1950–1975. During the postwar period, the differential was greatest in the latter half of the 1950s and has been narrowing ever since.

A warning must be added, however. The figures in the table do not indicate a clean wage differential, since other attributes of workers such as sex, age, education, and skill are not controlled for. We must recall that there is a considerable wage differential by age. The narrowing of the aggregate figures by size of establishment is a reflection, to an important extent, of the fact that large firms absorbed a greater proportion of young and cheap labor, relative to smaller firms. Faced with this competition, smaller firms were sometimes obliged to pay higher wages for young workers than larger firms. Thanks to these labor market pressures, interfirm wage differentials narrowed considerably during the 1960s and early 1970s.

When did such a differential start? Because we have no wage statistics for the prewar period comparable to the Basic Survey of Wage Structures, which was initiated in 1954, it is very difficult to give a reliable answer to this question. According to a careful comparison of the wages of skilled workers in a large plant and the wages of comparable workers in the same locality made by Odaka, wage differentials by size of firm appear to have emerged first in the 1920s.[40]

[39]Richard A. Lester, "Pay Differentials by Size of Establishment," *Industrial Relations* 7 (October 1967): 57–67; and Haruo Shimada, "The Structure of Earnings and Investments in Human Resources: A Comparison Between the United States and Japan" (Ph.D. diss., University of Wisconsin, 1974).

[40]Kōnosuke Odaka, "A Study of Employment and Wage-Differential Structures in Japan" (Ph.D. diss., University of California, 1967).

TABLE 5.20

Production Versus Nonproduction and Female Versus Male Worker Wage Differentials in Manufacturing Industries (in Percentages)

Year	Male production workers/Male nonproduction workers	Female production workers/Female nonproduction workers	Female nonproduction workers/Male nonproduction workers	Female production workers/Male production workers
1955	65.9	68.5	40.2	41.8
1960	62.2	67.9	37.7	41.2
1965	66.6	73.1	43.3	47.5
1970	71.1	72.8	45.2	46.3
1975	76.0	73.8	50.2	48.8

Source: Ministry of Labor, *Monthly Labor Survey, Annual Report,* (selected years).

TABLE 5.21
*Wage Differentials by Size of Establishment, Manufacturing
Industries, Monthly Cash Earnings (in Percentages)*

Year	Size of establishment by number of employees			
	500 or more	100 to 499	30 to 99	29 or less
1950	100	83.1	67.3	—
1955	100	74.3	58.8	—
1960	100	70.7	58.9	46.3
1965	100	80.9	71.0	63.2
1970	100	81.4	69.6	61.8
1975	100	82.9	68.7	—

Source: Ministry of Labor, *Monthly Labor Survey, Annual Report*
(selected years).

Negotiated Wage Increases

Finally, let us take a look at the outcome of wage negotiations. Concerted action aimed at increasing wages were organized by several industry federations of enterprise unions in late 1954, and the first concerted offensive was waged in the spring of 1955. This wage offensive has been repeated every spring and has been named *shuntō*.

Table 5.22 presents average wage increases both in terms of yen and percentages, together with a measurement of the dispersion of wage increases attained through *shuntō* from 1955, the first year of the movement, to 1977. Negotiated wage increases have grown remarkably every year since the beginning of the 1960s. This is in part a reflection of the tightening of the labor market under the rapid economic growth of this period. It should also be borne in mind that an increasingly large part of money wage gains has been offset by price inflation since 1970. Large wage increases were obtained in order to compensate for inflation.

An interesting feature of the outcome of wage negotiations is to be found in the fact, shown in the third column of Table 5.22, that the dispersion of wage increases reached at various negotiating units, mostly individual firms, narrowed remarkably until 1973 as *shuntō* movements prevailed throughout Japanese industry. This implies that one of the notable effects of the *shuntō* movement was intensified emulation among wage negotiators in different firms, unions, and industries, and as a consequence the stronger, quicker, and broader diffusion of negotiated wage increases throughout Japanese industry during the few months of the *shuntō* period every year.

Union Movements and Industrial Relations

The objective of this final section is to review chronologically developments in labor and union movements in a somewhat broad context of in-

TABLE 5.22
Negotiated Wage Increases in Shuntō *(Japanese Labor's Spring
Wage Offensive) 1955–1976*[a]

Year	Wage increase (in yen)	Rate of wage increase (in percentages)[b]	Coefficient of variation of wage increase[c]
1955	784	4.6	.98
1956	1,063	6.3	.57
1957	1,518	8.6	.39
1958	1,050	5.6	.58
1959	1,281	6.5	.39
1960	1,792	8.7	.34
1961	2,970	13.8	.27
1962	2,515	10.7	.26
1963	2,237	9.1	.31
1964	3,305	12.4	.20
1965	3,014	10.3	.31
1966	3,273	10.4	.24
1967	4,214	12.1	.13
1968	5,213	13.5	.14
1969	6,768	15.8	.13
1970	8,983	18.3	.12
1971	9,522	16.6	.14
1972	9,904	15.0	.15
1973[d]	14,910	19.8	.08
1974	28,981	32.9	.13
1975	15,279	13.1	.32
1976	11,596	8.8	.20
1977	12,536	8.8	.14

Sources: Surveys conducted by Trade Union Division, Bureau of Labor Administration, and Ministry of Labor. Quoted from K. Furuya, A. Nakamura, and T. Suzuki, *Chingin Hendō Yōin no Kenkyū* [A Study of Determinants of Movements in Wages], (Tokyo: G.P.O. 1969), p. 60 and Japan Productivity Center, *Katsuyō Rōdō Tōkei* [Active Labor Statistics], 1977, p. 72.

[a]Figures for 1955 to 1959 are averages of 72 to 84 major private firms, for 1960 to 1973, unweighted averages of 157 to 163 major private firms, and for 1974 through 1976, unweighted averages of 265 major private firms.

[b]The rate of wage increase is the percentage of average negotiated monthly wage increase per worker relative to the average monthly-regular wage before the wage negotiation.

[c]The coefficient of variation used here is .defined as: Wage increase of a firm at the third quartile − wage increase of a firm at the first quartile/the median of wage increases.

[d]Since the announced negotiated wage increase for the iron and steel industry in 1973 was specifically for a worker of age 35 with 12 years of length-of-service, it may not be treated, rigorously speaking, on an equal basis with the average wage increase of the various categories of workers for other industries. The average wage increase of all industries excluding the iron and steel industry in 1973 is 9955 yen, the rate of wage increase is 15.1% and the coefficient of variation is .11.

dustrial relations. It is also intended that this section should provide the reader with such basic quantitative information, relating to unionism and industrial relations, as changes in union membership, unionization ratios, labor disputes, and the like.

Early Developments in Unionism and Labor Movements

Before the end of World War II, trade unionism in Japan was placed under severe restrictions. Japan, as a late-comer among industrial societies, had to achieve industrialization as rapidly as possible. At the same time, it was necessary for Japan to construct a modern defense force quickly, because of the danger of colonization by the Western powers. These two targets could only be attained by the autocratic power of the Meiji Government, which was eager to maintain the political-social order as it was, strongly regulated and oriented for national strategies. Any social movement that disturbed the existing social order or undermined the national purpose had to be either severely prohibited or closely controlled by the police.

The government could not tolerate even a moderate type of unionism as advocated by Fustarō Takano, an admirer of Samuel Gompers. In 1900, the Public Peace Police Law was enacted, Article 17 of which made union activity virtually impossible. Except for Takano, union leaders of that time tended to become involved in the socialist movement, rather than the craft-union movement. The government's oppressive policy against the socialist or labor movement became stiffer after 1910, when a case of alleged "high treason" was brought against a group of anarchists led by Shūsui Kōtoku. This oppressive policy was maintained throughout the first half of the Taishō Era (1912–1926).

Union Movements and Industrial Relations During the Interwar Period

After World War I, the new ideas of liberalism, democracy, socialism, anarcho-syndicalism and communism flourished in Japan, and the labor movements' chances for growth seemed promising.

Under the then dominant social atmosphere of what was called "Taisho Democracy," the government announced the introduction of universal suffrage in 1925, with the first general election scheduled to take place in 1927. At the same time the government began to change its policy toward unionism from one of oppression to one of toleration, at least of moderate unionism.

This policy change was largely a result of a popular movement, particularly the workers' agitation for universal suffrage and the abolition of oppressive laws. These movements had been strengthened under the growing democratic tendency and had been stimulated by the Russian Revolution of 1917 and the nationwide "Rice Riot" in 1918. In 1926 the government repealed Article 17 of the Public Peace Police Law that had made union activities virtually illegal. However, the government enacted the Labor Disputes Mediation Act and the Public Peace Preservation Law in 1926, aimed at prohibiting the communist movement, which had been increasingly active since the foundation of the Japanese Communist party in 1922. On the other hand, attempts to give some protection to workers' right to organize failed when several trade union bills did not pass the Diet in 1926 and in 1931.

With the first general election (1928) close at hand, a movement was started to found a single labor-peasant party (Party of Propertyless People), with labor unions and peasant unions as its major supporters. However, while it was in the process of organizing, the union movement splintered into three ideological factions, each of which finally aligned with one of three separate political parties. The three groups were rightist, leftist, and middle of the road.

The rightist group, which continuously maintained an overwhelming majority position, tried to follow the pattern of British trade unionism. They placed emphasis on the bargaining function of unions and wanted to promote favorable labor legislation through a moderate right-wing socialist party. The group included Sōdōmei, the Seaman's Union, and other big unions in government-owned enterprises and large private firms.

The leftist group further divided into two factions: One was an illegal group under the direct control of the Communist party and subject to the Profintern (Red International of Labor Unions). Another was composed of legal leftists who were noncommunists but were strongly influenced by Marxist-Leninist ideology. The major unions of these leftist groups, both factions included, originally seceded from Sōdōmei in 1925 and formed Hyōgikai (National Council of Labor Unions), which played a leading role in founding the Labor–Peasant Party, a legal puppet party of the communists.

These leftist groups constituted a minority, with a membership of 30,000 at the most. However, their ideological influence has been significant in the Japanese labor movement as a whole. Quite a number of labor leaders in postwar Japan began their careers in these prewar leftist groups, and their way of thinking still has a legitimacy among contemporary labor leaders.

The middle-of-the-road group consisted of those unions that were either against rightist moderate reformism or against the extremely radical, unrealistic leftists. These groups seceded from Sōdōmei in 1926 and founded Kumiai Dōmei (Union Alliance). At the same time they established another separate political party called The Japan Labor-Peasant Party.

During the period from the end of World War I to the mid-1930s, unionism grew substantially, as can be seen from the statistical data in Table 5.23. The number of unions increased from around 300 in 1921 to 991 in 1935. Accordingly, union membership had more than quadrupled, from 103,000 in 1921 to 409,000 in 1935. The union organization ratio, too, had

TABLE 5.23
Unions, Union Membership (in Thousands), and Organization Ratios (in Percentages)

Year	Number of unions	Union membership	Organization ratios[a]
1921	300	103	—
1925	457	254	5.6
1930	712	354	7.5
1935	991	409	6.9
1940	49	9	.1
1945	509	381	—
1950	29144	5774	45.8
1955	32012	6166	34.7
1960	41561	7516	31.7
1965	52879	10070	35.0
1970	60954	11481	34.7
1975	69333	12473	34.5

Sources: Hideo Nakajima, "Senzen Sengo no Rōshikankei Shihyō no Suii" [Indicators of Labor Management Relations in Pre- and Postwar Periods], *Rōdōtōkei Chōsa Geppō* [Monthly Review of Labor Statistics] 29, no. 1, (January 1977): 13–26. Original sources: 1918–1937: Surveys by the Bureau of Society, the Ministry of Internal Affairs as reported in Bureau of Statistics, the Office of the Prime Minister, *Rōdōtōkei Yōran* [Handbook of Labor Statistics], March, 1976; 1938–1941: The same surveys as above, succeeded by the Bureau of Labor, and the Ministry of Welfare as reported in the same documents; 1945–1947: Bureau of Labor Administration, Ministry of Welfare, Statistics on Formation and Dissolution of Labor Unions; 1948–1975: Ministry of Labor, Basic Survey of Labor Unions.

[a]Estimates of organization ratios for the prewar period are the percentage of union membership relative to the number of workers, which in turn is based on relevant surveys of the Ministry of Internal Affairs and the Ministry of Welfare. See, Bureau of Statistical Survey, Ministry of Labor, "Tōkei Kara mita Wagakuni no Rōdō Sōgi" [Japanese Labor Disputes Viewed from Statistics] *Naigai Rōdō Shiryō* [Internal and External Labor Documents], December 1950, no. 29. Organization ratios for the postwar period are the percentage of union membership divided by the number of employees, which is taken from the Office of the Prime Minister, *Labor Force Survey, Annual Report* (selected years).

increased appreciably during this period, from 5.6% in 1925 to 7.5% in 1935.

The foundation of ILO also had a significant impact on both the labor movement and government's labor policy. The government softened its regulation of the unions and even tried to enact a trade union law in 1926 and 1931, although the bills could not pass the Congress, mainly because of opposition by employer organizations.

Another notable development during this period may be seen in the field of industrial relations, especially within the confines of large corporations. Large firms, including the government's enterprises, provided their employees with relatively high wages, as well as welfare and educational facilities, in order to retain workers of good quality for a long period and to secure their loyalty to the firm at the same time. Thus, in the 1920s, an industrial reward system began to spread among large firms under which wage increases and workers' promotions were determined largely by length of service, as well as by merit-rating. This industrial reward system was the prototype of what is called the *nenkō* system in postwar Japan. Derived as it was from the paternalistic personnel policy of employers, it was quite effective in limiting the growth of unionism.

When employers found it advisable, as a number of them did, to have some form of employee organization, they took the initiative in introducing joint consultation or works councils in place of unions. One of the most famous works councils was the Gengyō Iinkii (Workshop Council), established in the National Railway System in 1920, the largest state-owned enterprise at that time. This council functioned partly as joint-consultation machinery in the administration of welfare facilities and partly as a kind of grievance machinery. In the 1920s, the government also encouraged the spread of works councils in private industries. Unions, particularly leftist unions, tried in vain to convert such institutions into full-fledged unions by "boring from within" tactics.

Moreover, when the workers of large firms organized themselves, they tended to form unions based on the enterprise they belonged to. Typical cases were unions formed in such state-owned enterprises as arsenals, naval-shipyards, tobacco, municipal tramways, and water supply, and in large private enterprises in mining, steel, machinery, engineering, ship-building, copper refining, textile, electricity and city gas utilities.

In such enterprises, the *nenkō* system was more or less well-established, in which the common interest of the workers that had united them into a union had been founded primarily on an intra-firm basis, rather than on an industrial or occupational basis. Unions outside the large enterprises, whether rightist or leftist, found it increasingly difficult to organize these employees.

This relatively liberal and democratic period, however, was short lived, ending as Japan began its military expansion after the severe economic crisis of the early 1930s. As the political situation became more strained, the Japanese government no longer tolerated any labor or social movements that were contradictory to its military purpose. In 1940, right before the outbreak of World War II, even the right-wing unions that had survived the government's oppressive measures were at last forced to dissolve. In place of unions, the government organized Sampō, or Sangyō Hōkokukai (Association Dedicated to Serve the State Through Industrial Production) a patriotic, enterprise-based labor organization headed at the local level by the presidents of the respective firms.

Under such circumstances the labor movement in prewar Japan could not evolve on a widespread basis. The largest union membership ever acquired in that period was, at most, 420,000 in 1936, representing only 7% of employed workers. Also, the scope of union activities was quite restricted. Except for a very few well-established unions like the Seamen's Union, most unions were not able to bargain collectively with employers. Unions nevertheless did engage in concerted actions in labor disputes, including a number of bitter and prolonged strikes (see Tables 5.24 and 5.25). Most of the disputes, however, resulted in the unions' defeat and dissolution.

Postwar Growth of Unionism

Encouraged by the democratic labor policy of SCAP and the government, and promoted by the urgent necessity to protect their livelihood in the devastated land, workers started to organize themselves with vigorous enthusiasm. Within a few years after the end of the war, the number of unionists sprang from zero to over 6 million, representing over 50% of all wage and salary earners (see Table 5.23). The number of labor disputes and the number of workers involved also increased markedly (see Table 5.24). Union membership has continued to grow steadily ever since, except for a brief period between 1950 and 1952, and also one in 1976. The unionization ratio relative to employed workers gradually declined to around 35% in the mid-1950s, but this figure has been largely maintained since then, despite the rapid increase of employed workers as well as the massive changes in their industrial distribution. Occasional recessions that occurred during this period did not affect the union membership growth. In 1974, total union membership in Japan amounted to 12.5 million, second in the free world only to that of the United States (see Table 5.26).

So far as membership growth is concerned the Japanese union movement has achieved great progress, although, as shown in Table 5.27, workers in large firms are far more organized than workers in small firms.

TABLE 5.24

Labor Disputes[a] and Workers Involved (in Thousands)

Year	Number of disputes	Number of workers involved	Year	Number of disputes	Number of workers involved	Year	Number of disputes	Number of workers involved
1901	18	2	1926	495	67	1951	670	1386
1902	8	2	1927	383	47	1952	725	1842
1903	9	1	1928	397	46	1953	762	1743
1904	6	1	1929	576	77	1954	780	1546
1905	19	5	1930	906	81	1955	809	·1767
1906	13	2	1931	998	64	1956	815	1605
1907	57	10	1932	893	55	1957	999	2345
1908	13	1	1933	610	49	1958	1247	2537
1909	11	—	1934	626	50	1959	1193	1918
1910	10	3	1935	590	38	1960	1707	2335
1911	22	2	1936	547	31	1961	1783	1128
1912	49	5	1937	628	124	1962	1696	1885
1913	47	5	1938	262	18	1963	1421	1781
1914	50	8	1939	358	73	1964	1754	1634
1915	64	8	1940	271	33	1965	2359	2479
1916	108	8	1941	159	11	1966	2845	2298
1917	398	57	1942	173	10	1967	2284	1271
1918	417	66	1943	279	9	1968	3167	2340
1919	497	63	1944	216	7	1969	4482	3071
1920	282	36	1945	94	39	1970	3783	2357
1921	246	58	1946	810	635	1971	6082	3623
1922	250	41	1947	683	295	1972	4996	2657
1923	270	36	1948	913	260	1973	8720	4929
1924	333	54	1949	651	1240	1974	9581	5325
1925	293	40	1950	763	1027	1975	7574	4614

Sources: See sources cited in Table 5.23.

[a] Only those disputes that were accompanied by some form of dispute action, such as strikes and lock-outs, are listed here.

TABLE 5.25
Number of Working Days Lost by Labor Disputes (in Thousands)

Year	Number of working days lost	Number of working days lost per thousand nonagricultural employees	Year	Number of working days lost	Number of working days lost per thousand nonagricultural employees
1921	1173	—	1951	6015	456
1922	447	—	1952	15075	1096
1923	422	—	1953	4279	271
1924	613	—	1954	3836	236
1925	295	—	1955	3467	203
1926	698	—	1956	4562	249
1927	1177	—	1957	5652	288
1928	584	—	1958	6052	293
1929	572	—	1959	6020	278
1930	1085	—	1960	4912	216
1931	980	—	1961	6150	257
1932	619	—	1962	5400	214
1933	385	—	1963	2770	106
1934	446	—	1964	3165	117
1935	301	—	1965	5669	201
1936	163	—	1966	2742	93
1937	353	—	1967	1830	60
1938	41	—	1968	2841	91
1939	35	—	1969	3634	115
1940	54	—	1970	3915	119
1946	6266	—	1971	6029	178
1947	5035	—	1972	5147	150
1948	6995	572	1973	4604	129
1949	4321	364	1974	9663	270
1950	5486	454	1975	8016	233

Source: See sources cited in Table 5.23.

TABLE 5.26
Average Size of Enterprise Union

Year	Number of enterprise unions[a]	Total union membership (in thousands)	Average number of members per enterprise union
1953	18,228	5,927	325
1955	18,013	6,286	346
1960	21,957	7,662	349
1965	27,525	10,147	369
1970	30,058	11,605	386
1974	32,734	12,462	381

Source: Ministry of Labor, *Labor Union Basic Survey.*
[a]The number of enterprise unions is the number of Tan'itsu Kuniai according to the technical term of the *Survey.*

TABLE 5.27
Union Organization Ratios by the Size of Firm[a]

| | Size of firm (number of employees)[b] | | | |
Year	500 and over	100–499	30–99	Less than 30
1960	69.1	38.5	8.9	3.2
1963	61.3	37.6	10.4	3.1
1966	65.0	31.0	9.3	3.5
1969	63.0	33.5	9.8	4.9
1972	63.6	31.5	9.0	3.4

Source: Ministry of Labor, *Labor Union Basic Survey.*
[a]Unions in the public sector are excluded.
[b]Organization ratios are estimated using the number of employees as a denominator.

The Structure of Collective Bargaining and the Development of the Unions' Concerted Annual Wage Offensive

Because of the prevalence of enterprise unionism, almost all collective bargaining in Japan has been conducted exclusively between enterprise unions and their respective managements, with almost complete authority and autonomy on both sides. Except for a short period immediately after the war, when the government's control and regulation of industrial activities was strongly enforced, the participation of officers of the union's parental organization at the collective bargaining table was very rare. In general, employers in Japan have been, and still are, very reluctant to accept "outsiders"—the representatives of national, or local, industrial federations of unions—at the bargaining table to negotiate wages and other employment conditions that are considered "private matters," to be solved within each of the particular enterprises. Moreover, after 1949, Japanese business firms began to operate in freer and more competitive circumstances, and they developed increasingly wider differentials, both in terms and conditions of employment, between big enterprises and medium and small enterprises and even among big enterprises in the same industry. This tendency has prevented wages and other working conditions from becoming more standardized among industries, as well as among enterprises. The widening differentials in employment conditions have tended to solidify the structure of collective bargaining.

However, a significant change has taken place since the unions' annual spring wage offensive, or *Shuntō*, was initiated in 1955. In the beginning, the drive was organized by only eight national industrial federations, covering no more than 800,000 workers. Stimulated by rapid economic growth and structural changes in the labor market, the number of unions and their members participating in *Shuntō* has increased remarkably. In 1960, 4.4 million workers participated, and in 1975 the number increased to as much as 9.8 million, representing 77% of all union members in Japan. Thus, *shuntō* has become institutionalized as the most important wage-fixing practice.

Since the drive has been conducted by the concerted action of unions aligned on an industrial basis, with national centers playing a leading and coordinating role among the industrial federations, it has enhanced the authority and power of the national organizations over their affiliated enterprise unions. Also, industrywide and regionwide bargaining by some leading unions such as the Seamen, Coal Miners, Textile Workers, Private Railway Workers, and Synthetic Chemical Workers has been emerging. Even in the cases where officers of national industrial federations do not directly or formally sit at the bargaining table, as is common, a de facto industrywide bargaining still takes place. One of the most typical cases is de facto industrywide bargaining in the basic steel industry, where the outcome has a significant impact on wage negotiation in other industries.[41]

In this way, with the development of *shuntō* as well as increased involvement of the national industrial federation of the unions, the negotiated wage increase has tended to become more standardized than ever before (see Table 5.22).

Unions' Commitment to Political Activity and Their Alignment with Political Parties

The labor unions in postwar Japan have been characterized, as they were in prewar days, by a strong commitment to the political power struggle. When the union movement regrouped after the war, unions were unanimous in blaming the capitalist or imperialist system of Japan for leading the nation into a disastrous war. Supporting either Socialist or Communist parties, unions committed themselves to drastic social reform or revolution. In the process, however, interunion rivalry based on the ideology and political alignment of the prewar movements was revived and strengthened.

For several years after the end of World War II, Sanbetsu-Kaigi (Congress of Industrial Unions), the left-wing national federation that was strongly under the influence of the Japanese Communist party, and its affiliated unions, played a more active role than Sōdōmei (Japanese Federation of Trade Unions), the revived right-wing national federation that

---

[41]Shirai Taishiro, "The Changing Pattern of Collective Bargaining in Japan" *The Changing Pattern of Industrial Relations* (Proceedings of the Industrial Conference on Industrial Relations, Tokyo, Japan 1965, published by the Japanese Institute of Labor.)

supported the Japanese Socialist party. However, after the abortive general strike of February 1, 1947 and an order of SCAP of July 1948, which deprived employees of national enterprises, such as railroads and postal service, of the right to strike, Sanbetsu-Kaigi declined rapidly and was finally dissolved. In 1950, many former affiliates of Sanbetsu-Kaigi, and a leftist group formerly associated with Sōdōmei, formed Sōhyō (General Council of Trade Unions of Japan)—the largest national federation at present. However, within Sōhyō internal divisions soon developed over the issues of the Peace Treaty and affiliation with the International Confederation of Free Trade Unions (ICFTU). During prolonged strikes in the coal-mining and electric power industries in 1952, several union seceded and, together with Sōdōmei, they formed another national center, which later developed into Dōmei (Japanese Confederation of Labor), the second largest national federation.

Sōhyō supports the Japan Socialist party, and Dōmei supports the Democratic Socialist party. Mainly because of the party alignment of these two national centers, no less than 45% of Japanese unionists refused to join either federation (see Table 5.28). One of the major reasons why the Japanese labor unions, despite a membership size which is second only to that of the United States, do not function as a powerful pressure group, as unions do in other advanced industrial countries, is disunity and internal conflict. Disunity at the national and industrial levels tends to affect the solidarity of union members at the enterprise or plant level, resulting sometimes in union breakaways.

TABLE 5.28

Distribution of Union Membership by National Center, 1965 and 1975

National center	1965		1975	
	Membership (thousands)	Percentage of total	Membership (thousands)	Percentage of total
Sōhyō	4249	41.4	4573	35.2
Private sector	1784	17.4	1635	12.6
Public sector	2464	24.0	2938	22.6
Dōmei	1659	16.2	2266	17.5
Private sector	1555	15.2	2106	16.3
Public sector	103	1.0	160	1.2
Chūritsu-Roren	983	9.6	1369	10.6
Shin-Sanbetsu	61	0.6	70	0.6
Other	3300	32.2	4705	36.6
Total	10252	100	12953	100

Source: Ministry of Labor, *Labor Union Basic Survey.*

In spite of all these shortcomings and deficiencies, unions have supplied manpower as well as monetary resources to the Socialist and Democratic Socialist parties, and either by themselves, or jointly with these parties, they have formed a meaningful countervailing power to the government, which has been continuously monopolized by the conservative Liberal-Democratic party, except for the brief interlude of a coalition government in 1947–1948.

ACKNOWLEDGMENTS

In preparing this chapter, we are indebted to Dr. Ichiro Nakaya, the President, Fujio Yamashita, Director of the Research Department and other staff members of the Japan Institute of Labour for financial assistance and other relevant services. We are also grateful to Hideo Nakajima and Masami Hikita of the Ministry of Labour for providing us with indispensable help in compiling statistical data, and to Kazutoshi Kōshiro who read our interim report and gave valuable comments.

INDEX